Comparative and Transnational History

COMPARATIVE AND TRANSNATIONAL HISTORY
Central European Approaches and New Perspectives

Edited by
Heinz-Gerhard Haupt and Jürgen Kocka

Berghahn Books
New York • Oxford

First published in 2009 by

Berghahn Books

www.berghahnbooks.com

©2009, 2012 Heinz-Gerhard Haupt and Jürgen Kocka
First paperback edition published in 2012

All rights reserved. Except for the quotation of short passages for the purposes of criticism and review, no part of this book may be reproduced in any form or by any means, electronic or mechanical, including photocopying, recording, or any information storage and retrieval system now known or to be invented, without written permission of the publisher.

Library of Congress Cataloging-in-Publication Data

Comparative and transnational history : Central European approaches and new perspectives / edited by Heinz-Gerhard Haupt and Jürgen Kocka.
    p. cm.
    Includes bibliographical references and index.
    ISBN 978-1-84545-615-3 (hbk.)—ISBN 978-0-85745-603-8 (pbk.)
    1. Germany (West)—Historiography. 2. Germany—Historiography. 3. Europe, Central—Historiography. 4. Germany—Social conditions—Historiography. 5. Europe, Central—Social conditions—Historiography. 6. Transnationalism—Historiography. 7 . Acculturation—Historiography. 8. Social history—Methodology. 9. History—Methodology. 10. History—Comparative method. I. Haupt, Heinz-Gerhard. II. Kocka, Jürgen.
    D86.C65 2009
    907.2--dc22

2009025428

British Library Cataloguing in Publication Data

A catalogue record for this book is available from the British Library

Printed in the United States on acid-free paper.

ISBN 978-0-85745-603-8 (paperback)   ISBN 978-0-85745-604-5 (ebook)

CONTENTS

Preface — vii

Comparison and Beyond: Traditions, Scope, and Perspectives of Comparative History — 1
Jürgen Kocka/Heinz-Gerhard Haupt

PART I
Comparative and Entangled History in Global Perspectives

CHAPTER 1
Between Comparison and Transfers—and What Now? A French-German Debate — 33
Hartmut Kaelble

CHAPTER 2
A 'Transnational' History of Society: Continuity or New Departure? — 39
Jürgen Osterhammel

CHAPTER 3
Double Marginalization: A Plea for a Transnational Perspective on German History — 52
Sebastian Conrad

CHAPTER 4
Entangled Histories of Uneven Modernities: Civil Society, Caste Councils, and Legal Pluralism in Postcolonial India — 77
Shalini Randeria

CHAPTER 5
Lost in Translation? Transcending Boundaries in Comparative History — 105
Monica Juneja / Margrit Pernau

PART II
Transnationalization and Issues in European History

CHAPTER 6
The Nation as a Developing Resource Community:
A Generalizing Comparison 133
Dieter Langewiesche

CHAPTER 7
Birds of a Feather: A Comparative History of German and
US Labor in the Nineteenth and Twentieth Centuries 149
Thomas Welskopp

CHAPTER 8
Visions of the Future: GDR, CSSR, and the Federal Republic of
Germany in the 1960s 178
Jörg Requate

CHAPTER 9
Comparisons, Cultural Transfers, and the Study of Networks:
Toward a Transnational History of Europe 204
Philipp Ther

CHAPTER 10
Germany and Africa in the Late Nineteenth and Twentieth
Centuries: An Entangled History? 226
Andreas Eckert

CHAPTER 11
Losing National Identity or Gaining Transcultural Competence:
Changing Approaches in Migration History 247
Dirk Hoerder

Notes on Contributors 272

Select Bibliography 276

Index 291

≡ PREFACE ≡

Comparative history deals with similarities and differences between historical units, e.g., regions, economies, cultures, and national states. It is the classical way of transcending the narrow boundaries of national history. Comparative history is analytically ambitious and empirically demanding. The last decades have witnessed the rise of comparative history, but its practitioners have remained a minority, and its critics have not been completely convinced.

Entangled history deals with transfer, interconnection, and mutual influences across boundaries. It can be another way of moving beyond the limits of national history. Its rise is more recent. It has been fuelled by postcolonial perspectives, by a renewed interest in transnationalism, and by the intellectual consequences of globalization. It has been practiced in different contexts, e.g., in the overlap between French and German history, in the study of transnational migration, with respect to cultural transfer, or in the expanding areas of global history.

There is much tension, but there is also productive and innovative cooperation between comparative history and entangled history. German-speaking historians have dealt with these issues, over the last years, programmatically, empirically, and with new results. They were influenced by the international discussions, but also could build on their own traditions. Most of their research and debate has been conducted in German. Their approaches and results deserve to be brought to the attention of readers who do not have access to this language.

It is the aim of this book to introduce readers to this type of research and debate. It presents a selection of unpublished and published articles and essays dealing with comparative and entangled history. The introduction surveys the field and discusses issues of theory and method. It proposes different ways of cooperation between comparative and entangled history. Five contributions follow whose authors play an important role in the German debate about comparative and entangled history. Finally, six case studies are presented, which apply and frequently combine comparative and entanglement approaches. The focus is on European history in the twentieth century, but there is also attention to global contexts and their impact on European and German history. In one way or another, the contributions deal with the changing role of national history under the present conditions of Europeanization and globalization.

The editors express their indebtedness to a large number of discussants and commentators, particularly at the Berlin School for the Comparative History of Europe, the European University Institute Florence, and the University of Bielefeld. They want to thank Britta Schilling, Oxford, for carefully translating most of the texts from German into English, as well as Nancy Wegner, Berlin for working on the index and the proofs.

Florence and Berlin, July 2009
Heinz-Gerhard Haupt and Jürgen Kocka

Comparison and Beyond

Traditions, Scope, and Perspectives of Comparative History

JÜRGEN KOCKA and HEINZ-GERHARD HAUPT

The discussion on comparative history *(vergleichende Geschichte, histoire comparée)* is ongoing. Its value is praised; its benefits are acknowledged. But most historians are not interested in systematic comparison. Indeed, there is no lack of old and new objections to comparative history, or at least to certain types of comparative history. The topic remains controversial.[1] The current boom in transnational and transregional approaches—in the form of 'entangled histories' (*Verflechtungsgeschichte* or *histoire croisée*)— gives the issue of comparison a new timeliness. We can observe a certain upsurge in comparative history over the past decades; progress, however, has been limited, and comparison has remained a matter for a minority of historians.[2]

This introductory essay starts out with a discussion of what 'comparative history' means. We follow this up with a discussion of the different purposes and types of historical comparison in existence today, and we survey the role comparison plays in various narratives. We then discuss the tension between some classical historical methods and the principles of historical comparison, which help to explain why comparison has had such a difficult time internationally in historical studies. From this, we develop the traits that are or should be specific to comparison in historical studies. Finally, we discuss recent changes in the field of comparative history: the impact of cultural history, the changing units and spaces of comparison, and the opportunities and problems of transnational approaches that recently have moved into the foreground. Particular attention is given to the relation between *histoire comparée* and *histoire croisée*, i.e., comparative history and entangled histories (including connected and transfer history).

The chapter closes with an overview of the contributions to this volume. We pay most attention to the German literature and debate.

Definition and Goals of Comparison

Similarities and differences

In comparative history, two or more historical phenomena are systematically studied for similarities and differences in order to contribute to their better description, explanation, and interpretation.

By emphasizing the study of the similarities and differences of at least two comparative cases as centrally characteristic, comparative history is distinguished from studies devoting themselves to the analysis and interpretation of *one* constellation, as differentiated and comprehensive as it may be. There are excellent examples of transnational and transcultural works that are nevertheless not comparative.[3] When defined in this way, comparative history is also distinguished from entangled histories *(Verflechtungsgeschichte, histoire croisée)*, which does not seek similarities and differences between two (or more) units of research—e.g., between France and Germany, between Christianity and Islam, or between three village communities or several discourses—but, rather, insists on relationships, transfers, and interactions, i.e., the entanglements between them. However, it will be shown that *histoire comparée* and *histoire croisée* are compatible and have many points of contact.[4]

Studies that are comparative in the full sense of the term should also be distinguished from those in which comparisons show up only *en passant*, by the wayside or implicitly. Such implicit comparisons frequently appear. In the following, we will look at studies in which comparison plays a central methodological role and is a key element of research and narration. Finally, the above definition indicates that comparison in history is seldom an end in itself, but usually serves other goals.

On the most general level, one can distinguish between two basic types of historical comparisons, namely, between those which are aimed mainly at weighing contrasts, i.e., which are targeted at insights into the differences between individual comparative cases, and those which focus on insights into agreements, i.e., generalisation and, thus, the understanding of general patterns.

This distinction has been discussed repeatedly in the literature. John Stuart Mill already contrasted the 'method of difference' with the 'method of agreement'. A.A. van den Braembussche refers to Mill, as do authors such as Theda Skocpol and Charles Tilly, in order to distinguish between the 'contrasting type' and the 'universalising type' of historical comparison, only to situate various mixed forms between these main types.⁵ Otto Hintze made a similar distinction already in 1929: 'One can compare in order to find a generality upon which that which is compared is based; one can compare in order to more clearly comprehend one of the possible objects in its individuality and to distinguish it from the others'.⁶

Comparative historians usually do both in different combinations. The distinction made by Otto Hintze and others, however, is fundamental, and comparative studies can be differentiated according to the way they combine and weigh these two dimensions.

Methodological Functions

On a second level, which allows a somewhat more precise distinction, we can identify different methodological purposes that are served by historical comparisons:

a. In heuristic terms, comparison allows scholars to identify problems and questions that would otherwise be impossible or difficult to pose. Drawing from his own research, Marc Bloch provided an example from agrarian history to show what comparison is capable of uncovering. After investigating the English enclosures from the sixteenth to nineteenth centuries and assessing their functions, he thought it likely that comparable processes could have taken place in France, even if scholars had not yet uncovered them. Proceeding from the assumptions of French analogies or equivalents, as inspired by the English example, Bloch uncovered corresponding, if not identical, changes in agrarian property structures in Provence in the fifteenth, sixteenth, and seventeenth centuries. In this way, he contributed to a profound revision of this region's history. This productive act of scholarly transfer was based on the conviction that the problems of agrarian societies were similar on both shores of the English Channel. They called for parallel, if not identical, solutions if certain innovations—in this case, the emergence of a capitalistically managed agriculture—were to occur.⁷

b. In descriptive terms, historical comparison, above all, helps to apply a clear profile to individual cases and often to a single, particularly interesting case. For example, one discovers that the German workers' movement emerged as an independent force relatively early on only when compared to other workers' movements, such as those in England or the United States. The unusually powerful position, remarkable cohesion, and great historical impact of the German *Bildungsbürgertum* (educated middle classes) only become visible in comparison with other European societies. The delayed development of the West

German industrial city of Oberhausen only becomes apparent in contrast to other comparable places.[8] Historical peculiarities only become clearly visible when one refers to comparable examples, which are sufficiently similar in some respects, but differ in other respects.

c. In analytical terms, comparison makes an important contribution to the explanation of historical phenomena. On the one hand, it serves to criticize pseudo-explanations. Again, Marc Bloch provided a good example. When historians discovered by comparative studies that the intensification of pressure by the medieval and early modern manorial system in most regions of Europe took place more or less simultaneously (although in different forms), they took a sceptical look at all locally specific explanations of this phenomenon that local and regional historians had been quick to proffer. Instead of focusing on regional explanations, historians using the comparative method looked for more general explanatory models and, in this case, arrived at the declining ground rent and its causes.[9]

On the other hand, comparisons can serve as indirect experiments and can help to 'test hypotheses'. In this respect, it is important to think carefully about the 'experimental design'. When a historian attributes the appearance of phenomenon 'b' in a society to condition or cause 'a', he or she then can subsequently check this hypothesis by looking for societies in which 'b' appeared without 'a', or 'a' existed without leading to 'b'. In this way, one can either accept the hypothesis for the time being or continue refining it.[10] To be sure, this procedure can run up against tight limits, since historians—unlike natural scientists in their laboratories—rarely find the *ceteris paribus* condition sufficiently fulfilled between the constellations they compare.

Along similar lines, comparison helps to find or check generalizations. Thus, the comparative observation of specific forms of social protest in different societies can help determine the link between state power and social protest in the nineteenth and twentieth centuries. The comparison of different national cases can also demonstrate that and how the organizational ability of specific industrial workers was influenced by their system of work and by the structure of their communities.[11]

d. In paradigmatic terms, comparison can help to de-familiarize the familiar. When examined in light of observable alternatives, a specific development can lose the 'matter of course' appearance it may have possessed before. Comparison opens our eyes for other constellations; it sharpens what Robert Musil has called our *Möglichkeitssinn* (sense of the possible). It transforms one case into one among many possible cases. Comparison leads to de-provincializing historical observation.

As John H. Elliott put it: 'above all a comparative approach forces us to reconsider our assumptions about the uniqueness of our own historical explanation'.[12]

This has an impact on the atmosphere and style, the mood and culture of historical studies, including the way in which central terms are used. Frequently, comparison reveals their cultural specificities and historicity. A broad-based comparison with different, e.g., non-Western or historically remote, alien cultures can lead scholars to challenge the most general of terms. In this way, it is possible to highlight the cultural framework within which one works and which is often not discussed in noncomparative studies. Comparison encourages the historian to reflect on his own cultural foundations and on the culture of his own scholarly discipline.[13]

Comparison in different plots

Comparison is rarely practised in a pure form or for its own sake. Comparisons are usually built into different narratives or plots. There, they serve different functions within different contexts. Without any claim for completeness, we shall examine four different cases.

Asymmetrical Comparison

Frequently, one looks into another country, another society or another culture in order to better understand one's own. One hopes to understand the peculiarities of one case by looking at others. Often the other case (cases) is (are) used for purposes of background only, while intensive investigation is reserved for the area or problem in the centre of attention. This has been the way in which proponents of the German *Sonderweg* thesis usually looked into West European examples—or more generally 'the West'—in order to specify (and frequently criticize) 'German particularities'. This has been the way in which proponents of the 'American exceptionalism' thesis used to compare their findings with other cases in order to pinpoint (and frequently praise) particularities of US history. Max Weber's comparative studies were not completely void of this attitude when he looked into non-Western religions and civilizations with the purpose of understanding better what he termed 'Western rationalization' (or modernization).[14]

These are contrasting comparisons of an asymmetrical type. They are asymmetrical in that the cases used for the comparison merely get sketched in as background. Instead of a full-blown comparison, we are usually left with a national-historical analysis in a comparative perspective. Even this reduced form of comparison can be extraordinarily fruitful and has the added benefit of greater feasibility. However, it also runs a risk of excessively stylizing the history of the 'comparative case' or of the 'comparative cases', of homogenizing it or them without justification, and even systematically missing the point. One should also point to the danger that, in this way, the comparative historian may implicitly fall victim to those 'asymmetrical counterconcepts'[15] with which the nations, classes, and groups he or she studies distinguished themselves from others. Such a comparison may end up reproducing political and cultural self-definitions and stereotypes without analysing the mechanisms that brought them into existence in the first place. This was one of the main arguments advanced against comparative history by Michel Espagne, when he promoted transfer history approaches instead.[16]

But such comparative theses about specific patterns of national history frequently become starting points of challenging comparative questioning, leading into productive debate and research. This was the case when David Blackbourn and Geoff Eley started to criticize the German *Sonderweg* thesis, or when C.B.A. Behrens dealt with Franco-Prussian differences during the eighteenth century. Behrens argued that the French Revolution should not only be seen as a heroic moment of French history, but, when compared to the efficiency of Prussian politics, as the result of a failure of administration and governance during the eighteenth century. In another example, Roger Brubaker reaffirmed the importance of traditional German and French particularities when he compared principles of citizenship and opposed the German *ius sanguinis* to the French *ius solis*; the first being exclusive, the second more inclusive. But research done by Patrick Weill and Dieter Gosewinkel has shown that the differences between the two countries are not as clear from the beginning, and that the idea of the *ius solis* is shifting to France due to German influences. The construction of national differences or *Sonderwege* is questioned by these kinds of comparative studies, which in turn would not have come into being if the *Sonderweg* construction had not been presented in the first place.[17]

Comparison and Stage Theories

Comparisons have long been central to stage theory and, thus, to diachronic arguments. These are based on the assumption that institutions, economic systems, societies or even entire civilizations follow certain regular development patterns and, thus, are essentially comparable, even if they differ in terms of space, time, and details. Stage theories have rightly fallen out of fashion, not least because precise comparison has helped to demonstrate their untenability. One late example of this was Walt W. Rostow's influential and intriguing theory of industrialization. At its core lay the conviction that every industrialized country passes through the same phases of development with the same problems and similar solutions. Rostow's scheme was shored up with international comparisons at the beginning of the 1960s, but it was later challenged by more systematic international comparisons. Today, it is of only limited significance in scholarship, particularly since the history of industrialization has continuously moved the notion of comparison from the national to the regional level.[18]

Comparison and Typology

If comparison is intended to lead to a typology, then it is essential that it include at least three cases on a more or less equitable basis. One example for this approach is Theodor Schieder's old, but still influential study of the development of the nation state in western, central, and eastern Europe. By comparing national movements in Europe in the nineteenth century, he arrived at the following typology: while the national movements in the West of the continent emerged in the frameworks of already existing territorial states, in central Europe, e.g., in Germany and Italy, these movements aimed at assembling smaller existing territorial units into nation states. In the East of the continent, they turned against existing supranational empires in order to break them up and form nation states. According to Schieder, this was linked to profound differences in the national movements' respective programmatic-ideological orientation and 'timing', which can be examined through systematic comparison.[19] A different typology can be arrived at if one does not look for structural types, but, rather, for types of outcomes. In his study of the small states of central, eastern, and northern Europe, Miroslav Hroch set different caesuras depending on the social bearers and the respective spread of national ideas, and distinguished three phases leading up to the development of mass movements.[20] Both typologies have been strongly criticized by empirical research over recent years and have been revised to some extent. Ulrike von Hirschhausen and Jörn Leonhard summarize the current state of research under the programmatic title: 'From Typology to the Determination of Difference'.[21] They also use comparative analysis, although not with the intention of typologizing, but, rather, in order to challenge conventional typologies. Today, the anti-typological mood prevails. But it is ultimately focused on what it rejects. The value of comparative typologies lies not least in the way they provoke research and arguments with a critical thrust and thus contribute to the progress of knowledge.

One could cite other examples of successful typological comparisons. Scholars have examined variants of 'political modernization' of the nineteenth and twentieth centuries, establishing typologies that compare Western Europe with Russia, India, and Japan.[22] Despite decades of criticism aimed at modernization theories and concepts, the historical use of the terms 'modernization' and 'modernity' has recently experienced a new boom, modified by the pluralized notion of 'multiple modernities'.[23] Such studies frequently work on a comparative basis. The transition from totalitarian, authoritarian, and other dictatorships into various forms of representative democracy in the second half of the twentieth century is being researched from a historical perspective. Such studies cannot do without comparative typologies.[24] Researchers have recently discovered an interest in the development of European civil society in the period from the eighteenth to the twentieth centuries. There are many differences to be registered and explained—not only in regard to their content, bearers, and forms, but also their successes and failures. 'Path dependence' plays an important role, but so does the mutual impact of these different paths. A historical typology is the goal.[25]

While typological comparisons yield considerable benefits, they also create problems. Sometimes, they underestimate the multi-dimensionality, contingency, and openness of historical situations; they marginalize resistance to the general trends and cover up the non-realized alternatives that may have been present in a historical situation. Typological comparisons privilege the history of those trends that ultimately asserted themselves. The generally accurate notion that the nation state—and not the city or the empire—asserted itself as the historically most significant form of large-scale political organization in nineteenth-century Europe also led Theodor Schieder and others to belittle all efforts deviating from this goal as 'particularist'.[26] The comparative-typological approach frequently focuses on success and the conditions for success and not on the costs and victims of structural decisions and developments. Finally, studies taking a typological approach tend to insinuate that certain developments and structures are 'normal', such as English industrialization, Anglo-Saxon democracy, and Western civil society. In the process, such phenomena are often reduced to a few characteristic traits. They are even idealized and used as benchmarks in the study of different national and regional cases.[27] If one only measures the distance between one case (which has been stylized as a prototype) and other national or regional cases, one frequently ends up with the thesis of the (alleged) backwardness of the one behind the other. Such a characterization says and explains little. This methodological weakness can be reduced if one uses the argumentation model of the 'functional equivalent'. For example, Arnold Heidenheimer not only examined the different development rates of welfare state structures in France and Germany, but also pointed out that social pacification and the creation of mass loyalty, which was achieved in Germany by the welfare state, was attempted in France by means of a socially open, meritocratically organized educational system.[28]

Comparisons in Comprehensive Arguments

Comparison may appear as the centrepiece of analyses that exclusively do not argue comparatively, but also employ other approaches. This refers to comprehensive, empirically based, theoretically oriented, historical-systematic analyses with a comparative core, which are aimed at a broad, but spatially, chronologically, and thematically limited subject. These are studies that have traditionally been undertaken by social scientists rather than by historians. Karl Polanyi's study is one outstanding example of this. Michael Mann produces this type of ambitious analysis today.[29] Alexander Gerschenkron wrote a comprehensive analysis—one could perhaps say an empirically supported theory—of Europe's industrial development, which, while one would certainly criticize it empirically today, remains a scientific masterpiece in its structure. At its centre stands the comparison between national industrialization processes in Europe. Gerschenkron presents a list of their fundamental similarities and their significant differences, which he summed up in the phrase 'different solutions for identical problems and functional equivalents'. But Gerschenkron did not stop there. He conceived of the comparative cases he studied as components of a comprehensive system of European industrialization. He explained the differences between them by their different position in the overall system ('relative backwardness'); by their different timing on the one hand and by their mutual influence, i.e., the history of the relationship between them, on the other.[30]

Another outstanding example for the analysis of a comprehensive problematic with a comparative core is Barrington Moore's masterly study of the different paths to modernity taken by England, France, the US, China, Japan, and India in regard to the development of democracy and dictatorship. The general description, causal analysis, and interpretation of different developments are nicely linked up, the 'connected history' elements are all in place, and yet the comparison is the central motor of a comprehensive theoretical-historical line of argument.[31]

This also applies to recent works in the field of world history. The large-scale studies by Roy Bin Wong, David Landes, Gunder Frank, and Kenneth Pomeranz pursue the famous question, once asked by Max Weber and still timely today, of why and how the West achieved its modernization head start before other parts of the world. But unlike Weber, they are concentrating on economic modernization—self-sustaining growth and industrialization—and have come to notice that the European head start only became manifest in the eighteenth century. For example, it is difficult to speak of European superiority vis-à-vis China in previous centuries. This literature poses very complex causal questions, which are linked explicitly and implicitly with assessments of the success and costs of Western modernization in relation to other civilizations. This literature does not rely on comparison alone, but, rather, is based on highly diverse approaches toward analysis and interpretation. Unlike Weber, it also examines the interaction between the different regions of the world and enquires particularly into non-Western influences on the West's development. Comparison, however, plays an important role all the same. The question of which comparative units and benchmarks should be used becomes acute.[32] Without systematic comparison, this kind of broad-based, comprehensive, ambitious 'world history' would quickly fall prey to speculative and impressionistic commonplace. It revalorizes historical comparison.

The Whole and the Parts

Hartmut Kaelble, among others, has spoken in favour of global comparisons. He advocates the 'explicit and systematic comparison of two or more historical societies in order to investigate differences and similarities, as well as processes of divergent and convergent development.'[33] Indeed, numerous comparative studies have adopted such a macro-historical approach. But they have been criticized for concentrating too much on general social structures and functional contexts, rather than on the perspectives of affected and participating agents themselves. Increasingly, comparativists have learned to include the meso- and micro-historical levels.[34]

One typical example of comparing global structures is the already mentioned classic work of Barrington Moore (1966). While more recent agrarian historical studies have tended to emphasize the variety of situations in the countryside, Moore was concerned with a comparison of entire societies. Within them, he traced various expressions of rural structures and their consequences for the democratization process. Hartmut Kaelble pursued a similar logic when he sought the social-historical substrate of the political integration process in twentieth-century Western Europe.[35] On the basis of quantitative and qualitative evidence, Kaelble emphasized the tendencies toward convergence between European societies in fields such as urbanization, the family, and employment structures in contrast to the United States. It is preferred to use developmental-logical models or general theories in comparative studies of large-scale structures. References to the bourgeois revolutions, within the framework of which individual revolutionary uprisings are compared, belong just as much to the comparative historian's tool kit as the recourse to corporative or bourgeois society, as well as modernization, urbanization, and industrialization processes. The more strongly these models are exposed to criticism and empirical revision, the greater the chance that historical comparison can contribute to their specification, revision, and reformulation. The more rigid and inflexible the theoretical assumptions are, however, the greater is the danger that comparison will do nothing more than turn up illustrations of similar cases.[36]

Large-scale comparisons with broad and even global reach can have important functions. They can develop the distinctions and aspects that are necessary for historical-political orientation and hypothesis formation, without which individual studies would often remain systematically unlinked. For example, the successful large-scale global comparisons of B. Moore, R. Bendix, and others have, so to speak, pre-structured various fields of historical praxis and have thus served as systematic hypothesis-generators. However, this sort of research also reveals the narrow limits within which historians usually work. In globally conceived comparisons, empirical evidence can become a mere illustration of theoretical pre-decisions and used in a way that confirms the validity of the opening premise by necessity. While a holistic view of societies may well enhance the coherence of the demonstration, it can easily underestimate the highly differentiated composition of historical processes and structures. Particularly when applied to Europe as a whole, there is great danger of overemphasizing the continent's coherence and homogeneity.[37]

On the other hand, historical comparisons are often applied not to entire systems, but to partial aspects and partial areas that are clearly distinguishable in thematic, geographical, and chronological terms. The meaning of confessional identity in local elections, comparisons of various villages in different settlement regions of a nation state or the agrarian movements of various countries in the early phase of the European Revolution of 1848— these are examples of partial (limited) comparisons, which can be both international and intrasocietal.[38] The meso-level also provides numerous opportunities for comparative research. Social practices such as cooptation mechanisms, marriage, and social mobility patterns or association structures can be profitably compared with one another in a chronologically specific and locally transcendent manner.[39]

To be sure, the whole and its parts do not always fit neatly together. Their relationship can be determined analytically as long as the parts—to quote a succinct formulation by Pierre Vilar[40]—are interpreted as factors, results or indicators of the overall social context. Case studies can be used to find out to what extent and in which way specific aspects or objects were connected with general processes and structures: whether they were impacted by them, whether they can be seen in analogy to them, or whether they reacted upon and changed them. This broad anchoring of comparative studies is also desirable for comparative local studies, since it cannot be assumed that everything that is local has exclusively local causes.[41]

If individual phenomena or partial areas from various societies are compared with one another (which is the rule), one should realize that a single phenomenon can have different meanings in different contexts. *Mutatis mutandis*, this also applies to intrasocietal comparison. For example, evidence that, before 1914, aristocrats in many central and western European countries held leading positions in business means little as long as one ignores the different meaning of 'aristocracy' in, say, Galicia or Hungary, in France's largely de-aristocraticized society, and, by contrast, in German society, which was strongly influenced by aristocratic models. Behind what Arno Mayer called the 'persistence of the *Ancien Regime*' (1981), we can find hidden a wide array of lifestyles and strategies, channels of influence, and development processes.[42] That which looks identical can—depending on its context—mean something very different. Comparative studies must take this seriously.

The Peculiarities of Comparison in Historical Studies

Comparisons play a large role in the various social sciences and in the humanities—often more than in history. Whether in linguistics, law, sociology, political science, ethnology or literary studies, international comparisons are well known.[43] Depending on their national traditions, historical studies adopted internationally comparative questions in different countries to varying extents. In German historical studies, international comparison has been generally more widespread than in French or Italian scholarship. Today, the method is not limited to demographic or economic history, as in the 1970s, or to social history, as in the 1980s and 1990s; there are also numerous examples of comparison in cultural history.[44]

Does historical comparison possess certain peculiarities that distinguish it from comparative methods in other disciplines? We should set our sights on gradual and not fundamental differences.[45]

    a. Since the late Enlightenment, an attitude has been spreading among professional historians to the effect that historical research and presentation must adhere closely to the sources if they want to claim academic validity. Such an approach, historians hoped, would be particularly authentic. Since then, the critical reconstruction of past times from the vast array of different sources has been among the disciplinary standards of modern historical studies. Proceeding from the principle of proximity to the sources used, historians cultivate a healthy scepticism toward quick generalizations. We too see proximity to the original sources as an unassailable principle of the historical profession. Still, one has to differentiate. While it can be achieved in specialized studies, it is much less feasible in grand syntheses, and its value must not be one-sidedly emphasized vis-à-vis other fundamental principles of the discipline, e.g., the goal of understanding broader historical contexts.

b. Historians are always concerned with comprehending the transformation of reality over time. Our interests, explanations, and presentational patterns (even if they are of a systematic and argumentative nature) generally display a 'before and after' structure. The discipline is characterized by its special relationship to time. To many historians, their discipline is fundamentally committed to comprehending change over time in terms of *development*. This means that while new events occur over the passage of time, the new is not a repetition of the old, but, rather, the new emerges from the old. The old already contains the new as a possibility. The historical meaning of empirical findings does not become evident unless they are interpreted within their diachronic contexts. History is not a sum or sequence of cases that can be used to exemplify general laws. In this way, the great significance of the individuality principle in historical studies becomes understandable.

c. Historians assume that individual components of reality cannot be understood outside of their connection with other components of this reality. The perspectivist view of the differently interpreted whole is part of the understanding of the components. In turn, unless these components are reconstructed, no accurate understanding of the whole can be possible. Historical findings gain their meanings from their relationships within synchronic and diachronic contexts. Thus, the isolation of variables is less feasible and more limited in history than in economics or empirical social research.

The comparative approach maintains a somewhat tense relationship to these three principles of the historical method:

a. The more comparative cases are included, the smaller is the opportunity to adhere to the sources and the greater is one's dependence on secondary literature. But the use of secondary literature for comparative arguments is not without problems. If one does not want to uncritically repeat the vision a certain historiography is presenting on a certain problem or country, one has to immerse oneself thoroughly in the historiographical debates. If one studies a Spanish topic of the nineteenth century on the basis of original materials and compares it with a Japanese case of the same time, for linguistic reasons, the study of the Asian society may have to be based on secondary literature which, outside Japan, is published largely in English. A careful look at English and American studies of Japan becomes necessary and a reflection between this vision of Japan and the state of Japanese studies in the country itself would seem obligatory.

b. The notion of comparison assumes that the subjects being compared can be separated analytically, i.e., that the development context can, so to speak, be chopped up. Units of comparison are not normally seen as stages of one development or as moments of one complex constellation, but, rather, as mutually independent cases that are placed into relation with one another via general questions—according to similarities or differences in certain respects. Those who compare do not conceive of the objects of their investigation as individualities only, but as exemplary cases of a general phenomenon (*tertium comparationis*), which resemble each other in some respects and differ in others. Comparison shatters continuities and interrupts the flow of a narrative. Comparison usually does not deal with the passage of time, but, rather, with similarities and differences.

c. One cannot compare phenomena in their multi-layered totality—as complete individualities—but only in certain regards. Comparison thus assumes to some degree a selection, abstraction, and detachment from context. This necessity becomes particularly evident when one compares large numbers of cases. Someone who compares twenty industrialization processes or slavery in sixty countries has no choice but to examine the objects of investigation largely abstracted from their synchronic and diachronic contexts. Historians have reservations about this approach. The problem shrinks, but does not disappear altogether if one restricts oneself to just two or three comparative cases. In other words, comparison always means abstraction. Deborah Cohen is concerned about the costs of this reduction: 'While national historians' arguments tend towards the multicausal, drawing upon all of the factors that can explain a particular phenomenon, comparatists are often caught in a mono-or bicausal trap'.[46] This argumentation overstresses the totality of arguments within national history and understresses their selectivity. But it emphasizes the necessity for comparative historians to reflect on their selective procedures and the highly constructed status of their results.

This explains why, ever since the age of historicism, which helped bring the above-mentioned basic principles to the fore, historical studies have maintained a certain reserve toward comparison. Comparing is something for conceptually explicit, theoretically oriented, analytical historians with a certain distance to the classical historicist tradition. So far it has been the concern of a minority.[47]

But it also follows that historical comparisons should be of a certain kind that minimizes the tensions with the stated basic principles of historical studies. Historical comparisons differ and should differ from comparisons in the systematic social sciences to some degree in regard to the following characteristics: Historical comparisons tend to limit themselves to only a few cases, often just two or three. They are usually situated on an intermediate level of abstraction and go by the rule: as much abstraction as necessary, as much concretion and contextuality as possible. They usually place more value on contrasts than on generalizations and are more interested in the differences than the commonalities of the comparative objects. They strive to include changes in time and dynamics, whether by selecting processes as objects of comparison, by classifying non-processual comparative findings in terms of before and after, or by complementing comparison with other approaches. Finally, it is typical of historical comparisons that they frequently attempt to link structural-processual analysis with the reconstruction of experiences, perceptions and actions.

On the other hand, we find not only tensions, but also affinities between the principles of historical studies and the principles of comparison. The more analytical historical studies have become,[48] the more they have opened themselves up to comparison. There is a close and mutually helpful relationship between comparison and the analytical orientation in history. After all, when it is understood correctly, history's approach is always dependent on points of view, whether comparative or not. It is always selective and (re-)constructive. These attributes only become more manifest in comparison. As a matter of fact, historians always should define their units of investigation sharply in order to avoid misunderstandings and to achieve clarity. They only become particularly aware of this when making comparisons. For reasons of intellectual honesty, historians are called upon to reflect on their choice of terms and their references to non-scholarly conditions and consequences anyway. Comparison only forces them to undertake such a self-reflection in a particularly unavoidable way.

Comparative history is theoretically ambitious. It should constantly reflect on the conditions underlying its own approach. Among the questions its practitioners must consider and pass judgment on are the following:

a. Which comparative units are appropriate (nations, regions, cultures, epochs, crisis situations, institutions, groups)? While the decision may depend on the availability of sources, it particularly depends on the guiding questions. Take the history of the welfare state as an example. When its guiding principles and its origins were to be analysed, the comparative unit would be the nation state. If we were interested in the implementation of particular social laws, then the local level would be more promising.[49]

b. With what, and with whom, should the comparison be made? One says one should not compare apples with oranges. This means that one should not compare incomparable things. However, the comparability of two or more objects is primarily based on the question asked. So one should not compare apples and oranges if one wants to determine the benefits and drawbacks of different varieties of apples. However, one can and should compare apples and oranges if one's topic is fruit. Before beginning the comparison, one must know which aspects one wishes to compare, whether these aspects are relevant to the question being posed, and whether one's selection of 'comparison partners' is justified in regard to these aspects.

It also makes sense to ask whether the comparison undertaken today by the historians already has been practised by contemporaries in the past. Very often societies are defining themselves in relation to or against other societies. Social movements, towns or social groups do the same. It is useful to look comparatively at the categories at stake and the historical development of stereotypes, metaphors, and symbols. A comparative cultural history of comparisons as used by different historical actors is promising.[50]

c. However, even after solving the 'apple and orange' problem, the question of the appropriate 'comparison partner' is not yet completely solved. Should one contrast the German *Bürgertum* (middle classes) of the nineteenth century with western or with eastern European 'comparison partners'? The result will vary depending on the comparative perspective one ends up choosing. If, for example, one compares them with western European cases, then the German middle classes appear relatively weak and underdeveloped; if one compares them with eastern Europe, then they appear rather powerful and very bourgeois.[51] The selection of the comparative reference is often influenced by non-scientific experiences and valuations. One cannot always avoid this, nor will one always want to. But it is essential to reflect on this context and pay close attention to it.

d. Nor can the decision whether to make synchronic or diachronic comparisons be made *a priori*. Instead, it all depends on one's epistemological interests. If one wants to discover the development status of European societies in the twentieth century and compares them with respect to their blend of urban and rural elements, industrial capitalist and pre-capitalist structures, traditional and modern orientations, then it makes sense to insert one's probe at a specific point in time, such as 1848 or 1890, and thus to undertake a synchronic comparison.[52] If one wants to know how individual societies have solved concrete problems, then a time-staggered comparison may be necessary. On a time-staggered basis, one could examine how the individual European societies defined the 'social question' and how they dealt with mass poverty, housing problems, uncertain livelihoods, and old-age poverty. While the social welfare laws of the 1880s can be viewed as the core of Germany's development toward the welfare state, for France, the early decades of the twentieth century and the years following the Second World War, and, in the US case, the 1930s, would have to be examined.[53] The diachronic comparison can extend over short or long periods of time. Festivals during the Revolution of 1848 may be just as worthy of examination as the Revolution's long-term impact on the second half of the nineteenth century in Europe. Intertemporal comparison is less developed, although contrasting phenomena from ancient and modern history has proven to be highly intriguing.[54]

There is a close affinity between analytically oriented historical research and historical comparison. This explains the particular strength, the particular appeal, the particular difficulty, and—in our opinion—the particular desirability of historical comparison. History's present-day situation is characterized by high specialization and, still, a primarily national-historical orientation. The danger that too much will be compared and that the basic principles listed above will be deeply violated is minor. At the same time, in order to make history less nation-specific and Eurocentric and in order to make it more open and innovative, historical comparison deserves a higher status within historical studies than it has been accorded so far.[55]

Recent Changes in Comparative History

Impact of Cultural History

In the 1960s, 1970s, and 1980s, the majority of comparative studies by European historians were located in social and economic history. They usually privileged the comparative analysis of processes, structures, and institutions, among them social groups and classes, strike waves, divorce rates, welfare states, school systems, employment patterns, businesses, industrialization processes, urban structures, minorities, and modernization. In many cases, comparative studies used quantitative analysis, e.g., in the well-developed comparative history of social protests.[56] But over the last decades, historians' preferences for the analysis of structures, processes, and constellations have been deeply questioned. The reconstruction and integration of experiences, attitudes, and actions has gained a major place on their agenda. Different variations of cultural history have moved to the forefront. Symbolic forms, cultural practices, values, and meanings became important topics of historical research. Language has gained additional importance, both as an object of historical research, as well as a medium of historical studies upon which continuously to be reflected.[57] Confidence in quantitative data has been shaken. By reflecting on the ways in which statistical data have been produced, one has learned to perceive them as artefacts with sometimes very limited value. By stressing their categorical and definitional diversity, as well as their context-dependency, one has become more aware than previously that straightforward quantitative comparison may lead the historian astray.

In the course of these reorientations, which have reshaped the profession, as well as neighbouring disciplines, the contexts, objects, and methods of comparison have changed and continue to change.[58] Certainly, structures and processes must not be neglected. The reconstruction of experiences, discourses, actions, and ideas remains one-sided if not related to the structures, processes, and institutions with which they are usually interrelated in varying forms. This holds true for comparative history, as well as for historical studies without a comparative focus. Certainly, turning away from every form of quantification would be a tremendous loss for historical studies, whether comparative or not. Certainly, comparative history has never been predominantly quantitative, nor has it ever neglected the spheres of experience, perception, action, and culture altogether. But it is, on the other hand, clear that the comparison of cultures and cultural practices, of symbols and symbolic actions, of mentalities and ideas, stereotypes and orientations, memories and memorial sites has expanded and advanced.[59] Comparative studies have become more cautious and self-reflective as to the use of general concepts, the assumptions of comparability, and the acceptance of quantitative evidence. Historians have started to engage in the comparative history of concepts and semantic practices.[60] Along these lines much remains to be done. But it is beyond a doubt that comparative history neither masks experience and action in favour of structures and processes, nor is there any basic tension between comparative approaches and the reconstruction of cultures. Cultural history can profit from comparison as much as social, economic, and institutional history, as well as those numerous studies that cut across these distinctions.

Beyond the National Historical Framework

Traditionally, comparative history of the modern world has privileged comparison between national states or phenomena belonging to different nation states, e.g., social mobility in Germany and the US, or historiographies in different countries of Europe, or the relation between nationalism and feminism in a comparative perspective.[61] International comparison continues to be prominent. The most mature comparative history of Europe analyses similarities and differences in respect to convergence and divergence between national identities, national societies, and national cultures.[62] There are good reasons for such an approach that are related to the huge importance of national borders, identities, cultures, and politics in structuring both the life of the past and the present images of history.

But, clearly, regional and local identities have always played a role and continue to do so, both in structuring past realities and with respect to the frameworks of historical understanding today. And, clearly, in recent years both the Europeanization and the globalization of economic and political life, and culture and communication have created and intensified relations, connections, entanglements and constellations that extend beyond the borders between nation states, regions, and civilizations. Consequently, historical studies have continued to place their questions and answers within local and regional frameworks. Transnational approaches have recently gained much ground.[63]

Comparative history is not at all married to *international* comparison. Marc Bloch already stated that the decision about the appropriate spatial extension of the units of comparison varies with the questions asked and the problems investigated.[64] There have always been many comparisons between villages, cities, and regions. The recent rise of transnational approaches has given a new impetus to broad comparisons between world regions, cultures, and civilizations.[65]

Comparative History and Entanglement History

As argued above, comparative studies investigate differences and similarities, convergences and divergences for different purposes. This holds true for all sorts of comparison, including those moving beyond the borders of a specific national history by comparing between nations, cultures, and civilizations, or between phenomena of a transnational extension, such as many religions, international or transnational institutions, gendered phenomena or multinational economic structures. But in recent years, a different mode of extending historical study beyond national borders has gained much ground, in different forms and under different labels, such as history of transfer, entangled histories or history of entanglement, connected history, *histoire croisée* and *Verflechtungsgeschichte*. What these different approaches share is a common interest in the crossing of borders between nations, regions, continents or other spaces, in all kinds of encounters, perceptions, movements, relations and interactions between them, and in the way they perceived, influenced, stamped, and constituted one another. Interest in the cultural relations between two national states, particularly Germany and France, has been one of the roots of such approaches. Interest in the deeply asymmetric but entangled relation between colonial powers and colonies, between metropolis and periphery, between the West and other parts of the world has been another source for such approaches. They received an additional push by the recent upsurge of global history.[66]

The logic of comparison and the logic of entanglement history/*histoire croisée* clearly differ. While the comparative approach separates the units of comparison (in order to bring them again together under the viewpoints of similarity and difference), entanglement-oriented approaches stress the connections, the continuity, the belonging-together, the hybridity of observable spaces or analytical units and reject distinguishing them clearly (although, contrary to their self-understanding, they cannot do without distinguishing between them, either).

Some advocates of *histoire croisée* have rejected comparative history as too analytical, in the sense of drawing distinctions where they do not exist. They have stressed the incompatibility of *histoire croisée* and comparison. These positions are not convincing and have largely been given up.[67] But there continue to be many examples of *histoire croisée* and entanglement history that are satisfied with reconstructing relations and influences without practising a clear-cut comparison. This is problematic, because it is nearly impossible for transfer and entanglement historians to reach their aims if they shy away from precise comparison. As Johannes Paulmann put it: 'In order, as a historian, to recognize what is happening during a transfer, one must compare the following: the position of the object under investigation in its old context with that in its new context, the social origins of the intermediaries and of the affected parties in one country with those of another, terms in one language with those of another, and finally the interpretation of a phenomenon within the national culture from which it comes with that in which it has been introduced.'[68] Without explicit comparison, historical studies of transfers and of entanglements are in danger of becoming airy and thin.

On the other hand, comparative studies are not damaged, but improved by considering connections between the units of comparison wherever and whenever they exist. Apart from those interesting studies that compare societies very far removed from one another and unconnected,[69] comparative research can and must take connections between the compared cases into account. Such connections—i.e., mutual perceptions and influences, transfers and travels, migrations and trade, interaction, relations of imitation and avoidance, shared dependence from one and the same constellation or common origin—may contribute to explaining similarities and differences, convergences and divergences between the cases compared. This has been discussed theoretically, and good comparative studies have considered this in practice.[70] The rise of entanglement history has reconfirmed this methodological necessity. It is the task of the future to better combine comparative and entanglement history.[71]

It is in this sense that we are moving 'beyond comparison'. It means to better embed comparison in other intellectual operations and to modify it in this process. Historical comparison is changing and will continue to adjust to new needs and tasks. It is becoming more subtle and self-reflective. Comparative history and entanglement history are being combined in new ways. This is demonstrated by the following contributions to this volume, which show in which directions relevant work and debates of German historians are moving.

The Contributions to this Volume

The articles in this volume are either discussions on the scope and problems of comparative and transnational history or innovative case studies. The journal *Geschichte und Gesellschaft* in 2001 opened a discussion on the possibilities and limits of transnational history. Two of the most challenging articles published in this context are reproduced here. Jürgen Osterhammel, who not only demands for more internationally oriented writing and research in Germany but is practising it, continues to defend the methodological principles of comparative history, but would like to open social history research to broader transnational prospects. Migration history, for example, could be one of the more promising fields. In his article, Osterhammel does not abandon the national perspective, but wants to situate it in a global context, as does Sebastian Conrad. With a critical historiographic perspective, Conrad argues against the exclusion of colonialism from the main historical narratives, as well as against the assumption that Germany's short colonial experience did not have any pertinent effects on German society. Andreas Eckert takes up this argument and, based on recent studies on Africa, uncovers the layers of the historical relationship between Germany and its colonies. One of the underlying assumptions of these approaches is the 'entanglement' of histories in- and outside of Europe. Shalini Randeria criticizes a Eurocentric approach by stressing the variety of concepts of modernity and civil society used outside of Europe that also influenced European development. The different forms 'entanglement' can take are at the core of the article by Monica Juneja and Margrit Pernau, wherein the authors stress the importance of studying translations of concepts, as well as the lineages between historiographies.

Besides the debate initiated and developed by historians and sociologists working on extra-European history, a more Europe-oriented debate on the concept of 'cultural transfer' questions certain assumptions of comparative history. Hartmut Kaelble argues in favour of a comparative approach that takes into account linkages and relationships between the units of analysis and integrates them in a field of multiple contacts. In this context, Philip Ther makes the point that central European experiences should not be considered outside European history, but analysed in terms of transfers and communication processes with other European societies.

Among the comparative case studies, some of the most promising fields of comparative, transnational, and entangled history are presented. Dirk Hoerder shows the difficult integration of concepts of migration history into German historical narratives and argues not only for a comparative study of migration, but also for a careful study of the 'signs of migration in its many variants'. Jörg Requate, like Hoerder, combines comparative and transnational perspectives when he situates three different societies—the GDR, CSSR, and FRG—within a broad international discussion on planning, showing how each society was trying to implement economic plans and accept cultural pluralism. Arguing in favour of a broad, universalizing comparison, Dieter Langewiesche presents different features and functions of nationalism by following the arguments of B. Anderson, E. Gellner, and A. Smith. Thomas Welskopp, who chooses a national framework, compares the characteristics of German and US labour organisations over a long period of time and comes to some important conclusions. The two final articles thus show particularly that comparative history, in all of its different conceptualizations, remains important in the German discussion.

Notes

1. Cf. B. Z. Kedar, ed., *Explorations in Comparative History* (Jerusalem, 2009). C. Ragin, *The comparative method. Moving beyond qualitative and quantitative strategies* (Berkeley/Los Angeles, 1987). With comprehensive bibliographical information: Jürgen Kocka, 'Storia comparata', in *Enciclopedia delle scienze sociali*, 8 (1998): 389–96; Hartmut Kaelble, *Der historische Vergleich. Eine Einführung zum 19. und 20. Jahrhundert* (Frankfurt/New York, 1999); Heinz-Gerhard Haupt, 'Comparative History', in *International Encyclopedia of the Social and Behavioral Sciences*, vol. 4 (London, 2001), 2397–2403. D. Cohen and M. O'Connor, eds., *Comparison and History. Europe in cross-national perspective* (New York/London, 2004). - The following text is a thoroughly revised, enlarged and updated version of the introduction to: Heinz-Gerhard Haupt and Jürgen Kocka, eds., *Geschichte und Vergleich. Ansätze und Ergebnisse international vergleichender Geschichtsschreibung* (Frankfurt/New York, 1996), 9–45.

2. Surveys in Haupt and Kocka, eds., *Geschichte und Vergleich*, 47–130; Kedar, ed., *Explorations*, 1–28; Kaelble, *Der historiche Vergliech*, and Haupt, 'Comparative History'.
3. Cf. e.g., Fernand Braudel, *Civilisation matérielle, économie et capitalisme, XVe-XVllle siècle* (Paris, 1979); Eric J. Hobsbawm, *The Age of Extremes. A History of the World, 1914–1991* (New York, 1994); Immanuel Wallerstein, *The Modern World-System*, vols. 1–3, (New York, 1974–1989).
4. For a previous discussion of this relation cf. J. Kocka, 'Comparison and Beyond', in *History and Theory* 42 (2003): 39–44.
5. John Stuart Mill, *Philosophy of Scientific Method*, ed. E. Nagel (New York, 1881), 211–33; A.A. van den Braembussche, 'Historical Explanation and Comparative Method: Towards a Theory of the History of Society', in *History and Theory* 28 (1989): 2–24; Theda Skocpol/Margret Somers, 'The Uses of Comparative History in Macrosocial Inquiry', in *Comparative Studies in Society and History* 22 (1980): 174–197, esp. 176, 181; Charles Tilly, *Big Structures, Large Processes, Huge Comparisons* (New York, 1984), 80, 82.
6. Otto Hintze, 'Soziologische und geschichtliche Staatsauffassung' (1929), in Hintze, *Soziologie und Geschichte* (Gesammelte Abhandlungen, vol. 2) (Göttingen, 1964), 239–305, esp. 251.
7. Marc Bloch, 'Pour une histoire comparée des sociétés européennes' (1928), in Bloch, *Mélanges historiques*, vol. 1 (Paris, 1963), 16–40, esp. 20ff.
8. Cf. J. Kocka, ed., *Europäische Arbeiterbewegungen im 19. Jahrhundert. Deutschland, Österreich, England, Frankreich im Vergleich* (Göttingen, 1984); H.-U. Wehler, 'Deutsches Bildungsbürgertum in vergleichender Perspektive. Elemente eines 'Sonderwegs'?' in *Bildungsbürgertum im 19. Jahrhundert*, vol. 4: Politischer Einfluss und gesellschaftliche Formation, ed. J. Kocka (Stuttgart, 1989), 215–37; Heinz Reif, *Die verspätete Stadt. Industrialisierung, städtischer Raum und Politik in Oberhausen 1846–1929* (Cologne, 1993).
9. Bloch, 'Pour une histoire comparée', 5.
10. This aspect of comparison is strongly emphasized in William H. Sewell, Jr., 'Marc Bloch and the Logic of Comparative History', in *History and Theory* 6 (1967): 208–18.
11. Cf. Ch. Tilly et al., *The Rebellious Century 1830–1930* (Cambridge, MA, 1975); Th. Welskopp, *Arbeit und Macht im Hüttenwerk. Arbeits- und industrielle Beziehungen in der deutschen und amerikanischen Eisen- und Stahlindustrie von den 1860er bis zu den 1930er Jahren* (Bonn, 1994).
12. John H. Elliott, *National and Comparative History. An Inaugural Lecture delivered before the University of Oxford on 10 May 1991* (Oxford, 1991), 23.
13. Cf. J. Matthes, ed., *Zwischen den Kulturen? Die Sozialwissenschaften vor dem Problem des Kulturvergleichs* (Soziale Welt, special volume 8) (Göttingen, 1992), esp. 75–99. The value of comparison for the history of historiography and the social sciences has been demonstrated for different European countries: C. Conrad and S. Conrad, eds., *Die Nation schreiben. Geschichtswissenschaft im internationalen Vergleich* (Göttingen, 2002); P. Wagner, *Sozialwissenschaften und Staat, Frankreich, Italien, Deutschland 1870–1980* (Frankfurt, 1990).

14. Cf. Jürgen Kocka, 'Asymmetrical historical comparison: the case of the German "Sonderweg"', in *History and Theory* 38 (1999): 40–51; A.R. Zolberg, 'How many Exceptionalisms?', in *Working-Class Formation. Nineteenth-Century Patterns in Western Europe and the United States*, eds. I. Katznelson and A.R. Zolberg (Princeton, 1986), 397–455; Stephen Kalberg, *Max Weber's comparative-historical sociology* (Cambridge, 1994).
15. Reinhart Koselleck, 'Zur historisch-politischen Semantik asymmetrischer Gegenbegriffe', in Koselleck, *Vergangene Zukunft. Zur Semantik geschichtlicher Zeiten* (Frankfurt, 1979), 211–59.
16. 'Sur les limites du comparatisme en histoire culturelle', in *Genèses* 17 (1994): 112–21.
17. David Blackbourn and Geoff Eley, *The Peculiarities of German History. Bourgeois Society and Politics in 19th-Century Germany* (Oxford, 1984); C.B.A. Behrens, *Society, Government and the Enlightenment: The Experience of Eighteenth Century France and Prussia* (New York, 1985); A.R. Brubaker, *Citizenship and Nationhood in France and Germany* (Cambridge, 1992); D. Gosewinkel, P.Weill, and A.Fahrmeir, *Citizens and Aliens: Foreigners and the Law in Britain and German States 1789–1870* (New York, 2000).
18. W.W. Rostow, *The Stages of Economic Growth* (Cambridge, 1960); the regional historical approach in Sidney Pollard, *Peaceful Conquest. The Industrialisation of Europe* (Oxford, 1981). Patrick K. O'Brien, 'Industrialisation, Typologies and History of', in *International Encyclopedia of the Social and Behavioral Sciences*, vol. 11 (London, 2001), 7360–67.
19. Theodor Schieder, 'Typologie und Erscheinungsformen des Nationalstaates in Europa', in *Historische Zeitschrift* 202 (1966): 58–81.
20. Miroslav Hroch, *Die Vorkämpfer der nationalen Bewegung bei den kleineren Völkern Europas* (Prague, 1968).
21. Ulrike v. Hirschhausen and Jörn Leonhard, 'Europäischer Nationalismus im West-OstVergleich: Von der Typologie zur Differenzbestimmung', in *Nationalismus in Europa. West- und Osteuropa im Vergleich*, eds. Hirschhausen and Leonhard (Göttingen, 2001), 11–45.
22. Cf. Reinhard Bendix, *Nation-Building and Citizenship* (Berkeley/Los Angeles, 1977); Bendix, *Kings or People: Power and the Mandate to Rule* (Berkeley/Los Angeles, 1978).
23. Cf. Paul Nolte, 'Modernization and Modernity in History', in *International Encyclopedia of the Social and Behavioral Sciences*, vol. 15 (London, 2001), 9954–61; D. Sachsenmaier and J. Riedel, eds., *Reflections on Multiple Modernities. European, Chinese and Other Interpretations* (Leiden, 2002) (including a seminal contribution by S.N. Eisenstadt). Still important: H.-U. Wehler, *Modernisierungstheorie und Geschichte* (Göttingen, 1977).
24. Cf. Juan J. Linz and Alfred Stepan, *Problems of Democratic Transition and Consolidation. Southern Europe, South America, and Post-Communist Europe* (Baltimore/London, 1996).
25. Cf. Manfred Hildermeier et al., eds., *Europäische Zivilgesellschaft in Ost und West. Begriff, Geschichte, Chancen* (Frankfurt/New York, 2000); Jürgen Kocka,

'Civil Society in Nineteenth-Century Europe: Comparison and Beyond', in *Historical Concepts between Eastern and Western Europe*, ed. Manfred Hildermeier (New York/Oxford, 2007), 85–100; Jürgen Schmidt, *Zivilgesellschaft. Bürgerschaftliches Engagement von der Antike bis zur Gegenwart. Texte und Kommentare* (Reinbek, 2007).

26. Theodor Schieder, 'Partikularismus und nationales Bewusstsein im Denken des Vormärz', in Schieder, *Nationalismus und Nationalstaat. Studien zum nationalen Problem im modernen Europa* (Göttingen, 1992), 166–96.

27. Criticism of this approach can be seen in Jean Bouvier, 'Libres propos autour d'une démarche révisioniste', in *Le Capitalisme français. XIXe-XXe siècles. Blocages et dynamismes d'une croissance*, eds. Patrick Fridenson and André Strauss (Paris, 1987), 11–27.

28. A.J. Heidenheimer, 'The Politics of Public Education, Health and Welfare in the USA and Western Europe: How Growth and Reform Potentials Have Differed', in *British Journal of Political Science* 3 (1973): 315–40. Cf. the thoughtful essay of P. Baldwin, 'Comparing and Generalizing: Why all history is comparative, yet no history is sociology', in Cohen and O'Connor, *Comparison*, 1–22. Especially when comparison of organizations is intended, one should not just look for corresponding institutions in another society, but also ask how problems to which specific institutions try to respond are resolved by other means in other institutional, political, and cultural contexts. Cf. Kiran Patel, *'Soldiers of Work': Labor Services in Nazi Germany and New Deal America, 1933–1945* (Cambridge, 2005).

29. Karl Polanyi, *The Great Transformation. The Political and Economic Origins of Our Times* (1944) (Boston, 1957); Michael Mann, *The Sources of Social Powers*, 2 vols., (Cambridge, 1986, 1993).

30. Alexander Gerschenkron, *Economic Backwardness in Historical Perspective* (Cambridge, MA, 1962). In terms of criticism: P.K. O'Brien, 'Do We Have a Typology for the Study of European Industrialization in the XIXth Century?', in *Journal of European Economic History* 15 (1986): 291–334.

31. Barrington Moore, *Social Origins of Dictatorship and Democracy. Lord and Peasant in the Making of the Modern World* (Boston, 1966).

32. Cf. Roy Bin Wong, *China Transformed. Historical Change and the Limits of European Experience* (Ithaca/London, 1997); David S. Landes, *The Wealth and Poverty of Nations. Why Some Are So Rich and Some So Poor* (New York, 1998); Gunder Frank, *ReOrient: Global Economy in the Asian Age* (Berkeley/Los Angeles/London, 1998); Kenneth Pomeranz, *The Great Divergence, China, Europe and the Making of the Modern World Economy* (Princeton University Press, 2000). Cf. Peer H.H. Vries, 'Governing Growth: A Comparative Analysis of the Role of the State in the Rise of the West'. in *Journal of World History* 13 (2002): 67–138.

33. Kaelble, *Der Historische Vergleich*, 12.

34. Cf. Th. Welskopp, 'Die Sozialgeschichte der Väter. Grenzen und Perspektiven der Historischen Sozialwissenschaft', in *Geschichte und Gesellschaft* 24 (1998): 173–98; Jacques Revel, *Jeux d'echelles. La micro-analyse à l'expérience* (Paris: Le Seuil, 1996).

35. H. Kaelble, *Auf dem Weg zu einer europäischen Gesellschaft. Eine Sozialgeschichte Westeuropas, 1880–1980* (Munich, 1987). Cf. Kaelble, 'Europäische Geschichte aus westeuropäischer Sicht?', in Gunilla Budde et al., eds., *Transnationale Geschichte. Themen, Tendenzen und Theorien* (Göttingen, 2006), 105–17. Most recently: Hartmut Kaelble, *Sozialgeschichte Europas. 1945 bis zur Gegenwart* (Munich, 2007). But see P. Baldwin, *The Narcissism of Minor Differences. How America and Europe Are Alike* (Oxford, 2009).
36. Cf. H.-G. Haupt, 'Historische Komparatistik in der internationalen Geschichtsschreibung', in Budde et al., eds., *Transnationale Geschichte*, 142f.; J. Osterhammel, 'Sozialgeschichte im Zivilisationsvergleich. Zu künftigen Möglichkeiten komparativer Geschichte', in *Geschichte und Gesellschaft* 22 (1996): 143–64.
37. Cf. S.N. Serneri, 'L'Europa: identità e storia di un continente', in *Contemporanea* 2 (1999): 79–102.
38. Cf. Deborah Cohen, 'Comparative History: Buyer Beware', in *Bulletin of the German Historical Institute* 29 (2001): 23–33. See also J.L. McClain et al., eds., *Edo and Paris. Urban Life and the State in the Early Modern Era* (London, 1994); D. Lehnert, *Kommunale Politik: Parteiensystem und Interessenkonflikte in Berlin und Wien 1919–1932* (Berlin, 1991).
39. H.-G. Haupt, ed., 'Les mobilités dans la petite bourgeoisie du XIXe siècle'. Spec. Issue of the *Bulletin du Centre Pierre Léon d'Histoire économique et sociale* (1993).
40. P. Vilar, 'Croissance économique et analyse historique', in *Première Conférence internationale d'Histoire économique*, vol. 1 (Stockholm, 1960), 35–82.
41. Marc Bloch, 'Pour une histoire comparée'. C. Fumian, 'Le virtù della comparazione', in *Meridiana* 4 (1988): 197–221.
42. A. Mayer, *The Persistence of the Old Regime. Europe to the Great War* (London, 1981).
43. See the bibliographies in Ernst Wilhelm Müller, 'Plädoyer für die komparativen Geisteswissenschaften', in *Paideuma* 39 (1993): 7–23.
44. Overviews of comparative historical literature in Germany, England, and France can be found in: Haupt and Kocka, eds., *Geschichte und Vergleich*, 47–90; here, 91–130, a report by Hartmut Kaelble on comparative social history in the research of European historians.
45. On this issue, see also Kaelble, *Der historische Vergleich*, 93–113.
46. D. Cohen, 'Comparative History: Buyer Beware', in Cohen and O'Connor, *Comparison*, 63.
47. Some new developments within the discipline have not promoted the trend toward comparison. *Alltagsgeschichte*, which was discussed so exhaustively in the 1980s, and which concentrated on the reconstruction of experiences and lifestyles within a micro-historical framework, remained sceptical toward analytical approaches and produced few comparisons. Alf Lüdtke, ed., *Alltagsgeschichte. Zur Rekonstruktion historischer Erfahrungen und Lebensweisen* (Frankfurt, 1989). The most recent emphasis on 'entangled histories' and *histoire croisée* has led to a situation where scholars have shown less interest in similarities and differences than in relationships and transfers.

48. Especially in the 1970s and 1980s. Cf. Georg G. Iggers, *New Directions in European Historiography*, rev. ed. (Middletown, CT, 1984). For a spirited and convincing statement in favour of analytical (not necessarily quantitative) approaches in history, cf. Hans-Ulrich Wehler, *Literarische Erzählung oder kritische Analyse? Ein Duell in der gegenwärtigen Geschichtswissenschaft* (Vienna, 2007).
49. Cf. P. Baldwin, *The Politics of Social Solidarity: Class Bases of the European Welfare State, 1875–1975* (New York, 1999); G. Esping-Andersen, *The Three Worlds of Welfare Capitalism* (Princeton, 1990); D. Cohen, *The War Come Home. Disabled Veterans in Britain and Germany, 1914–1939* (Berkeley, 2001).
50. Cf. G. Sluga, 'The Nation and the Comparative Imagination', in Cohen and O'Connor, *Comparison*, 103–14.
51. Jürgen Kocka, 'The European Pattern and the German Case', in *Bourgeois Society in Nineteenth-Century Europe*, eds. Jürgen Kocka and Allan Mitchell (Oxford/Providence, 1993), 21–39.
52. See D. Dowe, H.-G. Haupt, and D. Langewiesche, eds., *Europa 1848. Revolution und Reform* (Bonn, 1998).
53. Cf. Jens Alber, *Vom Armenhaus zum Wohlfahrtsstaat. Analysen zur Entwicklung der Sozialversicherung in Westeuropa* (Frankfurt, 1982); S. Rudischhauser and B. Zimmermann, '"Öffentliche Arbeitsvermittlung" und "placement public" (1890–1914). Kategorien der Intervention der öffentlichen Hand. Reflexionen zu einem Vergleich', in *Comparativ* 5 (1995): 93–120. Christoph Conrad, 'Wohlfahrtsstaaten im Vergleich: Historische und sozialwissenschaftliche Ansatze', in Haupt and Kocka, *Geschichte und Vergleich*, 155–80.
54. Cf. Christian Meier, 'Aktueller Bedarf an historischen Vergleichen. Überlegungen aus dem Fach der Alten Geschichte', in Kocka and Haupt, *Geschichte und Vergleich*, 239–70.
55. Cf. also the argument in Haupt, 'Historische Komparatistik', 137–50.
56. Cf. the bibliography of comparative works by European historians put together by Hartmut Kaelble in Haupt and Kocka, *Geschichte und Vergleich*, 111–30.
57. This story has often been told. Cf. e.g., Lutz Raphael, *Geschichtswissenschaft im Zeitalter der Extreme. Theorien, Methoden, Tendenzen von 1900 bis zur Gegenwart* (Munich, 2003), chs. IX, XIII; Rolf Torstendahl, ed., *An Assessment of 20th-Century Historiography. Professionalism, Methodologies, Writings* (Stockholm, 2000); Doris Bachmann-Medick, *Cultural Turns. Neuorientierungen in den Kulturwissenschaften* (Reinbek, 2006).
58. Cf. Nancy Green, 'Forms of Comparison', in Cohen and O'Connor, *Comparison*, 41–56; Green, 'Réligion et éthnicité. De la comparaison spatiale et temporelle', in *Annales HSS* (2002), 127–44; Green, 'The Comparative Method and Poststructural Structuralism—New Perspectives for Migration Studies', in *Journal of American Ethnic History* 13(4) (Summer 1994): 3–22.
59. Cf. C. Tacke, *Denkmal im sozialen Raum. Nationale Symbole in Deutschland und Frankreich im 19. Jahrhundert* (Göttingen, 1995); Tacke, 'Feste der Revolution in Deutschland und Italien', in *Europa 1848. Revolution und Reform*, eds. D. Dowe et al. (Bonn-Bad Godesberg, 1998), 1045–88; H. Rausch, *Kultfigur und Nation. Öffentliche Denkmäler in Paris, Berlin und London 1848–*

1914 (Munich, 2006); J. Boutier and D. Julia, eds., *Passés recomposés. Champs et chantiers de l'histoire* (Paris: Autrement, 1995); M. Jeismann, *Das Vaterland der Feinde. Studien zum nationalen Feindbegriff und Selbstverständnis in Deutschland und Frankreich 1792–1918* (Stuttgart, 1992); E. Francois et al., eds., *Nation und Emotion. Deutschland und Frankreich im Vergleich. 19. und 20. Jahrhundert* (Göttingen, 1995); Arno Mayer, *The Furies. Violence and Terror in the French and Russian Revolutions* (Princeton, 2000); A. Lieske, *Arbeiterkultur und bürgerliche Kultur in Pilsen und Leipzig* (Bonn, 2007).

60. R. Koselleck et al., 'Drei bürgerliche Welten? Zur vergleichenden Semantik der bürgerlichen Gesellschaft in Deutschland, England und Frankreich', in *Bürger in der Gesellschaft der Neuzeit. Wirtschaft-Politik-Kultur*, ed. H.J. Puhle (Göttingen, 1991), 14–58; W. Steinmetz, 'Introduction. Towards a Comparative History of Legal Cultures 1750–1950', in *Private Law and Social Inequality in the Industrial Age*, ed. W. Steinmetz (Oxford, 2000), 1–41; I. Hamsher-Monk, K. Tilmans, and F. van Vree, eds., *History of Concepts: Comparative Perspectives* (Amsterdam, 1998); P. Wagner, ed., *The Languages of Civil Society* (New York/Oxford, 2006).

61. Cf. Hartmut Kaelble, 'Sozialer Aufstieg in den USA und Deutschland, 1900–1960. Ein vergleichender Forschungsbericht', in *Sozialgeschichte Heute. Festschrift für Hans Rosenberg*, ed. Hans-Ulrich Wehler (Göttingen, 1974), 525–42; Christoph Conrad et al., eds., *Writing National Histories. Western Europe since 1800* (London/New York, 1999); Ida Blom, 'Das Zusammenwirken von Nationalismus und Feminismus um die Jahrhundertwende. Ein Versuch zur vergleichenden Geschlechtergeschichte', in Haupt and Kocka, *Geschichte und Vergleich*, 315–38.

62. Hartmut Kaelble, *Sozialgeschichte Europas. 1945 bis zur Gegenwart* (Munich, 2007).

63. Michael Geyer, 'Historical Fictions of Autonomy and the Europeanization of National History', in *Central European History* 22 (1989): 316–42; Jürgen Osterhammel, *Geschichtswissenschaft jenseits des Nationalstaats. Studien zu Beziehungsgeschichte und Zivilisationsvergleich* (Göttingen: Vandenhoeck & Ruprecht, 2001); Patrick Manning, *Navigating World History. Historians Create a Global Past* (New York, 2003); C. A. Bayly, *The Birth of the Modern World 1780–1914* (Oxford, 2004); F. Osterhammel, *Die Verwandlung der Welt. Eine Geschichte des 19. Jahrhunderts* (Munich, 2009).

64. Bloch, 'Pour une histoire comparée', 37.

65. Cf. the contributions to Budde et al., *Transnationale Geschichte*; Jürgen Osterhammel, 'Transkulturell vergleichende Geschichtswissenschaft', in Haupt and Kocka, *Geschichte und Vergleich*, 271–314 (with many references); S.N. Eisenstadt, 'Die Dimensionen komparativer Analyse und die Erforschung sozialer Dynamik. Von der vergleichenden Politikwissenschaft zum Zivilisationsvergleich', in *Diskurse und Entwicklungspfade. Der Gesellschaftsvergleich in den Geschichts- und Sozialwissenschaften*, eds. H. Kaelble and J. Schriewer (Frankfurt/New York, 1999), 3–28; Hartmut Kaelble, 'Der historische Zivilisationsvergleich', in Kaelble, *Der historische Vergleich*, 29–52.

66. On transfer history see M. Espagne and M. Werner, eds., *Transferts culturels. Les relations interculturelles dans l'espace franco-allemand (XVII-XXe siècles)* (Paris, 1988); M. Espagne, *Les transferts culturels franco-allemands* (Paris, 1999); H. Lösebrink and R. Reichardt, eds., *Kulturtransfer im Epochenumbruch. Frankreich-Deutschland 1770 bis 1815* (Leipzig, 1997); L. Jordan and B. Kortlander, eds., *Nationale Grenzen und internationaler Austausch. Studien zum Kultur- und Wissenschaftstransfer in Westeuropa* (Tübingen, 1995); R. Muhs et al., eds., *Aneignung und Abwehr. Interkultureller Transfer zwischen Deutschland und Großbritannien im 19. Jahrhundert* (Bodenheim, 1998). Sebastian Conrad and Shalini Randeria, eds., *Jenseits des Eurozentrismus. Postkoloniale Perspektiven in den Geschichts- und Kulturwissenschaften* (Frankfurt/Main, 2002); R.J.C. Young, *Postcolonialism. An Historical Introduction* (Oxford, 2001); A.L. Stoler and F. Cooper, 'Between Metropole and Colony. Rethinking a Research Agenda', in *Tensions of Empire*, ed. A.L. Stoler and F. Cooper (Berkeley, 1997); H. Bhaba, *The Location of Culture* (London, 1994). Jürgen Osterhammel, 'Transnationale Gesellschaftsgeschichte: Erweiterung oder Alternative', in *Geschichte und Gesellschaft* 27 (2001): 464–79; S. Conrad, 'Doppelte Marginalisierung. Plädoyer für eine transnationale Perspektive auf die deutsche Geschichte', in *Geschichte und Gesellschaft* 28 (2002): 145–69; Conrad, *Globalisierung und Nation im Deutschen Kaiserreich* (Munich: Beck, 2006); S. Conrad and J. Osterhammel, eds., *Das Kaiserreich transnational. Deutschland in der Welt, 1871–1914* (Göttingen, 2004); Matthias Middell, ed., *Globalisierung und Weltgeschichtsschreibung* (Leipzig, 2003). Christoph Charle, *La crise des sociétés impériales. Allemagne, France, Grande-Bretagne 1900–1914* (Paris, 2001). S. Spiliotis, 'Wo findet Geschichte statt? oder Das Konzept der Transterritorialität', in *Geschichte und Gesellschaft* 27 (2001): 480ff.

67. Cf. the early works by Espagne and Werner in footnote 66 above with the more recent article by Michael Werner and Bénédicte Zimmermann, 'Vergleich, Transfer, Verflechtung. Der Ansatz der Histoire croisée und die Herausforderung des Transnationalen', in *Geschichte und Gesellschaft* 28 (2002): 607–26.

68. Johannes Paulmann, 'Internationaler Vergleich und interkultureller Transfer. Zwei Forschungsansätze zur europäischen Geschichte des 18. bis 20. Jahrhunderts', in *Historische Zeitschrift* 267 (1998): 649–85.

69. A classic example is Otto Hintze's comparison of feudalism in Europe and Japan. Cf. Hintze, 'Wesen und Verbreitung des Feudalismus' (1929), in Hintze, *Staat und Verfassung*, vol. 1, *Gesammelte Abhandlungen* (Göttingen, 1962), 84–119. Another example is James L. McClain et al., eds., *Edo and Paris: Urban Life and the State in the Early Modern Era* (Ithaca: Cornell University Press, 1994). An interesting discussion of this type of comparison in Natalie Zemon Davis, 'Beyond Comparison: Comparative History and its Goals', in *Swiat historii*, ed. Wojciecha Wrzoska (Poznan: Instytut Historii UAM, 1998), 149–57, esp. 152ff.; it is interesting that George M. Fredrickson concentrated his review of comparative history literature on the 'small but significant body of scholarship that has as its main objective the systematic comparison of some

process or institution in two or more societies that are not usually conjoined within one of the traditional geographical areas of historical specialization'. Cf. Fredrickson, 'Comparative History', in *The Past Before Us: Contemporary Historical Writings in the United States*, ed. M. Kammen (Ithaca, NY, 1980), 457–73, esp. 458.

70. Cf. H. Kleinschmidt, 'Galtons Problem. Bemerkungen zur Theorie der transkulturell vergleichenden Geschichtsforschung', in *Zeitschrift für Geschichtswissenschaft* 39 (1991): 5–22. As a practical example: Kaelble, *Sozialgeschichte Europas*; clearly, the author explains the observed convergences and divergences between the national societies of Europe by taking mutual perceptions and influences between them into account (among other factors).

71. Cf. Kocka, 'Comparison and Beyond'. J. Osterhammel is more sceptical about the fruitfulness of the linkeage in: J. Osterhammel, 'Transferanalyse und Vergleich im Fernverhältnis', in H. Kaelble and J. Schriewer, eds., *Vergleich und Transfer. Komparatistik in den Sozial-, Geschichts- und Kulturwissenschaften* (Frankfurt a.M., 2003), 439–66, esp. 466.

PART I

Comparative and Entangled History in Global Perspectives

≡ CHAPTER 1 ≡

Between Comparison and Transfers – and What Now?

A French-German Debate

HARTMUT KAELBLE

In recent years a lively and instructive debate about comparative history has reignited, with the jumping-off point of classical comparative history. Comparative history has come to be more widely practiced in both Europe and the US since the 1970s, though only by a minority of historians. It was well received among US historical sociologists, as well as exiles from Europe, and gained significant standing through a rediscovered essay by Marc Bloch from the 1920s. Since the 1990s comparative history has been practiced more often in Europe than in the US, particularly in Germany (Berlin and Bielefeld). Comparative history was one step in a stronger transnational orientation of European historiography, and it has been weighed over several times. In the classical sense, one can understand comparative history as the systematic search for differences and similarities—for divergences and convergences—between various means of comparison. The development of comparative typologies and their contextualization was bound to follow.[1]

After a quarter-century of comparative history, during which hundreds of comparative works were published, a debate began in the mid-1990s in which four concepts were developed: first, the concept of 'transfers'; then, the concept of 'entangled history'; after that the concept of *histoire croisée*; and, finally, the concept of a combination of comparative and 'relations history'. The development of these concepts sprang from each other and now contests historical doctrine.

Michel Espagne put forth the concept of 'transfers' in a 1994 article in the journal *Genèses*. He understood a transfer as the processes through which the norms, images and representations of one culture appear in another by the transmission of concepts. Such transmissions originate through migration, as well as through meetings and the reading of texts from another culture. In the article he called for more room to be given to studies of transfer in historical scholarship, since he argues that every nation is constituted not only by its own traditions, but also to a significant extent by such transfers from other nations. The history of a nation cannot be understood when the writing is limited only to its national history. He strongly criticizes classical comparison, because it possesses several weaknesses that transfer studies alleviate. It is obliged to first construct the objects of comparison in order to begin making a comparison. It must, therefore, considerably remove itself from reality, and often leave transfers from other nations or civilizations unconsidered. Transfer studies are not similarly constrained, and therefore more closely represent reality, since they follow change through the transmission of one culture into another. Classical comparison primarily concentrates on structures and institutions, and largely excludes experiences and history. Experiences, however, stand at the centre of transfer studies. Classical comparison, moreover, fails to adequately address the historian's central object: time. As a general rule, it compares societies from the same time period. By contrast, time is an essential element of transfer studies, since the studies are always analysing change.

Jürgen Osterhammel has argued very convincingly in a similar vein, but with important differences. In contrast to Espagne, Osterhammel is not primarily interested in transfers among European countries, but in transfers between Europe and Asia, as well as other non-European societies. His definition of the concept of transfer is broader than most others: transfers are not just cultural, but also political, social and economic developments.

'Entangled history' or 'shared history', as developed by the social scientist, Shalini Randeria, and the historian and specialist of Japan, Sebastian Conrad, raises a critique of classical comparison similar to that of Espagne but continues Osterhammel's line of thought in two respects. According to this concept, transfers join together and integrate not only adjacent countries, nor only members of similar cultures such as France and Germany, but also countries spatially separated from one another, such as Japan and Germany. Entangled history states that direct and indirect transfers take place everywhere and bind together all civilizations in the world. More significantly, it claims emphatically that colonizers and colonized societies are strongly bound to one another through transfers and not only through the much-researched transfers from the mother country into the colonies, but also, though less frequently noted transfers from the colonies to the mother countries. The concept of entangled history therefore stresses a shift in emphasis away from Europe.

In reaction to this argument French historian and German specialist, Michael Werner, and French political scientist, Bénédicte Zimmermann, constructed the concept of *histoire croisée*. Three key elements have contributed to the comparative history debate: *histoire croisée* is more or less grounded in a scepticism regarding the stand-alone existence of transnational spaces, movements, languages, values or institutions, and the nation is seen as a central point of orientation. As a result, this concept requires that transnational research of any kind take into account the fundamentally different perspectives of the different societies being compared and thus continually switch perspectives and become increasingly reflexive. Moreover, *histoire croisée* requires going beyond the predominantly *binational* orientation of comparative and transnational research to consider *multilateral* approaches and research. Finally, in the framework of this concept, the clear opposition between the disadvantages of classical comparison on the one hand, and the advantages of transfer studies, on the other, is reconsidered: it is argued that comparison and transfer share similar strengths and weaknesses.

Along with *histoire croisée* is a fourth concept: the combination of comparative and transfer studies. The basis of this idea is that transfer studies possess the same weaknesses as classical comparison. It argues that transfer studies must also construct their objects in order to define what constitutes a change through transmission from one culture to another. In addition comparisons, and not only transfer studies, operate across the dimension of time since they not only address similarities and differences, but also divergence and convergence. Comparisons are also argued to, indeed, deal with experiences. Moreover, transfer studies and comparisons rely upon and compliment one another. Comparisons require the consideration of transfers because transfers are a significant factor when addressing convergence and divergence. Without transfer studies, one overlooks an important explanation for divergences and convergences. Conversely, transfer studies require comparison because it is only through comparison that the delivering culture can be distinguished from the receiving culture; and it is only through comparison that the actual content of a change, which is at the core of a transfer, can be determined. For example, when one argues that the German nation largely consists of transfers from French culture, one must use comparison to figure out what is German and what is French. Finally, transfer studies further require comparisons, because comparisons become more a part of everyday thinking as the two societies are more tightly integrated, and as increased movements between them take place. Dealing with such everyday judgments and prejudices, explaining them, testing them and incorporating their influence, are considerable tasks for social scientists and historians, especially in a strongly integrated world.

In this debate, three things are noteworthy or worthy of critique:

1. This is not merely a methodological debate, but is part of a transnational reorientation of historical scholarship. This reorientation took

place in a time-specific historical context in Europe and would have had little chance to occur in earlier epochs. It has, without a doubt, been spurred on by massive anxiety over globalisation in times of growing unemployment and the decline of the European economy: falling behind Japan, Southeast Asia and the US; it was also encouraged by the recovery of the European Union since the 1980s, as European intellectuals came to see the EU as a significant transnational centre of European power; the process of individualisation, through which strong loyalties to European nation states were loosened in many European countries for citizens and historians alike and transnational values of international agreement and understanding came to be more highly prized; and, finally, through the new kinds of transnational wars since the 1990s, in which the main actors were no longer states alone and in which Europe, as a whole, was included. Without this time-specific historical context, the new transnational orientation of historians would remain incomprehensible. The debate, only briefly presented here, discussed different options for a transnational orientation of social and cultural history. Comparison was an alternative to transfer and relations studies. At the same time, the combination of both approaches was possible, because both options were concerned with the same goal of creating a more transnational historiography. They were not—and so as not to create any misunderstandings—the only options. The broader cultural and economic history of international relations, which was also developed during the 1990s, was another important, and not always clearly distinguished, option.

2. The debate under deliberation took place within a relatively small circle, and is not widely familiar outside it. It was limited to specialists of the last two and a half centuries and was not absorbed, for rather obvious reasons, by early modern historians or historians of the Middle Ages. It became increasingly a debate between social historians and Germanists, disciplines unfamiliar with one another and among whom there had not been close dialogue for a long time. Among the conventional partners of historiography—political science, sociology, ethnology, philosophy and law—the debate had little response. In these disciplines similar problems were discussed from time to time, usually under the topic of *Gattung* problems—in which one cannot compare objects that are tied in a close relationship. But the debate over *Gattung* problems was completely separate from the debate discussed here.

3. Up to this point in the debate no one has attempted to write a detailed scholarly history of historical comparison and historical transfer and relations. They certainly did not first begin in the 1970s, as is usually

thought in Europe. In the most interesting contributions on the subject the history of general social and cultural comparison is traced back to the Enlightenment, or even to Greek and Roman civilization (see the work of Peter Brockmeier, Lorraine Daston, Chris Lorenz, Lars Mjøset, Jürgen Schriewer).

What are the most significant challenges in the current status of the debate? How should historical comparison and relations history develop further?

The first, and most important, requirement has to do with the fact that this methodological debate precedes the practice of historical research. While the methodological works about classical historical comparison emerged at the end of a long practice of comparative history by historians, the discussion regarding the other concepts developed somewhat in reverse. Neither for 'entangled history', nor for *histoire croisée*, nor for the combination of historical comparison and relations history, are there a great number of empirical studies – and there are no internationally known, heavily cited and frequently translated model studies for future studies to engage. Transfer studies also do not a sea of research in which to swim. The immediate need for empirical research is imperative – otherwise the debate runs the danger of becoming lost in the abstract. Model studies, above all, often require many years of work.

A second requirement to further the debate is for abstract concepts beyond historical comparison to be reconciled with one another. How 'transfer history', 'integration history', 'relations history' and transnationality relate to one another is still too little considered, though there are proposals to do so. But the scholarly language also remains too unstructured. Should one abandon the term 'transfer history' in favour of 'integration', because the concept of transfer is too narrow and only means *changes* among concepts, experiences, and meanings through the transmission of these from one culture to another, while 'integration' is much more comprehensive? Or rather is 'transfer' a broader concept than 'integration', because transfers can take place between countries that are not tightly integrated and have little direct interaction? Or are both 'transfer history' and 'integration history' too narrow and should be dropped in favour of the neutral expression 'relations history' – which is not limited to changes through transnational transmission, and does not assume that all societies in the world are integrated and that foreign relations are an essential element of a particular society? Or is the concept of 'relations history' also too narrow for the transnational history of the twentieth century, because it cannot address important transnational developments such as international institutions – the World Bank, the United Nations, the European Union, the Catholic

Church – or transnational social spaces, movements, values, languages and discourses, as these cannot be reduced to relations between individual countries of societies, but, rather, possess their own, internal logic? Would it really be possible and sensible to break down the decision of the European Commission into French, British, German and Spanish contributions and relations, or to explain the decisions of the Catholic Church through reference to the relations among particular national daughter-churches? Does not the concept of relations history thus also have clear limits here? Would it be best to choose a kind of hierarchy among transnationality, relations history, integration history and transfers?

The third requirement: this debate needs to cease its exclusivity. It should be communicated more strongly to neighbouring disciplines, and they should be brought into the dialogue. Above all, the debate should move beyond its Franco-German exclusivity and open up into the Anglo-Saxon, Spanish-speaking and East Asian space. To this end, translations of key texts in English, Spanish, Chinese or Japanese would be necessary. The debate, which to this point has been bound tightly to the European context, would gain a new pulse through dialogue with these non-European historians.

Note

1. This essay appeared first as 'Die Debatte über Vergleich und Transfer und was jetzt?', in Geschichte.transnational (Forum), http://geschichte-transnational.clioonline.net/forum/id=574&type=diskussionen, 8 February 2005.

CHAPTER 2

A 'Transnational' History of Society

Continuity or New Departure?

JÜRGEN OSTERHAMMEL

The following text is a revised version of a contribution first published in the journal Geschichte und Gesellschaft *in 2001.[1] At that time, the editors were organizing a round table on the question of the desirability and possibility of a 'transnational' history of society. I was invited to provide a comment because of an academic background that is rather unusual for German historians. For a long time, my main fields of interest have been modern Chinese history and the history of the British Empire. In earlier articles, I had advocated historical comparisons occur not just between European countries or societies or even within the 'West', but across cultural borders and spanning wide spatial distances. What would a proponent of that kind of intercivilisational comparison have to say about the new catchphrase of 'transnational history'? The following text retains the gist of my arguments of 2001. It takes only selective account of the extensive debate that has taken place since then. Some of my earlier ideas would merit reconsideration in light of recent theoretical discussions, and, more importantly, of practical historiographical work that has been undertaken. My own basic convictions have remained the same: I am not persuaded that classical comparativism has been completely superseded and made obsolete by a programme of entangled history. Comparison and the analysis of intercultural and intersocietal transfers do not present a stark alternative. They complement one another, and there are numerous examples in recent historical scholarship for the successful combination of both approaches. Finally, I am not happy with a recent tendency to establish Transnational (with a capital T) History as a separate and perhaps even autonomous field. 'Transnational' refers to a particular perspective in the same way as 'national' does. It is always useful to ask whether new knowledge or insight can be gained from looking at a historical phenomenon in such a 'transnational' perspective. But this does not mean,* as has sometimes been suggested in the German debate, that transnational history is generally superior and preferable to national history.

* * *

Gesellschaftsgeschichte, the History of Society, has been one of the most successful paradigms in postwar German historiography. Its hallmark has been the infusion of social science theories into a tradition of social history that used to be basically descriptive. The original impetus behind *Gesellschaftsgeschichte* was not to demonstrate the usefulness of theory as such; it was more than just scholarly *l'art pour l'art*. The project was a political one: to develop a new interpretation of modern German history, carefully grounded in the fullest possible evidence, deploying the whole panoply of advanced research tools, and guided by a sense of tragic failure of German history with its 'special path' and ultimate, though ever fragile, democratic normality after 1945. Careful nurturing of these various elements allowed the mature achievements of *Gesellschaftsgeschichte* to emerge: an enormous output of monographs on all possible aspects on the history of the German bourgeoisie or (a wider concept) *Bürgertum*, Jürgen Kocka's multi-volume history of labour and labour organization in nineteenth-century Germany, and, the towering monument of the school, Hans-Ulrich Wehler's *Deutsche Gesellschaftsgeschichte*.[2]

The core group of *Gesellschaftsgeschichte* was surrounded by a larger group of pupils, sympathizers, and kindred spirits. Some of them, but not many, applied the basic approach of the History of Society to European countries other than Germany, especially France, Italy, and Russia. This is how far the school was prepared to go. Apart from an early interest of both Wehler and Kocka in the history of the United States, *Gesellschaftsgeschichte* was hardly ever transplanted into non-European contexts. Some of the reasons are obvious—*Gesellschaftsgeschichte*'s idea of society was closely linked to mature industrialism and its antecedents. Agrarian societies only entered the picture when germs of modernity were already visible. They were of interest only as belonging to the pre-history of modernity. 'Traditional' peasant societies as well as colonized societies all over the world failed to provide the elementary features of that type of social complexity that alone merited the attention of *Gesellschaftsgeschichte*. It has, therefore, always been a project centred on modern Germany and, to a lesser extent, Western and Eastern Europe. If 'transnational history' is also meant to be trans-European history, *Gesellschaftsgeschichte* will have to rethink its more or less unspoken assumptions.

However, it would be wrong to suppose that *Gesellschaftsgeschichte* has remained static. Once the foundations had been laid in the 1970s, the 1980s, as a period of 'extension', consolidated the initial achievement. This is how the leaders of *Gesellschaftsgeschichte* saw themselves, and *Erweiterung* became a favourite motto of the time. Extension of the basic paradigm was achieved by careful enlargement of *Gesellschaftsgeschichte*'s scope of action. *Gesellschaftsgeschichte* grew and prospered less through colonizing the outer reaches of historical scholarship than by the intensification of research and by the careful incorporation of adjacent thematic fields. This was a wise strategy, which allowed the paradigm to be tested and improved. From a position of unassailed self-confidence, *Gesellschaftsgeschichte* chose its own mode of extension. Some challenges, especially from *Alltagsgeschichte* or the history of material life and local experience, were fended off in an imperious manner. Elsewhere, concessions were made and new inspirations were welcomed and valued. Thus, a few new theorists were allowed to join the incomparable Max Weber in the pantheon of *Gesellschaftsgeschichte*'s thinkers of reference, first among them was Pierre Bourdieu (while Michel Foucault met with resolute refusal).[3] 'Agency' was added to 'structure'; 'culture', even if defined quite conventionally and narrowly, was taken on board; the method of comparison, famously pioneered by the great Max Weber himself, was recommended as the best method possible for absorbing new evidence and, at the same time, enhancing the power and rigour of explicative models.

By and large, such cautious attempts to keep up-to-date met with success and led to the revitalization of the project of *Gesellschaftsgeschichte*. In its mature form, it was much more than traditional social history. It included material production, social stratification, political power, and the institutions (much less the practices) of cultural expression. Yet anthropologists tell us that 'boundary maintenance' requires not just inclusion, but also exclusion; in other words, it requires drawing a line. Therefore, a few hoary antagonisms were left intact and were even confirmed: the history of international relations, apart from a brief flirtation with the study of imperialism, was flatly rejected; contemporary history with a strong narrative flavour was left to others; and the history of ideas, even in as novel a shape as 'intellectual history' or 'history of discourse', continued to be looked at with a considerable amount of suspicion, and seen as a vestige of old-fashioned *Historismus* in the tradition of Friedrich Meinecke.

Yet another kind of extension that was avoided was the enlargement of the spatial or horizontal sphere of reference. A careful critic of *Gesellschaftsgeschichte*'s house journal, *Geschichte und Gesellschaft*, has dubbed the whole tendency a 'nation-centred social history'.[4] This has been quite amazing from the point of view of the outside observer. A scholarly project that strongly opposed all forms of German (and any other) 'nationalism', that lost no opportunity to quote the great universalist thinker Max Weber, and that paid its respects to modern universalists such as Eric Hobsbawm,

Barrington Moore, Charles Tilly or Wolfgang Reinhard, felt surprisingly comfortable with its own provincialism.

In order to overcome such limits of vision, nothing seems to be easier than simply to add new geographic and cultural spaces. However, Hans-Ulrich Wehler has admitted that the guiding concepts of *Gesellschaftsgeschichte* are difficult to transplant into a seemingly familiar context such as the North American one.[5] It would be even more difficult to apply terminologies of Weberian sociology and modernization theory to non-Western social configurations. The indigenous self-description of such societies usually offers a rich repertoire of concepts, and the science of anthropology or ethnology provides additional instruments of study. At the same time, it would be wrong to deny the pertinence of European concepts to the rest of the world. Simple dichotomies of the West and the 'rest' should be a thing of the past. *Gesellschaftsgeschichte* might easily avoid a responsibility to extend its scope by playing the well-known game of 'othering the Other'. Yet, anthropology is of limited use for understanding the literate traditions of Asia, and holistic concepts of societal otherness such as the 'oriental mode of production' (Karl Marx) or 'oriental society' (John Stuart Mill) are no longer considered adequate for describing the complex hierarchies of traditional Asian societies, let alone their processes of modernization.

An obvious way out seems to lie in the development, in Max Weber's footsteps, of an integrated social science that develops flexible concepts for dealing with social phenomena across cultural boundaries, rather than to leave the 'Others' to special academic disciplines whose results can, from the point of view of 'normal' historians, safely be disregarded. Ultimately, one should aim at a kind of analytical two-way traffic. Just as ethnology and anthropology have been extremely helpful in enriching our understanding of Western societies, so the tools of Western social and historical science ought to be, perhaps in a modified way, applied to non-European societies.[6]

Such two-way traffic implies a heightened awareness of the history of European expansion and of the cultural interactions between Europeans and non-Europeans—subjects not normally within the purview of German historians. The history of German colonialism begins no earlier than 1884, and this brief episode was over by the end of the First World War. This had the historiographical consequence of the continuous insensibility of German historians toward the global dimension of European history. Yet, a brief look at countries such as Great Britain, the Netherlands, and Portugal, and even France and Russia, should reveal that, throughout the post-Columbian period, expansion has been a fundamental mode of existence for many parts of Europe. It is not Eurocentric conceit to say that overseas expansion and empire building are defining features of Europe's history. In many European countries, social processes transcended the boundaries of nation states. The spatial frame for solving social problems often extended the limits of the nation state. This may have been less so in Germany than elsewhere, although Germany could not escape the effects of earlier waves of globalization, and even became an active player in global games from the beginning of the *Kaiserreich* onward.[7] The best way to study those entanglements would be to take account of the most recent advances in migration history—a field strangely neglected by *Gesellschaftsgeschichte* proper.[8]

It has been suggested that border-transgressing relations and activities should generally come under the heading of a history of 'transfers'. The study of such transfers has already become a vibrant field of historical research. The crucial question is the reach of such an approach. A radical solution would be to abandon national history altogether in favour of a history of exchanges, networks, and hybridities. Suggestions of this kind are not entirely new. As early as 1967, the Swiss historian Herbert Lüthy pointed out that, up to the present, all history has been a history of colonisations and overlapping stratifications.[9] More than twenty years later, the sociologist Friedrich Tenbruck challenged the masters of *Gesellschaftsgeschichte* by juxtaposing the History of Society and the History of the World. Although the school of *Gesellschaftsgeschichte* rarely dodged a challenge, Tenbruck's critique went unanswered and unheeded.[10]

Tenbruck's article, nothing less than an intervention by one of Germany's leading sociologists, flatly contradicted the incremental model of slowly extending the scope of *Gesellschaftsgeschichte*. Tenbruck did not deny the relevance of the nation state as a unit of analysis, but he suggested that the most fruitful point of view for the historian to take was not inside the nation and the nation state; rather, it should be located at a higher level. External relations should not be secondary features of 'structures', whose principal dynamics were to be considered as internal and endogenous. Friedrich Tenbruck, completely untouched by 'postcolonial studies', suggested studying movements and transfers, migration and long-distance trade, along with conquests and the expansion of religions. Up to a point, this was Tenbruck's message—the 'structures' so beloved to *Gesellschaftsgeschichte* were crystallizations emerging from such a fluid reality. Published in 1989, these were prophetic proposals. Jürgen Kocka later arrived at similar, though less radical, conclusions, demanding 'the definition of problems within a global horizon'.[11] He went on to propose that historians should study 'the connections between local phenomena and global contexts'. The crux of the matter—radicalizing Kocka's point—is that one does not generally have to scale the ladder from the local to the global level. Instead, a historical analysis should begin from both ends at the same time. Joachim Radkau's global environmental history, written at the University of Bielefeld under the shadow of *Gesellschaftsgeschichte*, but in explicit distance from it, is a good example for this kind of 'polycentric' analysis.[12]

How do we get from here to a history of *society*? Basically, there are two possible ways for those who are not prepared to drop the concept of 'society' altogether and replace it with a loose collection of discourses and practices, identities and lifestyles. First, the permeability of bounded national and regional societies ought to be acknowledged. Not all social life is quintessentially 'entangled', but some kind of entanglement, even if quite limited in a particular case, is to be expected everywhere in modern history. This augments, rather than invalidates, a national perspective on modern history. Second, the methodology of comparison, as explained in other chapters in this book, can and should be used to determine whether there has been a distinctly European or, perhaps, 'Western' model of civilization and social organization. As long as this question is considered of any importance, comparison is indispensable. Even those who go far to avoid any kind of 'essentialism' cannot deny the existence of certain European peculiarities, which, of course, have been evolving over time and have been strongly influenced by the impact of economic and cultural globalization. For good reasons, historians are somewhat reluctant to engage in this kind of macro-comparison of entire national societies or even 'civilizations'. They prefer partial and topical comparisons to the very grand generalizations favoured by historical sociologists.[13] Still, the question of a typology of basic social forms in the world keeps lurking in the background and cannot be avoided. It should be discussed without any European triumphalism and sense of self-congratulation. In societal terms as well as in many others, non-Western societies are not just deficient losers of historical competition, lacking the essential aspects of Western modernity. This cannot be emphasized too strongly, given the limited interest of German historians in non-occidental history.

Comparison is one of the methods used by practitioners of 'transnational history'. A growing number of authors seem to know what 'transnational history' is, but upon closer inspection, few of them care to offer a definition. What does the adjective 'transnational' really mean? The concept was first used in the social sciences, but even there its specific content has often been left unclear. 'Transnational' obviously is different from 'supranational', a word that refers to the political development of (Western) Europe since about 1950: the emergence, unprecedented in history, of a separate sphere of political and administrative action distinct from, and, in a growing number of fields, superior to the sovereignty of the individual nation states.[14] On the other hand, 'transnational' should be distinguished from 'international', a term first used in 1780 by Jeremy Bentham. Originally, it referred to the relations between state actors within a plural system of militarized great powers.¹⁵ Current usage is much wider than that—'International Relations' also includes economic and cultural contacts and exchanges of the most varied kind. This is reflected in the vast body of literature in International Relations theory—a field of theoretical construction and reflection almost unknown to the great majority of historians. The additional connotation of cosmopolitanism, already present in Bentham's use of the word, has gained importance in recent decades. Since the establishment, in 1864, of the International Committee of the Red Cross, the world knows what today is called International Nongovernmental Organizations. Just one year later, the First International, as a transnational organization of militant European socialists, came into being. When historians speak today of 'internationalization', they do not mean horizontal relations between states, but the impact of higher levels on national societies. They use the term 'internationalism' to describe the rise of collective identities transcending the nation state, and, at the same time, they study the processes of internationalizing cultural, political, and economic practices that went hand in hand with the formation of national states during the nineteenth century.¹⁶ In respect to traffic, trade, and migration, such a process transgressed the boundaries of the European continent at an early point in time. In cultural terms, it mainly assumed the form of Westernization, and in the twentieth century, more specifically of Americanization. When Jürgen Kocka expects an imminent 'internationalization of the historical social sciences', he seems to indicate that these sciences will deal with transnational phenomena and, at the same time, that they will find a resonance all over the world. Both meanings can safely been accommodated within the word 'international'.

Yet, what is the advantage of introducing the special semantics of the 'transnational' alongside the established meanings of the 'international'? Sometimes, shifts in emphasis have been slow and almost imperceptible: multinational companies, for example, gradually came to be known as 'transnational corporations'. In the theory of International Relations, the term 'transnational politics' was introduced in the late 1960s.¹⁷ Initially, it encompassed all sorts of interdependent relationships in 'world politics', with the exception of the official relations between national governments. This later turned out to be impractically vague. Recent attempts at definition put an emphasis on 'clearly identifiable actors or groups of actors ... linking at least two societies'.¹⁸ This kind of formalism, typical for International Relations theory, however, is of little help for social historians.

Other approaches seem to be much more interesting. To give just two examples: sociological and ethnological studies of migrants in the present-day world have shown how it is possible to lead a life in a kind of permanent transgression of boundaries between persisting national cultures. People and communities 'in between' do not necessarily live in the rarefied world of a rootless cosmopolitanism, nor are they lost in a no-man's-land. Both options have, of course, existed in the past. But there is also the possibility of multiple identities, bilingualism, and the flexible enacting of roles. For this third type of cases, the concept of 'transnational social space' seems to offer an adequate solution. Spatial metaphors have the general advantage of addressing the problem of the 'framing' of social relations. They also open up the large fields of a history on the impact of political borders on social configurations.[19] In this sense, 'transnationalism' refers to a special category of social relations that unfold in tension with and in contradiction to the assertion of national sovereignties.

Secondly, it becomes more and more obvious that the social influence of religions is not contained within political boundaries. After a period when religion, in the sense of individual experience and piety, became one of the favourite subjects of *microstoria*, it is now being discovered as a factor of transnational cultural ordering. The old concept of 'ecumene' in the sense of large-scale communities of shared meaning assumes new importance. More and more, the nationalization of creeds and churches in post-Reformation Europe (much later in Catholicism than in Protestantism) is revealed as a very special case in the world history of religion.

It would not be difficult to continue like this. New developments in the contemporary world prompt us to take a new view of the past, and new theories help to detect or even 'constitute' new fields of inquiry. Both forces shaping the agenda of historians, the empirical and the theoretical one, have to be situated within larger historical contexts. Those who now advocate 'transnational history' should ask themselves what it is that motivates them to champion such a new 'turn'. It should also encourage them not to establish their new direction in an exclusive and sectarian way. Transnational history does not have to take sides in the long-term quarrel, so typical of German historical scholarship, between social historians and historians of international relations. On the contrary, transnational history could be an ideal bridge to bring together those 'two cultures' in historical studies.[20]

Finally, a small number of general points must suffice to outline the contours of a future transnational social history:

1. *Nationalgeschichtsschreibung*, the history of nations and nation states, has not been the 'normal' mode of historical writing. It emerged as a by-product of the formation of nation states in the mid-eighteenth century. David Hume, the Scottish-born historian of England, was the inventor of that genre. The call for a social history in a transnational perspective (abbreviated: TSH) responds to: (a) a new definition of problems and priorities in an age of continuing globalization; (b) a certain kind of exhaustion of the paradigm of *Gesellschaftsgeschichte* after three decades of specialized research; and, (c) the demand by major theorists

in the social sciences that 'notions' of society with a regionalist or national colouring are no longer acceptable from a theoretical point of view.[21]

2. TSH builds upon a program of social history in terms of structures and configurations, but supplements it with the idea of exchanges, flows, and streams. A central concept is that of the network.[22]

3. TSH takes leave of the scant regard for space in the German historiographical tradition of all schools and tendencies. While it would be an exaggeration to speak of a 'spatial turn', transnational history is much more sensitive to topics such as borders and boundaries, territoriality and the ordering of space, the natural environment of social and political processes, etc. The classical authors of sociology, with the exception of Georg Simmel, have, by and large, avoided such questions. Recent social science has taken them up again, and geography once again has to be taken seriously, as it was in the eighteenth century as a sister discipline of historiography.[23]

4. To praise the virtues of TSH does not imply a general denigration of the nation state as a unit of analysis. The nation state continues to be the most important institutional framework for the lives of most people in the world. National governments still have a decisive impact upon individual lives through legislation, law enforcement, taxation, public welfare, etc. Even the prototypical diaspora nationalities are striving for their own nation state—and have achieved it in cases such as Israel and Armenia. If a homogeneous European society slowly may be emerging, 'world society' is little more than a useful fiction, mainly limited to networks of elite communication.[24] It is not a sociological fact in the sense of Emile Durkheim's 'crystallized life'. A primacy of transnational or cosmopolitan norms and values is still limited to minorities and other small groups. There is, thus, no basis for transnationality in major social structures. On the other hand, conventional ideas of a *Gesamtgesellschaft*, with clearly demarcated boundaries and a high level of cultural uniformity, rapidly lose their attraction. Many societies in the world are heterogeneous societies constituted by immigrants, colonial, and ex-colonial 'plural societies' or simply 'multicultural' urban spaces. This needs no special mention for the United States, but in the case of Europe, closer inspection will help to discover the enormous importance of ethnic and cultural plurality, with all its concomitant tensions and conflicts.

5. For practical reasons, TSH will initially be mainly restricted to European history. However, such a limitation cannot be defended on systematic grounds. The old dichotomies Orient/Occident, Europe/non-Europe,

West/rest, civilization/barbarism, etc., are increasingly hard to maintain. Many arguments have been marshalled against them: from the critique of 'orientalism' to the latest theories of 'plural modernities'.[25]

6. There are numerous instances where not only those historians of Europe who are interested in overseas expansion and colonialism are well-advised to look beyond the confines of the continent, be it only to put Europe's alleged uniqueness into perspective. Thus, crucial features of 'European civil society' were, in fact, pioneered in other parts of the world. In 1893, the women of New Zealand, including the native Maori, received the vote. Australia's women followed in 1902, but female citizens of the United Kingdom had to wait until 1928. When, in 1935, property-owning women were enfranchised in India, the general vote for women in France was still nine years away. In all of these cases, local factors combined with 'transfers' from outside to achieve a specific outcome.[26] Europe did not always take the lead. This is also true for the development of the welfare state or for the modernization of urban space, where, again, some noteworthy innovations originated in Australia, a pioneer of suburbanization.

7. Is TSH identical with 'the history of transfers'? Of course, many transfers are transnational, but not all of these transnational transfers should be classed as social history. TSH does not include the disembodied movement of ideas or even some kind of abstract interaction of 'cultural codes'. In order to come to the attention of social history, transfers have to be connected to identifiable actors and institutions. It should be possible to study intentions, interests, and functions related to the transfers. Social historians are also interested in the effects of such transfers, and they want to explain where and why a specific transfer occurred and for what reasons it assumed the form that it did.

8. Does transnational history make a conventional history of society obsolete? Certainly not. A *Gesellschaftsgeschichte*, at least of the late modern period with its enormous importance of the nation state, cannot be based on networks, flows, and transfers alone. At the same time, some of the changes suggested by proponents of transnational history cannot be accommodated just by making minor adjustments to the given framework of *Gesellschaftsgeschichte*. The very concept of 'society' employed by its practitioners requires a fundamental overhaul. Hans-Ulrich Wehler's 'four dimensions'—the economy, social inequality, political domination, and culture (a residual category including religion, education, and the public sphere)—should perhaps be augmented by other central aspects of social life. In addition, *Gesellschaftsgeschichte*

might reconsider its narrow fixation on the rise of industry and industrial society. Industrialization took place in many different parts of the world, not just in Europe and North America. It failed to take root in many other quarters of the planet, some of which are unlikely ever to 'catch up' in the familiar sense of European development. And where industrialization happened, it did not necessarily result in fully articulated industrial societies. Therefore, *Gesellschaftsgeschichte* should broaden its range of types of society considered, and it should reflect once again on its ideas about the forms and temporal structures of social change. To look beyond Germany or even beyond Europe does not necessarily mean forfeiting one's own scholarly integrity and entering the extremely ambitious world of universal synthesis. Fortunately, there are many different ways of doing transnational history.

Notes

1. J. Osterhammel, 'Transnationale Gesellschaftsgeschichte: Erweiterung oder Alternative?', *Geschichte und Gesellschaft* 27 (2001): 464–79; for a broader treatment of the subject cf. Osterhammel, *Geschichtswissenschaft jenseits des Nationalstaats. Studien zu Beziehungsgeschichte und Zivilisationsvergleich* (Göttingen, 2001). Since the purpose of the present volume is to introduce the German debate, the following references will focus on German contributions. This should not mean that the international discussions are not being followed in Germany.
2. See P. Lundgreen, ed., *Sozial- und Kulturgeschichte des Bürgertums. Eine Bilanz des Bielefelder Sonderforschungsbereichs (1986–1997)* (Göttingen, 2000); J. Kocka, *Weder Stand noch Klasse. Unterschichten um 1800* (Bonn, 1990); J. Kocka, *Arbeitsverhältnisse und Arbeiterexistenzen. Grundlagen der Klassenbildung im 19. Jahrhundert* (Bonn, 1990); H.-U Wehler, *Deutsche Gesellschaftsgeschichte*, 5 vols. (Munich, 1987–2008).
3. The high watermark of this kind of 'extension' was a collection of articles: W. Hardtwig and H.-U. Wehler, eds., *Kulturgeschichte heute* (Göttingen, 1996).
4. L. Raphael, 'Nationalzentrierte Sozialgeschichte in programmatischer Absicht. Die Zeitschrift 'Geschichte und Gesellschaft. Zeitschrift für Historische Sozialwissenschaft' in den ersten 25 Jahren ihres Bestehens', *Geschichte und Gesellschaft* 25 (1999): 524–25.
5. H.-U. Wehler, 'What is the "History of Society?"', in *Conceptions of National History: Proceedings of Nobel Symposium 78*, eds. E. Lönnroth et al. (Berlin/New York, 1994), 277.
6. Important articles advocating the usefulness of anthropological approaches for the social history of Europe were published in *Gesellschaftsgeschichte's* main journal, e.g., U. Daniel, '"Kultur" und "Gesellschaft". Überlegungen zum Gegenstandsbereich der Sozialgeschichte', *Geschichte und Gesellschaft* 19 (1993): 69–99. For an attempt to apply categories of *Gesellschaftsgeschichte* to

an Asian country see J. Osterhammel, 'Gesellschaftsgeschichtliche Parameter chinesischer Modernität', *Geschichte und Gesellschaft* 28 (2002): 71–108.
7. See S. Conrad and Jürgen Osterhammel, eds., *Das Kaiserreich transnational. Deutschland in der Welt 1871–1914* (Göttingen, 2004); J. Osterhammel, 'Europamodelle und imperiale Kontexte', *Journal of Modern European History* 2 (2004): 157–81.
8. See D. Hoerder, *Cultures in Contact: World Migration in the Second Millenium* (Durham, NC, 2002); K.J. Bade, *Migration in European History* (Oxford, 2003).
9. H. Lüthy, 'Die Epoche der Kolonisation und die Erschließung der Erde' (1967), in *Universalgeschichte*, ed. E. Schulin (Cologne, 1974), 240.
10. F.H. Tenbruck, 'Gesellschaftsgeschichte oder Weltgeschichte?' *Kölner Zeitschrift für Soziologie und Sozialpsychologie* 41 (1989): 417–39.
11. J. Kocka, 'Historische Sozialwissenschaft heute', in *Perspektiven der Gesellschaftsgeschichte*, eds. P. Nolte et al. (Munich, 2000), 21.
12. J. Radkau, *Natur und Macht. Eine Weltgeschichte der Umwelt* (Munich, 2000).
13. The main themes of current historical sociology are surveyed in G. Delanty and E.F. Isin, eds., *Handbook of Historical Sociology* (London 2003); J. Adams, E.S. Clemens, and A.S. Orloff, eds., *Remaking Modernity: Politics, History, and Sociology* (Durham, NC, 2005).
14. G. Thiemeyer, 'Supranationalität als Novum in der Geschichte der internationalen Politik der fünfziger Jahre', *Journal of European Integration History* 4 (1998): 5–21.
15. See P. Friedemann and L. Hölscher, 'Internationale, International, Internationalismus', in *Geschichtliche Grundbegriffe. Historisches Lexikon zur politisch-sozialen Sprache in Deutschland*, eds. O. Brunner, W. Conze, and R. Koselleck, vol. 3 (Stuttgart, 1982), 367–97.
16. See M.H. Geyer and J. Paulmann, eds., *The Mechanics of Internationalism: Culture, Society, and Politics from the 1840s to the First World War* (Oxford, 2001).
17. See K. Kaiser, 'Transnationale Politik', in *Die anachronistische Souveränität*, ed. E.-O. Czempiel (Cologne/Opladen, 1969), 80–109; R.O. Keohane, ed., *Transnational Relations and World Politics* (Cambridge, MA, 1972).
18. T. Risse-Kappen, 'Introduction', in *Bringing Transnational Relations Back In: Non-State Actors, Domestic Structures and International Institutions*, ed. T. Risse-Kappen (Cambridge, 1995), 8.
19. From among a huge literature, see T.M. Wilson and H. Donnan, eds., *Border Identities: Nation and State at International Frontiers* (Cambridge, 1998).
20. See W. Loth and J. Osterhammel, eds., *Internationale Geschichte. Themen—Ergebnisse—Aussichten* (Munich, 2000).
21. N. Luhmann, *Die Gesellschaft der Gesellschaft*, vol. 1 (Frankfurt a.M, 1997), 31.
22. For a brief sketch of such an approach see J. Osterhammel and N.P. Petersson, *Globalization: A Short History*, trans. D. Geyer (Princeton, 2005).
23. J. Osterhammel, 'Die Wiederkehr des Raumes. Geopolitik, Geohistorie und historische Geographie', *Neue Politische Literatur* 43 (1998): 374–97; an impres-

sive plea for a spatially informed look at history is K. Schlögel, *Im Raume lesen wir die Zeit. Über Zivilisationsgeschichte und Geopolitik* (Munich, 2003).
24. For Europe see H. Kaelble, ed., *The European Way: European Societies during the Nineteenth and Twentieth Centuries* (New York, 2004); for the German debate on 'world society' see B. Heintz, R. Münch, and H. Tyrell, eds., *Weltgesellschaft* (Stuttgart, 2005).
25. See J. Osterhammel, '"Weltgeschichte". Ein Propädeutikum', *Geschichte in Wissenschaft und Unterricht* 56 (2005): 452–79.
26. I.C. Fletcher, L.E.N. Mayhall, and P. Levine, eds., *Women's Suffrage in the British Empire: Citizenship, Nation, and Race* (London/New York, 2000).

≡ CHAPTER 3 ≡

Double Marginalization

A Plea for a Transnational Perspective on German History

SEBASTIAN CONRAD

Double Marginalization[1]

'There can be no doubt', asserted the historian Hermann Heimpel of Göttigen at the end of the 1950s, 'that the time of a historical observation based exclusively on the nation state is over. The historical science must dare to jump into the planetary future, also in the recording of the past'.[2] This plea can still serve today, a half-century later, as a historiographic guideline. To be sure, one would not want to stylize Heimpel's as a postcolonial, transnational approach of the kind that I propose in the following chapter.[3] Heimpel's 'planetary future' has become in the meantime a globalized present, and worldwide communication has intensified to an extent that no one from Göttingen in the postwar period could have imagined possible.[4] The fundamental problem, however, has not lost its force: the writing of German history has been little altered by the surge of globalization. The interpretation of the German past, as a general rule, still stops at the national border.[5] The hegemony of this German-centric paradigm may have even been strengthened after 1989.[6]

This privileging of national history here will be challenged by a transnational perspective, which incorporates German (and European) history in a global interrelation and takes more seriously the relationship to regions outside of Europe than has traditionally been the case. Indeed, the traditional compartmentalization of the past according to national criteria leads to a loss of perspective on the manifold processes of integration and exchange and allows the nation to appear as an autarkic unit, an almost natural arbiter of events. The few attempts that have been made to deconstruct this model have tended to strengthen it even more: this applies, for example, to historical comparison, which through the process of doubling serves to relativize historiographical nationalism, but at the same time reproduces it—twice.[7] Similarly, transfer history, a dynamic comparison enriched through observation of reciprocal relationships, relies nevertheless on the framework of the nation state as the origin of historical contact.[8] Finally, approaches that expand the relevant frame of reference to European history often depend on the additive grouping of several national histories. [9] In particular, relationships with the extra-European world have been largely excluded from the writing of European history. The 'shared history' that binds Germany and Europe with Africa, Asia, and, since 1492, with the western hemisphere, plays at best a secondary role in traditional historiography.[10]

In this way, the obvious reality that contact with the extra-European world has increased sharply since the 'voyages of discovery', and even more since the middle of the nineteenth century, is ignored. Through trade, travel, slavery, diseases, wars, and colonial occupations, Europe was tightly bound with Africa, Asia, and America. These relationships led to long-lasting changes within the affected societies. For a long time, this process has been represented as the diffusion of European achievements throughout other parts of the world.[11] In the meantime, the insight has been made that these relationships in no way ran on a one-way street, but instead left behind long-lasting traces on Europe. But the stakes are higher: it is about more than the reciprocity of import, influence, and cultural exchange. The challenge is that taking reciprocal interrelationship between Europe and its 'others' seriously consists of observing that these exchange processes lay at the root of European modernity and were therefore constitutive in the development and self-understanding of Europe.[12] Without consideration for intercultural and colonial experiences within historical study, the understanding of German/European history necessarily remains partial and incomplete. Against this background, the demand for increased consideration of transnational interactions is not merely a plea to reconsider and call into question the artificial abstraction of national history, but also to understand that national history is a result of transnational exchanges.[13]

A 'shared history' that transcends the segregation of the national perspective can take on different forms. The consideration of intra-European border-crossings also contributes to a transnational writing of history.[14] For example, the attempt to reconstruct a *histoire croisée* between Germany and France demonstrated that 'units such as "France" and "Germany"' are to be regarded 'in part as the result of these common histories'.[15] In addition, the history of multinational political units, such as the Austro-Hungarian double monarchy, can hardly be written about without consideration for transnational processes. The extent to which interaction between Europe and the rest of the world is the focus of what follows is largely due to the fact that these connections have up to now been neglected. This applies in particular (but not only) to the experiences of imperialism and colonialism, which since the nineteenth century have shaped relations within the capitalistic world order, and to the experience of globalization. This could be called the suppressed unconscious of the European self-image. This is, in the German case, not merely the result of an inadequate engagement with Asian, African, or American history.[16] Rather, on a deeper level, it speaks to a double marginalization of the non-European dimension of German history. On the one hand, the concept of a 'shared history' has not up to now found its way into the theories that define our understanding of (European) modernity; on the other hand, German history counts as a special case, as it allegedly was less affected by the colonial experience than were other nations.

Blind Spots

That the majority of historical studies were composed from an internalist perspective, which makes it difficult to incorporate considerations of entanglements between different parts of the world, is connected with underlying axiomatic assumptions. In the *grand récits* of modernization, upon which concrete research explicitly or implicitly rests, non-European history remains a dark spot; as Michel-Rolph Trouillot once remarked, it often fills only a 'savage slot'.[17]

This applies to theories of modernization of a completely different provenance. Thus, the assumption of certain fundamental laws of history in Marxist historiography led to the view that development, as a general rule, was internally to be explained. Of course, predictions appear in the *Communist Manifesto* about the interconnectedness and the reciprocal penetration of the world. The idea of a common, global constitution of the modern world also appears in the work of Immanuel Wallerstein.[18] His approach remains ambivalent, however, because the history of the 'modern world system' can (and the concept came to be understood as such) also be read as a process of the gradual incorporation of the globe into a world order dominated by Europe.[19] In the practice of Marxist historical science, national developments have been frequently told, to use Lenin's phrase, as 'histories of a nation', histories of 'necessity', which proceed according to the dictated stages of world history.[20] Even the version of modernization theory, the genealogy of which traces back to the work of Max Weber, tends to pre-structure historical knowledge in such a way that European and non-European societies are conceived as separate entities. Of course, Max

Weber's work was as broadly diverse in its geographic and cultural scope as any other of his time (and even later). The great studies of Protestantism, Confucianism or Buddhism, however, are held together only through a common (fundamentally Euro-centric) theory and not through a common history. Above all, in approaches that rely on Weber, the perspective remains internalist; developments are explained internally; in the foreground stand changes over time within a society, not its interactions in space. Representative of this is the discovery of the 'early modern', a resource of indigenous modernization potential that nevertheless terminologically implies a later moment of 'fulfillment'. This prerogative of time over the category of space also remained definitive for the American modernization theories. Since the 1960s, under their influence, a large number of studies emerged that investigated the national pre-histories and indigenous traditions of a country and bestowed less significance on the interrelated constitution of modernity.[21]

Finally, in the work of Michel Foucault, which in recent years has been treated among historians as an alternative to traditional conceptions of modernization, the non-European dimension of European history also remains marginal. The great epistemic breakthroughs, sketched out in *The Order of Things*, follow an autarkic, occidental dynamic. The 'discovery' of man and subjectivity in the nineteenth century is presented as the sequel to the preceding 'period of representation'. That the European society at that very time was to overtake the entire globe played no role in Foucault's image of the epoch. But it also must be asked if the symbols of Foucault's modern age, the regime of sexuality or the panopticon, cannot themselves be conceived as products of another great watershed—colonial intervention. The extent to which 'disciplinary modernity' stands in a specific and global context has so far only begun to be addressed in scholarship.[22]

Stowaways

The systematic marginalization of Europe's colonial experience in different theories of modernity has contributed to the fact that, even in historiography, the reciprocal relationships among European nations have been pursued only in part. In this way, it is widely neglected that the emergence and development of modern societies in Europe are constitutively bound to their colonial interventions. Two important aspects of this relationship will be quickly sketched out here: firstly, traces of colonial encounters can still be read in a number of central categories of the social sciences. Supposedly neutral concepts are used to analyse relationships whose logic is already inscribed within them. Secondly, the non-European world has in many ways taken on the function of a 'laboratory of modernity' in which modern technologies (in Foucault's sense) are quasi-experimentally tested.

One of the most striking processes of the late nineteenth century, to come to the first point, was the unparalleled spreading of European knowledge throughout other regions of the world. Particularly in the form of modern science, this corpus of knowledge accrued an authority that frequently made it appear to be in line with the natural order of things. Universities were founded in the colonies and the few independent states outside of Europe, which classified and dispersed knowledge based on the model of European disciplines. The introduction of modern historiography—often modelled after Ranke's historism—was also an example of this. This diffusion process has been described often.[23] A fundamental problem has nevertheless been mostly overlooked: to what extent were the concepts and categories in which this knowledge was stored and negotiated themselves shaped by the colonial situation? Do the concepts and terms of social-scientific explanations carry the traces of the very 'hybridity' that shaped, according to some newer approaches, the nature of intercultural exchange?[24] Did the asymmetry of colonial power relationships perhaps manifest itself in the creation of categories that still shape our understanding of society and history today?

The consideration of this problem is still largely in its infant stage. So far, there have been few initiatives to research the relationship between colonialism and scholarship in this manner, which must also include a renewed history of concepts (*Begriffsgeschichte*). It is worth reflecting for a moment how considerations of this kind may contribute to our understanding of transnational history. Thus, Shalini Randeria observed that the disciplinary separation of sociology and anthropology in the eighteenth century reproduced the power gap between Europe and its 'other'. This Manichean ordering placed developing, 'modern' societies (the object of sociological analysis) in opposition to backwards or primitive tribes and peoples, which were solely accessible through anthropological research—social change on one side, stagnation and cultural singularity on the other. The academic ordering of knowledge is thus already inscribed with dichotomies, which, as 'stowaways', are part of the intellectual baggage with which we travel. [25]

Likewise, the process of consolidation of university disciplines, since the first half of the nineteenth century, has led to the virtual disappearance of non-European pasts from European historiography. To the extent that Asian civilizations were an integral component of the great universal histories of the Enlightenment period, this inclusion disappeared for the most part over the course of the nineteenth century, in which historiography specialized in the composition of national histories.[26] This disciplinary historical tradition is also connected to the exclusion of non-European regions from history—an expulsion that, in turn, remains unintelligible outside of the colonial context.

This geographic centering of history—which degrades whole continents to the status of 'history-less' regions[27]—was also carried out outside of Europe in the course of the global dissemination of history as an academic discipline. In Japan, where Ranke's young student, Ludwig Rieß, was in charge of constructing a historical faculty, academic historiography was devoted exclusively to European history.[28] This differentiation between a history of Europe and traditions and customs unworthy of history was closely connected to two primary concepts of European historiography also present outside of Europe: linearity and progress. The concept of a linear, continuous 'development', which conceived of the past as qualitatively different from the present and thereby made history a story of progress, was characteristic of European historiography of the nineteenth century. Outside of Europe, these concepts had to be incorporated into the vocabulary in order to make the concept of 'progress' terminologically possible.[29] This perspective was spread throughout the whole world in the form of 'Whig History': the national histories of India, Japan, and Argentina all were written from this perspective.[30]

Within historiography, such fundamental concepts are only discussed on the level of high theory, without a thorough historicization, that is, without a contextualization. Even in the *Begriffgeschichte* tradition of Reinhart Koselleck, the idea of progress was examined from within the secure fortress of the occidental history of ideas. The *Sattelzeit* remained, for him, an internal affair of Europe. Here as well, the question arises as to whether or not it would be more productive to broaden the perspective and to situate concepts such as *Sattelzeit* and progress in the process of western 'discovery' and colonization of the world, and thus add a postcolonial element to *Begriffsgeschichte*. The implementation of progress-oriented thinking does not merely rely on the 'acceleration' of occidental temporality, but, rather, may be a result of the increasing asymmetry in the relationships between Europe and the non-European world.[31]

In this sense, Johannes Fabian demonstrated that since the nineteenth century, travel to remote regions came to be understood as time travel: foreign cultures appeared to European observers to be in earlier stages of human history. In Europe's appetite for the 'foreign' and 'primordial', a longing for its own origin manifested itself as well. Europe and its others appeared as two worlds of different times. This 'denial of coevalness' was at the same time the foundation for the construction of a progress from the 'primitive' societies to the height of European civilization. The expansive new ordering of space in the nineteenth century was dependant on a fundamental reorganization of time. The colonialization of the world and the transformation of the past in histories of progress were codependent.[32]

Following the Darwinian revolution—and its mirror image, social Darwinism—a specific form of progress-oriented thinking had entered the social theories of the late nineteenth century. For Albert Wirz, there is a metaphorical aspect to the fact that Darwin did not come to his evolutionary enlightenment in his native London, but, rather, on an island in the Pacific.[33] Here, it is apparent that Europe's self-understanding was inseparable from its overseas exploits. But could Darwin's 'Galapagos' be more than a metaphor? It has been argued that the theory of evolution can also be read as a movement that brought the societal circumstances of post-Malthusian England into the animal world—a social 'survival of the fittest'—and therefore naturalized them.[34] But can this problem also be understood from a postcolonial perspective? If Johannes Fabian's analysis of European travel impressions can also serve as a description of Darwin's voyage on the *Beagle*, the discovery of the mechanisms of evolutionary progress in the Atlantic Ocean can hardly be surprising. European colonialism would have anticipated what *The Origin of the Species* read into the world of nature. The popularized Darwinism of the late nineteenth century therefore need not be seen as a simple justification of the colonial order, but also as its result.

Is the insight into natural historical and historical 'progress' (with its later incarnation as 'modernization' and 'development') a product of the colonial experience? Could it be, in other words, that this fundamental concept of historical understanding is loaded with the traces of the specific asymmetry that characterized the global exchange of goods and knowledge in the nineteenth century? The doctor Rudolf Virchow saw it that way. When faced with criticism of the practice of presenting people from foreign lands to the German public in the framework of animal parks and *Völkerschauen*, he insisted that this exhibition of the exotic would be to the 'greatest benefit of anthropological science'. 'Yes, in fact, these images of humanity'—representations of the kind of asynchrony that Fabian had described—'are very interesting for everyone who wants to know about the position of man in nature and about the development that the human species has achieved'.[35]

Laboratory of Modernity

The 'shared history' of Europe and the non-European world may have left behind deep epistemological marks in the concepts and categories that shaped the understanding of modern societies. Going beyond this discursive dimension, in order to come to the second point, cultural exchange found its expression following the expansion of Europe also in concrete forms of social practice. In many ways, the colonies represented an experimental field for the European colonial bureaucracy, serving as a testing ground for large-scale interventions and societal reforms. The colonies were in many ways not only the recipients of the accomplishments of occidental civilization, as an older reading suggested, but, rather, appeared in several regards as a type of laboratory for European modernity.[36]

Thus, the Caribbean historian Eric Williams posed the sweeping thesis that European capitalism had not developed in Europe alone, but, instead, must be traced back to the economic exchange of European colonial powers with the great plantations of the Caribbean islands. The enormous accumulation of capital that was necessary for the industrial manufacturing of textiles first became possible as a consequence of the exploitation of raw materials and labour in the colonies. The work of African slaves on the sugar plantations of the Caribbean could thus be seen as a catalyst of the industrial revolution.[37]

Much criticism has been directed at this thesis, which Williams first formulated in 1944.[38] Detailed investigation of capital flows and economic-fiscal interactions have cast doubts on the thesis, even though the argument is not yet entirely resolved. Kenneth Pomeranz has argued in recent years that Europe's developmental advantage since the nineteenth century cannot be explained internally. In his argument, capital does not play the central role. He shows that the scarcity of land in Europe was resolved through the slave trade and the emergence of a new form of periphery in the Caribbean: 'Forces outside the market and conjunctures beyond Europe deserve a central place in explaining why western Europe's otherwise largely unexceptional core achieved unique breakthroughs and wound up as the privileged centre of the nineteenth century's new world economy.'[39]

Similar relationships can be found in other areas. Richard Grove, for example, has characterized the inception of a sensibility for questions regarding environmental protection as an effect of European colonialism. He speaks of the 'central significance of the colonial experience in the formation of western environmental attitudes'. The first experiments with a systematic conservation of forests and with preventative measures against water pollution were implemented at the end of the eighteenth century overseas—in Mauritius, the Caribbean, and India.[40] The characterization of the colonies as the laboratory of modernity generally is not aimed, however, at the early period of European expansion, but, rather, at the mature phase of colonialism around the end of the nineteenth century. The colonial situation appeared here in many ways as an ideal testing ground for implementing large-scale reform plans and societal interventions. The notion that the social order could be reformed through planned, strategically motivated interventions won influence in political and administrative affairs toward the end of the century. This belief found scholarly support in the rising social sciences. The colonies appeared to many proponents of reform as the ideal location to put into practice this form of interventionist policies in light of the fact that in many cases, the resistance against extensive interference in Europe appeared insurmountable.

To the fields of systematic intervention belonged, for example, centralized city planning, the necessity of which had been increasingly emphasized since the turn of the century.[41] Gwendolyn Wright demonstrated that an array of city planning measures were implemented in French colonial regions with the purpose of testing concepts that could later be applied successfully in France. Urban reconfiguration was characterized not least by hygienic, sanitary, and transport technical requirements that would transform traditional city structures into modern urban centres. The reconfiguration of Moroccan cities, including Rabat and Casablanca, by Hubert Lyautey is the best-known instance of this socio-political policy of intervention.[42] The central tenet of the new urban design combined elements of traditional Moroccan cities with the modern, French style of *villes nouvelles*. In this way, the colonial projects demonstrated the ability of city planning on a grand scale without destroying local structures, a realization that was then transmitted back to France—urban modernization and the charm of small French cities did not have to be mutually exclusive.[43]

The colonies appeared thus as experimental fields for urban reconfiguration on a scale that still lacked societal acceptance in Europe. But colonial interventions did not always aim at such large-scale and conspicuous changes; they could also apply to marginal and seemingly ephemeral cases. Carlo Ginzburg has depicted in a fascinating essay an example of this form of micro-political experiment: the introduction of fingerprinting in the identification of criminals in Bengal in the late nineteenth century. The focus was not simply on criminological practices, which today find their consequent continuation in DNA tests; a specific understanding of the individual lay in this technical procedure, which met resistance in Europe. The identification of criminals, especially in repeat cases, by means of a fingerprint suggested ultimately that individuality—and even personality—could be determined based on a single external trait of the physical body: the lines of the fingertip.

In the colonies, however, this resistance did not appear to be significant. Since the 1880s, Sir William Herschel, administrative director of the Hooghly district in Bengal, made use of fingerprinting as an element of forensic practice. Local traditions, but also English perceptions of the lack of inherent individuality among the natives, may have contributed to the quick implementation. Its success in the colonial 'laboratory' led the doctor and anthropologist Francis Galton to recommend the same method for English law enforcement shortly thereafter. His hopes to determine racial differences between the peoples (Galton posited 'a more monkey-like pattern' among Indians)[44] were not fulfilled. Nevertheless, the functionality of the procedure in the identification process was obvious, and the dactyloscopic method was implemented within a short time in England and then later throughout the world.[45]

Historiographical Voids

The colonial experience has been neglected in social theories and in European history. A second level of exclusion is added to this general marginalization in the case of Germany. Even though the connections described above can hardly be assigned to a specific national history, the dominant opinion in historiography holds that the significance of the 'colonial adventure' in German history was particularly minor when compared to other European states. In light of the short duration of the German colonial empire, the small proportion of German settlers overseas, and the comparatively small economic profitability from the colonies, colonialism is considered for the most part to be a side note in German history.[46]

This assumption runs like a thread through the handbooks and syntheses of German history. In Klaus Hildebrand's comprehensive 900-page long overview of German foreign policy, in which one would expect an examination of the process of territorial acquisition in the framework of 'world politics', only four pages are dedicated to German colonial politics—and even here events happen almost exclusively in Europe. Notwithstanding a stubbornly maintained primacy of foreign policy, little meaning is ascribed to this specific aspect of foreign relations. Colonial politics remain a derivative field of political activity, a derivative of the European power constellation.[47]

This perspective can be found in other political-historical syntheses. Plans for the acquisition of overseas possessions in the middle of the 1880s were motivated within the context of European political strategies—colonial politics as a approchement with France or as a protection against England. Colonial politics is European politics, even 'by detour over Africa.'[48] Bismarck, who, upon looking at a map of Europe, remarked: 'That is *my* map of Africa,'[49] remains representative for German interpretations of things colonial, and historians too have largely remained within the parameters of this Prussian 'mental map'. The subsuming of colonial politics under internal conflicts among European powers follows, incidentally, a specific logic, as colonial history was typically told as a part of the pre-history of the First World War, the first great vanishing point for German historical teleology. Had German activity overseas sharpened the conflict within the European power system and advanced Germany's isolation? The colonial advances and retreats made by the Department of Foreign Affairs therefore depicted as were characterized by 'aimlessness' and elements of 'arbitrariness and improvisation'; compared to the other powers, they appeared as 'hectic and opaque' and made an 'anxious and unmethodical' impression.[50] Agadir, Tangier or Venezuela became, historiographically speaking, predecessors of Sarajevo.

Colonialism has also remained marginal in the social histories of Imperial Germany. To be sure, in the course of the worldwide protests against diverse forms of neo-imperialism since the late 1960s, an array of studies have emerged that critically have researched German imperialism in the years before the First World War.[51] Surprisingly, however, these approaches left virtually no trace in the analyses of German society. The abstraction of 'imperialism' seemed to warrant an inclusion of the Wilhelmian empire in an international (and also theoretical) context without it having to be proven in detail in social practice. In the multi-year Bielefeld *Bürgertum* project, questions regarding colonialism were never raised. In Hans-Ulrich Wehler's monumental *Gesellschaftsgeschichte*, as well, the consideration of colonial politics remains limited to a few pages.[52]

The marginalization of the colonial experience itself extends, interestingly, to the concept of 'social imperialism', a key concept of the 1970s. Bismarck's decision to acquire colonies is explained by Wehler as a strategy for deflecting internal social conflict overseas and, moreover, for motivating broad strata to agree to his Bonapartist reign. While both the plausibility of Wehler's thesis, as well as the effectiveness of social-imperialistic undertakings, depends decidedly on the popularity of the colonial projects, Wehler paradoxically emphasizes the lack of colonial enthusiasm among the population. How is Bismarck's system of securing his rule to be reconciled without mass support for colonialism? For Wehler, potential repercussions of colonial fantasies and hopes in German society play no role. The colonial visions of the enthusiasts among the ruling classes remained fundamentally a 'false consciousness' without support in the broader public.[53]

In both the primacy of foreign, as well as domestic politics, a historiographic exclusion of Germany's colonial experience can be observed. When colonial history then finally is taken up as a theme, the reader is not always protected from extremely stereotypical models. In Michael Stürmer's contribution to a book that is significantly dedicated to 'Germans and their Nation', the defeat of the Herero insurgence is reported. Here, the reader may be reminded of Edward Said's concept of 'orientalism': 'This war', so it goes, 'resembles in no way the image of war that soldiers and officers were raised with ... Instead of restricted, war was blind rage ... sources of water became places of ambush; imprisoned German peacekeepers were agonizingly martyred'. At issue is not the origin of this war of liberation or the motives of the insurgents; the perspective persistently remains that of the colonialists: 'The psychology of this war was, for the Germans, a nightmare'.[54]

The conflict in 'German South West Africa' was hardly a skirmish, but, rather, the largest war that the German empire pursued between 1871 and 1914. Throughout its course, more than 60,000 Herero and Nama were killed, along with 1,500 Germans; the Herero people were almost completely wiped out.[55] The Herero War achieved sad infamy through the 'annihilation order' of General von Trotha. Trotha had promised to carry out the war up to the complete elimination of the Herero, including male civilians, women, and children. It has been heavily discussed in historical research whether or not the imperial government in Berlin also pursued the war with genocidal intentions.[56] Hannah Arendt early on posited the thesis that the Herero War, with the practice of genocide and the construction of concentration camps, had anticipated the annihilation politics of National Socialism.[57] The thesis of continuity between colonial politics and the Holocaust has indeed been widely disputed and still in no way has been proven. Any trace of these connections, however, is missing from Stürmer's interpretation. The representation of genocide here degenerates into historiographic folklore: 'Every tactical teaching, every strategy of Europe was voided. The enemy was everywhere and nowhere, evaded the battle, and slammed shut from the darkness of the African night, helpless and at the same time insidious and cruel. War was not war in Africa, peace not peace'.[58]

Traces of Colonialism

In historiography, colonialism has for the most part remained an appendix to German history. In reality, exchange relationships with non-European cultures have played a much greater role than is apparent from the traditional perspective.[59] One should not be misled by the mere thirty-year duration of formal German colonial possession: both geographically and chronologically, the colonial imagination was not held to the limits of territorial possessions. This larger scope of colonial desire was in no way only a peripheral affair of colonial supporters; rather, it played a central and recognizable role in politics. The sought-after 'place in the sun' appeared to have territorial pretensions and spheres of influence around the globe as a precondition; German emigration to Brazil, the Krüger Dispatch, and

Wilhelm's 'panther's leap' to Agadir were issues that brought politics and the public under their spell. The colonial visions and political activities of the time transcended the geography of the German colonial empire.[60]

Even the year 1884, which marked the start of the German participation in the 'Scramble for Africa', was not a caesura in the history of German colonial fantasies. In fact, the founding of the nation state in 1871—commonly understood as a precondition of colonial politics—was in no way the origin for imperial aspirations.[61] In German history, since the late middle ages, there had already been a long colonialist tradition, predominately in the eastern European regions. Since the 1880s, eastern colonization and overseas imperialism have often been understood as complementary undertakings, even if the 'drive to the East' is qualitatively different from the imperialism of the nineteenth century.[62] Moreover, examples of colonial possession in Africa and South America played a significant role in the discussions of the nineteenth century.[63] Above all, however, colonial fantasies have had a long prehistory in Germany, as Susanne Zantop has shown. From cultural artifacts, a 'fictional German colonial history' can be distilled going back before the territorial expansion overseas, one which enabled 'great dreams and national myths' to enter the 'political consciousness' and, thus, set out a precondition for 'actual' colonial history.[64] In the empire of the imagination, therefore, colonial undertakings began earlier and were not limited to the topographical limits of the colonial empire that came 'too late'.

Finally, even with the formal end of German colonial rule through the Versailles treaty of 1919 (including the 'internal colonies'[65] now ceded to Poland), the colonial dream was not completely extinguished. In the Weimar Republic, the *Reichstag* was on few issues as unanimous as it was on colonial affairs and the demand for restitution of colonial territories.[66] The publication of colonial literature increased after 1918, and in particular Hans Grimm's 1926 novel, *Volk ohne Raum*, achieved large circulation. In the 'Third Reich' as well, colonial intentions—which included the infamous 'Madagascar Project'—played a great role and were only put aside in the course of the war against the Soviet Union.[67] In a peace plan from May 1941, Carl Goerdeler also suggested the 'restitution of German colonies'.[68] Finally, in the postwar period, colonial fantasies and projects were significant in the culture of the Federal Republic, even if postcolonial research is needed to reconstruct this continuity.[69]

Against this background, it appears particularly promising to take up the issue of the repercussions of imagined and real expansions into the non-European world. The effects and the legacy of the German presence in the colonies are seldom contested (even if their valuation varies). A transnational historiography could, however, move beyond this, toward the recognition that this intercultural contact left long-lasting marks on German society, which historians would be ill-advised to ignore. Franz Fanon's conjecture that fascism could be understood as European imperialism turned inward—which, not coincidentally, found its greatest resonance in Germany, which was deprived of its colonies after 1918—is only one possible vanishing point in the analysis of this problem.[70] The reciprocity of influence affected different parts of the society and left an impact on gender history, as well as on cultural history, the history of science, and social history.

For example, the conflict over gender roles in German society can also be embedded in this transnational context. The role played by German women in the colonies was for the most part ambivalent and over-determined; thus, the efforts to send more women to the colonies were aimed to no small degree at creating traditional forms of domesticity and family also in Africa.[71] There were also women, however, who viewed their presence and activities in the colonies as a contribution to female emancipation; to them, the colonies appeared as an experimental field that was less shaped by the traditional structures and mentalities of the Wilhelmian state. The writer Frieda von Bülow, for example, expected liberation from paternalistic ways from her stay in German East Africa, as well as the opening of a wide range of self-responsible, female activity.[72] The female activist Gertrud Bäumer later recognized Bülow's literature as a significant contribution to the feminist cause.[73]

Nevertheless, and this was not reflected by either Gertrud Bäumer or Frieda von Bülow, the racial hierarchy of the colonies remained completely and absolutely untouched. The equal opportunities for German women, which were made possible through domestic servants, helpers, and personnel, depended precisely on the continual subordination of the indigenous population.[74] Thus, it is even argued that racial segregation did not decrease with the arrival of women in the colonies, but instead was sharpened.[75] The supremacy of white Europeans appeared justified and confirmed through the natural order of things. In this reference to the naturalness of the social order lay, however, also the ambiguity of female emancipation in the colonial context. For ultimately, the institutionalization of gender differences in German society was likewise based on allegedly natural laws.[76]

Also a cultural history of Imperial Germany underlines the force of colonial images and representations.[77] Included in this are the many *Völkerschauen*, dioramas, and zoological gardens that shot up like mushrooms from the ground in the second half of the century and suggested not only the naturally given hierarchy between races and peoples, but also the naturalness of the societal order in Germany.[78] The great Berlin Colonial Exhibition of 1896 in Treptower Park demonstrated the popularity of the 'New

Germany' overseas.[79] Here, there was on display not just people, dances, and folklore, but also the material products of the colonial economy, which increasingly shaped the everyday lives of the population. The attraction of the colonial goods was based on their exotic flair; sometimes, though, the colonial origin of the goods faded, and the imported products were Germanized and 'naturalized'.[80] Finally, the copious broadening of literary works with colonial ambitions contributed to keeping colonial thoughts fresh in the minds of many. Included among these were the writings of authors such as Gustav Frenssen and Frieda von Bülow, who herself traveled in the German colonies and set her novels there.[81] The enormously popular works of Karl May—one thinks of his *Orientzyklus*—also carried colonial traits and helped shape the mentality of entire generations.[82]

The image of a society of 'its others' was not only created in works of fiction. Academic literature influenced the cultural memory of the time as well; scholars, for their part, were significantly affected by colonial encounters. The intellectual history of this time was deeply embedded in colonial structures. In particular, ethnology owed its rise to the German participation in the 'Scramble for Africa' and the partitioning of the non-European world.[83] Geography, as well, was for the most part, since the 1880s, established as a department in German universities and remained tightly linked to colonial expansion.[84] Similar interactions can be seen in other fields of academic research, most significantly in eugenics and racial studies.[85]

At times, the effects of colonial engagements on research were very concrete and can be traced to specific outcomes. In the history of science in Germany, there are examples of social experiments that transformed the colonies into 'laboratories of modernity'. Among these is large-scale vaccinations, which were used to immunize the Germany army against typhus at the beginning of the First World War. The collective precaution was not for nothing: the death rate was considerably lower than in the war against France in 1870/71. Incidentally, the large-scale prophylaxis measures were first tested in the colonies. In the Herero War of 1904–1907 in German South West Africa, German troop contingents for the first time systematically were immunized against typhus.[86] In light of the relatively short duration of the German colonial empire, the instances of social experimentation in the colonial 'laboratory' were distinctly less numerous than in the case of England or France. But, also in this regard, it would be reductionist to limit the effects, that the colonial governance of the world had on German society, exclusively to the territories of formal German colonial sovereignty.

Finally, colonial interaction was not without consequences for the great debates over social reform and societal organization that were led in Germany at the end of the nineteenth century. The new formulation of imperial and national citizenship in 1913 can only be understood in the framework of a perspective that goes beyond the geographical borders of the German nation-state. In the intense conflicts that ran up to the adoption of the bill in the Reichstag, specific colonial issues played a significant role. The focus was on the prohibition of 'intermarriage' and the possibility of building racial criteria into the citizenship law. On account of the administrative difficulties and the resistance in the Reichstag, however, these regulations did not find their way into the law.[87]

Another, less conspicuous regulation, however, overcame the political struggle in which the Ministry of Foreign Affairs was significantly involved, and was written into the amendment. In contrast to the 1870 law, the right to German citizenship no longer expired after ten years of absence from the motherland, but could now even be passed on to one's descendants. This stipulation was a reaction to the changing conditions of global migration: in the nineteenth century, the overwhelming majority of German emigrants (most going to the United States) had left the empire for good, and had thus been lost from the 'body politic' (*Volkskörper*). The acquisition of colonies since 1884 was not least motivated by this problem: those wanting to emigrate should be offered the opportunity to seek their luck abroad, without at the same time having to abandon the German nation (and national economy). The proportion of German settlers in the colonies had, indeed, remained much smaller than had been expected; in light of the political support for the settlement projects, it had to be ensured that the patriotic colonist did not pay for a stay of many years in the 'New Germany' with the loss of his nationality. The modification of the 'durability' of citizenship was thus a direct result of German colonial history.[88] This was not simply an issue of judicial cosmetics remaining meaningless in light of the quickly approaching end of the German colonial empire, but was, rather, a central dimension of societal self-understanding. Much later, the high number of 'resettlers' who, as a result of this stipulation, returned from the Soviet Union to the Federal Republic demonstrated the continuing significance of this legal provision and can also be understood as a result of the colonial legacy of German history.

Beyond the Tunnel Vision of National History

A transnational perspective, as is suggested here, could open a view to a relational history of modernity, which the paradigm of national history has tended to render invisible. This would also include considering the repercussions of colonial expansion in its fundamental meaning for the development of European societies. Included among these repercussions are, on one level, direct imports from overseas. The immediate influence of foreign cultures expressed itself above all, but in no way exclusively, in the cultural arena: the entrance of *japonisme* into European salons and exhibitions at the end of the nineteenth century may satisfy as an example.[89] Apart from these direct and obvious borrowings, however, two further mechanisms of the interrelationship between Europe and the non-European world have been discussed: firstly, a number of foundational assumptions, which must be understood as both conditions for and products of European expansion, have entered the vocabulary with which we have ordered the modern world. In this way, 'stowaways' travel in the conceptual baggage of modern social sciences, akin to passengers whose contribution to the course and direction of travel remains for the most part completely unnoticed. On the other hand, and more strongly related to the practice of imperialism, the colonies played a role as experimental fields for social intervention. In the period of urbanist and social science thinking, the colonial stage appeared as an ideal location for the testing and proving of interventions in societal structures; the colonies thus became, at least in certain cases, 'laboratories' of European modernity.

These complex interrelationships were not limited to particular nations and affected all (Western) European colonial powers in some form. They can be understood as an expression of the specific zeitgeist of the late nineteenth century and of the asymmetries of power of a capitalistic and imperial world. The principal of an 'entangled history' of the European and non-European world does not depend on the concrete proportion of colonies held by a country, even though the specific form of the relationship may have taken on different (national) colourings. Also in the case of Imperial Germany, we can observe the impact of the colonial experience—an impact that can be traced even after the end of the empire and beyond the caesura of 1945.

The colonial interactions considered here are only one part of the many forms of interaction and exchange that have shaped the world in the late nineteenth century. The decades before the First World War can be seen as an early high point of globalization in which the German empire was closely involved.[90] German industry exported beyond European borders; politics became 'world politics'; migration from, through, and into Germany increased markedly; and, above all, cultural entanglements left their mark on German society. To be sure, the colonies played a more limited role in Germany than in France, Holland or Great Britain; Western Europe remained a central point of reference for Germany. But Europe itself had changed and was increasingly embedded in global contexts; it can be only partially understood when uncoupled from the process of globalization. And in addition, the high period of global and colonial entanglements of the Wilhelmian empire coincided with a fundamental transformation of

German society and, at the same time, with a surge in the formation of European high modernity. In many societies at the turn of the century, there emerged basic social, political, and economic structures and conflicts that would shape Western industrial societies far into the twentieth century.[91] Therefore, the effects and repercussions of global/colonial interactions of this epoch are particularly relevant.[92]

A transnational, postcolonial or global historical perspective adds a vital dimension to the interpretation of the past and enables a broader contextualization outside the fixation on national societies. Sometimes, in this way, phenomena first become comprehensible in their complexity and global embeddedness. Of course, it is not to be assumed that anything and everything were related and 'entangled' to the same extent, in the same way, and at the same time. Different aspects of social life can be better understood within regional, national, international or transnational parameters; the level of global integration varies. Nevertheless, historiography would be well advised to overcome its tunnel vision of national history and take account of German history not only 'from the Rhine to the Memel'. It is necessary to take transnational relationships, also beyond Europe, seriously and, through this, to recover the suppressed unconscious of Europe's global past. Interactions, exchange, and circulations appear then not as 'contaminations' of national developments, but, rather, as the historical force that created the need for nation state boundaries in the first place—an ordering of the world from which historical thinking is only slowly recovering.

Notes

1. This essay first appeared in *Geschichte & Gesellschaft* 28 (2002): 145–69. Only minor changes have been made.
2. H. Heimpel, *Über Geschichte und Geschichtswissenschaft in unserer Zeit* (Göttingen, 1959), 22.
3. On the concept of postcolonialism, see L. Gandhi, *Postcolonial Theory* (New York, 1998); B. Ashcroft et al., eds., *The Post-Colonial Studies Reader* (London, 1995); R.J.C. Young, *White Mythologies. Writing History and the West* (London, 1990); R.J.C. Young, *Postcolonialism. An Historical Introduction* (Oxford, 2001).
4. On the attempts of West German historians of the early postwar period to disengage from National Socialism, see S. Conrad, *Auf der Suche nach der verlorenen Nation. Geschichtsschreibung in Japan und Westdeutschland, 1945–1960* (Göttingen, 1999).
5. See P. Nolte, 'Die Historiker der Bundesrepublik. Rückblick auf eine "lange Generation"', *Merkur* 53 (1999): 413–32. See also S. Berger, *The Search for Normality. National Identity and Historical Consciousness in Germany since 1800*

(Oxford, 1997). For the English historiography, see the findings of G. Eley, 'Playing It Safe, or How Is History Represented?', *History Workshop* 35 (1993): 206–20.
6. Examples of more recent overviews of German history include: H. Schulze, *Kleine deutsche Geschichte* (München, 1998); H.-U. Wehler, *Deutsche Gesellschaftsgeschichte*, 3 vols. (München, 1987–95); H.A. Winkler, *Der lange Weg nach Westen. Deutsche Geschichte*, 2 vols. (München, 2000); see also P. Nolte, 'Darstellungsweisen deutscher Geschichte. Erzählstrukturen und "master narratives" bei Nipperdey und Wehler', in *Geschichtswissenschaft im Vergleich*, eds. C. Conrad and S. Conrad (Göttingen, 2002), 236–70.
7. See H.-G. Haupt and J. Kocka, eds., *Geschichte und Vergleich. Ansätze und Ergebnisse international vergleichender Geschichtsschreibung* (Frankfurt, 1996); H. Kaelble, *Der historische Vergleich. Eine Einführung zum 19. und 20. Jahrhundert* (Frankfurt, 1999); J. Paulmann, 'Internationaler Vergleich und interkultureller Transfer. Zwei Forschungsansätze zur europäischen Geschichte des 18. bis 20. Jahrhunderts', *HZ* 267 (1998): 649–85.
8. See M. Espagne, 'Sur les limites du comparatisme en histoire culturelle', *Genèses* 17 (1994): 112–21; M. Werner, 'Maßstab und Untersuchungsebene. Zu einem Grundproblem der vergleichenden Kulturtransfer-Forschung', in *Nationale Grenzen und internationaler Austausch. Studien zum Kultur- und Wissenschaftstransfer in Europa*, eds. L. Jordan and B. Kortländer (Tübingen, 1995), 20–33; M. Middell, 'Kulturtransfer und Historische Komparatistik—Thesen zu ihrem Verhältnis', *Comparativ* 10 (2000): 7–41.
9. The most prominent example is the book series *Europa bauen*, which was published simultaneously in five European countries and portrays an essentialized image of Europe. Nevertheless, there are also conscious atttempts in this series to overcome the paradigm of national history. See M. Mollat Du Jourdin, *Europa und das Meer* (München, 1993).
10. S. Randeria, 'Geteilte Geschichte und verwobene Moderne', in *Zukunftsentwürfe. Ideen für eine Kultur der Veränderung*, eds. J. Rüsen et al. (Frankfurt, 1999), 87–96.
11. For a critique of the diffusion paradigm, see J. Blaut, *The Colonizer's Model of the World. Geographical Diffusionism and Eurocentric History* (New York, 1993).
12. See A.L. Stoler and F. Cooper, 'Between Metropole and Colony. Rethinking a Research Agenda', in *Tensions of Empire. Colonial Cultures in a Bourgeois World*, eds. A.L. Stoler and F. Cooper (Berkeley, 1997), 1–56; P. van der Veer, *Imperial Encounters. Religion and Modernity in India and Britain* (Princeton, 2001); see also S. Conrad and S. Randeria, 'Einleitung', in *Jenseits des Eurozentrismus. Postkoloniale Perspektiven in den Geschichts- und Kulturwissenschaften*, eds. S. Conrad and S. Randeria (Frankfurt, 2002), 9–49.
13. See A. Wirz, 'Für eine transnationale Gesellschaftsgeschichte', *GG* 27 (2001): 489–98. Critical to this: J. Osterhammel, 'Transnationale Gesellschaftsgeschichte. Erweiterung oder Alternative?', *GG* 27 (2001): 464–79.
14. S. Spiliotis, 'Wo findet Gesellschaft statt? oder Das Konzept der Transterritorialität', *GG* 27 (2001): 480–88.

15. C. Didry et al., 'Einleitung', in *Arbeit und Nationalstaat. Frankreich und Deutschland in europäischer Perspektive*, eds. C. Didry et al. (Frankfurt, 2000), 15–22, here 18. See also: M. Werner and B. Zimmermann, 'Beyond Comparison. Histoire Croisée and the Challenge of Reflexivity', *History and Theory* 45 (2006): 30–50.
16. J. Osterhammel, 'Außereuropäische Geschichte. Eine historische Problemskizze', *GWU* 46 (1995): 253–76.
17. M.-R. Trouillot, 'Anthropology and the Savage Slot. The Poetics and Politics of Otherness', in *Recapturing Anthropology. Working in the Present*, ed. R.G. Fox (Santa Fe, 1991), 17–44.
18. I. Wallerstein, *The Modern World System*, 3 vols. (New York, 1974–1989).
19. See M. Geyer and C. Bright, 'World History in a Global Age', *AHR* 100 (1995): 1034–60, esp. 1041n26.
20. See for example G.A. Hoston, *The State, Identity, and the National Question in China and Japan* (Princeton, 1994).
21. See Blaut, *Colonizer's Model*, 50–151. See also D. Chakrabarty, *Provincializing Europe. Postcolonial Thought and Historical Difference* (Princeton, 2000).
22. See T. Mitchell, *Colonizing Egypt* (Berkeley, 1991), esp. 35; and esp. A.L. Stoler, *Race and the Education of Desire. Foucault's History of Sexuality and the Colonial Order of Things* (Durham, NC, 1995).
23. See the chapter by A. Eckert, 'Dekolonisierung der Geschichte? Die Institutionalisierung der Geschichtswissenschaft in Afrika nach dem Zweiten Weltkrieg', in *Historische Institute im internationalen Vergleich*, eds. M. Middell et al. (Leipzig, 2001), 451–76; M. Mehl, *History and the State in 19th-Century Japan* (PalgraveMacMillan, 1998). Also W. Schwentker, *Max Weber in Japan. Eine Untersuchung zur Wirkungsgeschichte 1905–1995* (Tübingen, 1998); P. Duara, *Rescuing History from the Nation. Questioning Narratives of Modern China* (Chicago, 1995), esp. 17–50.
24. See H. Bhabha, *The Location of Culture* (London, 1994).
25. S. Randeria, 'Jenseits von Soziologie und soziokultureller Anthropologie: Zur Ortsbestimmung der nichtwestlichen Welt in einer zukünftigen Sozialtheorie', *Soziale Welt* 50 (1999): 373–82.
26. J. Osterhammel, *Die Entzauberung Asiens. Europa und die asiatischen Reiche im 18. Jahrhundert* (München, 1998).
27. The *locus classicus* is G.W.F. Hegel, 'Vorlesungen über die Philosophie der Geschichte', in *Werke* 12 (Frankfurt, 1970), esp. 129.
28. See S. Conrad, 'What Time is Japan? Problems of Comparative (Intercultural) Historiography', *History and Theory* 38 (1999): 67–83.
29. See R. Koselleck, 'Fortschritt', in *Geschichtliche Grundbegriffe*, eds. O. Brunner et al., vol. 2 (Stuttgart, 1975), 351–424.
30. See Chakrabarty, *Provincializing*; V. Lal, *The History of History. Politics and Scholarship in Modern India* (New Delhi, 2004); S. Tanaka, *New Times in Modern Japan* (Princeton, 2004).
31. R. Koselleck, *Vergangene Zukunft. Zur Semantik geschichtlicher Zeiten* (Frankfurt, 1979).

32. J. Fabian, *Time and the Other. How Anthropology Makes Its Object* (New York, 1983).
33. Wirz, 'Für eine transnationale Gesellschaftsgeschichte', 498.
34. Marx and Engels already observed this connection. See E. Lucas, 'Marx' und Engels' Auseinandersetzung mit Darwin', *International Review of Social History* 9 (1964): 433–69.
35. R. Virchow, 'Eskimos von Labrador', *Zeitschrift für Ethnologie* 12 (1880): 253–84, here 270.
36. Stoler and Cooper, 'Between Metropole and Colony', 5. See also P. Rabinow, *French Modern. Norms and Forms of the Social Environment* (Chicago, 1995). For the German case, see the skeptical argument of D. van Laak, 'Kolonien als "Laboratorien der Moderne"?', in *Das Kaiserreich transnational. Deutschland in der Welt 1871–1914*, eds. S. Conrad and J. Osterhammel (Göttingen, 2004), 257–79.
37. E. Williams, *Capitalism and Slavery* (Chapel Hill, 1944).
38. For a summary, see S. Drescher, 'Capitalism and Slavery after Fifty Years', *Slavery and Abolition* 18 (1997): 212–27. See also A. Wirz, *Sklaverei und kapitalistisches Weltsystem* (Frankfurt, 1984), 198–214.
39. K. Pomeranz, *The Great Divergence. China, Europe, and the Making of the Modern World Economy* (Princeton, 2000). Also the forum in *AHR* 107 (2002).
40. R.H. Grove, *Green Imperialism. Colonial Expansion, Tropical Island Edens and the Origins of Environmentalism, 1600–1860* (Cambridge, 1995), 3ff.
41. Compare to A. Sutcliffe, *Towards the Planned City. Germany, Britain, the United States, and France, 1780–1914* (Oxford, 1981).
42. See also J.L. Abu-Lughod, *Rabat. Urban Apartheid in Morocco* (Princeton, 1980). For English colonial politics, see. T.R. Metcalf 'Architecture and the Representation of Empire. India, 1860–1910', *Representations* 5 (1984): 37–65.
43. G. Wright, 'Tradition in the Service of Modernity. Architecture and Urbanism in French Colonial Policy, 1900–1930', *Journal of Modern History* 59 (1987): 291–316; G. Wright, *The Politics of Design in French Colonial Urbanism* (Chicago, 1991).
44. F. Galton, *Finger Prints* (London, 1892), 17.
45. Galton, *Finger Prints*, 17.
46. L.H. Gann, 'Marginal Colonialism. The German Case', in *Germans in the Tropics. Essays in German Colonial History*, eds. A.J. Knoll and L.H. Gann (New York, 1987), 1–17.
47. K. Hildebrand, *Das vergangene Reich. Deutsche Außenpolitik von Bismarck bis Hitler 1871–1945* (Stuttgart, 1995), 86–90.
48. K. Hildebrand, *Deutsche Außenpolitik 1871–1918* (München, 1989), 16.
49. E. Wolf, *Vom Fürsten Bismarck und seinem Haus* (Berlin, 1904), 16.
50. W. Baumgart, *Deutschland im Zeitalter des Imperialismus 1890–1914. Grundkräfte, Thesen und Strukturen* (Stuttgart, 1982), 65, 67, 70, 73. See also G. Schöllgen, *Imperialismus und Gleichgewicht. Deutschland, England und die orientalische Frage 1871–1914* (München, 1984).
51. H.-U. Wehler, *Bismarck und der Imperialismus* (Köln, 1969). Additionally, in the context of the empire debate (as a result of the Fischer controversy), which

can also be seen in Wehler's research, a series of special studies on German colonial history appeared. See especially H. Bley, *Kolonialherrschaft und Sozialstruktur in Deutsch-Südwestafrika 1894–1914* (Hamburg, 1968); K. Hausen, *Deutsche Kolonialherrschaft in Afrika. Wirtschaftsinteressen und Kolonialverwaltung in Kamerun vor 1914* (Zürich, 1970); D. Bald, *Deutsch-Ostafrika 1900–1914. Eine Studie über Verwaltung, Interessengruppen und wirtschaftliche Erschließung* (München, 1970); R. Tetzlaff, *Koloniale Entwicklung und Ausbeutung. Wirtschafts- und Sozialgeschichte Deutsch-Ostafrikas 1885–1914* (Berlin, 1970).

52. Wehler, *Deutsche Gesellschaftsgeschichte*, vol. 3, 977–90. See also W.J. Mommsen, *Der europäische Imperialismus* (Göttingen, 1979).
53. See H. Stoecker and P. Sebald, 'Enemies of the Colonial Idea', in Knoll and Gann, *Germans in the Tropics*, 59–72.
54. M. Stürmer, *Das ruhelose Reich. Deutschland 1866–1918* (Berlin, 1983), 232.
55. H. Gründer, *Geschichte der deutschen Kolonien* (Paderborn, 2000), 121.
56. See especially J. Zimmerer and Joachim Zeller, eds., *Völkermord in Deutsch-Südwestafrika. Der Kolonialkrieg (1904–1908) in Namibia und seine Folgen* (Berlin, 2003), with further literature.
57. H. Arendt, *Elemente und Ursprünge totaler Herrschaft* (München, 1986), esp. 307ff.
58. Stürmer, *Das ruhelose Reich*, 232.
59. See also A. Wirz and A. Eckert, 'Wir nicht, die Anderen auch. Deutschland und der Kolonialismus', in Conrad and Randeria, 'Re-*Orient*-ierung'.
60. See generally H. Pogge-v. Strandmann, 'Nationale Verbände zwischen Welt- und Kontinentalpolitik', in *Marine und Marinepolitik im kaiserlichen Deutschland, 1871–1914*, eds. H. Schottelius and W. Deist (Düsseldorf, 1972), 296–317; see esp. R. Chickering, *We Men Who Feel Most German. A Cultural Study of the Pan-German League, 1886–1914* (London, 1984).
61. This incorrect notion can be found in E. Said, *Orientalism* (New York, 1978), 19. But compare H. Fenske, 'Ungeduldige Zuschauer. Die Deutschen und die europäische Expansion 1815–1880', in *Imperialistische Kontinuität und nationale Ungeduld im 19. Jahrhundert*, ed. W. Reinhard (Frankfurt, 1991), 87–123.
62. The competition and the simultaneous interdependence between both forms of colonialization can be seen pronounced especially in National Socialist colonial politics, which focused on policies of segregation in its *Mittelafrika* plans that had been tested in 'Warthegau'. See A. Kum'a N'Dumbé III, 'Pläne zu einer nationalsozialistischen Kolonialherrschaft in Afrika', in *Aspekte deutscher Außenpolitik im 20. Jahrhundert*, eds. W. Benz and H. Graml (Stuttgart, 1967), 165–92.
63. H. Duchhardt, 'Afrika und die deutschen Kolonialprojekte der 2. Hälfte des 17. Jahrhunderts', *Archiv für Kulturgeschichte* 68 (1986): 119–33; M. Vogt, 'Brandenburg in Übersee', in *Entdeckungen und frühe Kolonisation*, eds. C. Dipper and M. Vogt (Darmstadt, 1993), 345–79.
64. S.M. Zantop, *Kolonialphantasien im vorkolonialen Deutschland, 1770–1870* (Berlin, 1999), 11f

65. See P. Ther, 'Deutsche Geschichte als imperiale Geschichte. Polen, slawophone Minderheiten und das Kaiserreich als kontinentales Empire', in Conrad and Osterhammel, *Kaiserreich*, 129–48.
66. H. Pogge von Strandmann, 'Deutscher Imperialismus nach 1918', in *Deutscher Konservativismus im 19. und 20. Jahrhundert*, eds. D. Stegmann et al. (Bonn, 1983), 281–93.
67. W.W. Schmokel, *Der Traum vom Reich. Der deutsche Kolonialismus zwischen 1919 und 1945* (Gütersloh, 1967); K. Hildebrand, *Vom Reich zum Weltreich. Hitler, NSDAP und koloniale Frage 1919–1945* (München, 1969); R. Lakowski, *Die Kriegsziele des faschistischen Deutschland im transsaharischen Afrika* (Ph.D. diss., Berlin, 1970); J. Dülffer, 'Kolonialismus ohne Kolonien. Deutsche Kolonialpläne 1938', in *Machtbewußtsein in Deutschland am Vorabend des Zweiten Weltkrieges*, eds. F. Knipping and K.-J. Müller (Paderborn, 1984), 247–70; A. Kum'a N'Dumbe III, *Was wollte Hitler in Afrika? NS-Planungen für eine faschistische Neugestaltung Afrikas* (Frankfurt, 1993).
68. Cited in Gründer, *Geschichte*, 218.
69. See M. Flitner, 'Vom 'Platz an der Sonne' zum "Platz für Tiere"', in *Der deutsche Tropenwald. Bilder, Mythen, Politik*, ed. M. Flitner (Frankfurt, 2000), 244–62. See also S. Friedrichsmeyer et al., eds., *The Imperialist Imagination. German Colonialism and Its Legacy* (Ann Arbor, 1998), esp. 233–336; D. Van Laak, *Imperiale Infrastruktur. Deutsche Planungen für eine Erschließung Afrikas 1880 bis 1960* (Paderborn, 2004).
70. See: Young, *White Mythologies*, 7f.
71. R. Chickering, '"Casting their Gaze more Broadly": Women's Patriotic Activism in Imperial Germany', *Past & Present* 186 (1988): 156–85. See also K. Smidt, 'Germania führt die deutsche Frau nach Südwest.' *Auswanderung, Leben und soziale Konflikte deutscher Frauen in der ehemaligen Kolonie Deutsch-Südwestafrika 1884–1920* (Magdeburg, 1997); B. Kundrus, *Moderne Imperialisten. Das Kaiserreich im Spiegel seiner Kolonien* (Köln, 2003), 77–95.
72. See R.A. Bermann, 'Colonial Literature and the Emancipation of Women', in Bermann, *Enlightenment or Empire. Colonial Discourse in German Culture* (Lincoln, 1998), 171–202.
73. G. Bäumer, 'Frieda von Bülow', *Die Frau. Monatsschrift für das gesamte Frauenleben unserer Zeit* (1908–1909), 407–12; See also P. Grosse, *Kolonialismus, Eugenik und bürgerliche Gesellschaft in Deutschland 1850–1918* (Frankfurt, 2000), 173.
74. L. Wildenthal, *German Women for Empire, 1884–1945* (Durham, 2001), 131–71.
75. See P. Spear, *The Nabobs. A Study of Social Life of the English in the Eighteenth Century* (London, 1963).
76. See generally D. Haraway, 'Teddy Bear Patriarchy. Taxidermy in the Garden of Eden, New York City, 1908–1936', in *Culture/Power/History. A Reader in Contemporary Social Theory*, eds. N.B. Dirks et al. (Princeton, 1994), 49–95.
77. B. Kundrus, ed., *Phantasiereiche. Zur Kulturgeschichte des deutschen Kolonialismus* (Frankfurt, 2003); A. Honold and K.R. Scherpe, eds., *Mit Deutschland*

um die Welt. Eine Kulturgeschichte des Fremden in der Kolonialzeit (Stuttgart, 2004).
78. Compare H. Gründer, 'Indianer, Afrikaner und Südseebewohner in Europa: Zur Vorgeschichte der Völkerschauen und Kolonialausstellungen', Jahrbuch für Europäische Überseegeschichte 3 (2003): 65–88; B. Staehelin, Völkerschauen im Zoologischen Garten Basel 1879–1935 (Basel, 1993).
79. See Arbeitsausschuß der deutschen Kolonialausstellung, ed., 'Deutschland und seine Kolonien im Jahre 1896. Amtlicher Bericht über die erste deutsche Kolonialausstellung', (Berlin, 1897). See also R. Richter, 'Die erste Deutsche Kolonialausstellung 1896. Der "Amtliche Bericht" in historischer Perspektive', in Kolonialausstellungen - Begegnungen mit Afrika?, eds. R. Debusmann and J. Riesz (Frankfurt, 1995), 25–42; Bezirksamt Treptow von Berlin, ed., Die verhinderte Weltausstellung. Beiträge zur Berliner Gewerbeausstellung von 1896 (Berlin, 1996).
80. J. Riesz, '"Kolonialwaren"—die großen Kolonialausstellungen als "exotische" Warenlager und Instrumente kolonialer Propaganda', in Riesz, Kolonialausstellungen, 159–78.
81. See J.L. Noyes, 'National Identity, Nomadism, and Narration in Gustav Frenssen's Peter Moor's Journey to Southwest Africa', in Friedrichsmeyer, Imperialist Imagination, 87–106; F. Eigler, 'Engendering German Nationalism. Gender and Race in Frieda v. Bülow's Colonial Writings', in Friedrichsmeyer, Imperialist Imagination, 69–86.
82. See N. Berman, Orientalismus, Kolonialismus und Moderne. Zum Bild des Orients in der deutschsprachigen Literatur um 1900 (Stuttgart, 1996).
83. G. Leclerc, Anthropologie und Kolonialismus (Frankfurt, 1976); W.D. Smith, 'Anthropology and German Colonialism', in Knoll and Gann, Germans in the Tropics, 39–57.
84. G. Sandner, 'In Search of Identity: German Nationalism and Geography, 1871–1910', in Geography and National Identity, ed. : D. Hooson (Oxford, 1994), 71–91; G. Sandner and M. Rössler, 'Geography and Empire in Germany, 1871–1945', in Geography and Empire, eds. A. Godlewska und N. Smith (Oxford, 1994), 115–27.
85. See P. Weindling, Health, Race and German Politics between National Unification and Nazism (Cambridge, 1989); P. Weingart et al., eds., Rasse, Blut und Gene. Geschichte der Eugenik und Rassenhygiene in Deutschland (Frankfurt, 1988); Grosse, Kolonialismus; N.C. Lösch, Rasse als Konstrukt. Leben und Werk Eugen Fischers (Frankfurt, 1997).
86. Even the 12,000 native prisoners who were not vaccinated were the object of medical observation and experimentation. Their sicknesses served as observational material and data for statistical inquiry. The high death rates of prisoners encouraged the idea among colonial doctors that: 'We Germans are called upon to bestow upon this land a history. That imparted a feeling of impartiality, which had its own allure', as the staff doctor Friedrich Zöllner admitted. See W. Eckart, 'Medizin und kolonialer Krieg: Die Niederschlagung der Herero-Nama-Erhebung im Schutzgebiet Deutsch-Südwestafrika, 1904–1907', in Stu-

dien zur Geschichte des deutschen Kolonialismus in Afrika, eds. P. Heine and U. van der Heyden (Pfaffenweiler, 1995), 220–35; see also W. Eckart, *Medizin und Kolonialimperialismus. Deutschland 1884–1945* (Paderborn, 1996).
87. Grosse, *Kolonialismus,* 160–68; D. Gosewinkel, *Einbürgern und ausschließen. Die Nationalisierung der Staatsangehörigkeit vom Deutschen Bund bis zur Bundesrepublik Deutschland* (Göttingen, 2001).
88. Grosse, *Kolonialismus,* 222f.
89. See K. Berger, *Japonismus in der westlichen Malerei 1860–1920* (München, 1980); S. Wichmann, *Japonismus. Ostasien-Europa. Begegnungen in der Kunst des 19. und 20. Jahrhunderts* (Herrsching, 1980).
90. See C. Torp, *Die Herausforderung der Globalisierung. Wirtschaft und Politik in Deutschland 1860–1914* (Göttingen, 2005); S. Conrad, *Globalisierung und Nation im Deutschen Kaiserreich* (München, 2006).
91. See P. Nolte, '1900: Das Ende des 19. und der Beginn des 20. Jahrhunderts in sozialgeschichtlicher Perspektive', *Geschichte in Wissenschaft und Unterricht* 47 (1996): 281–300; A. Nitschke et al., eds., *Jahrhundertwende. Der Aufbruch in die Moderne 1880–1930,* 2 vols. (Reinbek, 1990). For a European perspective, see G. Barraclough, *Introduction to Contemporary History* (Harmondsworth, 1967), 9–42.
92. See the chapters in Conrad and Osterhammel, *Das Kaiserreich transnational.*

≡ CHAPTER 4 ≡

Entangled Histories of Uneven Modernities

Civil Society, Caste Councils, and Legal Pluralism in Postcolonial India

SHALINI RANDERIA

In the heyday of modernization theory just thirty years ago, solidarities of caste, community, and religion were considered to be undesirable relics of the passing of 'traditional' societies destined for the dustbin of history. There were no communitarians then about who would have shared the widely prevalent belief in India that communities whose ways of life must be preserved and protected were shaped by individual identities. Theorists of social capital had yet to discover that dense social networks of any variety furthered civic ties and democratic values. Viewed with deep suspicion, religious communities on the subcontinent were believed to be an obstacle to the realization of a secularist ideal, which societies in the West were assumed to have achieved long ago. Affiliations of caste, solidarities of religion, parochial loyalties of language, ethnicity or region were seen as signs of backwardness, whereas ties of citizenship and nationhood were viewed as modern and desirable.[1]

An urgent task of the postcolonial state was seen to be the overcoming of diversity rather than the recognition of difference. By accepting several group-specific rights and devising a set of policies for the recognition of cultural differences in the public domain, however, the Indian constitutional experiment departed from the then current models of Western liberalism. It chose instead what Thomas Pantham has termed a 'communitarian-liberal democracy',[2] a postcolonial precedent that has been largely ignored in contemporary Western debates on minority rights and multiculturalism. Safeguards for religious and cultural minorities in the Indian constitution of 1950, including the provision of group-based quotas in education and public employment for members of disadvantaged communities, were a bold legal innovation without Western precedent. Such legal measures, which either granted minorities autonomy and equal treatment or sought to redress inequalities between groups, were then unknown in Western democracies.[3] Both the compensatory provision of numerical quotas for underprivileged communities and the right to one's own religiously defined family laws had their roots in colonial legacies of the institutionalization of difference. They were incorporated into the constitution of the new republic as temporary measures that were considered necessary to facilitate the transition to a mature modernity characterized by legal homogeneity and individual rights of citizenship.

Ironically, while Western societies, faced with a crisis of national political culture (as the chickens of the Empire came home to roost), began to discover multiculturalism and group rights, in India these constitutional measures came under serious attack in the name of cultural homogeneity and national integration. The militant Hindu nationalist attack against minority rights, especially the right of Muslims and Christians to be governed by religiously defined family laws particular to their own communities, is animated by the desire for a homogenous political community based on a unitary and uniform culture. Central to the rhetoric of political Hinduism is its insistence that only the religion of the Hindu majority can provide the legitimate foundation of a strong nation state modelled on the Western image. Couched in the vocabulary of religion, this is a highly modern statist project that aims to eradicate any legal and political recognition of cultural and religious differences. It thus includes plans for the reform of the Indian constitution in order to introduce a uniform legal code that would replace the plurality of civil codes of law for different religious communities. Such a conception precludes the possibility of a plurality of cultures in the public sphere. It also denies the desirability of a dialogue among communities out of which a shared national culture, which embodies more than only procedural commitments, could evolve. This is an issue that has exercised the political imagination in many Western societies as, for instance, in the German debate on *Leitkultur* or in French debates following the recent riots by urban immigrant youth. If it is assumed that the national culture should be the culture of the majority,[4] then the question of to whom the nation belongs culturally does not arise. However, if a shared and inclusive national culture appears just and desirable, such a composite culture must be the product of a dialogue between different communities with very different visions of the good life, irrespective of their group size, degrees of cultural similarity, and histories of migration or settlement in the country.

There remains an uneasy fit between the legal recognition of the collective rights of communities to their culture, which cements bonds of caste and religion, and the political process of nation building, which seeks to dissolve these very ties. The legal recognition of particularistic ties may well change their form, but not necessarily in the direction of universalistic ties of individual citizenship, as the case of India shows. A society with a plurality of religions, linguistic communities, ethnic groups, castes, and indigenous peoples, India strove for decades to find 'unity in diversity', to use the official vocabulary of nation building. But it also sought to wear the garb of modernity differently, as Nehru, the first Indian Prime Minister, put it.[5] Not only was this garb fashioned out of a traditional social fabric very different from that of Western societies, but it was also cut according to colonial design. These insights have led to a reconceptualization of the plurality of pathways and patterns of modernity in postcolonial societies such as India. Postcolonial theories as well as theories of regional modernities or alternative modernities have addressed the specific configurations of modernity in non-Western settings, the impure mixtures of Western ideas and institutions with a variety of traditions selected from the past and reconstituted in the complex process of historical and contemporary interaction with Europe.[6]

Recent attempts to pluralize modernity have been concerned with two sets of issues: (1) differences in the trajectories of modernity in different parts of the world; and (2) differences in the outcomes of these processes in different societies. Ideas of multiple modernities, such as those of Therborn or Eisenstadt, raise several questions concerning the relationship of European to non-European modernities.[7] What status would be accorded to the paradigm of 'Western' modernity (which must be pluralized as well) in a conceptualization that recognizes historical and contemporary entanglements between Western and non-Western societies under highly asymmetrical conditions of domination? As postcolonial theorists have argued, colonialism was not a one-way street that reshaped ideas and institutions in the non-European world. It was both a precondition for and a consequence of the modernization of economic and social processes in Europe. Standard comparisons in modern historiography, sociology, and political science are based on a conceptual nationalism that treats European metropole societies as if each one of them developed *sui generis* and compares them to one another. Or, in a modernization framework, European societies are compared to societies in the non-Western world in terms of the lacks and lags evinced by the latter. It thus narrates the history of non-Western societies in terms of what Mamdani has termed a 'history of absences or in terms of analogy with an idealized and reified "West".[8] Such a comparative approach neglects not only the relationship of European societies to one another as emphasised in the *histoire croisée* perspective,[9] but, more seriously, fails to situate the development of modern European ideas and institutions in a transnational and imperial framework. Such a perspective of entangled histories of modernities within and outside the West overcomes both the methodological nationalism and Eurocentrism of the social sciences by seeing colonialism as constitutive of, not external to, European modernity.[10]

Anthropologists working with the idea of a vernacularization of modernity[11] have usually emphasized the creative and selective appropriations of various aspects of Western modernities in different colonial and postcolonial contexts to produce a variety of hybrid outcomes. Once modernity is pluralized, it becomes possible to conceptualize trajectories and outcomes that diverge from the ideal-typical historical experience of a handful of western European societies. But, even more importantly, it is possible to analyse the unevenness of processes of modernization in different spheres *within* a society. Consequently, the idea of a homogenous Western modernity travelling, more or less imperfectly, to the rest of the world must be replaced by a messier and complex picture of what I have termed uneven and entangled modernities.[12] Rather than theorizing multiple or alternative modernities at the level of the nation state (Indian or Japanese modernity) or in terms of 'cultures', regions or religions (African modernity, Islamic or Confucian modernity), it would be more fruitful to explore interconnections in the reconfigurations of modernity both within and beyond nation state boundaries. Modernity has always been in tension with its others (the nonmodern or anti-modern), but it now also has become a contested concept with a multiplicity of meanings that vary with actors and contexts. As social experience, modernity varies in the understandings and practices of different groups of people within a society. Its status has, therefore, shifted from that of a teleological and a historical-philosophical category, as part of the Enlightenment project, to that of a part of the social imaginary that is acted and reflected upon.[13]

In the universal language of modern social theory, the history of the West is always written as world history. Of course, by globalizing the categories of Western modernity, capitalism and imperialism have lent some truth to this claim. But discourses of multiple or alternative modernities may, paradoxically, cement rather than destabilize the categories of Western modernity. The latter comes to be seen as a universal narrative against which the experiences of non-Western societies are juxtaposed as local narratives. The notion of entanglement that I propose would replace a comparison of societies in the rest of the world with those of the West by a relational perspective that foregrounds processes of historical and contemporary unequal exchanges, which shaped modernities in both parts of the world. Such a perspective would not privilege Western historical experience or trajectories and would be sensitive to the particularities of the non-Western society under study.

This chapter seeks to connect the sequestered histories of civil society and legal pluralism in the West and outside of it, and to locate them within the framework of (post)colonial governance. The first section delineates the entangled histories of civil society as the *locus classicus* of social ties independent of state and market.[14] Indian debates on civil society, which I discuss in the second section, interact with different Western imaginings of civil society and help one understand how local and translocal ideas, institutions, and workings of civil society are inextricably intertwined. Civic activism against the state and political debates, as well as scholarly ones, about it in many parts of the 'Third World' predate the rediscovery of this activism in the 'Second World'. A Eurocentric perspective on civil society often overlooks the fact that many of these debates in Latin America, Africa, and India are independent of the resurgence of interest in the idea of civil society in the West in the light of the East European experience.[15] A more cosmopolitan understanding of civil society would, therefore, include those debates along with analyses of the workings of civil society outside Europe.

The third section is concerned with what Dirks sees as the Indian variant of civil society instituted by colonial rule—the ties of caste.[16] Using Sudipto Kaviraj's distinction between traditional 'fuzzy' identities and modern enumerated ones, I examine critically the refashioning of multiple, fluid, contextually shifting personal identities and collective ties in pre-colonial India into monolithic, stable, and homogenous identifications and belongings based on common interest rather than social interaction. This process of transformation is illustrated with reference to the so-called 'untouchable' castes, or *Dalits*, as they prefer to call themselves collectively today. The status of these castes at the bottom of the social hierarchy is also examined with reference to the vexed issue of their inclusion in a pan-Indian 'Hindu' community, the boundaries of which were defined and shaped by the discourses and practices of the colonial state.

The final section of the chapter engages with the controversial issue of legal pluralism in the sphere of family law in India. The issue has been framed by its advocates and opponents in terms of the choice between community identity/autonomy, on the one hand, and national integration/social cohesion, on the other. In my view, both protagonists and detractors of legal pluralism have a narrow understanding of law in practice: they restrict the legal sphere to that of state law, thus according it a primacy it does not enjoy in social life. I look at the question instead from the vantage point of autonomous informal institutions of justice, outside the reach of the state, or in limited interaction with state courts, which set and adjudicate their own norms for the majority of lower castes among Hindus and Muslims in Western India.

My argument is that caste or *jamat* assemblies, as the sphere of the self-regulation of communities through an autonomous production and adjudication of family law, form an important domain of civil society in (post)colonial India. The workings of a civil society containing such collectivities challenge the liberal Western conceptualization of civil society as the sphere connecting autonomous individuals to the state. If civil society is, rather, understood as being concerned with establishing and maintaining bonds of social solidarity and as a sphere of relatively autonomous self-regulation, then castes and caste councils offer interesting material for thinking about civil society as being governed and organized in a very different way than from a liberal understanding of it. A liberal conception of civil society would include only formal associations based on voluntary membership—and on that criterion exclude from the ambit of civil society castes based on ascription. Caste councils do not merely reflect the 'tyranny of cousins' against the freedom to choose one's own individual identity, which Gellner sees as characteristic of modern civil society.[17] In my view, the modernist bias inherent in such a narrow and Eurocentric conception leads one to overlook rich forms of associational life in non-Western societies, just as it leads one to overemphasize the contrast between choice and ascription and to represent tradition and modernity as binary opposites.

Contemporary caste-based associations are as much traditional ascriptive bodies as they are modern organizations of colonial origin.[18] The form of these associations does not exactly reflect their purpose. Some of them own considerable property, have elected office bearers, have their accounts audited, are registered with the Commissioner of Charities, and publish regular newsletters. Many caste councils, which set norms and adjudicate family and marital disputes, are also associations that perform a variety of services for their members: they run secondary schools, colleges, and hostels for students in urban areas; provide scholarships for education; run *dharamshalas* (dormitories) at large temple complexes and places of pilgrimage; provide medical aid; form networks for political mobilization; and, organize meetings in large towns—announced in daily newspapers—at which marriages between younger caste members can be arranged by their families. A view of civil society in India that disregards these often lower caste organizations straddling the traditional-modern divide underestimates the often chaotic and messy pluralism of associational life even in modern Western societies. The modernist and individualist bias of such a liberal position, based on the trajectory of civil society in a few Western societies, precludes it—when, for example, judging which associations to include in civil society—from considering why the criteria of voluntary membership should take precedence over the criteria of autonomy from the state and internal self-regulation.

If, as my empirical material suggests, normative conflict *within* the local community of caste members is pivotal to its constitution, then multiculturalism and value pluralism cannot be understood in terms of the opposition between the state and communities. In arguing that processes of internal disputation and contestation of norms within each group—rather than the difference between 'traditional' or customary law and state law—are central to the collective identity of a caste, I question the communitarian representation of communities as internally culturally homogenous entities. If the state is a contested terrain, then communities are equally so contested. If one does not romanticize communities—as communitarian discourse often does—or read legal pluralism as a sign of a deficient modernity—as jurists often do—it is possible to map the changing contours and the intertwining of state and society, and the shifting boundaries between the public and the private spheres in the domain of family law. An analysis of the hybrid institutions in this domain reminds us of the unevenness of modernity in India, where social ties of caste have neither dissolved nor have been entirely transformed by state processes of codification and enumeration. If there is a convergence of Western and non-Western modernities, it is Western discourses of communitarianism and practices of multiculturalism that have come to resemble the uneven modernities of postcolonial societies.

Entangled Histories of Civil Society

Adam Seligman suggests that the idea of civil society in late-seventeenth- and eighteenth-century Europe developed in response to a crisis of social order not unlike the one that has led to its recent renaissance: the growth of market economies, the commercialization of land and labour, and the need to reconcile individual interests with the public good. It represented then, as today, an attempt to conceive of a new ethical model of the workings of society in the face of a crisis of social order. In eighteenth-century Europe, civil society came to be conceived of as the new moral source of social order in the wake of the questioning of God and King as transcendental and external foundations of order.[19] The preoccupation with the idea at the end of the twentieth century is clearly due to the dismantling of socialist states, the disappointment with the overreach of capitalist welfare states, and the disillusionment with the unfulfilled promises of modernizing postcolonial states. Debates about civil society are also debates about modernity, pluralism, social cohesion and value consensus, individualism, and communitarianism; they are about the shifting boundaries between the public and the private spheres.

Most recently—on the neo-liberal agenda of restructuring the state—civil society, whittled down to a depoliticized sphere of NGOs, is seen as a cheaper and more efficient alternative to the state. This redefined domain of civil society, represented as a domain of civic virtue and voluntary associations, communitarian solidarity, and self-help, excludes political struggles and challenges to state power. Instead, it is seen as a sphere of market-friendly institutions and service delivery agents outside and independent of the state. Such a vision overlooks the fact that civil society can hardly be a substitute for state functions, since it depends in part on state regulation for its functioning. A strong state is a necessary concomitant to a strong civil society, as Jürgen Kocka has pointed out.[20] Similarly, Neera Chandhoke has argued forcefully that state and civil society constitute, support, and may even impede one another.[21] De-linking the two to conceptualise them as separate and distinct spheres impoverishes our understanding of both.

Civil society is a relational term. It can only be understood in the matrix of a set of interdependent ideas and institutions—nation state, market, public sphere, citizenship, rights-bearing individuals. As John and Jean Comaroff remind us, these terms have had a highly chequered history in former colonies still struggling to free themselves of the intellectual and institutional legacies of European imperialism.[22] Concomitant with the setting up of the colonial state, the idea of civil society travelled to the colonies in the nineteenth century. It designated a sphere outside of the colonial state, either because the rulers sought to demarcate a sphere in which the state would not interfere or because colonial subjects, using this newly available political vocabulary, sought to delimit the influence of colonial rule with respect to certain areas of their lives.[23] If civil society in nineteenth-century Europe came to be defined within and in relation to the nation state, its emergence in the age of discoveries was related in part to the interest in very different modes and models of organizing social life in the non-European world.[24] Civil society in the colonies was a product of imperial rule with, from its inception, transnational referents.

John and Jean Comaroff have suggested that the broad contemporary transnational appeal of the idea of civil society as a 'trope for these uncertain times' is predicated upon the fact that it is not a concrete entity waiting to be explicitly defined and analytically demarcated once and for all.[25] Rather than view civil society, with Hall or Gellner,[26] as a unique Western achievement and its specific contours in non-Western societies as a sign of difference or deficiency, it may be important to see that the substance of the idea of civil society is inherently elusive, both in and outside the West. This is in part due to the complex intellectual history and uneven political realization of this ideal over several centuries in the West, as well as to the chequered history of its translation and conflictual domestication within the framework of colonial rule in most of the non-Western world. A preoccupation with the European roots of the idea often obscures an understanding of the routes through which various, often divergent and incompatible, ideas of civil society and the institutions it encompasses have travelled to, and been received in, other regions.

I think that it is important to emphasize that there is no single coherent idea of civil society that has travelled from the West and has been, or could be, replicated elsewhere. Its contours in Europe, and outside it, have been redrawn in various social and political theories of which it has been an element, and in political visions of which it has been mobilised to support. Various ideas of civil society were produced in Europe in the context of political practice answering specific historical needs, as Khilnani and Kaviraj have shown.[27] Their appropriation and cultural translation outside the West relate in creative ways to a diversity of Western traditions and were shaped by the political context in which they were forged—usually in opposition to colonial rule. The strategies of defiance crafted by Gandhi in the Indian national movement against British domination, for instance, owed as much to a recontextualization of Indian religious traditions of nonviolence and everyday strategies of domestic resistance as to Ruskin's writings on civil disobedience. But they were also a deeply deliberated civil response to the incivility of colonial rule. Asked once by a young British journalist, 'Mr Gandhi, what do you think of Western civilization?', Gandhi's famous reply was, 'I think it would be a good idea'.

Anthropologists have often cast doubts on the value of using an ethnocentric term such as civil society for comparative purposes.[28] They have made their own contribution to particularizing the term by exploring its very different referents in different societies, including various European societies.[29] The usual mode of engaging in a comparative exercise idealizes and abstracts from Western experience in order to then compare—negatively, more often than not—non-Western trajectories, transformations, and institutions of civil society as deficient or different. These narratives, whether Marxist or liberal, view social reality through the lens of binary oppositions (West/non-West, modern/traditional, societies with history/ societies without history, secular/religious). Non-Western societies, as the term signifies, are defined by negation. As André Béteille has argued, the dominant traditions of comparative research in the social sciences assign a priority to contrast over comparison, to difference over similarity, and to discontinuity over continuity;[30] all non-Western societies are compared in terms of their contrast to the West. The historical and contemporary experience of non-Western societies is understood in such a framework not in terms of what it is, but in terms of what it is not. But as Mamdani has suggested, an ahistorical essentialization takes place on the Western side of the binary opposition as well.[31] An idealized image of the West is created against which non-Western societies are measured and found wanting. Such an exercise partakes in a grand narrative of world history cast in terms of binary contrasts, in which, paradoxically, European historical experience is seen as both unique and universal, or at least universalizable.

One consequence of such a narrative is that it accords the European experience both an analytical value and a universal status, while regarding the non-European experience as marginal or residual. But if such a perspective caricatures the experience summed up as residual, it also homogenizes and mythologizes the experience postulated as normal. It ascribes a 'suprahistorical trajectory' of development to Western societies;[32] it posits a necessary rather than a contingent path unaffected by the struggles that produced it. It renders the experience of both European and non-European societies ahistorical by robbing them of their historical specificity. An exploration of these historical specificities would situate different meanings and trajectories of civil society in a framework sensitive to 'multiple modernities';[33] this approach would map the very different paths and patterns of civil society both *within* and outside Europe. Moreover, it would enable a delineation of the entanglements, of varying degrees and kinds, of different European societies with their imperial and colonial projects overseas at different points in time.[34] Viewing metropolitan self-understanding through the prism of the (post)colonial would enable a discussion of the complex play of inclusion/exclusion, disenfranchisement, recognition and exploitation of subjects and citizens, and the incivility of civil society not merely 'at home', but when intertwined with racism and violence abroad.[35] Drawing attention, for example, to the fervent missionary activities of modern Europeans in the colonies, a perspective which focuses on entanglements rather than comparisons between European nation states, would unsettle the modernist narrative of a progressive secularization of Europe, a narrative that makes it possible to overlook, or at least underplay, the role of the churches, missionary societies, and religious associations in modern Western civil societies and regard these as characteristic of backward or imperfect non-European ones.

A perspective of entangled histories would argue not only against seeing a single coherent idea of civil society as emerging fully formed in Europe, it would also show how various European ideas of civil society were used creatively and developed further outside of the confines of Europe and how these, in turn, affected metropolitan discourses and practices. After all, there is little in common between de Tocqueville's idea of civil society as a realm of secondary associations, Hegel's use of it as an analytical category to designate a sphere of ethics differentiated from the family and the state where societal ethics and individual morality can be reconciled, Gramsci's view of it as the sphere where the capitalist state establishes hegemony over society, and a Foucauldian perspective, which interrogates the neat demarcation between state and civil society through a conception of the state as a disciplinary formation whose capillary power flows into all social institutions and into the very constitution of its subjects. Therefore, instead of tracing the diffusion of the ideas and institutions of civil society as a near universal with purely Western roots, it may be more fruitful to analyse the contestation and deployment of various conceptions of civil society in the service of diverse theoretical positions and political agendas in both Western and non-Western societies today. These dialogues with Western modernity expand or modify some of its ideas, but remain in part uncomfortable with it, as the Indian debates on civil society I review briefly in the next section illustrate.

Traditional Solidarities vs. Modern Institutions: Civil Society as Contested Terrain

The current controversies about questions of civil society in India are fuelled by concerns about the nature of democratic politics and citizenship rights on the subcontinent, the widespread disillusionment with the failures of the postcolonial state to deliver the goods, fears that undue state interference undermines the functioning of intermediate institutions, and an interest in the revival or strengthening of indigenous traditions of civility. Activists and scholars alike have adopted the language of civil society to frame the legitimate rights of people in a democracy to make demands on the state, to render it accountable, to redress its malfunctioning, and to curb its authoritarian policies.

Rajni Kothari, the leading theorist of civil society in India, premises his call for a 'humane governance'—rooted in the subcontinent's own civilizational values and precolonial moral ordering of social relations—on a diagnosis of the ills of the modern state.[36] He views violence as inherent in the modern state, not merely as endemic only to its postcolonial formations. For him, the creation of civil society must draw 'upon available and still surviving traditions of togetherness, mutuality and resolution of differences and conflict—in short, traditions of a democratic collective that are our own and which we need to build in a changed historical context. This is the basic political task facing Indians—the creation of a civil society that is rooted in diversity yet cohering and holding together.'[37]

Critics of such a culturalist-communitarian perspective point out that its nostalgic and selective rendering of tradition overlooks the inequalities, hierarchies, and denials of individual freedom—continuing into the present—in these pre-modern traditions.[38] Such a sweeping critique, however, obscures the fact that these neo-traditionalist critiques of modernity do not advocate an unqualified romantic return to tradition. Rather, they emphasize the need for cultural moorings if alien institutions are to be successfully domesticated, a process that, in their view, requires sensitivity to traditions in order to recover their best characteristics. Ironically, the communitarian concept of civil society implies a return to a traditional moral ordering of community: the very hierarchical and pre-modern past from which Locke, Rousseau, and Hegel sought to break away from with the concept of civil society in order to move toward a shared public sphere of civic ties and trust among citizens/strangers.

Indian scholars of civil society[39] are not alone in privileging community ties over modern institutional arrangements. This seems also to be a relatively dominant trend in current renditions of civil society in Western scholarship. It is against a background of disappointment with state performance, or the perceived 'overreach' of the state, that a tendency to romanticize 'society' can be seen, especially those aspects of society least coloured by the (post)colonial or the welfare state—and, therefore, more 'civil' or authentic. Protagonists of this view of civil society tend to define the current malady in India as the result of the colonial rupture with tradition and the neglect of the subcontinent's distinct cultural roots when building modern institutions. Civil society, as Gupta has pointed out,[40] is thus understood as a realm before and/or outside modernity and the modern state. It is represented as a sphere sensitive to cultural plurality and social heterogeneity, a diversity that the state has sought to homogenize into a national monoculture.

An interesting contrast to this perspective is the view of the Indian sociologist André Béteille, for whom the social value of an idea or an institution exists irrespective of, and can never be reduced to, the idea's or institution's geographical origins.[41] His is a powerful critique of the search for more authentic ideas and institutions in tune with the cultural logic of Indian civilization. His argument for strengthening constitutional democracy in India emphasizes—following de Tocqueville—the role of modern intermediate and voluntary associations.[42] He sees the well being of modern institutions in India guaranteed only if civil societies are understood as comprising truly autonomous bodies—even if these bodies are of modern colonial origin.[43] For him, citizenship and constitutional democracy cannot be built out of primordial ties of caste, kinship, and religion, as these have formed the basis of a hierarchical social integration in the past. These traditional solidarities and exclusionary loyalties, therefore, are as responsible as is the intervention by the state for the fragility and malfunctioning of modern institutions. A plurality of inclusive, secular, mediating institutions, relatively autonomous from the state and insulated from particularistic ties, is indispensable for the development and functioning of democracy in India. The success of the modern project of nation building is predicated on the expansion of this realm of civil society.[44]

Placing himself squarely in the Hegelian tradition, Dipankar Gupta, also argues that a modern state—rather than traditional ties of caste and religious community, collective norms, and customary law—is indispensable for the functioning of civil society.[45] The primary task of civil society is, therefore, to constitute a community of citizens bound by the ethics of freedom, and not by the particularities of tradition or the calculus of market interests. At the centre of his discussion of civil society is the issue of individual freedom and citizenship, in contradistinction to the neo-traditionalist and communitarian views, which centre on the collective rights and autonomy of communities. From the neo-traditionalist or culturalist-communitarian viewpoint, a civil society based on the civilizational values of the subcontinent is the way to contain the violence of the modern postcolonial state. For modernists, liberals, and Marxists alike, it is important, instead, to strengthen intermediate rational-legal institutions. They advocate an expansion of the ambit of these institutions and the need to protect them both from the state and from the particularistic ties that corrupt their functioning.

For Gupta, civil society would include only those rational bureaucratic institutions compatible with individual freedom, equality, citizenship, deliberative procedures of decision making, autonomy, and the freedom of entry and exit. Partha Chatterjee concurs with this conceptualization of civil society, but argues that the history of modernity in non-Western settings is replete with the emergence of 'civil-social institutions' that do not conform to these principles and remain restricted to a small section of well-off citizens. The incomplete modernization of Indian state and society, which modernists like Gupta and Béteille would like to see completed along a Western trajectory, is, for Chatterjee, a distinctive feature of non-Western modernity and a marker of its colonial origins and its cultural difference.

Colonial Transformations of Caste Solidarities

The following two sections attempt to historicize and contextualize the ideas and institutions of civil society in India. By examining the workings of actually existing civil society—that is, the social practices of its inhabitants in a (post)colonial context—these sections explore some of the ambiguities and tensions inherent in the idea of civil society. The analysis laid out here also challenges a Western definitional monopoly on ideas and institutions that have travelled worldwide. It thus contributes to a less Eurocentric and a more cosmopolitan understanding of the uneven texture of contemporary modernities within India. Moreover, these sections explore the changing contours of ties of caste, which defy any neat classification in terms of the 'public-private' distinction, as these have been recast by the policies of the (post)colonial state in its interaction with communities.

The institutionalisation of group rights and legal pluralism in India is part of the entangled histories of liberalism in Western and non-Western societies. Western liberalism attempted to create homogenous universal citizenship in the metropolis while simultaneously instituting and cementing difference in the colonies. Unlike European polities conceived within a liberal democratic framework, colonies were never imagined as homogenous. As Dirks has argued, despite its rhetoric of universalizing modernity, colonial governance was concerned with the management, and often even the production, of difference.[46] Castes and religious communities as we know them today are very much a product of enumeration, classification, and categorization by the colonial state in the nineteenth and twentieth centuries.[47] Thus, the groups bearing collective rights in contemporary India and the kinds of rights they claim are shaped by processes of collective identity formation and community representation in colonial India. Whereas the ideology of colonialism pointed toward secular modern rights-bearing free citizenship and eventually nationhood, its reality dealt not only with the essentialization of racial inequality, but also with the institutionalization of an elaborate grammar of cultural diversity through bureaucratic and administrative practice.

There are two variants to the thesis that communalism in contemporary India is of colonial origin. The provision of separate electorates for religious minorities and the reservation of caste-based quotas in the administrative services have been regarded as powerful historical factors in the formation of caste and religious identities. Bipan Chandra has argued that these measures were an important instrument of the divide and rule strategy of the British, whereas Sarkar is of the view that the element of calculated incitement of communal hatred through these policies has been exaggerated.[48] More recently, the emphasis in historical scholarship has shifted from colonial policy to colonial discourse. Exploring the knowledge/power nexus, this scholarship has argued that colonial historiography, ethnography, cartography, and census operations shaped and strengthened the collective identities of castes and religious communities.[49]

The multiple identities based on cultural differences in pre-colonial India were fluid and flexible, not exclusive and exhaustive partitions of the world. The prevalence of overlapping and crosscutting idioms of difference meant that personal and collective identities were situational and segmented. For example, the community of Mole-Salam Garasia Rajputs in Gujarat had until recently a Hindu and a Muslim name for each of its members. There was no monolithic overarching ethnic identity cutting across caste, region, village of origin, religious denomination or sect. Moreover, the sense of distinctiveness on which each of these identities was predicated was not based on a reification of 'cultural' features that characterizes modern ethnicity. Kaviraj has argued that these *Gemeinschaften*, in Toennies's sense, were based on a sense of belonging and solidarity that had little to do with a convergence of economic or political interests.[50] In such a conception, pre-colonial communities are seen as based on organic bonds of kinship. They are seen as pre-political primordial groups bound by tradition rather than constituted through voluntary ties of association of a contractual legal nature.[51] As I argue in the final section, such a contrast misrepresents the nature of communities in that it overlooks that castes were, and most lower castes continue to be, largely self-governing local collectivities that have authority and jurisdiction over their members. Although ascriptive in nature and bound by multiple ties of social, marital, and gift exchange, they were nonetheless political and jural entities and have remained so.

Kaviraj has captured the difference between pre-modern, genuinely communitarian ways of conceiving a community and modern conceptions of it, in the contrast between 'fuzzy' and 'enumerated' communities.[52] 'Fuzzy' communities belonged to a world that was unmapped and unenumerated. These communities had fuzzy boundaries because some collective identities, such as caste or religion, were not based on territory. Their members were not concerned with drawing exact geographical boundaries of their communities, nor were they interested in unambiguously defining and counting all other members of the same region, caste, linguistic group or denomination. Numbers were not the basis of political legitimacy in pre-colonial India. It was only in the colonial and postcolonial states that they came to be used to bargain for economic resources and political privileges. Just how new the idea of exclusivist religious identities is can be seen from the fact that in the 1911 census, 200,000 Indians declared themselves to be 'Mohammedan Hindus'.[53]

Kaviraj suggests that the difference between fuzzy and enumerated communities has important consequences for the action-orientation of their members. Fuzzy traditional communities 'did not see historical processes as things which could be bent to their collective will if people acted concertedly on a large-enough scale'.[54] The enumeration of communities, introduced as part of colonial governmentality, brought about a radical change in this regard. Not only was enumeration a source of psychological strength regarding the size of the 'we' group, but numerical majority also became the basis of political legitimacy in the emerging nation state. It thus became imperative to define and draw precisely the boundaries of nations and regions and of communities within them. In the following section, I argue that an evolutionary view of the transformation of traditional multiple belongings and diffuse identities into modern monolithic interest-based ones obscures an important fact. Even in a world of enumerated collectivities, many castes continue to function as local, territorially demarcated groups of kin and affines with their own norms, procedures, and practices of self-government, which they jealously guard from state intervention. However, the fact that castes enjoy relative autonomy in the domain of family law does not prevent them from engaging in collective interest-based mobilization at elections in terms of the arithmetic of vote banks. Different kinds of ties based on different logics of connectedness are deployed by caste members in different contexts.

To return to the colonial context of the objectification of ties with the help of the technologies of counting and codification: in order to enumerate the entities that were to form the basis of colonial policies, unambiguous definitional criteria were necessary. That these were messy categories was often clear to those that administered them. Nevertheless, the colonial state adopted caste and religion for the purpose of census enumeration, for the allocation of seats in representative bodies, and for job appointments in the administration. For example, with regard to the term Hindu, the Madras Census Report stated as early as 1881: 'Regarded as a definition of religion, or even of race, it is more liberal than accurate'.[55] But, perhaps even more importantly, the decennial census operations and the policies based on them led to these categories becoming intensely contested. Being perceived as a member of a community was no longer a matter of changing interactional contexts, but, rather, was a matter of being subject to definitive bureaucratic classification. This not only touched on questions of self-identity, but involved high political and economic stakes for the elites of the different castes and communities. By the early years of the twentieth century, communal parties and caste organizations mobilized their respective all-India constituencies, created in the process of enumeration, in defence of their interests and for a greater share of political and economic power.

The logic and dynamic of the transformation of fuzzy local communities into enumerated regional or national entities can be illustrated with reference to the so-called 'untouchable castes' at the very bottom of the caste hierarchy. It is important to remember—as I have pointed out above—that this did not lead to the erosion of other modes of belonging, but added another dimension to them that could be deployed according to context. By separating out these communities and constituting them as an all-India category, colonial discourse and policy set in motion a process that acquired a dynamic of its own; this, in turn, had several unintended consequences. It had important consequences for the subsequent self-identity of these collectivities at the all-India level and for the formulation and implementation of state policies in relation to them even today. The reflexive process of social ties being moulded by the way they are conceptualized by the state is reflected in the hundred-year-old career of the term 'untouchable castes', which spans local, regional, national, and global levels.[56] Varying practices of discrimination against several communities at the margins of local caste hierarchies were first reified at a regional level in colonial ethnographies. They were then elevated in the census to form an all-India category embodying the essence of this discrimination in terms of 'untouchability'. The colonial policy of caste-based quotas, which continues in contemporary India, is a bone of contention for liberal secular intellectuals and the propounders of a Hindu nationalism alike. For the former, state policies based on particularistic identities contravene the principles of modern nation building based on the equality of all citizens; for the latter, a monolithic majoritarian Hinduism is difficult to maintain in the face of the politicization of caste identities and growing caste conflicts.[57]

Castes arranged in an orderly hierarchy were chosen by the British administration as the most important category with which to map and control Indian society. Although administrative necessity was said to be the official rationale for recording information on castes, nationalist Indians felt that it was part of the design 'to keep alive, if not exacerbate, the numerous divisions already present in Indian society'.[58] In order to collect 'objective' information, the fluid contours of a caste unit, as well as situational and segmented identities and belongings had to be resolved in favour of unambiguous categories. A standardization of caste names and definitional criteria became necessary in order to ensure all-India comparability. The groups separated out at the bottom of the local caste hierarchies as the repository of 'Untouchability' thus came to constitute a distinct all-India category embodying this essence. The group of castes thus demarcated became not only the object of missionary activity and conversions, of philanthropic practice and Hindu reformist zeal, but also of administrative interest and political concessions. In order to ascertain their numerical strength, a few defining features—out of the diversity of local cultural practices—were used to construct an all-India community.

The estimate of the 'Depressed Classes' population, as the 'Untouchables' were then called, varied widely depending on the specific criteria of ritual and social exclusion that were used—for example, non-access to temples, wells, association with an impure occupation or, more broadly, low status in the caste hierarchy. Around 1917, pollution by touch for the upper castes (that is, 'untouchability') came to be the chief criterion for inclusion in the category. I am not arguing that if castes had not existed, the British would have invented them. What the British did, however, was to use 'untouchability', an attribute of *all* inter-caste relations, to characterize and set apart as beneficiaries of political concessions and welfare measures a particular group of castes in every region. Once these categories were used for the conceptual reification of groups by missionaries, administrators, and Orientalists, however, they functioned in a recursive manner and—as ethnic labels—were appropriated by the people thus designated.

The boundaries of an all-India category of 'untouchable castes' were drawn once and for all in terms of a checklist of 'civic disabilities' (e.g., access to services of Brahmans, to 'public utilities' like wells and schools, to temples) put together by the Census Commissioner in 1931. However, to conceive of these exclusions in terms of 'civic disabilities' is to impose a modernist category. This category presupposes the existence of a civil society, not a world of caste divisions and interactions governed in different situations by different idioms of ritual ranking in which exclusion is a matter of degrees and contexts. Particular local practices did not reflect the *rights* of groups (which is what the state wanted to ascertain with regard to public utilities), but reflected, rather, continual contestation, claims, and counterclaims about ranking.

How far colonial rule and modern competitive politics were responsible for the reshaping of collective identities, and the role of indigenous agency in the process, remain matters of deep division among historians of modern India. But for this analysis, it is enough to have shown the historically changing character of ties of communities of caste and religion in interaction with the state. Recognizing the historical nature of processes of community formation does not, however, render contemporary identifications, belongings, and claims based on these as illegitimate. But it does point to a central dilemma inherited by the postcolonial Indian state: can the recognition of difference be institutionalized in a way that does not essentialize and cement difference? How can legal bureaucratic mechanisms for recognizing cultural heterogeneity take account of constructivist insights into the plurality and contextually shifting nature of identities? The Indian experience in this regard has much to contribute to Western debates—carried out without reference to non-Western experiences of diversity and pluralism—on differentiated citizenship, cultural rights of communities, and affirmative action. The unresolved tension between equality and identity continues to trouble the Indian model of communitarian-liberal democracy. One of the challenges for social and political theory in India and in the West is to address simultaneously claims based on these two principles.

Legal Pluralism and Autonomous Caste Councils

These theoretical debates among historians and social scientists in India serve to frame my discussion of local castes. Local castes and especially caste councils in western India are relatively autonomous institutional arenas for the setting, implementing, and interpreting of norms regarding engagement, marital conflicts, and affinal gift exchange, inheritance, divorce, remarriage, and the custody of children, as well as death rituals, funerary feasts, and obligations of gift giving to service castes on the occasion of these rites of passage. If civil society is the space of societal self-organization between family, state, and market,[59] it must—in the Indian context—include not only caste councils and associations, but also a variety of other non-state legal institutions of self-government and regulation of social life that are relatively autonomous from the state. Given the pre-colonial and colonial history of relative legal autonomy and pluralism in India, the state has never had a monopoly over the production, administration or interpretation of the domain that the British colonial administration subsumed under the sphere of personal law. Today, non-state institutions operating in this domain span a wide variety of institutions, from 'traditional' all-male caste councils in the villages and Gandhian or Jesuit organizations to 'modern' women's bodies and NGOs in urban areas. Although these organizations are not formally recognized by the state as legal forums for their decisions, based on norms woven together from a variety of sources, they are accepted and sometimes even sought out by lower state courts. These courts often exhibit greater similarity to community justice than to the higher-level judiciary in the field of family law. In contradistinction to upper courts, these lower level state courts, for example, rely on mediation by community elders or apply a community's own norms instead of state law. Nevertheless, non-state institutions usually enjoy not only greater legitimacy, but also elicit greater compliance from the disputants. For one, the parties involved in the conflict, usually along with the members of the larger community, have participated in arriving at these compromises. The community, moreover, is able to enforce these decisions in everyday social life using a variety of sanctions, including excommunication. But disputants also recognize these decisions as morally binding and closer to their own quotidian values and practices than court rulings.

Six distinct sets of phenomena must be distinguished analytically within the contemporary plurality of legal regimes and civil society institutions in the domain of family law in Gujarat:

1. The prevalence of separate religiously based family laws for members of different religious communities throughout the country (Hindu,

Muslim, Christian, Parsi). Codified by the British colonial state, and reformed by the postcolonial state in the case of the Hindu personal law, these are administered by state courts.

2. The *de facto* toleration by the state of a multiplicity of 'traditional' legal authorities and institutions, along with a multiplicity of 'customary' and scriptural sources of norms as administered by caste, 'tribal' or *jamat* councils (*panchayats*), which set, adjudicate, and administer these laws for the members of their own local communities.

3. The explicit constitutional provision for communities of indigenous peoples (so-called 'Scheduled Tribes') to be governed by their own set of customary family laws in state courts as well as their own autonomous forums.

4. The toleration by the state of the role of several voluntary organizations, including women's organizations, Gandhian institutions, and church-based NGOs, which seek to resolve family conflicts in accordance with a diverse set of legal norms using mediation.

5. The setting up by the state of 'people's courts' as a speedy, cheap, and accessible alternative to state courts and a way of lessening the pressure on the state system.

6. The introduction of 'women's courts' (*nari adalat*) by the '*Mahila Samakhya*' programmes (which were set up under a state-initiated programme for women's empowerment and gender justice funded by Dutch development aid).

All of these institutions operate parallel to and in varying degrees of interaction with state law and state courts. An analysis of their complex articulation with state-centred legal regimes would help to transcend the dichotomies in terms of which discussions of legal pluralism are often framed: tradition/modernity, state/community, state/civil society, and secular/religious. These relatively autonomous 'traditional' institutions, such as caste councils, fit neither the liberal model of civil society based on the individual rights of citizenship, nor the liberal assumption of the monopoly of the state over law. Nor do they fit Partha Chatterjee's idea of 'political society' discussed above, as they are not arenas of collective bargaining and negotiation with the state, but, rather, arenas in which communities govern their own internal affairs. My argument is that caste and community-based institutions should be seen as part of the specificity of the workings of civil society and of the uneven texture of postcolonial modernity in India. They should thus not be defined out of the public sphere of civil society as representing 'primordial' ties as opposed to 'civic ties', or be seen—as modernists like Dipankar Gupta are wont to—as administering 'customary law'.

An examination of the concepts and conduct of 'informal justice' in postcolonial India poses a challenge to liberal social and political theory derived from Western historical trajectories of individual rights of citizenship and the monopoly of the state over law. This examination also reveals a fracturing of sovereignty in the nation state, which contemporary academic and political debates about a uniform civil code in India obscure. By reducing law to state law, these accord to the latter a primacy and privileged status it does not have in practice. A rather narrow understanding of legal pluralism in academic and public debates in India has resulted from the focus on religiously based personal law of colonial provenance, administered in upper-level state courts alone. This focus on state law has eclipsed the role of civil society institutions such as NGOs and women's organizations, as well as the workings of caste councils in the field of family law. A mapping of the changing contours of state and civil society relations and of shifts in the boundary between the public and the private spheres must take account of the wide variety of institutions of informal justice and the heterogeneity of the legal landscape in contemporary India.

Nivedita Menon has argued that, from the point of view of gender justice, feminists should reject the homogenizing thrust of a uniform family law that seeks to subordinate women's interests in the name of national integration.[60] She cautions against the tendency to naturalize communities in order to claim rights in the name of primordial ties represented as prior to other identifications and belongings. As argued in the previous section, contemporary communities are far from immutable entities with unalterable contours and customs. Rather, they have been formed in the process of interaction with one another and the practices of the colonial state. Any attempt to subordinate the interests of women to the interests of communities defined as internally homogenous and conceived of as the collective bearers of rights is equally problematic. The rights of autonomy and difference, which communities claim vis-à-vis the state, must also be extended to women as members of communities. In this context, the right to exit from or choose whether or not to belong to a community—rather than simply ascriptive membership by virtue of birth—has come to define the community's civility for many feminists.

My ethnographic material—generated during fieldwork among the *Dalits*, or 'untouchable' castes, in north Gujarat (in Western India)—reminds us of the workings of local subdivisions of castes as communities of discourse.[61] Caste assemblies, comprising of adult men, set the rules and procedures by which they are collectively governed, commit them to writing, and interpret and change these norms in long, drawn-out processes of public negotiation. Legal and rhetorical skills are well distributed in the community, and the informal and nonprofessional nature of the proceedings ensures greater accessibility and participation for adult men of the caste. The caste assembly, or *panchayat*, composed of adult male members of a territorial unit of a caste, functions as the primary local unit of identification and belonging. Collective identity, patterns of solidarity, ties of kinship and affinity, but also community power structures and the authority of caste elders—all are constituted with reference to the *panchayat*. Following Moore, a *panchayat* can be understood more as a process with changing participants than as an institution or an event.[62] It is an important forum in which local community norms are subject to continual deliberation and periodic revision. Processes of internal disputation and contestation of norms within each caste—rather than the difference between community and state law—are central to the collective identity of a local sub-caste.

Each *Dalit* caste in north Gujarat is subdivided into several named local units constituted by a set of villages spread over a particular area. These local units, or *paraganu*, often do not encompass contiguous villages. Following Max Weber, Klass treats each subdivision of a caste as an autocephalous *Verband*, a corporate group with its own leadership and internal control mechanisms, which admits no other level of authority.[63] Rather than emphasize their corporate character, I have chosen to follow my *Dalit* interlocutors in conceiving of them as territorially defined, autonomous politico-jural units. These may function as units of endogamy, but their main function is the administration of all local caste matters, including the rules of connubium and commensality that bind members together. Interestingly, the Gujarati word for caste is either *nat* (derived from the Sanskrit *gynati*, meaning species), or *samaj* (society); these are used synonymously. The latter usage points to the fact that the social world of a caste is not conceptualized by its members as the arena of private particularistic interests—as opposed to a larger public sphere defined in relation to the state or seen as encompassing the entire nation. Caste members see the ties of solidarity marked by reciprocal food exchange and the exchange of women and gifts—exchanges that characterize castes as local communities—as belonging to the public sphere of sociality *par excellence*; they contrast this sphere with the private sphere of narrow individual self-interest.[64]

Each local caste unit, or *paraganu*, has its own written and printed 'caste constitution' (*bandharan*), which contains all of the rules of gift exchange with kin, affines, and service castes to be followed at life-cycle rituals. In addition, the *bandharan* contains the procedures and punishments for breaking an engagement, obtaining a divorce, the remarriage of widows and divorcees, and the custody of children. Caste assemblies legislate, administer, and adjudicate the internal affairs of the *paraganu*, enforce and interpret the norms, and punish transgressions and collect fines or even excommunicate the offending families from membership of the local caste. Written caste constitutions all over Gujarat seem to have been a response to the process of collection and codification of caste norms under colonial rule. In 1827, the British Collector of Ahmedabad, Borrodaille, launched a large-scale administrative enquiry to collate—through interviews with selected male caste leaders—the 'customs' of all castes in order to provide the colonial judiciary with information on which to base its decisions. This seems to have given a fillip to caste assemblies to commit to writing and publish their hitherto oral and highly contextual local norms. The form of present-day caste constitutions corresponds closely to the structure of the colonial questionnaires administered almost two centuries ago. The process of codification, however, did not completely freeze these highly flexible norms, which were and still are applied contextually. In the acrimonious public contestation of the rules and their interpretation at caste assemblies, the written document remains only one source of norms; others include, for example, precedent, as well as the practices of neighbouring subdivisions of the same caste.

Normative conflict *within* a spatially defined caste unit (*paraganu*) is pivotal to its constitution as a community, so that community justice is as contested a terrain as state law. Villagers told me in interviews that they often use both of these forums in parallel uses for different purposes. State courts are used to delay the resolution of a dispute interminably and demonstrate one's networks of influence outside the caste, or to harass an opponent and ruin him economically by pushing up the costs of a conflict through prolonged litigation. Justice is sought in the caste assembly with the support of one's network of kin and affines in accordance with the norms of one's community. There is a great deal of continuity between everyday social interaction and dispute settlement in caste assemblies. Even women, who may not speak for themselves in these forums, but have to be represented by their male relatives, prefer the familiar arena and idiom of caste assemblies embedded within their social world to the unfamiliar and distant world of state courts. Usually only young upwardly mobile men, resident in urban areas and with good salaries of their own, prefer to use state courts for divorces, in a bid to cut the ties of caste and to escape from family pressure. It is not that villagers prefer caste *panchayats* to courts as speedier or cheaper options; bribes have to be paid in both cases. But the money spent in caste assemblies builds on and strengthens multiple social ties and contributes to social capital, which can be used for other purposes in the future. Money paid to lawyers, judges, the police, and witnesses is seen, on the contrary, as a waste. It nurtures no social relationships, builds no new bonds of trust, and cannot be put to any other use in the future.

Unpacking categories such as civil society or community enables one to delineate some of the richness, the complexity, but also the ambiguities and paradoxes of contemporary processes of legal pluralism. Perhaps the uneven modernities of the semi-periphery make available political spaces for non-state actors—especially in the sphere of family law—eclipsed in the advanced industrial countries by a statist imaginary. Rather than merely seeing the existence of these non-state spaces as a sign of the weakness or failure of the state in postcolonial societies, one could also see these as a chance for justice to be realized by a diversity of actors with varying capabilities. The persistence of caste solidarities and the existence and transformation of non-state legal regimes is a reminder that 'traditional' ideas, values, and institutions are not residual traces of a vanishing colonial past in postcolonial settings; they are constitutive features of modern life. Veena Das has argued that all major institutions in India today have been reconstituted through their double articulation in tradition and modernity.[65] The material presented here on the plurality of the legal landscape bears witness to the diversity of sources of norms and arenas of conflict resolution in the domain of family law. It points to the easy quotidian intermingling of discourses and practices of 'traditional modernity', which theories of modernization posit as irreconcilable binary opposites.

The scholarly debates and everyday practices I have outlined here allow an analysis of the actual workings of civil society and the dilemmas of its actors vis-à-vis the state. State intervention in the lives of poor and marginalized communities in India is highly selective. The state recognizes the cultural rights of communities, but not their collective rights over natural resources (land, water, forests). The cunning state, as I have argued elsewhere,[66] chooses to exercise selective and partial sovereignty over its territory and its citizens. Highly interventionist in the domain of fertility control in poor families, for example, the Indian state has chosen to allow for diversity and relative autonomy of castes and religious communities in the domain of family law. However, what would appear in liberal theory and from a statist perspective as the failure of the state, or its weakness, can also be seen as an opportunity. The absence of state hegemony in some areas of social life, along with the state's inability, or unwillingness, to colonize completely the everyday life of its citizens, also provides a space for dissenting imaginaries. Rather than seek statist solutions based on Western models, the challenge for activists and social scientists is to be able to develop alternatives and to experiment with them as tools of a new moral and social imagination sensitive to the textures and rhythms of uneven modernities in India.

Notes

1. An earlier version of this chapter, which has been abbreviated and revised for the present volume, has been published in Yehuda Elkana et al., eds., *Unraveling Ties: From Social Cohesion to New Practices of Connectedness* (Frankfurt a.M., 2002).
2. Thomas Pantham, *Political Theories and Social Reconstruction* (New Delhi, 1975), 171.
3. Gurpreet Mahajan, *Identities and Rights: Aspects of Liberal Democracy in India* (Delhi, 1995).
4. Claus Offe, 'Homogeneity and Constitutional Democracy: Group Rights as an Answer to Identity Conflicts', in *Rules, Laws and Constitutions*, eds. S. Sabarwal and H. Sievers (New Delhi, 1998), 188–208.
5. Sunil Khilnani, *The Idea of India* (Delhi, 1997).
6. Sivaramakrishnan and Agarwal, *Regional Modernities: The Cultural Politics of Development in India* (Delhi, 2003); Dilip P. Gaonkar, 'On Alternative Modernities', in *Alternative Modernities*, ed. D. P. Gaonkar (London, 2001), 1–23.
7. Göran Therborn, 'Routes to/through Modernity', in *Global Modernities*, eds. M. Featherstone, S. Lash, and R. Robertson (London, 1995), 124–139; Samuel N. Eisenstadt, 'Multiple Modernities', *Daedalus* 129 (1)(2000): 1–29.
8. Mahmood Mamdami, *Citizen and Subject: Contemporary Africa and the Legacy of Late Colonialism* (Princeton, 1996).
9. Peter Wagner, Claude Didry, and Bénédicte Zimmermann, *Arbeit und Nationalstaat: Frankreich und Deutschland in europäischer Perspektive* (Frankfurt a.M, 2000).
10. Sebastian Conrad, and Shalini Randeria, eds., 'Geteilte Geschichte: Europa in einer postkolonialer Welt', in C.S. Conrad and S. Randeria, *Jenseits des Eurozentrismus: Postkoloniale Perspektiven in den Geschichts- und Kulturwissenschaften* (Frankfurt a.M, 2002), 9–49.
11. Bruce Knauft, eds., *Critically Modern: Alternatives, Alternities, Anthropologies* (Bloomington, 2002).
12. Shalini Randeria, 'Geteilte Geschichte und verwobene Moderne', in *Zukunftsentwürfe. Ideen für eine Kultur der Veränderung*, eds. J. Rüsen et al. (Frankfurt, 1999), 87–96; Shalini Randeria, 'Jenseits von Soziologie und soziokultureller Anthropology: Zur Ortsbestimmung der nichtwestlichen Welt in einer zukünftigen Sozialtheorie', *Soziale Welt* 50 (4)(1999): 373–82.
13. Shalini Randeria et al., eds., 'Konfigurationen der Moderne: Einleitung', in *Konfigurationen der Moderne: Diskurse zu Indien, Soziale Welt*, eds. S. Randeria, M. Fuchs, and A. Linkenbach, *Sonderband* 15 (2004): 9–34.
14. Shalini Randeria, 'Zivilgesellschaft in postkolonialer Perspektive', in Jürgen Kocka et al., *Neues über Zivilgesellschaft aus historisch-sozialwissenschaftlichem Blickwinkel*, WZB Arbeitspapier p01–801 (Berlin, 2001), 81–103.
15. Jean-Francois Bayart, *The State in Africa. The Politics of the Belly* (London, 1996); Mamdami, *Citizen and Subject* (1996); Rajni Kothari, 'Integration and Exclusion in Indian Politics', *Economic and Political Weekly* 23 (1988): 2223–27; Rajni Kothari, *State against Democracy: In Search of Humane Governance*

(Delhi, 1988); Kothari and Harsh Sethi, eds., *Rethinking Human Rights: Challenges for Theory and Action* (New York, 1989); D.L. Sheth, 'Grass Roots Initiatives in India', *Economic and Political Weekly* 19 (1984): 259–62; Dipankar Gupta, 'Civil Society or the State: What Happened to Citizenship?', in *Institutions and Inequalities. Essays in Honour of André Béteille*, eds. R. Guha and J.P. Parry (Delhi, 1999).

16. Nicholas Dirks, *Colonialism and Culture* (Ann Arbor, 1992).
17. Ernest Gellner, 'The Importance of Being Modular', in *Civil Society: Theory, History, Comparison*, ed. J. Hall (Cambridge, 1995), 32–55.
18. Shalini Randeria, *The Politics of Representation and Exchange Among Untouchable Castes in Western India* (Gujarat) (Ph.D. diss., Free University, Berlin, 1992).
19. Adam Seligman, 'Civil Society as Idea and Ideal', in *Alternative Conceptions of Civil Society*, eds. S. Chambers and W. Kymlicka (Princeton, 2002), 13–33.
20. Jürgen Kocka, 'Zivilgesellschaft als historisches Problem und Versprechen', in *Europäische Zivilgesellschaft in Ost und West. Begriff, Geschichte, Chancen*, eds. M. Hildermeier et al. (Frankfurt a.M., 2000), 13–39.
21. Neera Chandhoke, *State and Civil Society: Explorations in Political Theory* (Delhi, 1995).
22. John L. Comaroff and Jean Comaroff, eds., *Civil Society and the Political Imagination in Africa* (Chicago, 1999).
23. Sudipta Kaviraj and Sunil Khilnani, eds., *Civil Society. History and Possibilities* (Cambridge, 2001).
24. Seligman, 'Civil Society', 14f.
25. Comaroff, *Civil Society*, viii.
26. J.A. Hall, eds., *Civil Society: Theory, History and Comparison* (Cambridge, 1995); Gellner, 'Importance'.
27. Sudipta Kaviraj and Sunil Khilnani, eds., 'Introduction: Ideas of Civil Society', in Kaviraj and Khilani, *Civil Society*, 1–8.
28. Jack Goody, 'Civil Society in an extra-European Perspective', in Kaviraj and Khilani, *Civil Society*, 149–64.
29. Chris Hann and Elizabeth Dunn, eds., *Civil Society: Challenging Western Models* (London, 1996).
30. André Béteille, *Society and Politics in India* (London, 1991).
31. Mamdami, *Citizen and Subject*.
32. Ibid.
33. Eisenstadt, 'Multiple Modernities'.
34. Frederic Cooper and Ann Stoler, eds., *Tensions of Empire. Colonial Cultures in a Bourgeois World* (Berkeley, 1997).
35. Paul Gilroy, *Against Race: Imagining Political Culture beyond the Color Line* (Cambridge, MA, 2000); Edward Said, *Culture and Imperialism* (New York, 1993).
36. Kothari, *State against Democracy*.
37. Rajni Kothari, Rajni, 'Human Rights: A Movement in Search of a Theory', in *Human Rights: Challenges for Theory and Action*, eds. S. Kothari and H. Sethi (New York, 1991), 151–62.

38. Gupta, 'Civil Society'.
39. Kothari, *State against Democracy;* Sheth, 'Grass Roots'; Ashis Nandy, 'Culture, State and Rediscovery of Indian Politics', *Economic and Political Weekly* 19 (1984): 2078–83; Ashis Nandy, 'The Political Culture of the Indian State', *Daedalus* 118 (1989): 1–26; Partha Chatterjee, 'Beyond the Nation? Or Within', *Economic and Political Weekly* 32 (1997): 30–34; Partha Chatterjee, 'On Civil and Political Society in Post-Colonial Democracies', in Kaviraj and Khilnani, *Civil Society,* 165–78.
40. Gupta, 'Civil Society'.
41. André Béteille, 'Secularism and the Intellectuals', *Economic and Political Weekly* 29 (10)(1994): 559–66.
42. André Béteille, *Society and Politics in India* (London, 1991).
43. André Béteille, *Civil Society and its Institutions,* First Fulbright Memorial Lecture (Calcutta, 1996).
44. André Béteille, 'The Conflict of Norms and Values in Contemporary Indian Society', in *The Limits of Social Cohesion: Conflict and Mediation in Plural Societies,* ed. P. Berger (Colorado, 1998), 265–92.
45. Gupta, 'Civil Society'.
46. Dirks, *Colonialism.*
47. Bernhard Cohn, 'The Census, Social Structure and Objectification in South Asia', *Folk* 26 (1984): 25–49; Sudipto Kaviraj, 'The imaginary institution of India', in *Subaltern Studies VII,* eds. P. Chatterjee and Gyanendra Pandey (New Delhi, 1992), 1–40; Arjun Appadurai, 'Number in the Colonial Imagination', in *Orientalism and the Postcolonial Predicament: Perspectives on South Asia,* eds. C. Breckenridge and P. van der Veer (Philadelphia, 1993), 314–41.
48. Bipan Chandra, *Nationalism and Communalism in Modern India* (New Delhi, 1981); Sumit Sarkar, *Modern India 1885–1947* (New Delhi, 1983).
49. Bernard Cohn, 'Notes on the study of Indian society and culture', in *Structure and Change in Indian Society,* eds. M. Singer and B.S. Cohn (Chicago, 1968), 3–28; Cohn, 'Census'; Gyanendra Pandey, *The Construction of Communalism in Colonial North India* (New Delhi, 1990).
50. Kaviraj, 'Imaginary Institution'.
51. Amrita Shodhan, *A Question of Community: Religious Groups and Colonial Law* (Calcutta, 2001).
52. Kaviraj, 'Imaginary Institution', 20–26.
53. S.T. Lokhandwala, 'Indian Islam: Composite Culture and Integration', *New Quest* 50 (1985): 87–101.
54. Kaviraj, 'Imaginary Institution', 26.
55. Quoted in Jürgen Lütt, 'Hindus—a dying race. Census and Identity in India before the First World War', Paper for the Conference Identität im Wandel (Berlin, 21/22 October 1993), 1.
56. Randeria, *Politics of Representation.*
57. Shalini Randeria, '"Hindu-Fundamentalismus": Zum Verhältnis von Religion, Politik und Geschichte im modernen Indien', in *Kulturen und Innovationen: Festschrift für Wolfgang Rudolph,* eds. G. Elwert et. al. (Berlin, 1996), 333–61.
58. M.N. Srinivas, *Social Change in Modern India* (Berkeley, 1966), 100.

59. Kocka, 'Zivilgesellschaft', 4.
60. Nivedita Menon, 'Uniform Civil Code: Debates in Feminism Today', in *Sites of Change: The Structural Context for Empowering Women in India*, eds. N. Rao et al. (Delhi, 1996), 445–59.
61. Randeria, *Politics of Representation*.
62. Erina Moore, 'Law's Patriarchy in India', in *Contested States: Law, Hegemony and Resistance*, eds. M.L. Black and S. Hirsch (New York, 1994), 89–117.
63. Morton Klass, *Caste: the Emergence of the South Asian Social System* (Philadelphia, 1980).
64. Shalini Randeria, 'Kings, Brahmans, 'Untouchables': Caste-Hierarchy and Gift-Exchange Western India', in *Wissenschaftskolleg Jahrbuch* 1990–1991, ed. W. Lepenies (Berlin, 1992), 294–312; Shalini Randeria, 'Mourning and Mortuary Exchange: the Construction of Local Communities among the Dalits of Gujarat', in *Ways of Dying Death and its Meanings in South Asia*, eds. E. Schombucher and Claus Peter Zoller (Delhi, 1999), 88–111.
65. Veena Das, *Critical Events: An Anthropological Perspective on Contemporary India* (Delhi, 1995).
66. Shalini Randeria, 'Cunning States and Unaccountable International Institutions: Legal Plurality, Social Movements and Rights of Local Communities to Common Property Resources', *European Journal of Sociology* 44 (1)(2003): 27–60.

=== CHAPTER 5 ===

Lost in Translation?

Transcending Boundaries in Comparative History

MONICA JUNEJA AND MARGRIT PERNAU

Introduction

Comparative history, especially in Western Europe, views itself as transcending the traditional focus on nation states and opening up to a new, global perspective of the world.[1] By extending the space given in university studies and in research first to Eastern Europe, but in the longer perspective also to non-European countries, it sets out to overcome not only provincialism, but also the power structures ingrained in historical research. Practitioners of comparative history, Hannes Siegrist claims, generally consider themselves specialists of a dialogue between cultures conducted on an equal footing.[2]

On the other hand, historians of non-European countries, particularly those researching on India, do not cease to remind us of the ways in which comparative studies have contributed to anchoring the supremacy of European history, reducing the rest of the world to the status of 'not-quite' or at least of 'not-yet'. Far from being conducted on an equal footing, the history of comparison—beginning with the founding fathers of Oriental studies at the end of the eighteenth century—of the theories of modernization that have not yet lost their intellectual hold over researchers' minds, shows that comparison very often leads to a hierarchization and, hence, tends to stabilize rather than disrupt existing power structures.[3]

To reflect on the interrelationship between power and knowledge is not in the first instance an outcome of what is sometimes perceived as an 'apologetic stance' of the younger generation of Western scholars toward the Third World.[4] A historiography that seeks to legitimize itself solely on the grounds of its political underpinnings and evades the question of an adequate description of historical reality altogether is no longer distinguishable from myth.[5] Yet even if we were to set aside the discussion on the political responsibility of the historian, the question of the interrelation between power and knowledge persists at the centre of all comparative research—irrespective of political correctness. Ignoring this relationship would lead to distortions in the perception of both of the units meant to be compared and would obscure their interrelatedness. In modification of Talleyrand's famous dictum, one might venture to say that such an oversight would lead not only to indefensible politics, but worse, to bad historiography.

This chapter, hence, proceeds in four steps. Firstly, we will briefly review the history of comparative studies in the Western historical tradition, bringing out the entry points into intercultural comparison that this method offers, as well as the questions it does not address and the gaps that remain. Secondly, we will follow up on the implications of the linguistic turn for comparative studies. If all of our thinking is deeply influenced by language, how can we write about two different cultures in one language? How do translation and representation in another language affect the possibilities of a comparison, which aims at something different from an appropriation? Which language and which concepts do we need for writing transnational, and even more so, transcultural history?

Thirdly, comparisons have traditionally been worked out between entities that were deemed to exist independently of each other. However, the urge to pay close attention to transfer processes has raised certain methodological problems that still completely have not been resolved. The relations between the metropolis and the colony, however, as the evolving new imperial history has shown, go much further than any transfer, even if the latter is thought of as a reciprocal process. What are the implications for comparison if encounter does not only bring about a change within the entities to be compared, but creates them in the first place? How, on the other hand, can we evaluate the impact of entanglement; how can we distinguish between endogenous and exogenous factors without resorting to comparison?

In the fourth and final part, we will present a project that we have been working on for some time, which tries to transcend historiographical boundaries—in other words, it seeks to take entanglement into the domain of historiography with a view of evolving a common language through encounter and dialogue between historians and historical traditions.

Historiography in Western Europe—Comparison, Transfer, and Globality

Since the late eighteenth century, comparison was regarded as a sign of modernity within the scientific discourse of the West. A key role was ascribed to the comparative approach at the turn of the eighteenth century, a time when a reorganization of the social sciences was underway. A comparative mode of reflection was held to bring about new ways of conceptualization, accompanied by a number of methodologically fruitful operations, such as drawing analogies, locating and defining relationships, and drawing parallels while identifying difference.[6] While providing a scientific basis to a range of newly formed disciplines, the horizon of comparative studies extended during the eighteenth century beyond the limits of Europe, so that concepts such as culture and civilization came to be defined in relation to plurality, and observed and textualized in a proliferation of literary and scientific genres.[7] The focus shifted a century later to the state or nation states, to subjects related in one way or the other to nation building—the comparative study of legal frameworks, constitutions, administrative apparatuses, and so on. The comparative method was premised on the constitution of autonomous units from which all forms of interdependence and interrelationships were abstracted, units defined not only through the boundaries of the nation state, but also through a process of internal homogenization.[8]

The revival of comparative history during the last two decades, particularly in Germany, initially continued with many of its older assumptions still intact, though in recent years these have been increasingly subject to critical scrutiny as part of the effort to respond to the challenges of globalization. When Hans-Ulrich Wehler spoke in 1972 of comparison as the highest form of historical research in order to 'test the validity of either very general or very specific hypotheses', he had primarily the debate on the German *Sonderweg* in mind. This debate provided the impetus for a spurt of large, comparative projects in the 1980s and the 1990s, notably the project on the history of the European bourgeoisie located at the University of Bielefeld. The themes of comparative history, as they developed in Western Europe during the past two decades, mostly have resided within the framework of the nation or the region. The subjects investigated cover a wide range—professions, education, family forms, bureaucracies, legal institutions, labour—and, in more recent times, have been extended to include political rituals, festivals, symbols, and myths.[9] The historical approach was mainly that of social history marked by both quantitative, as well qualitative, analysis. While lip service has been paid to extend the comparative mode to include the analysis of discourses,[10] there has on the whole been little systematic engagement with problems of language and discursivity, which are indispensable to any engagement with multiple cultural contexts.[11]

Historical comparison was by its very nature confronted with several hurdles of a pragmatic and institutional kind—it necessitated, to begin with, linguistic and cultural competence for more than one region and access to more than one set of sources and archives, which demanded a proportionately higher budget of time and finances. It also required familiarity with a multiplicity of historiographical traditions and an institutional anchoring within existing university structures. One consequence of such difficulties has been that many of the 'comparative' studies ended up resorting to what has been described as 'asymmetrical comparison'.[12] In such comparisons, one of the units is not investigated in equal depth as the other; rather, it serves as a foil of sorts to highlight the 'peculiarities' of the other unit. Criteria for the selectivity operating with regard to the choice of what is compared and in what depth the study is carried out are not always made transparent. Yet, even though this form of comparison was, strictly speaking, an 'abuse' of the method, it was not ruled out completely, as it was regarded as at least opening the view to alternative historical developments.

Comparative history—as it has been by and large practised among a group of historians in Germany, together with colleagues in France and England and, since the 1990s, with those in Eastern Europe—rests on the juxtaposition of two or more units regarded as autonomous, investigated so as to yield conclusions about their similarities and differences. This method, on the whole, has been believed to have advantages outweighing the problems it poses. Drawing up a balance sheet of structural similarities and differences—for the approach addressed structures more than processes—appeared to replicate and ensure the precision of methods practised in the natural sciences. Comparative history continues to be viewed as an important corrective to nation-centric perspectives, enabling access to culturally alien units and sensitizing the historian to multiple perspectives. Depending on the choice of 'partners' that are compared, the national perspective can be relativized in more than one way.[13] More recently, comparative history has also been ascribed the virtue of being able to induce dialogical competence and heightened self-reflexivity.[14] Yet in recent years, this mode of constituting units of comparison without reflecting on the criteria of their constitution, as well as the reduction of complexity that this method is forced to undertake due to the need to iron out those aspects that cannot be directly explained through comparison, have brought on a number of challenges and critical questions.

At the heart of this critique lies the position taken by the advocates of comparative history until recently: that comparison must be decoupled from a study of relationships that may proliferate between the units being compared.[15] According to these advocates, the two approaches—the search for similarities and differences on the one hand, and the study of interrelationships, on the other—are to be kept 'methodologically apart'. In this, they draw upon the authority of Marc Bloch, who, in his pioneering essay of 1928, is supposed to have argued against such a 'mixing' of perspectives.[16] However, it was Bloch who made a distinction between two types of comparisons: a comparison between units marked by contiguity of time and space, and between units separated by such great distance both in time and space so as to preclude all interaction between them.[17] In the first case, Bloch actually cautioned that not integrating the history of interactions within a comparative frame could produce distortions. His reference was, however, to Europe, to geographically and culturally contiguous regions, whereas regions separated by greater distance fell into the second category. Even this latter position can today be questioned in the light of global perspectives.

The issue of relationships existing between the units being compared has become an important debate within the field of comparative history during recent years, although Friedrich Tenbruck broached it earlier.[18] Many of these questions have been stimulated by newer historiographical trends, such as global and transnational history, postcolonialism, and the linguistic turn. In the forefront, however, are those historians who argue for the interconnectedness between the history of transfers and the comparative mode, as the latter on its own appears too narrow and often too static to find explanations for similarities and differences. The study of transfers and their varied reception—the multiple interpretations, reworkings, questionings, and subversions that occur in the wake of the movement of goods, concepts, norms, and practices from one cultural context into another—brings with it the need to contextualize and so allows for greater complexity, rather than the reduction that a pure exercise in comparison involves. Comparative history must therefore, so the argument goes, open itself up to the study of transfers, as similarities and differences are likely to be an outcome of interrelationships or intersections of one kind or another.[19] This would also mean a greater degree of sensitivity to the constructed nature of the units, both in the cases of comparison as well as in the study of transfers. An argument in this direction has been put forward, calling for the exploration of conceptual categories that transcend the national: trans-societal or transcultural comparisons.[20]

A question that, however, remains unaddressed here is the way in which units of comparison are constituted in the first place. What role do global entanglements play in the formation of such units, in the creation and shifting of boundaries? Global perspectives in historiography force us to address this question. Not only the new imperial history (as discussed below), which argues for intertwined histories that connect the metropolis and the colony, but also studies of the early modern period make a persuasive argument for 'connected histories'. In all of these contexts, there exist numerous possibilities of comparison—of urban forms, structures of political authority, forms of sociability, the symbolic repertoire of different cultures, to name only a few areas—which were, however, themselves more often than not constituted through the 'connectedness' of regions and cultures.[21] Thus, although the integration of transfers and comparison is a welcome paradigmatic elaboration that could deepen the interpretive potential of comparative history, it does not address a number of issues that are of crucial value once comparative history is practised beyond the boundaries of Europe. Comparisons with non-European cultures and regions are often couched in terminology such as *Zivilisationsvergleich*, which, although they ostensibly seek to depart from a Eurocentric view, end up defeating their purpose, as the criteria for constructing a unit termed 'civilisation' remains obscure.[22] There is, to begin with, the obvious problem linked to research: comparisons between civilizations that are seen as totalities are empirically almost unattainable and would inevitably lead to essentializing models or purely impressionistic observations and generalisations. Units of comparison are constructs created both by modern historians and by contemporaries as part of their strivings toward self-definition. Therefore, the comparative mode would need to investigate boundaries as part of these constructs. Similarities and interrelationships would effect a blurring of boundaries on the one hand, yet, on the other and at the same time, the highlighting of difference would define, or perhaps constantly redefine, frontiers. One response to the problem of boundaries fluctuating in the wake of reciprocal movements between the units of comparison has been a concept of transnationalism. This notion draws its impulses from sociological-cum-ethnological studies of migrant populations, those who develop multiple identities realized through a constant transgression of boundaries between social and political units. Transnationalism, therefore, is conceptualised as a particular category of social relationships created in opposition to limits imposed by national boundaries.[23]

A problem of a different kind is posed by the suggestion that, in cases of diachronic comparisons between Europe and regions of the non-European world, conditions prevailing in the latter during the first half of the twentieth century might be 'usefully' compared (or viewed as parallel) to those of the 'early modern' period in Europe.[24] As long as the conceptual criteria underlying comparison are not made transparent, the dangers of opening the back door to one more form of Eurocentrism while throwing the master narrative of Kantian universalism out of the front door, cannot be ruled out. Is 'modernity' here implicitly a notion grounded in European experience that relegates non-European societies to the 'waiting room of history', as Dipesh Chakrabarty has pointed out?[25]

The opening up of comparative history to areas beyond Europe leaves many questions open, the most important of these being the question of the language and concepts with which this history is written. In an evidently pragmatic move, practitioners of the new 'Global History' begin by approaching non-European areas by being equipped with a conceptual apparatus rooted in the particularity of the European experience, though one that is blandly assumed to possess universal normative significance. The crucial question is, what follows this initial pragmatic approach to an alien field, a way of seeking to access the unknown through the familiar? Do European concepts then become a yardstick for measuring societies and cultures across time and space? Do non-European societies then present a case of 'incomplete transformations' or 'absences' if they do not measure up to the criteria implicit in conceptual categories coming from a European context? Does the alien get completely subsumed within the familiar and therefore lose its identity, or does it get excluded from mainstream discussions because of the difficulties encountered while trying to cast unfamiliar histories in a familiar mould? Is the alternative to this dilemma a form of 'multi-perspective' writing, praised by practitioners of global comparisons,[26] which privileges a multitude of indigenous concepts for each region written about, concepts that are marked by greater accuracy, on the one hand, but that on the other hand serve to fix the alien once and for all in unapproachable alterity? The divide between the European approach, that claims universality, and the individual non-European approach, that clings to its particularity, is replicated at the institutional level in the separation between 'mainstream' departments of History and the so-called 'area studies', each preserving its domain and practising its craft in isolation of the other. The relationship as it exists in German academia is, however, one of asymmetrical power, as the authority to represent the 'global' has come to rest with the mainstream. The institutional isolation of area studies is partly a form of self-exclusion and partly an outcome of an unequal distribution of power.[27]

This brings us to the central question of whether narratives of comparative history in a global frame as we know them today are indeed a peculiarly Western or Eurocentric form of knowledge. Sensitivity to the issues at stake in the use of concepts and language when operating across cultures, while underlining the necessity for a comparative history of discourses, has been shown in the European context by Steinmetz and others.[28] The linguistic turn has sensitized us to the ways in which comparison comes to be configured through language, to the insight that the comparative exercise does not precede conceptual categories, but is dependent upon them. While Siegrist elevates dialogue and sensitivity of multiple perspectives to a central position in modern comparative approaches, these virtues are of little use without the accompanying reflection on the interpretive categories through which sources in different languages are read and interpreted, and assimilated within a master narrative. If comparison is also a 'representation' of one culture or history by the practitioners of another, the question of who enjoys the authority to 'represent' becomes relevant. To what extent do practitioners of comparative history today reflect upon the ways in which their own academic location and practice structure their analytic procedures? Does dialogue take place in a space purged of the workings of power? The linguistic turn in the social sciences has drawn our attention significantly to the way power intervenes in transactions that 'translate' intellectual productions from one context into another.

Translation and Representation

Every comparison between two phenomena originally described in different languages implies translation. In the original meaning of the word, translation stood for the carrying over of meaning from one language into another. This process might require the effort of a specialist, yet it was neither deemed impossible to express the same meaning in different languages, nor was this procedure of translating held to affect either of the languages. The linguistic turn, however, has sharpened our awareness of the extent to which our perceptions of the world are shaped by language. What gets lost in translation is not only a part of the meaning,[29] but also the possibility of creating different conceptual categories and definitions, of drawing up different boundaries. Concepts and categories in any given language are intimately related to social and cultural experience, and there is no direct path that would lead from particular experience to universal categories. The attempt to nevertheless deploy such 'particular' categories in a 'universal' vein may well end up denying to the other the possibility of self-representation.[30]

However, the power structures embedded in translation can work both ways.[31] The first translations on the Indian subcontinent, brought about by colonialism, were linked to the endeavours of the founding fathers of Oriental scholarship, who were working from Fort William College in Calcutta at the end of the eighteenth century. Marked by the ethos of the Enlightenment ideal of a common history of mankind, they strove to recover texts in Sanskrit, Persian, and Arabic, but also in the modern vernaculars, and translated them into English for a European audience. These translations were supposed to neither transform the target language nor alter the fundamentals of European knowledge, but, rather, add to the archive of available information. They contributed to rendering the Orient understandable and, hence, controllable.[32] At the same time, this was the period of the great comparative projects, notably in linguistics, which led to the discovery of the common origin of the Indo-European languages. In the meantime, however, Indians were deemed to have degenerated from this common origin in the Aryan period. A renewal was believed to be possible only through a return to untainted sources, not through interaction with the modern European world. The idea of a common origin was matched by the underlining of radical difference in the present, a difference that the colonizers strove to maintain. The 'white Moghuls',[33] those British officers who dressed like Moghul nobles, married local women, were fluent in the vernacular languages, and recited Persian poetry, have been presented as agents of cultural contact. This should not make us forget that, while they were willing to take in a selected Orient, they refused reciprocity—the Orient had to be kept Oriental. Appropriation and othering thus went hand in hand; translating Indian texts into English was a means of creating and stabilizing power.

Much maligned in recent times, the Anglicist project from the 1830s onward was a reaction against this exclusion and therefore able to draw on the support of a considerable number of Indian scholars and reformers. India, in their eyes, might have been different in the past, but it had the possibility for development and might one day hope to catch up, even with England. Instead of translating Indian texts—now considered useless both for the indigenous and the European audiences—Macaulay and his allies started a campaign for translations from English into the vernaculars. From 1840 onward, the Delhi College became an example of this reforming urge, teaching mainly Western knowledge, but through the medium of Urdu in order to facilitate the acculturation of the new information. Unlike the translations emanating from Fort William College, the Delhi College translations aimed, from the beginning, to change the target language. Besides the conscious creation of a new vocabulary to convey new meanings and to talk about new subjects, it was hoped that the Urdu language would, through the intimate contact with English, be cleansed of its tendency toward exaggeration and hyperbole and rendered chaste and clear.[34] This new language was then envisaged as a possible vehicle for the expression of new ideas. Through comparison and translation, it was the Indian reality that was to be changed, as translating English texts into Indian vernacular was also a means of creating and stabilizing power.

So if comparing across cultures, as well as refusing this comparison, if incorporating the concepts and categories of the other culture into our narrative, as well as translating them, are all tainted with the exercise of power, how do we proceed? What way and what language can we find for comparison?[35] One suggestion has been the use of analytical concepts stemming from neither culture and might thus be seen as bridging the gap between them. If, however, we take the link between experience and language seriously, even scholarly language itself will not provide us with an archimedal point situated outside culture, language, and experience.[36] On the contrary, analytical terms can be viewed as one of the ways in which the West described itself—be it the opposition of society and community, of ascribed and acquired status or even concepts such as politics or religion.[37]

This problem has been a subject of intense discussion among anthropologists for a considerable stretch of time. How do we represent the other; how do we translate cultures without either appropriating them into our own categories or excluding them from common humanity as fundamentally different and, hence, incomprehensible?[38] Translation here has been viewed not primarily as an academic exercise, but as a social act in which both sides are involved.[39] Representation thus remains no longer a unilateral activity, but is transformed into a part of a dialogue in which the representation of the self, both of the anthropologist and his partner in the field, and of the other, again, of both sides, intertwine and bring forth something new. It is the dialogue that permits the sharing of experience and, hence, the emergence of a new language through 'translating and being translated'.[40]

A dialogue may be difficult for anthropologists, but perhaps not impossible. But how can this concept be of use to historians, whose potential dialogue partners have passed away a long time ago? It is our argument that comparison may well come to perform a similar function und substitute for the creation of common experience through dialogue, thus successively bringing forth the language it needs. This presupposes a view of language not as fixed, not as a prison house of meaning,[41] but as adaptable and constantly evolving. In this case it might make sense, when writing for a European audience, at the beginning to base comparison on European concepts and experiences. However, what is important is not to stop there, but to use this comparison to include non-European experiences. Unlike a translator of literary texts, the historian has the possibility continuously to discuss his translational activity. While he may take his readers' European preconceptions as a point of departure, he will quickly reach a stage where the historical evidence cannot be encompassed any longer by the original concepts. What would be a sign of failure in a literary translation here can be taken as an opportunity for pointing out different ways of conceptualising and of drawing boundaries and, most importantly, for attempting to explain the reasoning behind them. Far from 'nostrification', this kind of comparative approach may enhance the awareness of the presence of different forms of self-representation without, however, essentializing them and excluding the other from the framework of a shared history.

While starting from different methodological assumptions, in the end this comes quite close to what Homi Bhabha proposes as the creation of an 'In-Between' of cultures, of a 'Third Space' that belongs to neither of them.[42] What is at stake is not the obliteration of cultural differences, but, on the contrary, the preservation of their 'enunciative disturbance',[43] as well as the refusal to contribute to a solidification of the fluid boundaries between languages and between cultures. This space is not a given, but constantly brought forth and redrawn—translation and comparison, as we understand them, both presuppose and create it. In the words of Salman Rushdie: 'Having been borne across the world, we are translated men. It is normally supposed that something always gets lost in translation; I cling, obstinately, to the notion that something can also be gained'.[44]

The fundamental difference with regard to traditional comparative analysis, which poses the construction of a *tertium comparationis* as the precondition to comparison, is that we claim that both the language and the commonality needed to evolve only in the course and as a result of comparative activity. This is not a new invention, of course, but has been practised, more or less systematically, within Western European history for quite some time. An example is the seminal work edited by Jürgen Kocka on the European *Bürgertum*, which, without erasing the differences between, for example, the French *bourgeoisie*, the English middle classes, and the German *Bürgertum*, still used language in such a way as to cover all three phenomena, with the author changing his readers' understanding and inner images of the concept of *Bürgertum* as he went along.[45] Hence, every successful translation and comparison brings forth its own requirements and simultaneously lays the groundwork for further comparison.[46] If this sounds overly optimistic, critics may perhaps be reminded that we have no alternative but to work as if communication were possible, even while recognising that power relations continue to be at work and influence our research, and then set out to improve what we are doing.

At the same time, it is important to open up academic structures for reciprocal translations. If we aim at a third space, it will not be reached starting from one side only; multiperspectivity[47] must be based on dialogue between historians who are representatives, as well as on mixtures of different historiographical and cultural traditions.[48]

Comparison, Entanglement, and the Problem of Boundaries

The central theme in the *Satanic Verses* by Salman Rushdie, is the transformation the main character experiences once he is confronted with the representation of his self as seen by the British, a representation backed by power, which leaves him no choice but to become who he is imagined to be.[49] However, it is not only the Indians who are 'translated men', who are no longer able to disentangle the colonial other from their self, but the British as well. 'The trouble with the Engenglish is that their hiss hiss history happened overseas, so they dodo don't know what it means'.[50] If the 'mutual encounters'[51] between India and Britain have led to such an entanglement,⁵² to such a transformation of both sides that the boundaries between the self and the other are no longer recognizable, if one cannot be perceived without the other, what does that imply for the possibility of comparing the two countries? Does comparison presuppose boundaries—either given boundaries, or at least the possibility for the historian to construct them according to some identifiable criteria?

From the beginning of the colonial period, Indian history has been written as a history of transfer, foregrounding the agency of the British. This way of seeing informed a range of writings, first among them the self-congratulatory narratives of colonial writers, who pointed to the transformation of the subcontinent through the encounter with British culture, notably in the field of language and political norms, and the introduction of the British legal system, which in their eyes led to the reform of Indian society and finally to the awakening of the nation led by an English educated elite.⁵³ It also informed nationalist critics, who underlined the drain of wealth following from the colonisation of the economy, transforming the production system of the country to suit Britain's requirements.⁵⁴ Finally, it influenced a first generation of historians who were working out the implications of Edward Said's critique of Orientalism for the Indian context, thereby locating the moving force of history exclusively among the colonial actors and their construction of knowledge.⁵⁵

This unilateral attribution of agency, however, did not go very far in explaining historical processes and developments. India was not a clean slate upon which the British inscribed their categories, nor was the colonial power ever so self-sufficient as to be able to forgo the support of collaborating elites: princes and nobles, when and where indirect rule seemed to further British interests most, or administrative specialists where they chose to rule by records.⁵⁶ Indian systems of knowledge thus entered colonial constructions, reworked, reconfigured, and changed, sometimes beyond recognition, not by colonial officers thinking and writing in splendid isolation, but rather in a process that involved both Indians and the British, a process in which the British were not the only ones to use knowledge to consolidate their power and to situate themselves within the larger fabric of Indian society. The dialogue that ensued among the different actors was certainly neither free nor equal, but it was far from being the monologue historians had been focusing on earlier.⁵⁷

While this approach led to a closer consideration of an entanglement taking place in India, British history hardly came into the picture, unless it was to explain developments taking place elsewhere—the rise of evangelicalism and utilitarianism, the influence of Gladstone on the introduction of elected municipal councils, the importance of Labour's electoral victory after the Second World War for Indian independence. Britain influenced

India, but was hardly influenced in turn; British history, so it was believed, could still be understood in and from within Britain alone. This is exactly the proposition that the New Imperial History has called into question in the last ten years. Pointing out the interrelation between the different categories of differentiation, notably between class, race, and gender, these works began to investigate the ways and the extent to which developments in the colonies reflected back on the metropolis.[58] Was the manliness of the British middle-class men constructed only in relation to British women, or to Oriental men as well? How did the prohibition of the burning of Indian widows—'white man saves brown women from brown men', as Gayatri Spivak has aptly named it[59]—influence the way British men and women, not only in the colonies, but also 'at home' viewed themselves and devised their own place in the world? Can the development of the British middle class as a social und cultural category be understood without reference to their colonies any more than without reference to the working classes? Does the civility of civil society make sense without its other, the 'barbarian' to be civilized? Can there be a concept of modernity without relegating tradition not only to the past, but to another place as well?

Much work needs still to be done before these questions can be answered with a certain degree of confidence, but it is already becoming apparent that the processes of mutual reconfiguration went far beyond what might be subsumed under intercultural transfer, both in terms of their extent and their depth. This has two important consequences for historical research. Firstly, if developments both in the colony and in the metropolis originate in or are shaped to a large extent by their mutual encounters, it no longer makes sense to study them as separate entities, which afterwards may or may not be brought together. History is 'connected history', or relational history first and foremost.[60] If this can be translated into historiographical practice, it might well amount to a change in paradigm.[61] Secondly, as it is, the history of transfer could only be integrated into the classical theory and method of comparison with difficulties.[62] Comparing presupposes the existence of at least two entities with a minimum of stability. If the boundaries between them cannot be identified or underwent considerable change within the period under consideration, the identification of differences and similarities, not to speak of conclusions aimed at generalization, is rendered difficult, if not impossible. The development of the history of transfer into a relational history further compounds these problems. If the causes for which we aim to elucidate lie not in the entities themselves but in their entanglement, a comparison can certainly still be drawn, but will yield no valuable explanation.

However, entanglement, even under colonial rule, was never complete and all encompassing. Neither country was invented from nothingness through encounter. Entanglement does reconfigure the perception of a culture's past, but it does not completely obliterate that past and its workings. If we want entanglement to develop into a useful analytical concept, one which goes beyond the vague feeling that everything is related to everything else, the first step would be to differentiate as to its extent: was the metropolis affected by entanglement in the same way as the colonies were? While both sides were re-imagined through the encounter, and we have some idea of how this re-imagination worked for the colonies, we are only beginning to have a look at the way European countries were impacted by the colonies. If the colonial perception was very present in the colonies and backed by power, what did the metropolis react to—was it the 'writing back' of the empire or, more often, their own imagination? Only comparison can shed light on the different ways in which entanglement worked under conditions of power or of subjection.

Furthermore, can we distinguish phases of intense entanglement from others in which the pendulum swung back? Did entanglement work in a different way in different areas, say, in economics and in culture? Were different groups of persons entangled to a different extent? To all of these questions, answers can be provided only through a comparative approach, which would throw into relief the differences and similarities of the starting position from which both entities enter entanglement and the different or similar ways they engage with each other. This need not imply an essentialization. However, persistent differences, the creation of new differentiations, as well as the unequal reconfiguration of boundaries and representations should form one of the central platforms of our enquiries. Not only does comparison facilitate this approach, it constitutes an important, if not the only way to keep the focus on inequality in relational history.

Up until now, it has been taken for granted that transcultural comparisons would necessarily take place between colonies and their former colonizer. This will certainly constitute one of the important areas of research for years to come. However, it should not remain the only one. Comparisons between different non-European countries or regions, which, for instance, underwent either different forms of colonialism or no colonialism at all, would permit historians to gauge the influence of colonial entanglement in a much more precise way. Such comparisons have been underway for a long time, yet they still form notable exceptions.[63]

Another possible line of comparison would be between those European and non-European countries that were never linked by colonialism and, hence, entangled to a much lower extent and in a more indirect way. Here, all of the advantages ascribed to the more classical forms of comparison continue to hold true—its heuristic value, its possibilities for the testing of hypotheses of causality, and the enlargement of the historian's sense for very different answers to a common problem.[64] At a meta-level, finally, it would only be the comparison between comparative studies with and without entanglement that would lead to a possible evaluation of entanglement's impact. Once again, it will be the practice of comparison that will bring forth its own pre-conditions and then render possible new levels of comparison.

Interweaving Historiographies

The relationship of asymmetrical power between the practitioners of European and non-European history that finds institutional articulation in the quasi-hermetic frontiers separating the so-called *Allgemeine Geschichte* in German academia from the area studies—Indology/South Asian studies, Chinese, Japanese or Islamic Studies, to name a few—has resulted in the creation of parallel historiographies. This separation or, rather, absence of dialogue replicates itself at the international level, where in today's world of unprecedented mobility and exchange, historiographical interaction is also regulated through specific channels that can claim scientific authority over it.[65] The implications of such separation go beyond the marginalisation of area studies from the 'mainstream' in German academia, as observed earlier. In the long term, it is to be feared that non-European histories, as written by specialists in non-metropolitan locations, would be rendered 'invisible' at the global level in a situation where these histories defy the categories of representation and analyses deployed in the new narratives of transnational and transcultural history. What forms of self-reflexivity are required, which would create a space for more elastic concepts representative of cultural plurality, both within a regional and a transnational frame? It is our conviction that an important move in this direction would involve traversing historiographical boundaries. We would need to explore the terrain of academic cultures beyond the frontiers of the Western world and engage with historical paradigms within non-European histories that have produced over the years—at least in the case of the Indian subcontinent, an example with which we are most familiar—a rich output of research and writings on a range of subjects: religion, identities, the nation state, to mention only those that fall into our particular fields of research. In our view, putting into practice the idea of writing histories cast in a terminologically neutral (i.e., non-Eurocentric) frame requires a methodological dialogue between these perspectives with a view of identifying the hurdles of translation from one context into another, followed by the question of whether and to what extent the perspectives that have been determined for non-Western histories could provide fresh and useful impulses for understanding and perhaps reframing issues of German/European/Global History.

An attempt in this direction has been made by us in the form of a project that began as a small workshop—*Religion and the negotiation of boundaries: South Asia and Germany in comparative perspective*, in Heidelberg, 22–25 October 2003—and has grown since then into a more comprehensive collection of essays.[66] The idea of bringing together specialists from what may, at first glance, seem to be widely disparate, unrelated, and even incompatible fields of study was acknowledged to be an unusual one. It was an unusual occurrence in German academia for a number of reasons: it could not be situated within the 'normal' format of comparative or transnational histories focusing either on comparisons within Europe or else on regions connected through a history of transfers, nor were practitioners of 'area studies' comfortable with the unfamiliar idea of a close interaction with specialists outside of the 'area'.[67] Furthermore, the choice of South Asia and Germany appeared difficult to accommodate within a common frame, as the two regions were not united by an entangled colonial past that could then be investigated for its 'mutually constitutive' character. Yet, since issues of religious and other identities have been a richly researched area of Indian history, the interaction of experts from different academic cultures offered a stimulus for questioning the historiographic boundaries within which we work and for sensitising all of us to the plurality of meanings—at times overlapping, at times discordant—transported by concepts, while communicating in a common international language. It further opened the way to a discussion on which concepts were required and could be rendered in a common historical language and which ones were 'untranslatable' and needed to be retained in their culture-specific designations.

Rather than summarise here the results of the workshop, it will suffice to show through two examples, drawn from our research, how dialogue across academic frontiers could work its way toward entwined historiographies more sensitive to the plurality of practice and open to a cross-fertilization of concepts. The first example is a comparative study of the German Catholic *milieu* and the Indian Muslim community. A study of both groups calls into question the concept of the nation state as demarcated by territorial borders by introducing two problems at the same time: that of internal divisions and that of extra-territorial solidarities transcending national borders. In the case of both of these groups, academic research and popular perceptions long have been governed by the assumption that religious identity, clearly defined through sacred texts claiming a monopoly of definition, constituted the most important, if not the only, form of identity of believers at the personal and social level.

This notion of a theologically delimited and homogeneous community has been challenged in the last two decades, both in Germany as well as in India, though in very different ways. Research on the Muslim community in South Asia has pointed out, on the one hand, the many similarities between Muslims and Hindus hailing from similar social and regional backgrounds, even in those domains—family structures, caste, and gender relations—where religious teachings were supposed to shape everyday life.[68] This, in turn, allows for a re-contextualization of religion within the framework of multiple identities, each of which brings forth different communities and draws different and overlapping boundaries. On the other hand, the border between religions itself has been problematized, showing that clearcut demarcations between religious groups are blurred by a realm of liminality[69] in which people either adhere to different faiths at the same time (being both Hindu and Muslim) or shift their allegiances according to circumstances (Hindu women going on pilgrimage to Muslim shrines, Christians and Muslims invoking the goddess of smallpox, Christian priests exorcising Muslims possessed by Hindu spirits, etc.).

Research on German Catholicism, conscious of the fact that the *milieu* was not a given, but a space that was carved out in the wake of modernization processes of the nineteenth century, has concentrated on the ways in which theology sought to bring about homogeneity. Studies have highlighted the processes of hierarchization and bureaucratization in the Church, as well the integrative role of both the Centre Party and associational life that buttressed the above processes. Writings taking seriously the proliferation of multiple identities (e.g., Mergel's work on middle-class Catholics[70]) continue to be rare; more often than not, the border is viewed from one side only, and usually the Catholic side. The historiographic exchange between the different research traditions can open up the way to reframing one's enquiry on both sides of the academic encounter, finding explanations for empirical material that had earlier resisted accommodation within a given paradigm[71] and, above all, comparing the significance of conceptual categories in different cultural contexts and finding ways in which those rooted in one context alone could be made more elastic. At the same time, one becomes aware of the limits of such 'elasticity' through understanding and the ability to explain difference.

The second example is that of missionary enterprise and conversion, by its very nature a case in which religion operates in a context of entanglement. Both missionaries and their converts populated a space that could be designated as liminal, one that cuts across the inside/outside divide, a space that was neither wholly contained within a state or a cultural boundary nor exclusively part of an international network, but one that animated both. Here, we can study both the de-localising of a phenomenon and its embedding within another set of local traditions and meanings, bringing together comparison, difference, and connectedness within the framework of a social history. Marked by overt asymmetries of power, transfer in the context of a mission is a more entangled issue, marked simultaneously by resistance and rejection, as well as adoption and appropriation. The viewing of Christian missions from the perspective of the Indian subcontinent comes as a useful corrective against simple binaries that have tended to dominate perceptions of missionary history, namely, oppositions between Hindu or Muslim/Christian, or between a state-driven conversion and an authentic indigenous religion. The problematization of the Indian experience of Christianity has helped to break up monolithic constructs such as those relating to the figure of the missionary, the convert, and the religious community. By drawing attention to internal differences and dissensions among missionary societies and at the same time unravelling the complicated textures of communicative encounters with an alien populace whose 'difference' had to be both constituted and then levelled out through conversion, these histories have managed to pluralize missionary work and theology. This, however, is only a beginning; a next step would be a polycentric exercise comparing approaches to conversion and Christianization in different continents, which may or may not be connected through common networks.

Above all, the study of Indian Christianity and its trajectories over many centuries brings sharply into focus the difficulties of using concepts such as conversion, religion or identity as anthropological constants. Engagement with the history of Christianity on the Indian subcontinent and with the self-perceptions of converts ends up unsettling the notion of identities as being firmly ensconced within bounded communities. Moreover, it opens up the way of analysing intersecting forms of inequalities and boundaries that constantly intersect as part of a historical process.[72] The porous nature of the boundaries marking the social landscape of regions where Christianity, over many centuries, had been among the religious groupings has been an established outcome of research on the Indian subcontinent.[73] Yet new forms of entanglement brought on changes in India as well, resulting out of conflicting cultural and social definitions of the notion of identity and community, which were changing both in the metropolis where the missionary societies were located and in the colony, which was undergoing a new experience of encounter at many levels. Conversion came to be understood in a multiplicity of ways: as an accumulation of identities, as embodied plurality rather than an exclusivist gesture that rejects and abandons one identity for another, and as the individual convert's search for an autonomous space from which he is able to question relationships within the community he has joined.[74] At the same time, the act of relocating the self within a new faith also had to find ways of accommodating a history of breaks, difference and rejection, along with traditions of sharing. Such perspectives and understandings can provide useful insights for the practice of transnational history in different parts of the Western world. Since the latter focuses on the issue of identities within a multicultural context shaped by migration, it continues to implicitly assume the presence of one culturally dominant community. An engagement with Indian historiography, on the other hand, would serve to shake up such a notion and even suggests conceptualising the nation as a field of dispersed identities, continually being traversed by communities that may be both autonomous and overlapping, with live traditions of exchange, as well as histories of fracture and rejection.

Interweaving historiographies across cultures can be a step toward scrutinizing and deconstructing the operations of translation through different stages, beginning with the ways in which materials get canonized as 'primary sources' through to the operations of writing history contingent on questions, concepts, and language. The difficulties and communicative barriers posed by such a process must not, however, be underestimated—these range from elementary aspects, such as the conditions of academic work and research facilities prevailing in different parts of the world, to paradigmatic differences and the peculiarity of problems with which the practice of history in the non-European world often has to deal. One major example of the latter is the challenge posed by religious fundamentalisms and xenophobic nationalism that both constrains and defines the agendas of scholars in ways that those of us located in the West find difficult to imagine. Yet a negotiation of many of these local constellations is a vital part of intercultural understanding that directs our attention toward and forces us to grapple with multiple entanglements and the plurality of languages and methods that make up the configuration of historical narratives. While such a dialogue will never be an entirely symmetrical equation of power and advantage, we hope it will be an important step not only toward relativizing the hegemonic status enjoyed by historiographical traditions emanating from the West, but equally toward ensuring that the authority they enjoy as practitioners of 'global history' rests on greater methodological rigour.

Notes

1. We would like to thank the participants of our panel on 'Concepts in transcultural history' at the First European Congress of Global History, Leipzig, 2005, and the members of the 'Forschungsgruppe Zivilgesellschaft, Citizenship und politische Mobilisierung' at the Wissenschaftszentrum, Berlin, for their critical and helpful comments on some of the central issues of this essay.

2. H. Siegrist, 'Perspektiven der vergleichenden Geschichtswissenschaft. Gesellschaft, Kultur und Raum', in *Vergleich und Transfer. Komparatistik in den Sozial-, Geschichts- und Kulturwissenschaften*, eds. H. Kaelble and J. Schriewer (Frankfurt a.M./New York, 2003), 305–39, quotation 338.
3. D. Chakrabarty, *Provincializing Europe. Postcolonial Thought and Historical Difference* (Princeton/New Delhi, 2000).
4. J. Osterhammel, 'Transferanalyse und Vergleich im Fernverhältnis', in Kaelble and Schriewer, *Vergleich und Transfer*, 439–65, ref. to 440.
5. J. Osterhammel, 'Kulturelle Grenzen in der Expansion Europas', in J. Osterhammel, *Geschichtswissenschaft jenseits des Nationalstaats. Studien zu Beziehungsgeschichte und Zivilisationsvergleich* (Göttingen, 2001), 207. Another approach seems to be taken in the discussion between G. Prakash, 'Writing Post-Orientalist Histories of the Third World. Perspectives from Indian Historiography', *Comparative Studies in Society and History* (1990): 383–408 and R. O'Hanlon and D. Washbrook, 'After Orientalism. Culture, Criticism and Politics in the Third World', *Comparative Studies in Society and History* (1992): 141–67, and the reply of G. Prakash, 'Can the "Subaltern" Ride? A Reply to O'Hanlon and Washbrook', *Comparative Studies in Society and History* (1992): 168–84.
6. J. Schriewer, 'Problemdimensionen sozialwissenschaftlicher Komparatistik', in Kaelble and Schriewer, *Vergleich und Transfer*, 9–54.
7. J. Osterhammel, *Die Entzauberung Asiens. Europa und die asiatischen Reiche im 18. Jahrhundert* (Munich, 1998); J. Fisch, 'Zivilisation, Kultur', in *Geschichtliche Grundbegriffe. Historisches Lexikon zur politisch-sozialen Sprache in Deutschland*, eds. O. Brunner, W. Conze, and R. Kosselleck, 7 vols. (Stuttgart, 1972–97), vol. 7: 679–774.
8. Schriewer, 'Problemdimensionen sozialwissenschaftlicher Komparatistik', 37.
9. For an overview, J. Kocka, *Bürgertum im 19. Jahrhundert: Deutschland im europäischen Vergleich*, 3 vols. (Göttingen, 1995).
10. H.-G. Haupt and J. Kocka, 'Historischer Vergleich: Methoden Aufgaben, Probleme. Eine Einleitung', in *Geschichte und Vergleich. Ansätze und Ergebnisse international vergleichender Geschichtsschreibung*, eds. H.-G. Haupt and J. Kocka (Frankfurt a.M./New York, 1996), 35.
11. See on this point the critique formulated by R. Koselleck, U. Spree, and W. Steinmetz, 'Drei bürgerliche Welten? Zur vergleichenden Semantik der bürgerlichen Gesellschaft in Deutschland, England und Frankreich', in *Bürger in der Gesellschaft der Neuzeit. Wirtschaft—Politik—Kultur*, ed. H.-J. Puhle (Göttingen, 1991), 14–58, esp. 19ff., where the authors underline the historical agency of language.
12. J. Kocka, 'Asymmetrical Historical Comparison: The Case of the German *Sonderweg*', *History and Theory* 38(1) (1999): 40–50.
13. H. Kaelble, 'Interdisziplinäre Debatten über Vergleich und Transfer', in Kaelble and Schriewer, *Vergleich und Transfer*, 472–73; Kocka, 'Asymmetrical Historical Comparisons', 49.
14. Siegrist, 'Perspektiven der vergleichenden Geschichtswissenschaft', 333ff.

15. Haupt and Kocka, 'Historischer Vergleich', 10ff.
16. Ibid.
17. M. Bloch, 'Pour une Histoire comparée des Sociétés européennes', in M. Bloch, *Mélanges historiques*, vol. 1 (Paris, 1963), 16–40; Trans. by M. Aymard and H. Mukhia, eds., as *French Studies in History*, vol. 1: The Inheritance (New Delhi, 1988), 35–68.
18. F.H. Tenbruck, 'Gesellschaftsgeschichte oder Weltgeschichte?', *Kölner Zeitschrift für Soziologie und Sozialpsychologie* 41(3) (1989): 417–39; English version as 'Internal History of Society or Universal History?' *Theory, Culture and Society: Explorations in Critical Social Science* 11(1) (1994): 75–94.
19. Osterhammel, 'Transferanalyse und Vergleich'; M. Espagne, 'Sur les limites du comparatisme en histoire culturelle', *Genèses* (17, Sept. 1994): 112–21; M. Espagne, 'Transferanalyse statt Vergleich. Interkulturalität der sächsischen Regionalgeschichte', in Kaelble and Schriewer, *Transfer und Vergleich*, 419–38; C. Eisenberg, 'Kulturtransfer als historischer Prozess. Ein Beitrag zur Komparatistik', in Kaelble and Schriewer, *Transfer und Vergleich*, 399–418; a persuasive case for a history of intersections, a *histoire croisée*, has been made by M. Werner and B. Zimmermann, 'Vergleich, Transfer, Verflechtung. Ansatz der *Histoire croisée* und die Herausforderung des Transnationalen', *Geschichte und Gesellschaft* 28 (2002): 607–36.
20. T. Welskopp, 'Stolpersteine auf dem Königsweg. Methodenkritische Anmerkungen zum internationalen Vergleich in der Gesellschaftsgeschichte', *Archiv für Sozialgeschichte* 25 (1995): 339–67, here 343; Siegrist, 'Perspektiven der vergleichenden Geschichtswissenschaft', 321ff.
21. S. Subrahmanyam, *Explorations in Connected History. From the Tagus to the Ganges* (Delhi, 2005); S. Subrahmanyam, *Explorations in Connected History. Mughals and Franks* (Delhi, 2005); M. Juneja, '"Early modern" oder "precolonial?" Die Problematik der Zeitzäsuren in der indischen Geschichte', paper presented at the conference 'Die frühe Neuzeit als Epoche', Erlangen, 15–17 September 2005.
22. H. Kaelble, 'Eine besondere Zielsetzung: der historische Zivilisationsvergleich', in H. Kaelble, *Der historische Vergleich. Eine Einführung zum 19. und 20. Jahrhundert* (Frankfurt a.M/New York, 1999), 79–92; J. Osterhammel, 'Sozialgeschichte im Zivilisationsvergleich. Zu künftigen Möglichkeiten komparativer Geschichtswissenschaft', *Geschichte und Gesellschaft* 22(2) (1996): 143–64. While Osterhammel does suggest resorting to smaller units of comparison, the mode and criteria of selection have not been made explicit.
23. J. Osterhammel, 'Transnationale Gesellschaftsgeschichte: Erweiterung oder Alternative?', *Geschichte und Gesellschaft* 27(3) (2001): 464–79, here 472ff.
24. Osterhammel, 'Sozialgeschichte im Zivilisationsvergleich', 153.
25. Chakrabarty, *Provincialising Europe*, 9.
26. Such as Siegrist, 'Perspektiven der vergleichenden Geschichtswissenschaft'.
27. This question has been discussed by both of us in different contexts: M. Pernau, 'Transkulturelle Geschichte und das Problem der universalen Begriffe. Muslimische Bürger im Delhi des 19. Jahrhunderts', in *Area Studies und die Welt :*

Weltreligionen und mene globalgeschichte, ed. B. Schäbler (Wien, 2007), 117–50; M. Juneja, 'Mission, encounters and transnational history—reflections on the use of concepts across cultures', in *Halle and the Beginnings of Protestant Christianity in India*, 3 vols. (Halle a.d. Saale, 2006), 1025–46.

28. Koselleck, Spree, and Steinmetz, 'Drei bürgerliche Welten?' While comparative research has, on the one hand, responded to this plea for differentiating between and integrating inner-European particularities also at the discursive level within its analytic frame, there has emerged, on the other hand, a construct of a 'universal' European language in relation to regions beyond the frontiers of Europe.
29. S. Rushdie, 'Imaginary Homelands', in S. Rushdie, *Imaginary Homelands. Essays and Criticism 1981–91* (London, 1991), 9–21, quotation 17.
30. This is, of course, the central theme of E. Said, *Orientalism* (New York, 1978).
31. S. Shimada, 'Zur Asymmetrie in der Übersetzung von Kulturen. Das Beispiel des Minakata-Schlegel Übersetzungsdisputs 1897', in *Übersetzung als Repräsentation fremder Kulturen*, ed. D. Bachmann-Medick (Berlin, 1997), 260–75.
32. B. Cohn, *Colonialism and its Forms of Knowledge. The British in India* (Delhi, 1997).
33. W. Dalrymple, *White Mughals. Love and Betrayal in eighteenth century India* (London, 2002).
34. For a more detailed analysis of the translation processes involved see M. Pernau, ed., *The Delhi College. Traditional Elites, the Colonial State, and Education before 1857* (Delhi, 2006).
35. S. Hoeber Rudolph, 'The Imperialism of Categories. Situating Knowledge in a Globalizing World', in *Perspectives on politics* (2005), 5–14.
36. This problem has already been pointed out by M. Bloch, 'Pour une Histoire comparée'. One example of this approach to comparison is the collection P. Feldbauer, M. Mitterauer, and W. Schwentker, eds., *Die vormoderne Stadt. Asien und Europa im Vergleich* (Vienna/Munich, 2002), in which the concluding chapter by Schwentker ('Die "vormoderne" Stadt in Asien und Europa. Überlegungen zu einem strukturgeschichtlichen Vergleich') is a heroic *post facto* attempt to encompass the contributions on individual regions within a comparative frame. While Schwentker problematizes the issue of language, he resorts to the solution of drawing upon a terminology ('zentrale Orte', 'Funktionszusammenhänge', 'Netzwerke') drawn from the social sciences and implicitly considered more neutral.
37. S. Shimada, *Die Erfindung Japans. Kulturelle Wechselwirkung und nationale Identitätskonstruktion* (Frankfurt a.M., 2000); J. Matthes, '"Zwischen" den Kulturen?', in *Zwischen den Kulturen? Die Sozialwissenschaften vor dem Problem des Kulturvergleichs*, ed. J. Matthes (Göttingen, 1992), 3–13; J. Matthes, 'The Operation called "Vergleichen"', Matthes, *Zwischen den Kulturen*, 75–103.
38. For an excellent introduction into the problematic see E. Berg and M. Fuchs, eds., *Kultur, soziale Praxis, Text. Die Krise der ethnographischen Repräsentation* (Frankfurt a.M., 1999).
39. Unlike G. Spivak, this approach presumes that the subaltern—or whoever occupies a subaltern position vis-à-vis the social scientist—can speak and that

his representation, not only of himself, but also of 'his other', can be recovered. G. Spivak, 'Can the Subaltern Speak?', in *Marxism and the Interpretation of Culture*, eds. C. Nelson and L. Grossberg (Urbana, 1988), 271–313.
40. M. Fuchs, 'Übersetzen und Übersetzt-Werden. Plädoyer für eine interaktions-anaytische Reflexion', in Bachmann-Medick, *Übersetzung*, 308–28; M. Fuchs, 'Soziale Pragmatik des Übersetzens. Strategien der Interkulturalität in Indien', in *Übersetzung als Medium des Kulturverstehens und sozialer Integration*, eds. J. Renn, J. Straub, and S. Shimada (Frankfurt a.M., 2002), 292–322.
41. S. Shimada, *Grenzgänge—Fremdgänge. Japan und Europa im Kulturvergleich* (Frankfurt a.M., 1994), 36.
42. H. Bhabha, *The Location of Cultures* (London, 1994).
43. W.J.T. Mitchell, 'Translator translated. An Interview with cultural theorist Homi Bhabha', *Artforum* 33 (1995): 80–84, http://prelectur.standford.edu/lecturers/bhabha/interview.html, accessed 6 November 2003.
44. Rushdie, *Imaginary Homelands*, 17.
45. Kocka, *Bürgertum im 19. Jahrhundert*.
46. The same way of proceeding that has been explained here with reference to concepts and categories may also be applied to historical methodology. Neither the position of radical critics such as V. Bahl and A. Dirlik, who see all of historiography as a form of Western imperialism (A. Dirlik, V. Bahl, and P. Gran, eds., *History after the Three Worlds. Post-Eurocentric Historiographies* (Lanham, 2000)), nor the stance of A. Nandy, who pleads for the replacement of historiography by new myths (A. Nandy, *The Intimate Enemy. Loss and Recovery of Self under Colonialism* (Delhi, 1983)), nor the argument of J. Osterhammel that no new methodology is needed for the study of non-European societies and their inclusion in transcultural comparisons (J. Osterhammel, 'Transnationale Gesellschaftsgeschichte') seem to take into account the fact that historical methods are not closed, but open systems, which change in response to new challenges. New concepts need to be envisaged not as a starting point, but as a result of dialogic transcultural studies—this approach, we wish to argue, will in all probability lead not only to a new conceptual language, but to new methods of research as well.
47. J. Schriewer, 'Problemdimensionen sozialwissenschaftlicher Komparatistik'.
48. For a more elaborate discussion of this argument, see next subsection.
49. S. Rushdie, *The Satanic Verses* (London, 1988)—as opposed to what the Fatwa against Rushdie suggested, the novel has much less to do with Islam than with colonial and orientalist representations of both the religion and its practitioners.
50. Ibid., 343.
51. J. Malik, ed., *Perspectives of Mutual Encounters in South Asian History 1760–1860* (Leiden, 2000).
52. The notion of entanglement is a basic analytical insight that informs postcolonial writing of the past decade or more, and more recently, the new imperial history. It was practiced with exemplary skill by M. Sinha in her monograph, *Colonial Masculinity. The 'manly Englishman' and the 'effeminate Bengali' in the Late Nineteenth Century* (Manchester, 1995). This methodological perspective has also marked the writing of C. Hall over the past many years, be-

ginning with *White, Male and Middle-class: Explorations in Feminism and History* (Cambridge, 1992), and more recently, *Civilising Subjects: Metropole and Colony in the English Imagination 1830–1867* (Oxford, 2002). Entanglement was brought in as a programmatic objective in S. Conrad and S. Randeria, *Jenseits des Eurozentrismus. Postkoloniale Perspektive in den Geschichts- und Kulturwissenschaften* (Frankfurt a.M./New York, 2002).
53. J. Mill, *The History of British India*, 6 vols. (London, 1840).
54. D. Naoroji, *Poverty and Un-British Rule in India* (London, 1901).
55. Most explicitly by G. Viswanathan, *Masks of Conquest. Literary Study and British Rule in India* (New York, 1989).
56. R. Saumarez Smith, *Rule by Records. Land Registration and Village Custom in Early British Punjab* (Delhi, 1996).
57. This approach profoundly is linked with the name of C. Bayly and his school in Cambridge; as an outstanding example, see his *Empire and Information. Intelligence Gathering and Social Communication in India, 1780–1870* (Cambridge, 1996). It has been taken up and developed by a number of scholars, among whom the work of J. Malik, *Perspectives of Mutual Encounter*, and E. F. Irschick, *Dialogue and History. Constructing South India 1795–1895* (Berkeley, 1994), deserve special mention.
58. C. Hall, *White, Male and Middle Class*; C. Hall, *Civilizing Subjects*; A. Burton, *Burdens of History. British Feminists, Indian Women and Imperial Culture, 1865–1915* (London, 1994); K. Wilson, ed., *A New Imperial History. Culture, Identity and modernity in Britain and the Empire* (Cambridge, 2004).
59. Spivak, 'Can the Subaltern Speak?', 297.
60. S. Subrahmanyam, *Explorations in Connected History*.
61. For a different opinion: K.K. Patel, 'Transnationale Geschichte—ein neues Paradigma?', http://geschichte-transnational.clio.online.net/forum/id=573&type=artikel (2004).
62. M. Espagne, 'Sur les limites du comparatism en histoire culturelle',; Kaelble and Schriewer, *Vergleich und Transfer*.
63. See for instance the two volumes of comparative studies on family relationships in Africa and India: C. Risseeuw and K. Ganesh, eds., *Negotation and Social Space. A gendered Analysis of changing Kin and Security Networks in South Asia and Sub-Saharan Africa* (Delhi, 1998); R. Palriwala and C. Risseeuw, eds., *Shifting Circles of Support. Contextualising Kinship and Gender in South Asia and Sub-Saharan Africa* (Delhi, 1996); and the smaller-scale comparison of L. Dube, *Women and Kinship. Comparative Perspectives on Gender in South and South-East Asia* (Delhi, 1997). Very interesting results are also to be found in C. Büschges and J. Pfaff-Czarnecka, eds. *Die Ethnisierung des Politischen. Identitätspolitiken in Lateinamerika, Asien und den USA* (Frankfurt, 2007).
64. H. Kaelble, *Der historische Vergleich*; H.-G. Haupt and J. Kocka, *Geschichte und Vergleich*; H.-G. Haupt and J. Kocka, 'Comparative History. Methods, Aims, Problems', in *Comparison and History. Europe in Cross-National Perspective*, eds. D. Cohen and M. O'Connor (London, 2004), 23–39.

65. Hierarchies in international academia today are no longer decided purely according to the color of one's skin or passport. Rather, it is the institutional location and the authority the location carries that determine which voices shall be heard. For instance, the selection of articles in the collection Conrad and Randeria, *Jenseits des Eurozentrismus*, is confined exclusively to those voices emanating from metropolitan locations, which have come to enjoy, over the past two decades or more, the status of a 'master discourse' on postcolonialism, whereas more critical, relativizing positions that in recent years have contributed to the debate on the relevance of postcolonial perspectives from non-metropolitan locations have not been given space. One outstanding example of an empirical study in this context is R. Singha, *A Despotism of Law. Crime and Justice in Early Colonial India* (New Delhi, 1998). For a theoretical engagement, S. Sarkar, 'Postmodernism and the Writing of History', in S. Sarkar, *Beyond Nationalist Frames. Postmodernism, Hindu Fundamentalism, History* (New Delhi/Bloomington, 2002), 154–94.
66. M. Juneja and M. Pernau, eds., *Religion und Grenzen in Indien und Deutschland. Auf dem Weg zu einer transnationalen Historiographie* (Göttingen, 2008).
67. 'Can you compare apples and oranges?' was a reaction from a representative of the 'Area Studies'. The exception, however, were participants from ethnology and anthropology, disciplines where transcultural communication is a central plank of research practice.
68. I. Ahmad, ed., *Caste and Social Stratification among Muslims in India* (Delhi, 1983); I. Ahmad, ed., *Family, Kinship and Marriage among Indian Muslims* (Delhi, 1976); I. Ahmad, ed., *Ritual and Religion among Muslims in India* (Delhi, 1981); I. Ahmad, ed., *Modernization and Social Change among Muslims in India* (Delhi, 1983).
69. On the application of this concept to Indian history, S. Mayaram, *Resisting Regimes. Myth, Memory and the Shaping of a Muslim Identity* (New Delhi, 1997); see also essay by S. Mayaram, 'Of Syncretism and Liminality: Religious Being in South Asia and Beyond', in Juneja and Pernau, *Religion und Grenzen* (Göttingen, 2008), 55–77.
70. T. Mergel, *Zwischen Klasse und Konfession. Katholisches Bürgertum im Rheinland, 1794–1914* (Göttingen, 1994).
71. For instance, T. Mergel, 'Konfessionelle Grenzen und überkonfessionelle Gemeinsamkeiten im 19. Jahrhundert. Europäische Grundlinien', in Juneja and Pernau, *Religion und Grenzen*, forthcoming.
72. S. Chandra, '"Seventy Times Seven" – The Sin of "Christian Manhood" in a Colonial Situation', in Juneja and Pernau, *Religion und Grenzen* (Göttingen, 2008), 145–68.
73. See for instance S. Bayly, *Saints, goddesses and kings: Muslims and Christians in South Indian society 1700–1900* (Cambridge, 1989).
74. This shift can be plotted by comparing the two case studies on conversion to Christianity: M. Juneja, 'Mission und Begegnung – Gestaltung und Grenzen eines kommunikativen Raumes', and S. Chandra, '"Seventy Times Seven"', both in Juneja and Pernau, *Religion und Grenzen* (Göttingen, 2008), 123–44 and 55–77.

# PART II

Transnationalization and Issues in European History

CHAPTER 6

The Nation as a Developing Resource Community

A Generalizing Comparison

DIETER LANGEWIESCHE

Generalizing Comparison in Nationalism Research[1]

Generalization is one of the basic forms of historical comparison.[2] In scholarly research on nationalism, this approach has been used for some time. It is one of the central insights of all nationalism research—even when used as an instrument for nationalist purposes. Comparison relies upon generalization, and generalization is open for application to different forms of comparison, which are discussed and tested here.[3] The most influential courses of study, however, aim for a generalizing comparison that reveals the effects of both national ideas and practices. The nation's model of development, as well as the intentions, perceptions, and beliefs of its actors are also examined in the best studies. The focus of a generalizing comparison, though, is not always on national particularities; instead, it is concerned primarily with identifying commonalities, which may be used to define the fundamental models of national thinking and behaviour that may be observed in all national societies. Benedict Anderson, Ernest Gellner, and Anthony D. Smith, to name only three extraordinarily influential authors, aim for such generalizing comparisons. Characteristically, they combine the geographic and temporal breadth of their perspective on the history of nationalism with a focus on a single central factor, the effect of which they consider to be crucial.

For Anderson, the creator of the nation as an 'imagined community' is language, whose influence he traces through institutions such as schools and universities and in the mass market of the public.[4] He views national identity as emerging from 'two profoundly contrasting types of seriality'. While he locates 'unbounded seriality' in the 'print market' and in 'the representations of popular performances', he ascribes institutions such as the census and the election to 'bounded seriality'.[5]

Ernest Gellner, in contrast, examines the roll of nationalism in governance processes. Centralization of power disposes people to view their world through nationalist eyes. The state and nationalism, as well as their symbiosis, are not, in contrast to culture and organization, universal and unfading. From Gellner's global perspective, nationalism fulfills the task of adapting society to the conditions of modernity. The nation state organizes a highly sophisticated educational system that prizes and cultivates national high culture and at the same time guarantees its members exclusive access to this new societal power centre. This territorial identification of culture and state serves as a national imperative to view foreign cultures within the nation state as a dishonour and to see their removal as a task of collective self-preservation. In Gellner's socio-anthropological theory, cultures within a nation state qualifying as foreign must either be nationalized or purged. The nation state, a creation of nationalism according to Gellner, appears as a cultural homogenization machine supported by, and organized around, power structures.

While the majority of generalizing nationalism research, such as that done by Anderson and Gellner, describes nationalism as a temporally and geographically limited phenomenon, Anthony D. Smith presents it within a framework of supertemporal continuity.[6] His archetype is the Jewish nation, which since its Old Testament beginnings through today has survived the Diaspora and has not been dependent on the existence of a Jewish state.[7]

Why do nations die so hard? Smith attempts to explain this riddle of the supertemporal continuity of national ties in his most recent book, *Chosen Peoples*. Comparisons, in the sense of transfer or integration (*histoire croisée*), are not in a position to deal with this question. This is because they require that their research objects communicate with one another. This is not a given for the nations that Smith examines from a temporally universal perspective. Smith therefore chooses a generalizing comparison, but nevertheless engages with different comparative conceptions.

Among the five universal-historical approaches that Jürgen Osterhammel identified in the nineteenth century, one can assign Smith's universal history, which attempts to uncover the 'sacred foundations'[8] of nations, to 'philosophical history'.[9] Smith examines selective cases of collective religious attitudes from biblical time through the twentieth century that enable the strength and resilience of the 'modern belief-system of nationalism,'[10] independent of ethnicity, language, and state. The nation unites elements of belief and ethnic community, which over time creates 'a national community of faith and belonging' through religious attitudes and rites.[11] Modern nationalism turns this belief in a 'sacred communion' into secular authenticity—the sanctum of the national cult. The tabernacle of this cult contains the bread upon which this identity feeds: community in space and time, charged and sanctified with centuries of cultural significance. It is only because nationalists tap into these sacred traditions that they can politicize ethnic groups and their cultures and thus create 'the new kinds of society, polity, and modernized culture that we call nations'.[12]

No nation exists without religion—religion, following Emile Durkheim, is functionally understood as the convictions and practices that differentiate the holy from the everyday and produce a community of believers. Smith thus defines the nation as 'a community of faith',[13] within which he distinguishes four forms. In the Israel of the Old Testament, he presents the prototype of faith in being chosen by God.[14] Among the medieval Armenians and Ethiopians, as well as the Boers and the Jewish Zionists of the late nineteenth and early twentieth centuries, he examines the concept of a people (*Volk*) who have made a covenant with God ('peoples of the covenant'). As examples of 'missionary peoples', who, in contrast with those of the covenant, turn themselves toward the outside and want to change the world, he chooses Russia, France, and England, as well as medieval Scotland and Wales.

In generalizing comparison, as Smith practices it in the style of philosophical history, the concern is not with origins and historical development. Instead, it examines the means of argument employed by national cults that are not tied to a specific period of time. At the core of the national cult, according to Smith, is the conception of a sacred homeland, a golden era, and a glorious death. Through these images, the nation imagines a sacred destiny, which unites it and directs it toward a common future. The nation thus gives a place to the sacred in a secularizing world, and provides a religiously pregnant, politically, and culturally uniting force, which cannot be achieved by world ideology.

Such an extra-temporal, world-historical perspective—limited nevertheless to the Judeo-Christian realm—would not be possible within the framework of a transfer- or integration-based approach, as the nations that Smith takes up in his generalizing comparison do not have contact with one another. The comparative perspective is created by the observer; it does not arise from developments in the field of observation. This broadly impressive approach, however, also creates problems that are related to the concept of generalizing comparison, though not necessarily resulting from it.

Smith understands the nation, as does the majority of research to this point, as an outcome of cultural practice.[15] In his wide overview, however, he cannot consider how it functions. Smith offers no cultural history that analyses cultural practices, but, rather, a history of ideas that examines conceptions as they can be found in 'sacred texts'. Through them, the religion of the people is made available. Practice, with its dense network of relationships among actors, only can be dealt with minimally in a generalizing history. But practice should not be so decidedly blocked out as it is in Smith's work. What follows is an example to highlight why this is the case.

As Smith defines religion functionally, he can equate political religions, whose promises relate to the present world, with religions that prepare for the afterlife. This can be helpful for incorporating social practices into the approach. But Smith does not pose the decisive question: do the political religions of this world overcome political failures in the same way as religions of the afterworld?[16] Religious faith does not depend on success; political faith does. Political faith can only survive a certain measure of defeat.[17] The defeat of the Boers, to take a historical example that Smith considers, destroyed their national identity, but their religious faith remained undisturbed. The persistence of religious faith is thus not, as Smith claims, in general a guarantee for the survival of the constructions of national identity. A secular-religious foundation is only *one* factor giving the model of a nation its strength and persistence. The interplay of factors demands analyses that take practical experience into account. Such analyses are lacking in Smith's analysis, but are not foreign to the method of generalizing comparison. It is nevertheless difficult for a generalizing perspective precisely to define actors, as is done in more recent nation-oriented research, which examines how local and regional action arenas are connected to the national arena. Smith defends against this at the outset by claiming only to be able to regard *long durée* by means of ethnic history, which he assigns to the fields of memories and myth, as opposed to professional history. That is a misunderstanding, as historiography also plugs away assiduously at these fields. Smith does not use these methods for examining myths and memories, nor for illuminating their significance for cultural and political experience. He writes a history of ideas without considering how it is practised today.

Smith describes the historical narrative of nationalists, what they understand to be history, and how they construct from this 'maps for the road to national destiny'.[18] In particular, he analyses splendidly their conviction of 'no destiny without history'.[19] Thus, an image of the past emerges from the perspective of these actors. It becomes apparent how nationalists from different eras and societies saw themselves and their world. Smith reconstructs impressively their self-image. Therein lay the strengths, but also the limits, of his new work and his form of generalizing comparison. That generalizing comparison can, however, overcome these limits in that it must not follow nationalist narratives is demonstrated by the approaches of Anderson and Gellner, as well as Otto Bauer in his excellent work from 1907 about questions of nationality in the Habsburg monarchy.[20]

Nation as a Resource Community

In the nineteenth century, the nation and the nation state became *the* decisive forms of state order. All other forms lacked legitimacy. This new order emanated from Europe and began a worldwide triumphal procession. It was not, however, simply absorbed by other parts of the world. Recently, Christopher Bayly impressively laid out the multifaceted varieties of nations, nation states, and nationalism in his world history of the nineteenth century. As in other accounts, globalization here also signifies a similar growth in both homogeneity and complexity.[21]

Why, both at that time and today, is political thinking so strongly determined by the idea of the nation that even the notion of a supranational, supragovernmental, united Europe continues to be thought of through the analogy of the nation—that is, as an entity not only dependent on common governmental institutions, but also on cultural homogeneity? Some argue against the acceptance of Turkey into the European Union on the basis of this requirement of homogeneity, in this case under the European flag. Others, who also argue for this, rely not on the necessity of an internal unity analogous to a nation, but, rather, refer to the already achieved convergence of legal systems in the EU and the likelihood that this trend will continue in other areas. The goal is always the ideal of the most homogeneous society possible as a prerequisite of a united, functional state order for all members of the European Union. The historical model of cultural and political homogeneity is the nation and the nation state in its modern form of organization.[22]

Why has this ideal of the nation been able to achieve such a commitment? Which advantages and successes does it promise? These questions will now be discussed in a generalizing comparison with the aim of defining the nation as a *resource community*. Even though the development of various nations and nation states proceeded very differently, the idea of the nation always promised the same thing to its members: a fair chance at participation in the collective political, social, economic, and cultural success of the nation. The nation thus displayed its unique attraction as a resource community. And this promise can only be realized when the nation is organized as a state and equipped with legitimate enforcement power. Thus, nation and state are difficult to separate. The idea of the nation and the state as its operational instrument functionally are tied together.

The Defence and Power Community

Which common goods are produced according to which rules was and continues to be extraordinarily variable. Security against the outside is always among them: in this view, the nation is a *defence community* as well as a *power community* dependent on expansion. This expansion surge reached a high point in the nineteenth century, during the age of imperialism, when the individual nation, in competition with other nations, could only assert itself as a power-state through colonial power. But, from the very beginning, securing and growing power was one of the hallmarks of nation building. The nineteenth century sought to exclude less powerful states from the new nation state European order—but to no avail. But it was the 'proven ability to conquer', as Eric Hobsbawm formulated poignantly, that established the right of a nation to its own state.[23] Isaiah Berlin, in his comparisons in intellectual history—which may also be called generalizing—characterized this test of power, which every nation on its way to becoming a state must pass, as 'Frankenstein's Monster': not to be restrained by its creators.[24]

Otto Bauer already attempted to do just this before the First World War by incorporating the nation as a central pillar of human collectivization in Marxist theory. He spoke of the 'fighting vehicle (*Kampfwagen*) of the nation'[25] and campaigned, like his Austro-Marxist comrade Karl Renner, for a 'multinational state of equal nations',[26] in order to defuse the conflict-producing ideal of homogeneity. But even they justified the multinational state in relation to the nation state, which they were convinced was power-political at least up until the end of the First World War. The nation state pays for its fiction of homogeneity with a limitation on its power resources, while the multinational state could convert its territorial size, to the extent it was capable, into economic superiority. Power instruments were to be used in the 'rage of aggrandizement',[27]—this was the formula of Elias Canetti, who recognized therein the main hallmark of the twentieth century. Canetti also sees the role of the nation in this expansionist mandate.[28] As power-machines, they compete and wage war against one another.

The Legal and Political Community

Security against outside threats has its counterpart in the demand for internal security. Early on, this became a common goal and gradually was implemented: internal security against the abuse of power by individuals or groups through a national *legal community*. Whoever was ranked among the legally equal went unchallenged. But all who fought for their entry into this circle of those fully endowed with rights adhered to the equality commitment, with which the nation was fascinated. Otto Bauer colourfully named those excluded from this circle as the 'back seat of the nation'.[29] The promise of equality, to which they appointed themselves, allowed the 'imaginary order' of the nation to assume the highest level of legitimacy, which all who demand the promise of participation called upon.[30]

The demand for political equality for all members of the nation, which long was limited only to men, commonly followed as the next step toward legal equality. Recognizing all as political equals, regardless of ethnic, religious or social identity, was a large step in the drawn-out emancipation process in the name of the nation: the nation as a *political community*. Its main criterion, against which the convergence toward this ideal was measured in the nineteenth century, was suffrage.

Culture, Solidarity, and Environment Community

A conception of the nation as a *culture community* also belongs to the idea of the resource community. Education for all was its leading idea and continues to be so today. But it is important to understand how this has changed starkly and in varied ways over the last two centuries. It began first with the right and the obligation to obtain an elementary education for all and was then expanded to the opportunity for all who are intellectually capable of obtaining a higher education. Here, as well, 'all' meant 'all men' for a long time. In addition—as was recognized early on in principle, but remains varied and disputed in concrete execution to this day—is the ideal of the nation as a *solidarity community* for socialized security in cases of sickness and invalidity, in old age, and, finally, also in unemployment. The latter came late and was not implemented everywhere, but it was demanded early on.[31] Finally, as early as the nineteenth century, the idea of the nation as an *environment community* emerged. Here, the nation pushed on its formal boundaries, as the territorial space of the nation state showed itself to be too small for effective environmental policy. Nevertheless, it is again in this case the nation state that fulfils transborder obligations for its members.

Competition and Performance Community

Comparison has always played a central role in the orientation of all nations. Thus, they have always understood themselves as a *competition community*—a subcategory of power community. Competition with other states has always been a part of the imperative of the nation state to possess and expand power. The perspective looks not only toward the outside, but also considers internal capabilities. This competition—here, a unified point for transnational studies, which investigate relationships and integration—was the primary reason that the expansion of nation state's catalogue of duties and responsibilities proceeded so much in parallel across Europe. The demand for an increase in resources, which is anchored to the equality postulate of the nation, put the nation state under pressure to perform. Nations would be measured according to what competitors could afford their members. The enormous build-up of the social state after the Second World War had much to do with this competition and was additionally intensified by the system competition between the two great blocs of the liberal states in the West and the communist states.[32]

This competition of systems encouraged everywhere the expansion of the *performance community*. This development was carried out within the framework of the nation state itself. Today, the leading economies of Europe face for the first time an opposing movement. Global competition now poses an argument for the scaling back of the nation state's performance catalogue. But here, too, the aim is to preserve the capacity of the nation to compete. If the nation state loses its old power of performance, regardless of the reasons, then the logic of national community thinking requires collective efforts and sacrifice. Europe did not come to know this side of globalization in earlier globalization processes.[33] But Europeans are, as are all nations, familiar with the nation as a *suffering and sacrifice community*.

Suffering or Sacrifice Community

The nation as a *suffering or sacrifice community* is historically bound to the experience that the emergence of all nations is based in war. War is the father of the nation state and, as co-creator of the nation, belongs among the empirical lessons taught by world history.[34] Only the history of the Jewish nation appears not to conform to this world-historical constant, although only during the time of the Diaspora. During the era of its statehood, the Jewish nation also included a history of war similar to all nations.[35] Bayly points out the significance of war for the power-political differentiations during the globalization process of the nineteenth century. Indeed, he writes about the notion of 'Western exceptionalism', but without relativizing the privileged position attained by 'the West'. He sees the main reason for this privileged position, which first became dominant in the nineteenth century, in the superiority achieved in European weapons technology and war strategy. It was not the European 'spirit', but, rather, its 'efficiency in killing other human beings'[36] that tipped the scales. Without the 'second military revolution', there would be no European domination of the world. Bayly supports this view socio-historically by examining which social conditions the emergence of the modern nation state was dependent upon, with its instruments of power, both externally and internally.

In war, the nation has always viewed itself as a *sacrifice community*, which included the demand to give one's life for the good of the nation. The idea of glorious death indeed has been long a part of the religious bonding strength of the nation, as Anthony D. Smith recently noted. But it has only been the modern nation, since the French Revolution, that enters its wars as a *sacrifice community* that imposes the same obligation of sacred death upon each member. This is demonstrated by the fact that every fallen soldier, no matter how simple, wins a claim to the eternal memory of the nation. In the memorial, the nation awards eternity to all of its dead. In the words of Reinhart Koselleck:

> Since the introduction of general conscription, beginning with the *levée en masse*, the name of every fallen soldier became worthy of remembering, and since the world wars, the names of women and children are remembered as well. All have offered their lives for the nation or the people, whose identity is authenticated with their death—thus reads the memorial message, and thus will it be experienced as long they are ritually cared for. Parallel to this, in all constitutional forms, there has been a democratic trend. Equality in death is claimed by the living: to be prepared to die, and to be responsible for the same thing for which up to now life has been sacrificed. This cult of death slowly undermined the ruling dynasties in Europe, and accompanying them at first, until finally replacing them completely.[37]

Koselleck called this an 'authentic case of secularization': 'The hope for the afterworld is transposed into earthly hope for the future into the community of political action, bringing the promise of eternity to light'. The nation takes over the task of the court of judgment: 'what was once entrusted to the church mass, the other-worldly welfare of the soul, becomes the task of the political cult of the dead. The death of every individual is justified as long as it serves to secure the political welfare of the entire people for the future. And that is why he must be remembered'.[38] This democratization of remembering the dead for the nation became a part of all political regimes, including authoritarian ones. The promise of equality in death for the nation belongs also to the tomb of the Unknown Soldier. Through this, the nation remembers all of the dead who were torn up on the battlefield and thus individually cannot be remembered. No one can be excluded from memoriam, because all are equal before the nation, as stated previously, in 'the uncompromising finality of death'.[39]

The Openness of the Equality Promise of the Resource Community in Principle

The idea of the nation as a resource community comprises many facets and is being considered more and more comprehensively. An end of its expansion cannot be seen, as the nation state continues to be the most effective instrument for realizing collective demands for participation and use of common resources. It was not the state itself that developed into a vehicle of emancipation for claims to equality. It was the idea of the nation that forced upon the state this obligation in revolutionary fashion and then further developed it toward a potentially unlimited resource community.[40] Thus, the idea of the nation also became the central idea behind decolonization. The nation as a fundamental promise of equality could not be limited anywhere in the long run, in no area of society and in no part of the world. The nation thus became the ideal of emancipation par excellence. As an attempt to transfer this ideal into a normative institution capable of action, the nation state was constructed in the nineteenth century as one state, according to the core idea that comprised the entire nation and only this one nation. 'One nation—one nation state' was the credo of the nineteenth century, and this heritage continues to define national thinking today. It was and is, despite all of the violence unleashed,[41] a way of thinking focused on emancipation and equality. Only on account of this could the *nation* become the most influential idea of modernity, unrivalled in attractiveness, first in Europe and the United States, then in Latin America and Asia, and, finally, worldwide.

Unrivalled in attractiveness was, above all, the combination of exact spatial boundaries and the openness of goals. The nation state as a unique, delimited space enabled the promise of equality, which included ever more spheres within the nation state: security and power, law and politics, gender, culture, society, and, finally, the environment. The nation acts as a vehicle of equality that is always seeking out new spheres of influence, open for new developments in the society, and thus, in principle, unlimited.

The idea of the nation as a resource community of equals is thus open to the future. The demand for equality is not once and for all set in stone, but can, rather, be moved around. A narrowing is also imaginable and can be legitimized through the idea of the nation as a resource community. Cutting back, however, would break outside the development path established up until now, which has tended toward expansion. How difficult it is to step outside this point of view is demonstrated by the current debates in many European states over how to develop a new foundation for a welfare state in which certain spheres are removed—for instance, if care for the elderly is no longer designated as a national obligation, but, rather, an individual task. Political decisions of such magnitude appear to fall back into the realm of the nation state even in Europe, where the European Union is without an appropriate historical precedent.[42] In the public debates and in institutional decision making, determining how far the catalogue of responsibilities of the nation as a resource community can expand in the future is always of concern. Varying answers appear not only in the course of history; today, also, nations take different positions on the issue. But it is common to all nations that they alone have the exclusive right to make these decisions, and that their members grant them this monopoly on decision making.

The Nation as a Combat Community Prepared for War

How could the nation state become a *combat community*, which views war as an instrument of action toward the outside world, and be developed out of an emancipated community-based vision of a nation, which aims for internal equality of opportunity and security of existence in competition over resources? Two main reasons helping to explain the war history of modern nations on their way to becoming nation states have been recognized by international research: the first looks inward toward the nation and the second looks toward the outside political environment.

A Look Inward

A general explanation—from a world-historical perspective in the sense of a generalizing comparison, as it is represented here—is offered by Ernest Gellner in his unique, internationally influential work mentioned above, *Nations and Nationalism*. His image of the nation state as a power-supported cultural homogenization institution is not new—it suffices to remember Moritz Arndt and Max Weber. Arndt had already, in 1813, in his work, *Über Volkshaß* (*On the Hatred of Peoples*), evoked in emotionally stirring language that which Gellner analytically lays out. Arndt's religiously formulated sermon on the 'hatred towards the French, not simply for this war', but, rather, 'for a very long time',[43] voiced a central insight for modern nation research: the nation recognizes itself in its enemy. In the enemy, the nation finds its 'point of unity'.[44] 'Hate, revenge, wars of revenge, wars of life and death, and the demand to exterminate without mercy all foreigners found within its borders'[45]—this is not un-Christian or inhuman, as the laws of nature also apply to the cultural actions of humans. 'It lives alone and is created alone through an eternal war and fight for power'.[46] With this claim, Arndt complied with the main current of bourgeois-liberal thinking of the nineteenth century: fighting is the elixir of life and the source of progress. He called for the Germans to form their nation—whose political greatness was still at this time a vision of scholars—as a political entity capable of action against *the* French. At the same time, he saw in 'national hate' a general principle according to which humanity became peoples and nations, in that they were separated from others. Each nation is different and has 'a right to exist'.[47] In addition, national pride and 'national hatred' are equally necessary in order to prevent 'uninhibited mixing with the unequals'. But to believe that one is better than others is, for him, 'a prejudice'. One must not ask, 'Why do the Turk, the Pole, the Spaniard and the Englishman exist' and why are they so different; 'rather, we must believe that they can be there, because they are there'.[48] Their otherness is 'a bright mirror' for the others and at the same time 'a beneficial partition'.[49]

What Arndt saw is summarized in Max Weber's definition of the nation in analytical language: 'a specific type of pathos, in which a group of people, bound together through a language-, confessional-, convention- or fate-based community, connects with its own, either already existing or envisioned organization of political power'.[50] Weber understands the nation, like many before and after him, as a homogenization machine that achieves internal unity by means of separation from the outside. Violence is used in the pursuit of this goal both internally and externally. This is almost always unavoidable if other groups, who consider themselves to be nations, live within the nation state claimed by a particular nation. In these cases, violence almost always arises. Ethnic cleansing as an obligation for the rise of the dominant nation, as well as other violent means of purging including extermination, have a long historical tradition. Ethnic cleansing is, in this view, not an unfortunate case of history, but, instead, part of the 'nationalist imperative' of national-cultural or even national-ethnic homogeneity.

A Look Outward

There is a danger of war everywhere where different groups understanding themselves to be nations live together in a territory. As soon as these nations want to establish their own nation state—which all nations strive to do, as only a separate state can fulfil the promises of the national ideal—and compete with other nations over a specific territory, there is a threat of war. Peaceful solutions through broad accommodations for minorities occur seldom and could, for the most part, only be achieved at a late stage. Even then, they are rare. Here, the nation state appears to push on a limit of its instruments for action, which is difficult to overcome within the construction principles of the nation.

The United Nations is tasked with overcoming this problem worldwide. It stands in the tradition of supra-state agreements and institutions, presupposing the nation state as the standard state form, which wants to domesticate its propensity for war. War as a means of achieving state interests should no longer qualify as the peak of state sovereignty. The European Union, by contrast, seeks a radical departure from a history of state and nation, which was also always a history of war. It does not represent a departure from the nation, but, rather, from the sovereign nation state. This union of states of a new form, as the German Constitutional Court has called it,[51] offers the chance that conflict between nations will no longer become conflicts between states, with the danger of weapons becoming involved in the conflict. The union of states does not replace the nation state, but it obligates all member states to comply with a nonviolent framework for conflict resolution, in which a growing portion of state sovereignty is transferred to the supra-state institutions with the power to enforce sanctions against member states and exercise power over individual citizens. The monopoly on violence, which the state possesses in order to limit violence among its citizens, is transferred to the EU, so that it gains the qualities of a state. Violent conflicts among its nations are not permitted. The EU is an internal instrument for peace and is designed to end the history of war of the *combat community* nation. It is without historical precedent and is a break of global historical significance in the laboratory of nations that is Europe. The historical symbiosis between nation and war will be dissolved, it is hoped; however, only internally. Externally, the institutional structure of the EU aims in an opposite direction, which has always been connected to state building: being able to go to war.[52] Generalizing comparison offers a suitable instrument for analysing these developments in their state and trans-societal models. The fact that it thereby rules out other approaches is something it shares with other conceptions of comparison.[53]

Notes

1. For the following chapter cf. D. Langewiesche, 'Nationalismus - ein generalisierender Vergleich', in G. Budde et al. (eds.), *Transnationale Geschichte, Themen, Tendenzen und Theorien* (Göttingen, 2006), 175–189.
2. See H.-G. Haupt and J. Kocka, 'Historischer Vergleich: Methoden, Aufgaben, Probleme. Eine Einleitung', in *Geschichte und Vergleich. Ansätze und Ergebnisse international vergleichender Geschichtsschreibung*, eds. H.-G. Haupt and J. Kocka (Frankfurt, 1996), 9–45.
3. See various contributions to J. Osterhammel, *Geschichtswissenschaft jenseits des Nationalstaats. Studien zu Beziehungsgeschichte und Zivilisationsvergleich* (Göttingen, 2001).
4. B. Anderson, *Imagined Communities. Reflections on the Origin and Spread of Nationalism* (London, 1983).
5. B. Anderson, *The Spectre of Comparisons. Nationalism, Southeast Asia and the World* (London/New York, 1998), esp. 30–45.
6. A.D. Smith, *Chosen Peoples. Sacred Sources of National Identity* (Oxford, 2003).
7. On the shifts in internal Jewish notions of the Jewish Nation, the source text is: M. Brenner, A. Kauders, G. Reuveni, and N. Römer, eds., *Jüdische Geschichte lesen. Texte der jüdischen Geschichtsschreibung im 19. u. 20. Jahrhundert* (München, 2003); see also A. Funkenstein, *Perceptions of Jewish History* (1993).

8. Smith, *Chosen Peoples*, 4.
9. Osterhammel, '"Höherer Wahnsinn": Universalhistorische Denkstile im 20. Jahrhundert', in Osterhammel, *Geschichtswissenschaft jenseits des Nationalstaats*, 170–82, 178. Osterhammel identifies the other four types as social evolutionism (e.g., I. Wallerstein), natural scientific history (e.g., J. Diamond), divergent-convergent thinking styles (e.g., F. Fernández-Armesto), and the economic perspective (e.g., W. H. McNeill, Gellner, Diamond).
10. Smith, *Chosen Peoples*, 5.
11. Smith, *Chosen Peoples*, 23.
12. Smith, *Chosen Peoples*, 43.
13. Smith, *Chosen Peoples*, 24.
14. See A. Mosser, ed., '"Gottes auserwählte Völker". Erwählungsvorstellungen und kollektive Selbstfindung in der Geschichte' (Frankfurt a.M., 2001).
15. Similar also were the Austro-Marxist studies of nationalism up to 1900, which equally were based empirically and theoretically reflective. Otto Bauer und Karl Renner are the primary representatives who strongly influenced Hans Kohn, Eugen Lemberg, Ernest Gellner, Walker Conner, and Eric Hobsbawm, all of whom are tied strongly to the multinational Habsburg Monarchy in their approaches, even though this was not always made explicit. See D. Langewiesche, '"La socialdemocrazia considera la nazione qualcosa di indistruttibile e da non distruggere". Riflessioni teoriche dell'austromarxismo sulla nazione intorno al 1900 e il loro significato per la ricerca attuale sul nazionalismo', in *La Nazione in Rosso. Socialismo, Comunismo e 'Questione nazionale': 1889–1953*, eds. M. Cattaruzza and S. Mannelli (2005), 55–82.
16. F.W. Graf references this in: 'Die Nation—von Gott "erfunden"? Kritische Randnotizen zum Theologiebedarf der historischen Nationalismusforschung', in *'Gott mit uns'. Nation, Religion und Gewalt im 19. und frühen 20. Jahrhundert*, eds. G. Krumeich and Hartmut Lehmann (Göttingen, 2000), 285–317, 298. Regarding the connections between nation and religion in German and European history, see H.-G. Haupt and D. Langewiesche, eds., *Nation und Religion in Europa. Mehrkonfessionelle Gesellschaften im 19. und 20. Jahrhundert* (Frankfurt a.M., 2004); Haupt and Langewiesche, eds., *Nation und Religion in der deutschen Geschichte* (Frankfurt a.M., 2001).
17. See H. Carl, H.-H. Kortüm, D. Langewiesche, and F. Lenger, eds., *Kriegsniederlagen. Erfahrungen und Erinnerungen* (Berlin, 2004).
18. Smith, *Chosen Peoples*, 217.
19. Ibid., 216.
20. O. Bauer, *Die Nationalitätenfrage und die Sozialdemokratie*, 2nd ed. (Vienna, 1924; 1st ed. 1907).
21. C.A. Bayly, *The Birth of the Modern World 1780–1914* (Malden and Oxford, 2004).
22. See, with the most important literature, D. Langewiesche, 'Zentralstaat—Föderativstaat: Nationalstaatsmodelle in Europa im 19. und 20. Jahrhundert', *Zeitschrift für Staats- und Europawissenschaften* 2(2004): 173–90.

23. E.J. Hobsbawm, *Nationen und Nationalismus. Mythos und Realität seit 1789. Mit einem aktuellen Vorwort des Autors u. einem Nachwort von Dieter Langewiesche* (Frankfurt a.M., expanded ed. 2004; English trans. 1990), 51.
24. I. Berlin, 'Kant as an Unfamiliar Source of Nationalism' (1972), in *The Sense of Reality. Studies in Ideas and their History* (New York, 1996), 232–48, 234.
25. O. Bauer, 'Unser Nationalitätenprogramm und unsere Taktik ("Der Kampf" 1, 1907/08)', in Bauer, *Werkausgabe*, Band 8 (Vienna, 1980), 67–78.
26. K. Renner, 'Oesterreich-Ungarn und seine Völker', in Renner, *Oesterreichs Erneuerung. Politisch-programmatische Aufsätze* (Vienna, 1916), 25–30, 28.
27. E. Canetti, *Masse und Macht* (Frankfurt a.M., 1980; 1st ed. 1960), 524.
28. Ibid., 185ff.
29. Bauer, 'Die Nationalitätenfrage und die Sozialdemokratie' (1907), in Bauer, *Werkausgabe*, Band 1 (Vienna, 1975), 49–622, 44.
30. See the work of R.M. Lepsius, who also employs a generalizing comparison, *Interessen, Ideen und Institutionen* (Opladen, 1990).
31. For an extraordinarily stimulating generalizing comparison focused on Europe: R. Castel, *Die Metamorphosen der sozialen Frage. Eine Chronik der Lohnarbeit* (Konstanz, 2000; French: Paris, 1995).
32. A generalizing worldwide comparison is offered by E. Hobsbawm, *Das Zeitalter der Extreme. Weltgeschichte des 20. Jahrhunderts* (Munich/Vienna, 1995; English trans. London, 1994).
33. On the globalization of the eighteenth and nineteenth centuries see Bayly, *Birth of the Modern World*; for a more succinct overview: J. Osterhammel and N.P. Petersson, *Geschichte der Globalisierung* (Munich, 2003).
34. As an overview: Langewiesche, 'Zum Wandel von Krieg und Kriegslegitimation in der Neuzeit', *Journal of Modern European History* 2(2004): 5–27; N. Buschmann and Langewiesche, eds., *Der Krieg in den Gründungsmythen europäischer Nationen und der USA* (Frankfurt a.M., 2004); in terms of global history M. Mann, *The Sources of Power. Vol. II: The rise of classes and nation-states, 1760–1914* (Cambridge, 1993).
35. An excellent collection of sources on Jewish-national self-determination and its changes: M. Brenner, A. Kauders, G Reuveni, and N. Römer, eds., *Jüdische Geschichte lesen. Texte der jüdischen Geschichtsschreibung im 19. und 20. Jahrhundert* (Munich, 2003).
36. Bayly, *Birth of the Modern World*, 469.
37. Kosselleck, 'Einleitung', in *Der politische Totenkult. Kriegerdenkmäler in der Moderne*, eds. Kosselleck and Michael Jeismann (Munich, 1994), 12.
38. Koselleck, 'Einleitung',14.
39. Ibid.
40. See for this—also a generalizing comparison—W. Reinhard, *Geschichte der Staatsgewalt. Eine vergleichende Verfassungsgeschichte Europas von den Anfängen bis zur Gegenwart* (Munich, 1999).
41. See an attempt at a generalizing comparison-based history of ideas: Langewiesche, 'Nationalismus als Pflicht zur Intoleranz', in *Intoleranz im Zeitalter der*

Revolutionen. Europa 1770–1848, eds. A. Mattioli, M. Ries, and E. Rudolph (Zürich, 2004), 281–302.
42. See Langewiesche, 'Zentralstaat—Föderativstaat'.
43. E.M. Arndt, 'Über Volkshaß' (1813), in *Grenzfälle. Über neuen und alten Nationalismus*, eds. M. Jeismann and Hennig Ritter (Leipzig, 1993), 319–34, 332.
44. Ibid.
45. Ibid., 320.
46. Ibid., 324.
47. Arndt, 'Volkshaß', 331.
48. Ibid.
49. Ibid., 330, 334.
50. Ibid., 330, 334.
51. See P. Hommelhoff and P. Kirchhoff, eds., *Der Staatenverbund der Europäischen Union* (Heidelberg, 1994). For the 'integrated state' as a new state consciousness, see R. Wahl, *Verfassungsstaat, Europäisierung, Internationalisierung* (Frankfurt a.M., 2003), 17–52, 22.
52. On the historically based hope that in the future, democratization will limit the willingness for violence both within and without, see the globally applicable investigations in R. J. Rummel, *Power Kills. Democracy as a Method of Nonviolence* (New Brunswick/London, 1997); Rummel, *Death by Government* (New Brunswick/London, 1994).
53. As an example of a comparative method that presents itself as better than all others: M. Werner and B. Zimmermann, 'Vergleich, Transfer, Verflechtung. Der Ansatz der histoire croisée und die Herausforderung des Transnationalen', *Geschichte und Gesellschaft* 28 (2002): 607–36.

CHAPTER 7

Birds of a Feather

A Comparative History of German and US Labor in the Nineteenth and Twentieth Centuries

THOMAS WELSKOPP

Ever since Werner Sombart posed his famous question, 'Why is there no socialism in the United States?', the comparative view on the history of labor in Germany and the US has stressed marked differences between the two countries, if not completely divergent paths of development.[1] Whereas the German case has been represented, preferably in Marxist terms, as a historical role model on a global scale when it comes to the strength and ideological aptness of the organized labor movement, the American storyline always alluded to the US's deficiencies and failure to live up to that alleged standard. In the current debate about the ostensible 'clash of cultures' between a US 'hire-and-fire capitalism' and a 'cozy' German 'Rhenish capitalism' characterized by the harmonious corporatism of employers, unions, and the state, labor relations play a crucial role. The truly important differences between styles of industrial relations we can observe at present are all too easily projected back into history in order to create the simplistic picture of an ever-widening gap between the two countries that originated a long time ago.[2]

Yet a more fine-grained analysis comparing the labor histories of Germany and the US over a long time—i.e., from the beginnings to the present—has so far not been undertaken. This chapter devotes itself to such a groundbreaking task. It will reveal that the history of labor in Germany and the US cannot be portrayed as a linear development of divergence or as a continuously widening gap that has led to almost polarized or antagonistic systems of industrial relations in the respective countries. Rather, it will attempt to document and explain this parallel history as a sequence of much more subtle mutual approximations and deviations.

Beginnings to 1890s: The Artisanal Phase

In 1890, labor as an organized force could already look back on a history of more than sixty years. These formative six decades had shaped both the structure and make-up of labor movements on either side of the Atlantic Ocean and the respective systems of labor relations between employees and employers. Those foundations would influence the times to come—not necessarily as enduring patterns in a continuous progression, but sometimes as path dependencies channeling processes of fundamental change.

The years around 1890 were not the starting point for organized labor; they actually marked the end of its first era of existence. The decades that followed witnessed the demise of the *artisanal phase* of the German and US labor movements.[3] In both nations (Germany, indeed, became a nation state only in 1871), the first labor organizations did not form in response to early industrialization, but as a reaction to the increasing commercialization of traditional artisanal trades. Small master artisans and journeymen found their skills depreciated on markets where capital increasingly dictated the terms and the value of work, and degraded, in the words of contemporaries, the 'skilled art' of the artisan to just another commodity. In the larger cities of the US East and northern Midwest, workshops grew in size, and single masters employed a multiplying number of journeymen. As a result, masters in trades such as tailoring, shoemaking, metalworking, printing or construction came to resemble small capitalist entrepreneurs who delegated their former manual and supervisory tasks to hired foremen and progressively focused on financial management, customer acquisition, and sales. They fashioned the production of their establishments according to the projected demand of an anonymous buyers' market, rather than to individual customers' orders.[4] Journeymen, meanwhile, felt condemned to a lifelong existence as dependent wageworkers. They deemed mounting commercial pressure responsible for deteriorating working conditions. The swelling ranks of immigration further undermined their position, either because immigrants proved willing to work for less than the customary wages, or because they set up small workshops on their own, competing for an embattled market by exploiting compatriots under 'sweatshop' conditions.

The early trade union movement originated in this social and economic environment. After the Massachusetts Supreme Court had ruled trade unions and their strike activity to be legal in 1842—before, courts had traditionally banned such organizations as 'conspiracies' according to common law doctrine—they became a major force in employee-employer relations.[5] Trade unions organized along narrowly conceived craft lines. They erected more or less rigid barriers against certain ethnic minorities—mostly the latest immigrant arrivals—and were not interested in including unskilled workers. They appealed to the pride and group ethos of the union's potential members, which was based on shared skills, and moulded this elitist group consciousness into a considerable fighting power. Sharing a common craft background secured the group's unity of interests, accumulation of generous funds, and arcane knowledge of the craft-specific labor markets. The aim of craft unionization was to control local or regional labor markets by establishing 'closed shop' or 'union shop' rules that either made only union members eligible for employment or made joining the union mandatory for all workers upon entry. This way, solidly organized workforces became a formidable strike weapon, since they could not be replaced by unskilled strikebreakers. Consequently, they were able to secure good wages and working hours if the overall economic situation was favourable.[6]

Craft unionism of this type gained a firm foothold in some early expanding industries, most notably in coal mining, iron and steel making, the railroads, metalworking, 'mule spinning', or textiles, and printing. Here, craft-specific skills played a dominant role in organizing production. Work groups exercised a great deal of autonomy, and often they managed the work process for themselves under various models of 'subcontracting'. Moreover, skilled teams forming rigid internal hierarchies controlled apprenticeships and advancement of junior workers through the ranks. Craft unions in early industries proved successful as long as company sizes did not surpass a certain limit and competition among a sizable number of firms in neighbouring locations remained strong.

Germany also faced the spreading forces of capitalist commercialization. The development affected the same trades as in the US, but in slightly different ways. Prussia abolished the guild system between 1807 and 1810, but here, as elsewhere, the guild tradition lingered on until the freedom of trade was decreed by the North German Federation (*Norddeutsche Bund*) in 1869. The guild tradition was a major barrier for the capitalization of workshops. This meant that workshop sizes remained considerably smaller than in the US, except in the construction industry. Commercialization advanced even under these conditions, but, instead of generating larger economic units, it led to a proliferation of small shops that further inflated a severely overcrowded artisanal market. For many sons from the generation of 'paupers', an apprenticeship in crammed trades such as tailoring or shoemaking still promised upward mobility. Yet working conditions for journeymen and small masters alike were deteriorating because of their influx. Better-off masters still used guild regulations to subdue rebellious journeymen and competing small masters. In most workshops, the masters themselves still worked manually and did not concede to their (few) journeymen the degree of autonomy that their US colleagues enjoyed.[7]

These circumstances proved unfavourable for unionization. Characteristically, the first union organizations in Germany, the associations of printers and cigar makers, founded in 1848, originated in trades that both came closest to the US expansion of shop sizes and were least hampered by the guild legacy. Yet for most German tradesmen, trade unions appeared as a counterintuitive model of organization, reminiscent of the worst facets of the guild. They preferred associations modelled after the bourgeois clubs (*Vereine*), which included members of all trades and even small masters and shopowners (and intellectuals), provided that they did not exploit the manual laborers. These workers' associations (*Arbeitervereine*) or workers' educational associations (*Arbeiterbildungsvereine*) became the centres of social life for thousands of young, male members of dozens of artisanal and commercial occupations. After an appearance in the revolution of 1848, they mushroomed again in the early 1860s, clustering in regions such as Saxony, Hamburg, Frankfurt, the Southwest, the lower Rhine, and—rather late—Berlin. Despite their 'universal' self-image, however, workers' associations were not actively recruiting industrial workers; they excluded women even where the law did not prohibit female membership, and they remained unresponsive toward the agricultural population.

Given the explosive nature of public life in a post-revolutionary, pre-national Germany still governed by more or less reactionary monarchical autocracies, the workers' associations were immediately swallowed up by conflicting factions of the bourgeois liberal movement struggling for a unified German nation. Thus, the German labor movement was politicized almost from the outset. In contrast to the US, it originated not as a trade union, but as a political party movement. The workers (by the definition of their associations) soon drifted to the left, radical democratic wing of the nationalist mainstream and eventually began to emancipate themselves from bourgeois liberal hegemony. In 1863, Ferdinand Lassalle founded the General Workers' Association of All Germany (*Allgemeine deutsche Arbeiterverein*) explicitly as a political party fighting for universal male suffrage.[8] Until 1869, a rival Social Democratic party organization emerged under the leadership of August Bebel, a small master wood turner from Leipzig, and Wilhelm Liebknecht, a journalist who had taken part in the revolution of 1848 and spent years of exile in London before repatriating to Saxony.

Although both parties rivalled for recognition by Karl Marx, who was still in exile in London, German Social Democrats saw him as a moral rather than as an ideological authority. Marxist doctrine entered the Social Democratic discourse only on a tactical, but not on a programmatic level, even when the factions united to form the Socialist Workers' Party in 1875. Instead of embracing Marx's revolutionary theory, the Social Democrats heralded an 'associational socialism' firmly rooted in the experiences and worldviews of an artisanal small workshop universe that was ostensibly collapsing under the 'double yoke of the powers of capitalism and the powers of the [autocratic states'] bayonets'.[9] Since capitalism was perceived as a financial vampire draining the lifeblood from honest production, rather than as the driving force behind industrialization, anything short of its wholesale destruction could only appear as palliate. The solution to the 'social question' had to be political. For Social Democrats this meant overthrowing the autocratic state by means of a revolution that they depicted as a—more successful—reprise of 1848 and replacing it with a true democratic republic (*Volksstaat*). When a unified Germany became an unwanted reality in the Prussian-dominated *Deutsches Reich* in 1871 and Otto von Bismarck introduced universal male suffrage on the federal level, Social Democrats soon developed outstanding capabilities as election campaigners. Until 1878, when the party was banned under the Anti-Socialist Law (*Sozialistengesetz*), the Social Democrats managed to win up to thirteen seats in the Reichstag, and they mobilized up to 440,000 supporters, or roughly 8 percent, of the popular vote.[10]

Whereas commercialization had produced a predominantly trade union-oriented labor movement in the US (early and not entirely unsuccessful experiments with Workingmen's Parties had been absorbed into the Democratic Party under the popular presidency of Andrew Jackson), the German context firmly established a predominantly political path for labor. Trade unions in Germany saw themselves cornered between a party hegemony that during the 1870s still threatened its very existence and a strike movement across most urban trades that virtually swept aside the feeble union organizations in the boom of 1869 to 1873. A comparison of the US (1883) and Germany (1877/78) reveals that union membership in the US exceeded the German figures by a rate of five to one (with populations of roughly the same size). Iron and steelworkers, coal miners, and cigar makers made up the largest union contingents in the US, while no major industry had yet been organized in Germany. In Germany, cigar makers still accounted for the largest portion of membership, while printers claimed the highest percentage of organized workers (50 percent), with construction and metalworking slowly catching up. Yet only 1.5 percent of all artisanal and industrial workers belonged to a trade union in 1877.[11] Furthermore, party hegemony had led to a schism along ideological lines into Social Democratic 'free' trade unions, liberal unions, and, later on, Catholic unions (*Christliche Gewerkvereine*), which placed a heavy and long-lasting burden on the German trade union movement.

Werner Sombart's classic question as to why there was no socialism in the US could, therefore, well be countered by the quip that there were only weak trade unions in Germany before 1890. That socialism was entirely absent on US soil, however, would be a slight misrepresentation. Such a view would ignore The Noble and Holy Order of the Knights of Labor, a federation of local workers' associations, trade unions, and cultural organizations that had been founded as a secret society in 1869, but by 1883 had flourished into a mass movement 'whose membership is not known publicly, but it runs into the hundreds of thousands'.[12] At its height in 1886, when the Haymarket bombing charged to anarchists in Chicago and a failed general strike broke its momentum, the Knights of Labor claimed to have about one million supporters, mainly from the ranks of white craftsmen and skilled industrial workers, but also of unskilled workers, African Americans, and women. Except for this decidedly greater inclusiveness, the Knights became the labor organization in the US that bore the closest resemblance to German social democracy. The Knights of Labor also embraced an ideology of 'associational socialism' that depicted banks, monopolies, stockbrokers, and 'corrupt politicians' as their main adversaries. Although revivals of local Workingmen's Parties remained short-lived—albeit not without success—the Knights had a political vision. At the same time, the revolution they propagated was supposed to be a cultural revolution brought about by the self-education of the workers.[13]

The Knights were a political mass organization without a firm foothold in US party politics—a recurrent theme in US labor history, as we will see. Therefore, on the apogee of their power in 1886, the Knights called a general strike, the 'Great Upheaval', in order to win the eight-hour day, a central political demand, by means of trade union activity. The strike failed, but had been most effective in the centres of craft union organization. This experience brought the craft unions—as International Brotherhoods (international meaning that Canadians were recruited as well) or Amalgamated Associations (federations of several even more exclusive crafts) loosely affiliated with an umbrella organization called Federation of Organized Trades and Labor Unions—to abandon the cultural and political course of the Knights and to reorganize in an association strictly devoted to business unionism, the American Federation of Labor (AFL), founded in 1886. Deprived of their strong craft union wing and the East Coast radicals (after the Haymarket incident), the Knights continued to exist in the small towns and agricultural belts of the Midwest, where they paved the way for the Populists and later on for the Socialist Party.

1890 to the First World War: Craft Unionism and Centralization

By 1890, the AFL's craft union strategy had fully evolved. Its premise was that unions had to rely on their own strength. This strength lay in the 'union shop', which guaranteed 100 percent organization of skilled workmen on the shop floor. This strategy mobilized sufficient power to win labor contracts by means of strike threats or actual walkouts in direct negotiations with individual employers. Union policies focused on 'bread-and-butter' issues; their objective was a 'pure and simple unionism', as AFL-leader Samuel Gompers, an immigrant cigar maker, put it. The AFL served as an umbrella organization for its constituent craft unions, which acted with full autonomy in order to play out their inherent strengths on the level of individual enterprises. According to Gompers, relations between the AFL and the individual unions resembled the relationship between the federal government and the individual states.

'Pure and simple unionism' reflected a widespread frustration of US labor with politics. The fragmented structure of the political system in the US discouraged ventures from establishing a nationwide labor party with a strong programmatic orientation, such as the Social Democrats in Germany. This was true even when the American Socialist Party, with its presidential candidate Eugene V. Debs, a railroad clerk from Indiana, won 6 percent of the popular vote in 1912. Twenty Socialists served in nine state legislatures by that time, and seventy-four US cities had elected Socialist mayors by 1911.[14] US politics remained local and state-based. Early universal male suffrage had increased the number of public offices and soon led to the infamous patronage networks of the cities' political machines. Consequently, labor organizations developed a pragmatic approach to politics by backing individual 'labor-friendly' candidates or tickets of the two major parties. This amounted to the non-partisan, but nevertheless political strategy 'to reward [labor's] friends and to punish [its] enemies'. It supported protective labor legislation with very limited success, since what had been achieved in one legislative body could always be nullified by another. Furthermore, since labor regulation was a state affair and the federal government only had jurisdiction over interstate commerce, the rivalry among states for economic growth resulted in a 'race for the bottom' that eventually freed US employers from most employment restrictions or compensatory obligations.

Another primary objective of labor engagement in politics would have been to secure the right to organize collectively, to strike and to picket, because only this guaranteed that the AFL craft unions could bring to bear their full strength in labor conflicts. This, however, was difficult to achieve given the fragmented structure of the political institutions. Labor rights were of little value if they could not be secured on a nationwide level. Finally, the most formidable adversaries of labor were not city and state legislatures, but the courts. State Supreme Courts ruled out as unconstitutional all workers' compensation laws enacted by several states prior to the First World War. Courts at all levels of the legal system vexed the unions with freely administered 'injunctions' against strike actions and picketing. After Congress had passed the Sherman Anti-Trust Act in 1890, federal courts, following the violent Pullman strike of 1894, turned this law, which prohibited restraint of trade by conspiracies among businesses, against nationwide union organizations, particularly when they tried, as had been advocated during the 1880s in order to protect unions, to incorporate in a business manner.

Therefore, union strategy before the First World War was determined by reliance on the 'union shop' and expansion of membership. AFL-affiliated unions grew and reached a rate of unionization that surpassed 12 percent in 1904, a level that was almost twice as high as the level of unionization in Germany. The most active union, the International Association of Machinists, tripled its membership between 1900 and 1910, counting 61,000 cardholding metalworkers by that date. The year 1904 already had marked a turning point, however. Whereas union membership continued to grow steeply in Germany, the rate of unionization increasing to 20 percent by 1914, the US level fell to under 10 percent by 1910 and stagnated until the war effort began to stimulate the economy around 1915. The reason for this reversal of trends was that the 'union shop' doctrine was probing its limits as the expanding big corporations systematically began ousting the unions from their mills, and resistance of smaller employers against union rule stiffened.

The first symptoms of a change of atmosphere date as far back as 1892, when the Amalgamated Association of Iron, Steel, and Tin Workers was resoundingly defeated by the Carnegie Steel Company in the bloody strike at its Homestead works near Pittsburgh.[15] The Amalgamated Association was the largest craft union at that time, accounting for roughly 24,000 members in almost three hundred local lodges across the steelmaking centres of the US.[16] Yet, Carnegie had also grown into the largest and most rapidly expanding US steel producer. On the brink of a giant merger, in 1901, that was about to produce the US Steel Corporation, Carnegie had implemented new steelmaking technology whose economizing potential he saw impaired by the union. Consequently, the steel company mobilized its superior resources, starving the Homestead steelworkers into submission during a four-month work stoppage. It was not the replacement of skills by new technology and management techniques, but the concentrated power of new giant corporations that crippled the steel union in one mill after the other. Already by 1895, membership was cut in half; after the unsuccessful attempt to strike for the complete unionization of the US Steel mills in 1901, the Amalgamated lost further territory. Playing non-unionized against unionized mills during economic slumps, US Steel finally claimed victory with its radical 'open shop' policy by 1909.[17]

The fate of the Amalgamated signalled that the 'union shop' doctrine would run into ever-stiffening resistance as corporations grew and competition remained cutthroat. After an initial period of expansion, when craft unions spread throughout industries with a more medium-sized structure, a greater number of competing firms, and less rapid growth—as was the case with the machine building industry into the first years of the new century—the tide turned. Mergers and endogenous expansion created corporations such as International Harvester, whose resources were powerful enough to confront the unions head-on. The 'union shop' policy changed from being a tool promoting new membership to a defensive measure in desperate struggles to hold embattled territory. Defensive strikes for union recognition replaced 'bread-and-butter' disputes, and each defeat meant a strongpoint lost for the union. Small and medium-sized producers in major industries, finding themselves cornered between non-unionized big corporations and the unions entrenched in their establishments, aggravated the process by starting a militant 'open shop' drive in the late 1890s. In 1903, the National Association of Manufacturers reorganized into a nationwide anti-union institution devoted to protecting its members' 'open shop' policy and supporting their attacks on the union. Although employers were, under US legal conditions, unable to regulate prices and cushion competition, the pressure to free themselves from union influence made collaboration, at least in terms of anti-union solidarity, possible—and effective.[18]

In Germany, the union movement barely survived its close affiliation with social democracy, as forms of both organizations were declared illegal and prosecuted alike under the Anti-Socialist Law (*Sozialistengesetz*), which remained in effect until 1890. Yet, both organizations eventually turned their outlaw status into a success: the Social Democrats, whose participation in campaign activities was legal even under the ban, won almost 20 percent of the popular vote in the Reichstag election of 1887 and became the party with the greatest public appeal in Germany, mobilizing 1.4 million supporters to flock to the polls. The Social Democrats, meanwhile, had developed into a party of industrial workers, mostly skilled, yet with their former artisanal core intact. In the early twentieth century, the party basically organized a heterogeneous socio-cultural urban milieu in the working-class neighbourhoods of big and medium-sized cities. In its centres of influence, it also began opening up for more small businessmen, white-collar workers and intellectuals than had been considered previously in historical accounts. In the January elections of 1912, the Social Democrats gained their greatest victory before the First World War, collecting 4.2 million votes, or 35 percent of the electorate, and winning 110 seats to become the strongest parliamentary faction in the Reichstag. Despite its numerical strength, however, the Social Democratic Party remained politically isolated and excluded from the governmental bodies of the *Reich*.

Although the political wing of the labor movement was strongly developed, it was also hampered in its influence on the actual political decision process and was torn time and again by the highly ideological debates between 'revolutionaries' and 'reformers'. German unions thus saw themselves in a situation not much different from that of their US colleagues, as German unions also lacked effective political representation. Labor legislation was slow and depended on intricate scheming among the liberal, conservative, and Catholic *Zentrum* (Centre) factions in the Reichstag, where the labor movement only played the part of an absent 'other'. Bismarck's early welfare measures, which were aimed at alienating the workers from Social Democracy, grossly failed to achieve this objective and produced only miniscule real social effects. Therefore, German trade unions had to rely on their own strength and work to expand their membership.

The key to this effort was a sufficient degree of political independence in a trade union spectrum divided by ideological and party lines. The trade union movement had been reinvigorated during the later years of the Anti-Socialist Law by local grassroots organizations in trades and industries such as metalworking or construction, which officially appeared as politically neutral 'professional associations' (*Fachvereine*). Given the political impotency of social democracy even after the ban had been lifted, a separate, independent organizational structure for 'free' trade unions became imperative. This was all the more urgent since party and union clientele were far from identical: a statistical survey showed that in 1910, 20 percent of all industrial workers in Germany were members of trade unions, but only 7 percent belonged to the party. Among the union members, a good third were also registered Social Democrats. Tuning down party rhetoric, therefore, was a prerequisite for attracting recruits more interested in union activity than party politics. Union leader Carl Legien declared in the late 1890s: 'In the economic struggle all forces need to be concentrated without enquiring into the political creed of the individual'.[19]

The decisive difference between the German and US trade union movements before the First World War, then, was a matter of strategy. AFL craft unions relied on the 'union shop', the full autonomy of local lodges, which hoarded their accumulated funds, and a decentralized structure that rendered union presidents weak and the AFL leadership almost without resources. The 'free' trade unions in Germany, in contrast, adhered to a central organization. Whereas the individual workshop or plant in the US served as the basis of union organization, German trade unions were weak on the shop floor but had access to strong central institutions and their pooled funds. For them, recruiting new members was even more important than for their US colleagues, since accumulated dues made up the organization's main power resource. Characteristically, union locals in Germany were termed 'dues collecting stations' (*Zahlstellen*). Consequently, nationwide 'central associations' (*Zentralverbände*) headed the individual unions, which were still organized along craft lines and attracted skilled rather than unskilled workers. The district units of all 'free' unions represented in a city formed 'community cartels' (*Ortskartelle*) in order to pool resources for local activities. A major breakthrough in the establishment of a politically independent central organization occurred when the General Commission for German Trade Unions (*Generalkommission*) was founded as the strategic policy articulating body in 1890.

This organizational development accounted for the steep and continuous growth of German trade unions between the second half of the 1890s and the First World War. The Social Democratic 'free' trade unions doubled their membership every five years. In 1904, their affiliated unions counted one million dues-paying workers, with the *Christliche Gewerkvereine* (300,000) and the liberal *Hirsch-Dunckersche Gewerkvereine* (100,000) a distant second and third. In 1913, membership of the 'free' trade unions surpassed 2.5 million workers. The key to their success was that the centralized structure allowed trade unions to strategically focus—and discipline—strike activity all over Germany. Organized strikes planned and financed generously by the central union institutions proved to be powerful even where shop floor unionization was not strong. Some major walkouts failed, such as the textile workers' strike in Crimmitschau in 1903/04, which had been called to spearhead the ten-hour workday drive. Overall, though, trade union strategy was very effective.[20]

The lack of militancy that the 'union shop' doctrine had promoted in the US, furthermore, made German employers more willing to compromise. To be sure, the big corporations in heavy industry or in the 'new' chemical and electric engineering industries were as hostile to unions as their US counterparts. The steel industry was called the 'citadel of anti-unionism' by August Bebel, and coal mining experienced several militant strike waves with hundreds of thousands of participants, but was not organized effectively before the war. The main difference with the US was, rather, that small and medium-sized enterprises in machine building, metalworking, and other decentralized, export-oriented industries legally cooperated with each other in Germany. Instead of mounting an equally militant 'open shop' drive as the US had done, they often settled for wage and hour contracts with the unions that covered entire regions. The number of such collective agreements (*Tarifverträge*) in Germany more than quadrupled from 3,000 in 1906 to 13,500 in 1913. By that time, 2 million German workers, and a third of all union members, were covered by collective labor contracts.

The First World War and Aftermath: Strikes, 'Red Scare', and Industrial Unionism

The necessity to abandon craft unionism in favour of a new industrial unionism was felt earlier and with more contemplation by German trade unions than by the US AFL organizations. Whereas the latter became more and more content with defending their niches of organized shops in an increasingly marginalized part of the great industries, the imperative to actively recruit members forced their German colleagues to look beyond an all too narrow conception of crafts. In 1891, the German Metalworkers' Association (*Deutscher Metallarbeiterverband*, DMV) was founded explicitly as an 'industrial union' with jurisdiction over all metal trades, including iron and steel, at all skill levels. The idea behind 'industrial unions' was that in modern industrial plants, workers from a variety of occupations could be employed. Since labor had lost control over skill acquisition anyway, it made sense to organize all workers cooperating in one workshop in the same union, in accordance with the principle 'one plant—one union'. Until well after the First World War, the union, in fact, represented little more than a federation of associated skilled occupations, and its progress into heavy industry remained slow. It proved very successful, however, in organizing the small and medium-sized, export-oriented machine building and tool making workshops that had become the backbone of the German economy. By 1900, the DMV counted a dues-paying membership of 500,000 metalworkers and ranked as the largest single trade union in the world.

The First World War lent this issue even more urgency. In both countries, the need to rally a strained workforce thinned out by army service behind the war effort fostered the states' readiness to intervene into collective labor relations and accept organized labor as partners in the process.[21] In Germany, the Patriotic Service Law (*Vaterländisches Hilfsdienstgesetz*) of 1916 introduced mandatory workers' councils on the plant level of industrial enterprises. For the price of suspending the 'union shop' doctrine for the duration of the war, the AFL was accepted by state and employers as a collective bargaining agent in the National War Labor Board (NWLB, 1918), a joint arbitration board that oversaw thousands of such boards on the regional and local level. The state-controlled National War Labor Policies Board formulated model solutions for labor agreements in the armament industries, but remained dependent on the associated corporations' voluntary compliance. The employers attempted to dodge the NWLB's drive to establish bona fide collective bargaining under its jurisdictional umbrella by initiating Employee Representation Plans (ERP), powerless company unions under complete control of the management. The dismantling of the NWLB in 1919 marked the withdrawal of the state from labor interventionism in favour of 'normalcy'. This removed political pressure from corporations, which immediately returned to their previous autocratic labor regimes.

Meanwhile, however, the war years had seen an unprecedented soaring of union membership, most impressive in heavy industry, the former 'Hindenburg line of anti-unionism'. Advanced mechanization had altered the forms of workers' cooperation on the shop floor and actually upgraded skill levels, while reducing the unskilled workforce and curbing turnover. New bonds of workplace solidarity also signalled that the second generation of immigrants had been integrated into US industrial culture. The surge in membership was largely a grassroots phenomenon. The AFL unions, and most prominently the Amalgamated Association, were not willing to adapt to an industrial structure in order to accommodate this new force. They feared of being overwhelmed by masses of presumably radical alien workers. Therefore, the AFL only half-heartedly contributed to the National Committee for the Organization of Iron and Steelworkers (NCOIS), which staged a belated and—in major steel centres such as Pittsburgh—incomplete organization drive in the autumn of 1918. In September 1919, the NCOIS called an industry-wide strike for union recognition, with 365,000 steelworkers responding. The Great Steel Strike was met with determined resistance by the big corporations and military interventions by state militias. As in other large industries, the strike petered out after almost four months. The physical isolation of the steel centres from the metropolises of the East and West had contributed to the fact that public opinion turned quickly against labor. For the public, the strike was not a sign of advanced assimilation, but, on the contrary, a symptom of un-American alien radicalism. Press coverage of the steel strike became part of the 'red scare' that suspected all immigrants of having communist or anarchist intentions.[22]

The leaders of the steel strike were charged with anarchist conspiracies or affiliations with the Industrial Workers of the World (IWW), an internationalist organization that appealed to all workers, but actually spread only among truly international occupations, such as the maritime personnel of commercial ships, longshoremen, and dock workers. It also gained some following in the West and among travelling casual laborers ('tramps') as a cultural network, rather than a proper trade union organization.

German workers—as conscripted naval servicemen or as strikers in industry—spearheaded the November revolution of 1918, which brought down the *Kaiserreich* and paved the way for the new German republic. They staffed the workers' and soldiers' councils that sprung up in factories and communities all over the country. Yet for them—as for the labor movement as a whole—the revolution's consequences were a mixed blessing. Fear of socialization had caused German employers to compromise. The

Stinnes-Legien agreement of 1918 accepted the trade unions as legitimate collective bargaining agents even in heavy industry, and the Central Collaboration Committee (*Zentralarbeitsgemeinschaft*) was created as a clearing forum for voluntary negotiations between representatives of employers and unions. At the same time as they were winning formal recognition, however, German trade unions faced the detrimental effects of the proliferating schisms in the political labor movement on the one side, and a growing militancy of 8 million (1920) mostly newly won members on the other. The division within the Social Democratic Party (1917–1922) and the separation of the Communist Party (1918/19) translated into conflicts between 'reformers' and 'revolutionaries' within the unions, especially with regard to the demand to socialize the basic industries, above all coal mining. Consequently, unions resorted to policies that were designed to bring the workers under political control. This met with a grassroots unionization movement in formerly unorganized industries, like chemicals or iron and steel, which demanded structural adaptation of organizations to their industrial background and determined leadership in direct shop floor action. As the trade unions failed to provide either, workers' militancy broke out of containment in thousands of wildcat strikes.

The political schism and organizational shortcomings within the German unions brought together political radicalism and workplace militancy as rather strange bedfellows. In the Ruhr, for instance, a syndicalist movement sprang up that, on the one hand, represented grassroots sentiment in favour of effective union organization and direct action in order to gain material rewards. Food supply, indeed, was still critical, and inflation was making itself felt. On the other hand, the syndicalist movement, especially among the coal miners, focused on the socialization of basic industries and rallied behind political radicals who led them into a bloody civil war for military control of the region in 1920. Syndicalism was a highly volatile, short-lived movement that oscillated between a political radicalism eventually swallowed up by Communism and a workplace militancy that expended itself in local strikes out of disappointment over union policies. The result was a dilemma that placed a burden on labor and industrial relations for the remaining years of the Weimar Republic. The unions were weakened by internal political conflict and had lost much loyalty in the ranks of new recruits, who, in turn, saw themselves increasingly stripped of their collective power on the shop floor. Workers' militancy had caused the employers to mistrust deeply both their potentially destructive workforces and unions that had failed to keep them at bay. Employers also found that the value of unions as partners in negotiations had decreased decisively, precisely because they no longer seemed to be in control of their members. The political rifts, finally, slowed down the process of the unions' structural adaptation to industrial unionism.[23]

1920s and 1930s to the Second World War: The Decisive Role of the State

Hyperinflation and the concomitant rush into large-scale investments and acquiring material goods had postponed the demobilization of the German war economy until 1924, whereas the US and Great Britain had experienced already a sharp postwar recession in 1920/21. The crisis immediately swelled the ranks of the unemployed, and a substantial lack of jobs even during the recovery years around 1928 (2 million unemployed) continued to characterize the German economy until the bottom fell out of employment in the Great Depression. By 1932, the number of jobless persons easily surpassed the 6 million mark. Structural unemployment, however, further eroded union power. Although union membership, with 4 to 5 million cardholders between 1924 and 1933, remained twice as high as during the late *Kaiserreich*, the trade unions proved incapable of staging independent industrial action. And despite the consolidation of the 'free' trade unions, which had absorbed the syndicalist workplace militancy by 1924, the political conflicts between Social Democrats and Communists still bore down on union strength and on the degree of loyalty the unions could expect from grassroots networks on the shop floor.

The German trade unions' defensive stance is best illustrated by the fact that the largest open industrial conflict during the Weimar years was forced upon trade unions by employers. West German steel and metalworking corporations answered wage demands following the termination of a labor contract in October 1928 with the lockout of 240,000 workers. With this 'Iron Dispute on the Ruhr' (*Ruhreisenstreit*) of 1928, employers clearly aimed at weakening decisively the unions and at bringing down the 'trade union state' (*Gewerkschaftsstaat*) that they felt the Weimar Republic had become. Weimar politicians, however, came to the rescue. In November, the Reichstag voted to support the locked-out workers by public welfare, a measure that relieved the unions' finances and strained the employers' resources. Both sides of the conflict agreed to succumb to arbitration by Carl Severing, Social Democratic Minister of the Interior, in December 1928. He ruled for a small wage increase and the re-instatement of all locked-out workers and their elected representatives.[24]

The struggle on the Ruhr showed that the status of organized labor in Weimar Germany had become totally dependent on the permanent commitment of the state to safeguard its rights. Although the Social Democrats only participated in four of the twenty-one short-lived Weimar administrations, they exerted a continuous influence on Weimar labor and welfare legislation. Not only did they back up liberal-bourgeois/*Zentrum* minority regimes in return for favourable labor policies, but they also staffed the specialized parliament committees with legally trained experts. The Works

Councils Statute (*Betriebsrätegesetz*) of 1920 institutionalized union participation in plant-related labor relations, and although vigorously disputed within the ranks of the unions and their rank-and-file membership, the *Betriebsräte* remained the most important link between the organization and their popular base throughout the Weimar years. The Grand Coalition under Chancellor Hermann Müller (1928/30) instituted nationwide state-controlled unemployment insurance (*Reichsarbeitslosenversicherung*) in 1928, a social-political innovation that would falter under the pressure of the Great Depression only four years later.

The Weimar state guaranteed collective bargaining in Germany. It set up state councils with prominent politicians—ministers, members of parliament, heads of the German *Länder*—which settled labor disputes if free negotiations failed. Their settlements were binding. After the consolidation of German industry, employers assaulted this system of compulsory arbitration by the state (*Zwangsschlichtung*) head-on. Their strategy was twofold: first, employers tried to push arbitration boards more and more toward settlements favorable to industry; secondly, employers did everything they could to undermine the legitimacy of state arbitration as a system. When the Great Depression began, employers exacted consent for enormous wage cuts and layoffs by state arbitration boards and still complained about the Weimar *Gewerkschaftsstaat* they now openly set out to destroy.

The Great Depression practically brought the power of the state to safeguard labor's rights to an end, even if some institutions continued to exist until 1933. Yet it had become clear that the trade unions were no longer able to defend more than the chance for members with higher seniority to extend their employment and get the young recruits to industry and the elderly fired first. The final years of the Weimar Republic, consequently, were marked by an increasing political fragmentation and radicalization of German workers that polarized the political landscape. Even if it is true that industrial workers remained underrepresented in the National Socialist electorate, a substantial, mostly small-town clientele in ill-organized trades did turn to the right, social outcasts flocked to the paramilitary SA, and staunch resistance before 1933 concentrated in the traditional centres of the labor movement. Here, the growth of the Communist Party after 1930 fed mainly on the influx of young unemployed males, who had dropped out of the Social Democrat milieu.[25]

The National Socialists outlawed the Communist and Social Democratic Parties during the first months of their reign, and they cracked down on the trade unions the very day after holding the first nationwide May Day celebrations, complete with a Hitler speech, on 2 May 1933. Except for networks of underground resistance, the organizations of the German labor movement had been crushed without a fight. The National Socialists installed an all-embracing workers' organization lavishly financed by the appropriated funds the trade unions had accumulated over generations. This German Workers Front (*Deutsche Arbeitsfront*) was not a substitute for the unions, but a mechanism to sustain party control over the workers whom the Nazis deeply mistrusted. When rearmament and preparation for war made labor supply scarce after 1936, German workers resorted to informal shop floor coalitions and individual bargaining to successfully regain material rewards. A majority of German workers retained a measure of loyalty to the regime—which had been won by Hitler's early foreign policy coups and *Blitzkrieg* victories—as long as the supply situation remained favourable and the war was not yet felt severely on the home front. Stalingrad marked a turning point. Yet even as total defeat became imminent in the spring of 1945, many workers continued to acquiesce to—or to collaborate in—the exploitation of forced labor in German factories.

The German case has demonstrated that the credible commitment of the state to guarantee labor rights is the single most critical variable that determines the chances of trade unions to organize workers on a permanent basis and to gain sustained acceptance as collective bargaining agents in industrial relations. Against this background, the story of US labor during the 1920s and 1930s at first glance looks like a simple reversal of its German counterpart: whereas the Weimar Republic institutionalized collective bargaining, the Republican administrations of Warren G. Harding, Calvin Coolidge (who had come to fame when he crushed the Boston police strike of 1919 by military force), and Herbert Hoover stood for a 'hands off' policy of the state that gave employers all possible freedom to shape their labor relations as they saw fit. And whereas the National Socialists oppressed the German labor movement after 1933, Franklin Delano Roosevelt's New Deal for the first time established a state-backed system of collective bargaining in the US. On a deeper theoretical level, however, an asynchronic comparison of 1930s labor relations in Germany with the 1920s in the US, and of Weimar Germany with New Deal America, will reveal important structural parallels.

The 1920s were aptly termed 'the lean years' by labor historian Irving Bernstein.[26] This was not only true for the meagre income increase workers successfully extracted from the bountiful riches of the 'Coolidge prosperity'.; the decade was also a particularly bleak one for US organized labor. After the great strikes of 1919 and 1920 had ended in utter defeat, the 'open shop' had become a reality throughout all but the most marginalized sectors of US industry. US workers now saw themselves thrown back on localized industrial action, if they could be mobilized at all by the decentralized and severely weakened unions. In the large cities on the East Coast and the industrial Midwest, the fragmented nature of labor relations offered a venue for organized crime to intrude and overtake control of local employment conditions—not without violence, and at a price.[27] Labor racketeering eventually developed into one of the most profitable lines of illegal business during the last years of National Prohibition.[28] It exemplified the idea that 'warlord' authority tends to take charge under conditions where the state is conspicuously absent from or hostile to the regulation of labor relations.

Only the textile workers, predominantly female since the late war, countered the overall trend. The Amalgamated Clothing Workers, under the leadership of pragmatic Sidney Hillman, made substantial headway in organizing women in the men's clothing industry over the course of the 1920s. Yet other sectors set a rather different tone for the decade. The 'big railroad strike' of 1922, a walkout of more than 400,000 employees of all railway occupations in reaction to severe wage cuts, was brought down by the most sweeping court injunction in US labor history. Harding's Attorney General, Harry Daugherty, had made the state's doctrine in regard to labor disputes unequivocally clear even before the railroad men had heeded the strike call: 'I will use the power of the government within my control,' he declared, 'to prevent the labor unions of the country from destroying the open shop.'[29]

It has often been overlooked, however, that US workers, as the decade proceeded, underwent a process of profound politicization. Although beaten by Hoover in a landslide win in the presidential elections of 1928, New York Governor Al Smith—Catholic, labor friendly, and a product of New York's Tammany Hall Democratic machine—had managed to win 'a larger popular vote, as the losing candidate, than any other Democratic presidential candidate, successful or unsuccessful.'[30] The elections sent a clear signal that industrial workers in the northern metropolises, many of them second-generation immigrants, were increasingly rallying behind a Democrat labor ticket that would bring Franklin Delano Roosevelt into office in 1933, when he succeeded in winning back the Democratic Old South. Although the major mobilizing issue for immigrant workers had been opposition to Prohibition, their politicization gained momentum as the Great Depression set in and became a catalyst in bringing about the New Deal.[31]

Roosevelt carried the 1932 elections with a landslide majority of 57 percent of the popular vote. This gave the new administration the authority to intervene into labor relations on an unprecedented scope. Roosevelt's New Deal sparked off a barrage of heterogeneous initiatives and measures; a multitude of new state agencies mushroomed. Yet all of these activities basically fell into three categories: emergency measures for immediate relief, social legislation and a neo-corporatism that called for the constructive collaboration of employers, and organized labor under the guidance of the state. With the Social Security Act of 1935, the Roosevelt administration laid down the foundations for—among other welfare measures—

nationwide unemployment insurance and old age pensions. The National Industrial Recovery Act (NIRA), passed within the first hundred days of the new administration, became the manifesto of neo-corporatism. It made cooperation among businesses of the same industry legal by having them pledge compliance with codes of 'fair competition'. Further, it established the National Recovery Administration (NRA), an agency staffed by experts that settled labor disputes by arbitration and encouraged companies to recognize unions and to sign codes fixing 'fair' prices and minimum wages. It called for active labor market management by the state (Congress approved a new, federal US Employment Service). Finally, its Section 7a maintained the workers' right to organize and bargain collectively through representatives chosen in company-wide elections.

In 1935, the US Supreme Court struck down the NIRA as unconstitutional because it interfered with interstate commerce. Yet in the same year, the Roosevelt administration reiterated its will to provide a new legal basis for industrial relations. The National Labor Relations Act (NLRA), authored by Senator Robert F. Wagner, confirmed in even more unequivocal words the right of workers to organize in bona fide trade unions and to bargain collectively through representatives of their own choosing. A newly established National Labor Relations Board, comprised of labor and employer members, replaced the NRA as a surveillance, regulation, and arbitration agency. Contrary to the hopes of employers, the Supreme Court upheld the Wagner Act. The Court ruled that workers were entitled to the same rights as employers and that, since all modern business had an interstate dimension, federal regulatory powers were no longer constrained by the commerce clause. The Roosevelt administration, in sum, provided the state's credible commitment to safeguard labor's rights, which had become a necessary condition for the firm establishment of collective bargaining mechanisms.

The weight the Wagner Act gave bona fide trade unions in its statute was more than justified. In reaction to the NIRA, large corporations—if they did not refuse completely to comply with it while waiting for a Supreme Court decision—had revitalized their company union programmes as their rather unilateral interpretation of the workers' right to organize. Yet the history of the ERPs demonstrated that the post-New Deal upsurge in industrial unionism neither had to build union strength from scratch, nor was it solely the effect of favourable state legislation. Over the course of the 1920s, new forms of cooperation in fully mechanized mass production industries had provided fertile ground for the spread of a new workplace solidarity that brought forth informal labor leaders, often second- and third-generation immigrants, with great authority among their shop floor colleagues. Soon, networks of this kind began infiltrating the company unions. The ERPs became the Trojan horses of industrial unionism. Company unions often served as covers for recruiting union members long before the union started an official organization drive. To the shock of many hard-nosed employers, company unions declared themselves independent and elected officers from their own militant rank-and-file. ERPs then liaised with bona fide union organizers or called company elections in which the union ticket usually won by wide margins.[32]

The New Deal did revitalize trade unions that had suffered the most serious losses during the 1920s. Under the NRA, the United Mine Workers counted 300,000 new members within a few months and won recognition in the previously non-union coal regions of Kentucky and Alabama. The International Ladies Garment Workers tripled its membership to 200,000, and the Amalgamated Clothing Workers added 50,000 new recruits. It was from this reinvigorated centre of industrial unionism within the AFL that the demand for openly organizing along industrial lines was brought forward, and an active unionization drive in the mass production industries was launched. Since the existing craft unions within the AFL refused to give up jurisdiction over unorganized trades and declined to join in the aggressive organization drives in the steel, rubber, automobile, and textile industries, seven AFL-affiliated unions joined ranks with John L. Lewis, president of the United Mine Workers, and founded the Committee for Industrial Organization in November 1935.[33] In 1936, AFL president William Green expelled these unions on the grounds that they 'fostered dualism', but, in fact, it was the AFL that split the US trade union movement into a traditional craft union wing and a rapidly growing group of industrial unions. The latter established a permanent organizational structure under the name of Congress of Industrial Organizations (CIO).

The success of the CIO drive was spectacular. The Steelworkers Organizing Committee (SWOC) began to invade the steel centres, which had been softened up by subversive ERPs, in the summer of 1936. By March 1937, SWOC had won recognition by the US Steel Corporation, the nation's largest producer. By the summer of 1937, 'Big Steel', or 75 percent of the workforce employed in the industry, worked in organized plants. The aborted, bloody 'Little Steel Strike' of 1937 was only a temporary setback. With the steel mills running full blast in preparation for war, the 'Little Steel' corporations, one by one, succumbed to the union around 1941. In 1942, SWOC renamed itself United Steelworkers of America. The workers in the automobile industry gained recognition of their union by staging an unprecedented 44-day 'sit-down strike' in December 1936, refusing to leave their workplaces and virtually occupying their plants at General Motors in Detroit. This signified the importance of new loyalty bonds among workers, shaped by the cooperation in fully mechanized plants. State influence again played a decisive role, however. General Motors obtained a Michigan court injunction ordering the workers to leave 'private property', but Governor Frank Murphy refused to enforce the verdict by calling in the militia. Instead, he arbitrated a meeting of company officials and delegates of the United Auto Workers, who negotiated union recognition and a labor contract. When Chrysler and other big auto corporations followed suit within a year, another 'open shop' industry had been unionized. The auto workers' 'sit-down' tactics were copied by colleagues in rubber and textile factories, and 'lie-downs'—for lack of places to sit—even spread to department store chains like Woolworth's.

The Second World War saw the US trade union movement at the apogee of its power. The first peace-time year, 1946, was marked by a nationwide strike wave that shut down almost every major industry. 4.8 million workers participated in the walkouts; 116 million workdays were lost. Union membership had grown from 8 million (1940) to 14.5 million. By 1947, 'one-third of the nonagricultural labor force was unionized. Two out of five manufacturing workers, more than three out of four miners [and steelworkers], and more than seven out of eight construction workers' belonged to CIO- or AFL-affiliated unions.[34]

1950s to 1970s: The 'Gilded' Decades

The Second World War was also a turning point, however. The miners' strike of 1943, called by the United Mine Workers, had prompted a patriotic Congress to overrule Roosevelt's veto and pass the War Labor Disputes Act, which restricted strikes in times of national emergency and prohibited unions from funding candidates for political office. The War triggered public anti-union sentiment. Although the CIO had created, with the Political Action Committee, an influential political lobbying organization that had an impact on the Presidential and Congress elections of 1944, its pairing with the Democratic Party backfired in 1947, when the Republicans won majorities in both houses of Congress in reaction to the strikes of the previous year. Dependence on state guarantees thus made the unions vulnerable to the changing tides of party politics so long as labor-friendly legislation was not rooted deep enough in a general consensus of all parties. The Republicans hurried to initiate a rollback against organized labor. In 1947, Congress passed over a veto by President Truman, and legislated the Labor-Management Relations Act (Taft-Hartley Act), written by Senator Robert Taft, son of the former President and Supreme Court justice.

The system of institutionalized industrial relations that the NLRA had enacted already suffered from serious flaws. Unlike the works councils in

Germany, which communicated directly with corporate managers, US workers and their plant representatives had to resort to bureaucratic grievance procedures or appeals to the NLRB if they wanted conditions of employment changed. This made employee-employer interaction cumbersome and litigious. Although the NLRB had called for large bargaining units, collective bargaining remained decentralized. Most agreements were negotiated for individual companies or corporations, or even single shops. This forced the unions to continue their 'union shop' strategy. The Taft-Hartley Act now made centralized bargaining for entire regions or industries impossible. Its section 14b empowered the several states to ban not only the 'closed shop', but also the 'union shop'. The Act intervened deeply into the internal affairs of the unions, such as the 'check-off' of union dues and the collection of welfare provisions, and it obligated unions to file their constitutions and financial statements with the Labor Department. It curtailed eligibility for union membership and, for instance, proscribed foremen to join up. Strikes in times of emergencies or 'injurious to public health or safety' were placed under severe restrictions. The law also rehabilitated court injunctions that could postpone work stoppages for months.

Union lobbying for outright repeal of this 'slave labor statute' was intense but futile. Opposition soon concentrated on eliminating the particularly objectionable section 14b, which, indeed, eventually would weaken decisively the US trade union movement. The Taft-Hartley Act encouraged the individual states to enact labor relations laws that went far beyond its own regulations. States could ban not only union shop agreements between unions and employers, but also maintenance-of-membership clauses and other measures of union security that unions depended on in a system of fragmented collective bargaining. Predictably, the states, especially in the underdeveloped South, which was to become the fastest growing labor market after 1950, engaged in a 'race for the bottom' in terms of labor rights. Already by the end of 1947, twelve states had passed laws banning the 'union shop', and eventually all southern and southwestern states enacted 'right-to-work laws', which either destroyed local unions or made it impossible for them to get a foothold in local industry in the first place.

In 1955, the two rivalling union organizations settled their disputes and reunited to form the AFL-CIO, at that time still a massive force commanding 15 million dues-paying members. Union membership already had peaked, however, in 1953/54. The AFL-CIO remained entrenched in the industrial heartlands of the North. Here, industrial relations, although strained by major strikes, continued uncontested as long as the economic boom lasted, domestic demand grew, and comparatively high production costs could be passed on to the consumer. Yet the post–1945 era was marked by the fact that new, innovative, and labor-intensive industries—like aviation and defence—no longer settled in the industrial North, but migrated to the South and the West, which in the meantime had become mostly non-union territory. In the late 1960s, moreover, established industries started shifting capacities to the South. This not only stopped any further expansion of union membership, but also resulted in its steady decline.[35]

The importance of a social-political consensus beyond partisanship for the establishment of a stable, permanent system of organized industrial relations has nowhere been more clearly demonstrated than in Germany after 1945. Here, the experience of Weimar and National Socialism convinced the authors of the German Basic Law (*Grundgesetz*) to grant constitutional status to the right to organize (to both employees and employers) and to engage in industrial disputes for economic improvement. Article 9, section 3, became the legal foundation of the so-called 'collective bargaining autonomy' (*Tarifautonomie*), which meant that the state only guarantees the legal framework for agreements, which employee organizations and employers have to negotiate without state interference. Employees and their organizations were granted the right to enforce their positions by means of work stoppages; in return, the trade unions had to abstain from strikes as a political weapon. Elaborate strike procedures developed over the next decades in an interplay of pragmatic interaction in labor disputes and the positive evolution of case law in labor-related legal proceedings. Combined with centralized organization and the binding character of collective agreements for entire industrial districts, *Tarifautonomie* contributed greatly to the creation of large bargaining units and the emergence of 'forerunners', test negotiations between unions and employers in a single industry that then set the tone for the whole series of collective bargaining in other industrial sectors. All of this combined to greatly reduce the strike rate. Between 1955 and 1987, there were only five years in which the number of open industrial disputes exceeded 1,000, while in thirteen years less than one hundred strikes each occurred.[36] Germany's postwar economic ascent was doubtlessly fuelled by the most peaceful labor relations found across all of Europe.[37]

Immediately after the end of the war, grassroots union networks had again sprung up in most industries. Especially in heavy industry, they collaborated closely with employers in a combined effort to avert the projected dismantlement (*Demontage*) of production facilities by allied forces. This common resistance was successful in the three Western zones of occupation, whereas the Soviet Union enforced dismantlement in its own zone of occupation, the later German Democratic Republic (GDR). This new, more cooperative and trusting relationship between workforces and management translated into the revitalization of works councils (*Betriebsräte*), which now gained acceptance by employers throughout the major industries. The federal Works Constitutional Law (*Betriebsverfassungsgesetz*) of 1952 gave the works councils a legal basis and obligated them to play a constructive role in joint labor management. Furthermore, the law introduced labor co-management at the corporate level: it ruled that employee representatives were entitled to a third of the seats in corporate boards of directors. The Co-Management Law (*Mitbestimmungsgesetz*) of 1976 extended the number of labor representatives in the boards, but fell short of what the trade unions had achieved in heavy industry by means of free bargaining: the Basic Industry Co-Management Law (*Montanmitbestimmungsgesetz*) of 1951 prescribed that boards were staffed by five representatives of labor and employers at par, and that an eleventh member of the board had to be a neutral person elected by both parties (*paritätische Mitbestimmung*). One labor representative complemented central management in the rank of 'director of labor affairs' (*Arbeitsdirektor*). Unlike the US model, the German model of co-management embedded labor participation in the structure of corporate governance.

These legal entitlements to laborers and the expansion of the trade unions went hand in hand. Yet the ground for this unpredicted expansion was provided by a decisive political decision that finally liberated the unions from the *Kaiserreich* and Weimar legacy of ideological disunity. In 1949, the *Deutsche Gewerkschaftsbund* (DGB)—as the umbrella organization of, at that time, sixteen German industrial unions—was founded according to the principle of political unity (*Einheitsgewerkschaft*) that crossed party-political lines, even if the small white-collar workers union (*Deutsche Angestelltengewerkschaft*) defected as a special interest group, and the DGB would display a slight inclination to lean towards the Social Democratic Party (SPD) over the following decades. In the early 1950s, DGB membership already surpassed the 6 million mark. It rose continuously until 1981, when trade union membership peaked at about 8 million. Far into the 1970s, the DGB unions still remained a predominantly male organization; only then did women join ranks in substantial numbers, accounting for a fifth of total trade union membership in 1981.[38]

This long-term linear expansion stands out as another contrast to the more arc-shaped US development with its apogee in the early 1950s. The differential impact of the Taft-Hartley Act in the US and co-management in Germany was doubtlessly responsible for this increasing divergence. In some German industrial districts, most notably those shaped by heavy industry, chemicals or machine building and tool making, a close-knit network of ties between workplace peer groups, works councils, local union functionaries, and community politicians spread and came to dominate local social life and local politics for at least two generations. This was the basis of the rather late but thorough 'social democratization' of the Ruhr district during the 1950s, for instance. Big cities such as West Berlin, Hamburg, Cologne or Stuttgart developed very similar structures of patronage and mutual exchange. Here, trade union influence on the public sector was especially strong. In trade union and SPD strongholds of this kind, the degree of unionization in individual plants almost reached a 'union shop' level. Again, the centrality of the workplace for social life expressed itself in these developments at a time when industrial expansion still reigned supreme. This development was mirrored in the GDR, where the workshops fulfilled even more additional functions as welfare agencies and cadre units of local party and union organizations. The excessive burdening of the workplace with non-economic tasks—sometimes more persons acted as functionaries than worked in production—overcharged the GDR economy in the long run. During the 1950s and 1960s, however, the centrality of the workplace accounted for the closest approximation of the state-socialist to the 'Rhenish capitalist' regime of production.

As for labor and social legislation, the GDR played the role of an 'absent other' in the West German discourse. Its very existence made governments and employers more conciliatory to labor in matters of welfare and industrial relations. Neither this nor the accession to power by the SPD in the Grand Coalition after 1966 and the social-liberal coalition from 1969 to 1982, however, made it easy for the trade unions to win substantial legal concessions or place achievements reached in collective bargaining on a firm legal footing. Length-of-workday regulations never became law. Some statutes like the *Montanmitbestimmungsgesetz* of 1951 only retrospectively sanctioned a standard defined in free negotiations between employees and employers. Other laws, such as the reformed *Betriebsverfassungsgesetz* of 1971 or the *Mitbestimmungsgesetz* of 1976, fell far short of the unions' demands. Therefore, unions had a hard time in Germany, too, when they tried to push legal regulation beyond the minimal social consensus that guaranteed their very existence and ascribed them their role in society. They still had to rely on their own strength in order to maintain political clout.

1980s to Present: Under Attack by Globalization

The oil price shock of 1973 marked a turning of the economic tide in both nations. Yet in the US, industrial recession began earlier and ran deeper than in Germany. The old core of industrial America in particular came under existential pressure. During the 1980s, iron and steel and the automobile industry in the soon-to-be-called 'rust belt' of the East and industrial Midwest were shaken, as corporations with a long-standing tradition collapsed. Their workers faced mass layoffs, and a substantial number of the former prominent one-industry-towns, which had housed large factory complexes, now decayed to depleted wasteland. The US unions failed to meet this challenge. They proved unable to shelter their members in endangered plants from unemployment. Paradoxically, militant unions like the United Auto Workers still succeeded in winning favourable contracts for the works not yet eradicated by Asian competition. However, they lost ever more territory as the decade dragged on.

At the same time, industrial migration to the South and West continued on an even greater scale. The iron and steel industry shifted a substantial proportion of its capacities to modern 'mini-mills' in the non-union South, while closing down their giant, but dated plants in Pennsylvania, Ohio, and Indiana.[39] New industries, such as the computer and IT business, which would boom in the 1990s, chose locations near prestigious universities and clearly preferred a non-union environment. Since then, the 'offshoring' of jobs has affected all but the most high-tech of industries. Although deregulations during Ronald Reagan's presidency destroyed unionism in some public service sectors such as air traffic control, public service remains a sector with a comparatively high degree of unionization. This may coincide with the recent tendency of members of occupations commanding a high measure of expertise and individual indispensability to begin to discover unions as a powerful tool to further their collective interests. One could probably call this phenomenon the resurgence of craft unionism on a completely new level. As professional organizations, the US trade unions have gained remarkable success in staging unionization drives in formerly impenetrable territory. This has been true for the Latino agricultural laborers in California and the southwest after 2000. A major organization campaign is still under way in the retail industry, with Wal-Mart as a prime target.

In Germany's heavy industrial districts, structural crisis deepened during the later 1980s. Here, the tripartite coalition of unions, employers, and regional governments attempted to manage the 'structural change' (*Strukturwandel*) without recourse to mass layoffs. Early retirement schemes cushioned the massive reduction of workforces during the 1980s and 1990s. These policies prevented the emergence of industrial wastelands and ghost towns on a scale one could find in the US. Yet they severely burdened the welfare systems already pressured by demographic decline. Other regions, not protected by similar political coalitions, faced a more rapid and aggressive downsizing of their industries. In both types of territories, new businesses, such as the new media business around Cologne or software development industry in the vicinities of major technical universities and schools of applied science, replaced the 'old' industries, and sometimes occupied their deserted locations. But since these new economic activities revitalized only small patches of these vast industrial areas, they were only able to absorb a much lower number of people than had been employed during the heyday of industrialism.[40]

These developments have eaten away continuously at union membership since the early 1980s. German unification in 1990 has aggravated this situation. On the one hand, the downfall of the GDR removed the 'silent alternative' that had prompted employers and the state to uphold high welfare standards for political reasons, even in dire economic times. Therefore, the end of the Cold War opened Germany up for the unrestricted infiltration of globalization. On the other hand, unification resulted in the complete collapse of the industrial economy in the East. A whole generation of East German workers swelled the ranks of the unemployed, which had grown steadily in the West since the 1980s. Record unemployment and early retirement overburdened the welfare system even more. Resources for slowing down the 'de-structuring' of East German development were diverted from the West, but failed to stem the tide. The unions suffered severely in the process. They have withdrawn to a defensive position against both cuts into the welfare system, which all major parties are promoting in the face of exhausted public budgets, and an outright attack by neo-liberal political forces in Germany on the social-political consensus that was a central foundation of the old Bundesrepublik.

Notes

1. W. Sombart, *Warum gibt es in den Vereinigten Staaten keinen Sozialismus?* (Tübingen, 1906).
2. W. Abelshauser, *Kulturkampf. Der deutsche Weg in die Neue Wirtschaft und die amerikanische Herausforderung* (Berlin, 2003).
3. B. Laurie, *Artisans into Workers. Labor in Nineteenth-Century America* (New York, 1989).
4. The Civil War marked the introduction of confectionary sizes for clothes, shoes, and hats; after that, production for an anonymous market became possible on a large scale. See W. C. Davis and B.I. Wiley, eds., *The Civil War* (New York, 1983/1984).
5. C.L. Tomlins, *The State and the Unions. Labor Relations, Law, and the Organized Labor Movement in America, 1880–1960* (Cambridge, 1985).
6. D. Montgomery, *The Fall of the House of Labor. The Workplace, the State, and American Labor Activism, 1865–1925* (Cambridge, 1987).
7. F. Lenger, *Sozialgeschichte der deutschen Handwerker seit 1800* (Frankfurt a.M., 1988).
8. T. Offermann, *Die erste deutsche Arbeiterpartei. Organisation, Verbreitung und Sozialstruktur von ADAV und LADAV 1863–1871* (Bonn, 2002).
9. Quoted in: T. Welskopp, *Das Banner der Brüderlichkeit. Die deutsche Sozialdemokratie vom Vormärz bis zum Sozialistengesetz* (Bonn, 2000), 592, 640.

10. Ibid., 495.
11. Ibid., 288f.
12. US Senate Committee on Education and Labor, *Report upon the Relations between Labor and Capital*, vol.1 (Washington, DC, 1885), 316.
13. R.E. Weir, *Beyond Labor's Veil. The Culture of the Knights of Labor* (University Park, PA, 1996).
14. Figures from: D.B. Robertson, *Capital, Labor, and State. The Battle for American Labor Markets from the Civil War to the New Deal* (Lanham, MD/Oxford, 2000), 24.
15. P. Krause, *The Battle for Homestead, 1880–1892. Politics, Culture, and Steel* (Pittsburgh/London, 1992).
16. Figures and detailed analysis in: T. Welskopp, *Arbeit und Macht im Hüttenwerk. Arbeits- und industrielle Beziehungen in der deutschen und amerikanischen Eisen- und Stahlindustrie von den 1860er bis zu den 1930er Jahren* (Bonn, 1994), 166ff.
17. Robinson, *Capital, Labor, and State*, 104f.
18. J. Rees, *Managing the Mills. Labor Policy in the American Steel Industry during the Nonunion Era* (Dallas, 2004).
19. Quoted in: Robinson, *Capital, Labor, and State*, 70.
20. F. Boll, *Arbeitskämpfe und Gewerkschaften in Deutschland, England und Frankreich. Ihre Entwicklung vom 19. zum 20. Jahrhundert* (Bonn, 1992).
21. I. Steinisch, *Arbeitszeitverkürzung und sozialer Wandel. Der Kampf um die Achtstundenschicht in der deutschen und amerikanischen Eisen- und Stahlindustrie 1880–1929* (Berlin/New York, 1986).
22. D. Brody, *Labor in Crisis. The Steel Strike of 1919* (Philadelphia/New York, 1965).
23. W. Plumpe, *Betriebliche Mitbestimmung in der Weimarer Republik. Fallstudien zum Ruhrbergbau und zur chemischen Industrie* (Munich, 1999).
24. Welskopp, *Arbeit und Macht im Hüttenwerk*, 661ff.
25. K.-M. Mallmann, *Kommunisten in der Weimarer Republik. Sozialgeschichte einer revolutionären Bewegung* (Darmstadt, 1996).
26. I. Bernstein, *The Lean Years. A History of the American Worker 1920–1933* (Boston, 1972).
27. G. Adams, *Age of Industrial Violence 1910–15. The Activities and Findings of the United States Commission on Industrial Relations* (New York/London, 1966).
28. J. Landesco, *Organized Crime in Chicago. Part III of The Illinois Crime Survey 1929* (Chicago/London, 1968).
29. Quoted in: M.B. Schnapper, *American Labor. A Pictorial Social History* (Washington, DC, 1972), 439.
30. 'What Hoover's Smashing Victory Means', *Literary Digest* (17 Nov. 1928): 6.
31. L. Cohen, *Making a New Deal. Industrial Workers in Chicago, 1919–1939* (Cambridge, 1990).
32. Welskopp, *Arbeit und Macht im Hüttenwerk*, 610ff.
33. I. Bernstein, *Turbulent Years. A History of the American Worker 1933–1941* (Boston, 1970).

34. Robertson, *Capital, Labor, and State*, 261.
35. J.P. Hoerr, *And The Wolf Finally Came. The Decline of the American Steel Industry* (Pittsburgh, 1988).
36. Figures in: M. Schneider, *Kleine Geschichte der Gewerkschaften. Ihre Entwicklung in Deutschland von den Anfängen bis heute* (Bonn, 1989), 500.
37. G. Müller, *Strukturwandel und Arbeitnehmerrechte. Die wirtschaftliche Mitbestimmung in der Eisen- und Stahlindustrie 1945–1975* (Essen, 1981).
38. J. Angster, *Konsenskapitalismus und Sozialdemokratie. Die Westernisierung von SPD und DGB* (Munich, 2003).
39. Hoerr, *The Wolf Finally Came*.
40. W. Hindrichs et al., *Der lange Abschied vom Malocher. Sozialer Umbruch in der Stahlindustrie und die Rolle der Betriebsräte von 1960 bis in die neunziger Jahre* (Essen, 2000).

CHAPTER 8

Visions of the Future:

GDR, CSSR, and the Federal Republic of Germany in the 1960s

JÖRG REQUATE

Since the collapse of the SED regime, calls for a comparative embedding of GDR history have been raised ever more, and have been in part fulfilled. Three perspectives are to be differentiated: firstly, a comparison with 'the other German dictatorship'; secondly, a comparison with other socialist states; and, thirdly, a comparison with the Federal Republic. Most theoretical and methodological approaches have been concerned with comparisons of dictatorships.[1] Despite extensive agreement in principle that such comparisons are sensible and necessary, their not insubstantial methodological problems have been emphasized, so that empirical work in this area has, up until now, remained limited to a few aspects.[2] Comparisons between the socialist states of the Eastern Bloc are relatively less problematic methodologically and have increased in recent years.[3] More than concrete comparisons, such studies have tended to explore and emphasize transnational processes and influences. Key themes in this area are 'Sovietizing' processes on the one hand, and, on the other hand, anti-Americanism, both approaches that notably permit cross-systemic perspectives.[4]

For research regarding the two German states, questions about opposing 'divisions and overlaps' have proven to be a promising source of contrasting comparisons.[5] Comparisons that take Western democracies as the standard of measurement and, above all, challenge the deficits of dictatorial regimes may be politically legitimate, but even at their best do little to take into account the particular momentum of non-democratic societies. A pure comparison of particular developments would be more suitable, but would nevertheless lack, in the underlying sense of the comparison, that *tertium comparationis*. Such comparisons emerge when one assumes that both systems encountered similar challenges, to which they responded in very different manners. Not long ago, Kaspar Masse remarked correctly that such an approach relies on the assumption that both German societies were concerned with industrial societies and saw themselves facing cross-systemic demands of modernization.[6] Such approaches found their defining expression in so-called 'convergence theory', which, at the time, came to have significant meaning for political scientists and economists, as well as policy advisors. The theory is based on the premise that both great societal systems—especially in the form of their main representatives, the USA and the USSR—were concerned above all with industrial societies, regardless of their political differences. This also implied the assumption that both societies faced ultimately similar conditions and needs, which in turn were defined to a great extent by technical progress on the one hand, and the necessities of efficient organization, on the other. Because the adherents of this theory assumed further that these external 'material conditions', along with increasing scientification at the core of both systems, would lead to similar solutions, the convergence of both systems appeared from this perspective as a logical outcome.[7]

That history took another course is known and requires no repeating here. The notion that a convergence of systems—the capitalist-orientated Western democracies and the socialist-based dictatorial systems of the 'Eastern Bloc'—should have occurred appears from today's perspective as, at a minimum, adventurous. From the perspective of the 1960s, it appeared differently: the theory that the two great systems were facing similar problems, which would lead them to develop similar solutions, and from a certain standpoint could therefore come to a 'convergence', possessed considerable attraction for many political scientists and sociologists at the time. It makes little sense now to uncover the error of these theories in a retrospective engagement. The interesting question, instead, is which real historical developments led to the acceptance of convergence theory, and whether, at the time, there were actually cross-systemic developments and perspectives on developments that appeared to substantiate a convergence of systems, or at least would take on a common set of developmental processes. Thus, the thesis reads that convergence theory deliberations reflected the primacy of a thought process in line with feasibility and 'planability', which was, in turn, based on a conception of perpetual economic growth and technical progress. From the US perspective, the historian David Farber describes the 1960s as the 'age of great dreams'. He saw the basis for these dreams in the interplay of a strong and steady economic growth with manifold hopes for social and cultural change.[8] Burkhard Lutz similarly characterized the first thirty postwar years as a perpetual dream of prosperity, and Jean Fourastié in France termed them *trente glorieuses*.[9]

Even though these diagnoses were posed from a Western point of view, it should be emphasized that they comprised the perspective of a global economic boom that included both the West and the East. The problems of convergence assumptions from the Eastern perspective will be addressed. From the Western perspective, however, it appeared in the 1960s that even the socialist industrial states in no way occupied a precarious economic position, but, rather, shared in a clear-cut, long-term phase of prosperity that included societal systems on both sides of the 'iron curtain'. Lyndon B. Johnson's 'Great Society', Erhard's *Formierte Gesellschaft* (Formed Society), and Ulbricht's 'Socialist Human Community', taken separately, exhibited great differences. But they were similar in that they were relatively contemporaneous, appearing in the first half of the 1960s, and, moreover, because they comprised common visions of a social future.[10] On this basis, convergence theory assumptions were also based on a spirit of prognosis, which was expressed in future-oriented ideas specific to the 1960s.

These cross-systemic 'revolutions in the future' will be examined further in what follows.[11] The GDR and the Federal Republic of Germany thus build a core to which other countries, in particular the CSSR, can be added. From the system-comparative perspective, Czechoslovakia proves to be an especially illuminating comparison with the GDR. Because of discussions about economic reforms, which were held also in other socialist states in the 1960s, these debates continued most conspicuously in Prague and Bratislava. Methodologically, the inclusion of a comparison between countries of the same 'bloc' in a comparison of systems has an invaluable advantage, because generalizations on the basis of a particular country can be avoided. Practically, however, this requires a limitation to discrete aspects. For this purpose, a short overview of convergence theory approaches will be given. Subsequently to the overview, four areas will be discussed, in which, at least for a certain time, there were cross-systemic developments. To a certain extent, on account of classical economic framing conditions, the debates about and approaches to new economic concepts and reforms make up the first main point. The reciprocal and particularly provocative disposition of market and planning-based concepts will play an important role. The second focus will be on the scientific, political, and fictional levels of the explicitly future-oriented characteristics of both societal systems during the 1960s. A central element of their conception of the future was 'scientification', that is, the concrete, scientifically based planning of social processes. The third focal point will concentrate on these debates and their related problems. The debate about the forced creation and appointment of experts as 'human capital' will take up a central role and be considered along with contributions from various perspectives.

Even though the influence of Rostow was a cornerstone of convergence theory—inasmuch as the view was held that socialist societies would ultimately develop into consumer societies and that they would conform to 'the

West'—questions about lifestyle in a wider and cultural sense rarely played a role. The 'cultural revolution' (Hobsbawm) of the 1960s was nevertheless clearly a transnational phenomenon, whose relationship with technocratic orientation toward the future is admittedly difficult to define. In a fourth point, therefore, questions about these relationships will be raised, and at the same time it will be made clear how differently the respective social systems in the East and West were able to integrate the cultural uprisings that occurred.

Convergence of Systems? Memories of a Lost Theory

Similar to the 'theory of the modern' and in many ways related to it, convergence theory is less a contained theoretical construct than a conglomerate of different theoretical approaches and assumptions that rest on a common basis. These primary assumptions state that all developing industrial societies, independent of their political composition, are confronted principally with the same social prerequisites and challenges. To what extent and in which way the systems assimilate under these conditions remains controversial—not least in relation to the political implications that are tied to them. Besides sharing the same common basic theoretical assumptions, the theories are also similar in that they both are bound closely to political valuations of the systems' development.

This was entirely obvious to one of the founding proponents of convergence theory, the US economist Walt Whitman Rostow, who belonged to the John F. Kennedy Braintrust and, at the end of the 1950s, who formulated his considerations about the 'phases of economic growth', with the unmistakable purpose of breaking the monopoly of Marxist social theory on conceptions of the future.[12] Rostow proposed a type of phase model of economic growth, at the end of which stood the highly developed consumer society. The path to this point, however, could be laid out differently. The Marxist path stood more or less on the same level as the liberal-democratic alternative. Rotstow's central argument stated, however, that societies only would be ripe for, and vulnerable to, Marxism during the first phase of the industrialization process. In this sense, Russia was a model case for his argument. The collapse of Russian society in the First World War was met with a phase of strong economic growth. This constellation, according to Rostow, created particularly fertile ground for the rise of the Communist Party. Rostow saw the initial process of further industrialization in the communist states as not hindered, but rather, even under great brutality, fuelled by dictatorship. In the last phase of industrialization, the phase of mass consumption, however, dictators would not survive due to the democratizing effects of this process, according to Rostow. Communism was, in Rostow's perspective, a 'transitional sickness' that would be overcome in the age of mass consumption.[13] This all spoke in favour of the view that further economic growth would bury Communism. The leadership of the Soviet Union, which had already grasped this in principle, tried, in the 1950s, to prevent an economy of high mass consumption primarily in order to protect the dominance of the Communist Party.[14]

From the Marxist perspective, such analyses relied not only on 'false notions about historical progress, and the character and structure of societies', but, at the same time, also appeared as 'new versions of imperialist strategic planning'.[15] The fact that Rostow and other representatives of similar ideas were in the senior staff of the Kennedy administration appeared, from this perspective, as evidence that no pure scientific opinions would be found there. Rostow's thoughts, rather, possessed from this perspective a clear 'counter-revolutionary function' of imperialist intention.[16]

This rejection of Rostow's position from the Marxist perspective is, however, in retrospect much less surprising than the predicted type of demise. For it is not due to economic weakness, as Rostow prophesized, but, rather, economic success that Communism eventually perished. Zbingiew Brzezinski and Samuel P. Huntington, therefore, also remarked in their debate with convergence theory that in this perspective, the United States appeared as 'prosperous and free', but also ultimately as 'static' in contrast with the dynamic Soviet Union.[17] In reality, one can hardly emphasize enough that the foundation of convergence theory is to be found in the shared belief on the Western side that Communism was an enormously successful economic system. The—at least official—growth figures for the Soviet Union were certainly perceived as impressive in the West, and the Sputnik shock of 1957 contributed to the image of a highly technically and economically developed system.[18] US politics and political counsel became concerned thereupon with downright fearful amazement at the development of the Soviet economy. At a Congressional hearing in 1959 regarding a comparison between the US and Soviet economies, CIA Chief Allen Dulles testified that the growth rate of industrial production in the USSR in the last eight years had been twice as great as in the USA. If the growth rate of Soviet industry remained at 8 or 9 percent for the next decade and the US economy continued to grow as it had, the industrial gap between the economies of both countries nearly would be closed.[19]

Against this background, convergence theory approaches also experienced a change in perspective. In place of Rostow's prophecy of a pivoting of communist regimes toward the liberal-democratic pattern of Western systems, ever more voices emerged that conceived of a real convergence between West and East, instead of a single-sided pivoting of the socialist systems toward the capitalist models. In this vein, the US economist John

Kenneth Galbraith published in 1967 his writing about 'the New Industrial State' and provoked a furore well beyond the academic community.[20] Galbraith explicitly suggested that capitalism make use of one of the central elements of socialist economies, namely, planning. The reason for his suggestion was rooted less in a particular sympathy for the socialist states than in a belief in their efficiency. Indeed, the increased demands for a turn toward a more planned economy that one finds in Galbraith and others certainly should not be interpreted as an orientation toward Soviet methods of economic governance. The apparent success of the Soviet economy made it seem advisable in the eyes of many economists to once again turn to theorists—primarily John Meynard Keynes—who regarded global interference in the economic process as necessary and beneficial. Against the background of the Sputnik shock, the reference to the Soviet growth figures played primarily a provocative role in promoting the concept of planning and paving the way for new economic-political methods. Technical progress and rational planning were guarantees of success for both systems, and not just in Galbraith's view. The race to space and to the moon symbolized policies targeted at the future for both systems. These policies not only held the future closely in view, but also made it 'able to be planned'.

Tightly bound to the belief in the growing influence of technology and planning was also a notion that the power of technicians and planners was increasing, even in the communist states and, therefore, the power of ideology would be diminished. Here lay perhaps the most fatal error of convergence theory. As the following examples will demonstrate, no debates over economic reforms, the shape of the future or the necessity of a strengthened management would lead to the rise of a 'non-political' techno-planning elite. There were, indeed, as will be shown next in a comparison between Czechoslovakia and the GDR, different forums for 'technical', 'non-political' debates. Nevertheless, the level of 'anti-politicization' was always only relative, and not just in the communist states.

On the Way to a Fusion of Market and Planned Economies?

Even though the convergence theory approaches sketched out above had their origins and were most intensively discussed in the US, this in no way means that Europe was not present in the discussions. The French sociologist Raymons Aron made one of the most significant contributions to the subject outside of the US in his 1963 book, *Société industrielle*.[21] The debate was received broadly and collectively across Europe.[22] Nevertheless, in many convergence theory works of US origin, the geographical distance between the United States and the 'Eastern Bloc' played a significant role, as the actual economic problems of the socialist states were taken infrequently into account. An intensive engagement with the real economic situation of the Warsaw Pact states would possibly have yielded a less threatening image. The shift toward planned concepts in the West, despite ever higher and more constant growth figures, can hardly be explained as the result of an actual crisis. Economists in the East, in contrast, precisely due to growing economic problems, looked for opportunities to integrate market instruments into the planned economy.[23] One need only look at Poland, Czechoslovakia or the GDR to gather that in all three countries at the end of the 1950s and beginning of the 1960s, questions about reforms and changes to the planned economic system were being posed.[24] After the economies in all three countries initially gained momentum under Soviet-style planned economy and, in part, even achieved high growth figures, political and economic crises increasingly began to emerge. Common to the reform debates in all three countries was that they would not proceed without reference to the Soviet Union. A basic assumption, thereby, was increasing de-Stalinization, in particular after the XX Party Congress of the Communist Party. More strikingly, however, was that, in all three countries, the 'reformers' argued more and more with Soviet authors in order to legitimize their reform positions. The second overall commonality was that the debates always ended and provoked backlashes when discussed and suggested measures were perceived as attempting to form a new system. Thirdly, and lastly, the question of in which organs, from which persons, and in which public division the reform issues would be discussed played a major role. Where, however, the borders lay in detail and in which forums the debates would be made available, differed among the three countries in question. But at the outset, it can be held that, in light of the chronology of the debate, the GDR and the CSSR were decidedly more similar than Poland, where, already considerably earlier and in particular in 1956, a kind of 'reform euphoria' had taken hold and subsequently died down.

When one turns to the GDR and Czechoslovakia, the work of André Steiner for the GDR and Maria Köhler-Baur for Czechoslovakia appear to be in agreement that the origin of the reform debate can be found in a deep economic crisis, the resolution of which was tightly tied to the political legitimacy of the regime.[25] The recognition that the pressing problems could not be solved with instruments of the existing economic system led to a search for new methods of political economy and the approach to reform in both countries. Common to the debate was also that, in a certain mirror image analogy to the West, the at times taboo concept of the market formed a partially explicit and partially implicit reference point in the efforts to reform. The debate in the GDR was, thereby, in several respects under much greater constraints than in neighbouring countries to the south. Applying a clever use of Khrushchev's notion of a decentralized economy, a group of economists, including the Prague Academy of Science, developed visions of reform that broke away from the thought schema outlined above. That the academy in this time frame had become a sort of reservoir of experts and researchers who did not conform to the official party line played a significant role. Indeed, the debate in Czechoslovakia remained limited for the most part to the academic community and academic institutions, in which it could evolve comparatively 'freely'. 'Free' in this sense meant, above all, that the concept of the market could be discussed openly and even beyond the limits of basic systemic foundations without discussions being brought to an end. 'Freely' also meant that the participating researchers could represent their thoughts relatively unhindered in foreign journals. The influence of these debates and of the concrete visions of economists on policies nevertheless remained minor in Czechoslovakia. In 1965, the Economic Commission of the Central Committee of the Communist Party, indeed, did seize the initiative to reform the current system and made verbal arguments to Ota Šik at the suggestion of the economists at the Academy of Sciences. In the end, though, the taboos of the socialist economic system remained undisturbed, and 'reforms' were limited to a few small corrections within the system.

Notwithstanding this, and, above all, in comparison to the GDR, the openness of the academic discussion in Czechoslovakia remained remarkable. In contrast to Czechoslovakia, the scholarly debate in the GDR remained more tightly bound to politics. A similar space for comparatively free discussion did not develop, therefore, in the GDR.[26] Indeed, on the contrary, the state and party leadership were involved closely in the considerations of reform. Thus, more meaning was attributed to economic rationality in the phase of the debate over a 'new economic system' than in earlier periods. The reforms that were actually implemented, however, remained clearly within the framework of the planned economic status quo. 'Market-economic' elements could serve to make the plan more efficient, but should in no way develop their own momentum. The possibility of a 'self-regulating device' remained, even in the reform phase of the 1960s, greatly limited. When one looks at Poland and at the reforms that were actually introduced there, it is not surprising that they soon pushed on the limits of the existing system. The comparison with Poland, however, is enlightening from a different perspective: as mentioned previously, the chronology of the debate in Poland progressed quite differently than in the GDR and CSSR. The strike of 1956, as well as the election of Gomulka as party chief of the Polish Workers' Party only shortly after being released from prison, led, already in this phase, to reforms of economic policy, which relied principally on approaches that were later employed in the CSSR. Even in Poland, these attempts at short 'reform euphoria' were nevertheless bogged down or were simply undone.²⁷ During the 1960s in other socialist countries, there was an atmosphere of revolution in economic policy, whereas in Poland, the 1960s were characterized by disenchantment. The reform debates of the 1960s—in certain ways parallel to the other socialist states—were present in Poland, but because the economic situation there was distinctly better than in comparable countries at this time, these debates were limited for the most part to academic circles. If Poland's position in the years before 1968 had been precarious and isolated—as was the case in the other socialist states—the discussion about 'market-based elements' in the planned economy would have ceased entirely.

Looking at the Federal Republic, one sees a mirror image reversal of this debate, as mentioned previously. There was also in the Federal Republic a removal of taboos and a semantic shift in connection with the notion of planning.²⁸ Despite the undeniable upsurge in economic circles that the notion took, 'Keynesian', 'global-steering' schools of thought in reality played a clearly subordinate role in the macroeconomic academic debate. Georg Altmann, in a new publication about the economic and labour market politics of the 1960s, also rejects the notion that, under the influence of a possible generational or elite transition, there was a sharp shift in economic policies from a liberal, Erhardtist slant to a Keynesian, Schillerist slant.²⁹ The Stability Act of 1967 appeared in continuity with longer, gradual developments, and not as the result of a sudden change in course. The apparent success of the law, to which overcoming the economic crisis of 1966/67 was attributed, contributed significantly to a vision of the controllability of the economy, which would be deflated by no later than 1973. Thus, Altmann attributes, with good reason, the high expectations for the 'plannability' of the economy that were held for a short time in the Federal Republic much more to the general incipient scientific and future-oriented planning euphoria than to the change in general economic conditions or a paradigm shift in the scholarly economic debate. It was only against this background that the 'East' and 'West' actually moved closer together than in the real economic questions, as will be shown in both of the following sketched out themes. In the area of economics, the alternating uses of market and planning concepts indeed served, up to a certain level, as a targeted provocation in the respective debates. The general conditions for the debates, however, differed greatly, and the economic systems remained in tact.

Technocracy and Future Prognosis

Although futurology and its fictional treatment had its origins long before the 1960s, the boom of scientific, popular, and fantasy-based engagement with the future grew unmistakably during that era.³⁰ Far more apparent than the convergence tendencies of economic systems, this constituted an array of phenomena and developments characterizing the 1960s similarly in both the 'West' and the 'East'. A fundamental difference should nevertheless be pointed out here: the socialist systems, as is known, were based on the notion of being on the side of constant scientific progress and thus were on the way toward a principally predictable future. Here lay a basic difference compared with the essentially open view of the future held in the Western democracies. All the more striking, then, was that in the 1960s, both systems viewed the future with a new quality that, at least in part, displayed astounding parallels. The reasons behind this were of both an economic and a technical nature: the fast reconstruction following the Second World War was paired with groundbreaking technical innovations, which were particularly visible in the area of space travel and served to greatly expand the imagination of what was feasible. Against this background, the year 2000 formed a kind of magic date that symbolized the future and its rapid approach, encompassing both its promise and its threat.[31] Thus, parallel to the undeniable optimism toward progress, a consciousness of the risks and the potential threat of future developments arose, at the height of which stood demographic changes and a predicted population explosion. From this position between optimism about progress and insight into potential threats, on both sides of the 'iron curtain', there developed a fixation on the future with the consideration that its planning is necessary, as well as possible.

This boom of future-orientation was demonstrated, among other things, in the founding of a multitude of 'think tanks' and *Ideenagenturen*, which specialized increasingly in prognoses in a comprehensive sense.[32] In France, the Commissariat Général du Plan, as the highest-ranking administrative official since the end of the Second World War through the 1970s, coordinated French national economic planning.[33] Similar planning and development commissions existed in Belgium, the Netherlands, and Sweden. Even in Great Britain, the framework of the National Plan between 1964 and 1970 was developed through the work of national or half-national institutions, such as the Committee on the Next Thirty Years of the Social Science Research Centre or the National Economic Development Council. In Eastern Europe, in the USSR, the GDR, Poland, Romania, and the CSSR, prognostic, planning-based studies also emerged at the end of the 1960s, though they were admittedly carried out less within institutions founded for that purpose than conducted within the framework of their existing scholarly communities.[34] In methodological as well as contextual hindsight, US institutes, such as the RAND Corporation (founded 1948) or the Hudson Institute (founded 1961), were leading the world in such studies. At the same time, they served as models for Western European institutes, such as the Paris-based *Association Futuribles Internationale*, founded by

Bertrand de Jouvenel in 1960, the British-American Institute for the Future and, finally, the Berlin *Zentrum für Zukunftsforschung* (1968–1981). From an international perspective, this comparatively late internationalization, which had already been lamented by contemporaries, underscored once more the permanent separation of the Federal Republic from the GDR. The negative image of the 'planned economy' in the 'Eastern Bloc' and particularly in the GDR discredited general concepts of social planning in public opinion far into the 1960s.

In part through direct connection with the institutions mentioned above and in part independently, there developed an array of specifically future-oriented periodicals, such as *Futuribles* in France, *Futures—The Journal of Forecasting and Planning* in England, *Analysen und Prognosen über die Welt von Morgen* and the monthly journal *Atomzeitalter. Zeitschrift für Sozialwissenschaften und Politik* (1959–1971) in the Federal Republic. Moreover, there was an extraordinary boom in the book market for future studies. A complete and current bibliography in the middle of the 1970s would show that, during the end of the 1960s and beginning of the 1970s, between eighty and 120 publications in the English language alone were released that were focused predominately on questions about the future. The years 1970 and 1972 evidenced the highest rate of publication. A list of the most significant works of future-oriented research identifies a figure of around seventy-five authors, who not only wrote the most important works of future-oriented research, but also at the same time campaigned intensively for its institutionalization.[35]

In addition, general political institutions worked more and more with prognoses and predictions. A survey by the Organisation of Economic Cooperation and Development (OECD) from the beginning of the 1960s identified at least one hundred organizations worldwide that in some form systematically engaged with prognoses. A survey between 1968 and 1970 of the Council of Europe regarding long-term prognoses identified a count of around three hundred (national, semi-national or private) organizations, including general think tanks,[36] which, while not specialized in future research, nevertheless had a prognostic focus.[37] Furthermore, it is noteworthy that, at this time, the fictional counterpart of futurology, science fiction, experienced a boom in both the East and the West. Behind and outside the 'iron curtain', this literature inspired by technology and a belief in progress, which also dealt with the subjugation of foreign galaxies and defence against enemy attacks, experienced a remarkable upswing. In both societal systems, science fiction, or *wissenschaftliche Phantastik*, as the genre was called in the GDR in accordance with Russian language conventions, was not limited to these topics, but, rather, took on an increasingly sociopolitical dimension.[38] The range of 'social fiction' proved to be much wider in the West, however. Here also it is evident that the particular type of future-orientation of the 1960s, together with the obvious parallel developments of 'scientific progress' in both the East and the West, raised significant problems for precisely the system it had promised to improve. This was made clear in the criticism aimed at 'scientific progress' from the orthodox position: critics complained that 'fantasy' literature did not account for the evolution of communism. As these perspectives on visions of the future fell by the wayside, so did the clear differences between the visions of the future of both systems.

The extent to which a great convergence in the 'scientification' of the world became precarious from the perspective of the socialist states can be seen in the temporary boom of cybernetics. Cybernetics symbolized the tendency in both systems to subject social development to scientifically verified regulation. The notion of a regulation based on permanent feedback—which contradicted the laws of thermodynamics—created a dual problem in the socialist states, and particularly in the GDR, which was made clear through the fate of the prominent GDR cyberneticist Georg Klaus.[39] First, Klaus repeatedly referred to the development of cybernetics in the West, not least in order to emphasize the comprehensive trend of this specific form of scientification. He also emphasized, though, fundamental systemic differences: while the West turned to cybernetics as a method of regulation, so the argument goes, it nevertheless missed the proper goal of regulation. Only Marxism-Leninism could claim to have done this. This argument succeeded, at least temporarily, in fending off the suspicion of ideological weakening through excessive reliance on technocratic approaches. This fundamental suspicion nevertheless remained in existence, especially as the idea of cybernetics brought along a second problem. Feedback ultimately meant co-determination from below, because regulation could only function when the appropriate information came back from the system. However, in this lay the fundamental problem of the system in general, because this would have meant that one would have to confront empirical problems. These problems applied not only for ideas of cybernetics, but also for the notion of scientification generally. Because its consequential implementation would inevitably have led to a surrender of power from the parties to experts, systemic questions would quickly be raised. Thus, it is no wonder that in the GDR, as in the CSSR after the abolition of the Prague Spring, the programme of scientification was put to rest.

'Human Capital' and Scientification

Both of these concepts belonged to the 'plastic words' of the 1960s, in which objectives and diagnoses mixed. Following the postwar boom in the

East and the West, the belief that the scientific revolution was necessary in order to enable economic growth on a broader stepladder, to meet social demand through increased production, and to expand policy capabilities united politicians, planners of the future, and scientists. Tied to these assumptions about development was the necessity to assemble qualified manpower and to make science the determining productive factor in the planning of change. The case of France demonstrates how differently these tendencies were incorporated in individual societies. There, already at the beginning of the 1960s, a new working class was being spoken of in industrial sociology, which was different from traditional industrial workforces and instead composed of technical intelligence.[40] Planning on the other side of the Rhine—other than in the Federal Republic—could not have implemented any process of removing taboos, otherwise its dictatorial form would have been bared and adopted into Gaullism in order to promote the economic and social modernization of the country. Sketching out the differing responses of individual national societies to the problems in question forms an interesting chapter in a comparative history of the 1960s.

The transfer from a socially exclusive system of education to a general right to education occurred in the GDR in the postwar period and in the 1950s and led not only to an increase in the number of graduates from secondary schools, but also to a democratization of entry to universities.[41] In the 1960s, this edge gained by the GDR over the Federal Republic diminished, because the necessity of stronger educational efforts was henceforth recognized west of the Elbe. In the GDR, by contrast, starting from the end of the 1960s and onward, a massive advancement in technical intelligence turned out to be in contradiction with political aims and was therefore driven back. In this way, the debates over education differed considerably during this period in both German states. Although the protagonists of the debates in both states shared the belief that the future of the societies in systemic competition depended upon the general level of education, the education debate in the GDR remained tightly limited to a circle of experts, while in the Federal Republic it was led broadly and controversially in the public. Georg Picht's 1964 critique of the 'German education catastrophe' was famously the origin of a public debate that was informed by international comparison.[42] It was precisely against this background that the traditional, civic vision of education, which in the postwar period led to the restoration of the three-level school system and universities, appeared to be overhauled.[43] The promotion of what had become the proverbial 'Catholic girl from the country' remained, indeed, for the most part simply a lip service of education politics, but at least demonstrated how deeply principles of social justice had affected the education debate in the Federal Republic; while in the GDR, they had tended to lose meaning. For the most part, as the GDR society defined itself as 'classless', questions about 'underprivileged' strata were no longer posed, which as a result led to an increasing self-recruitment of the 'cadre'. Even if the education system in the Federal Republic actually had not been open to the masses, as the permanent refrain of 'equal opportunity' suggested, the catchphrase 'education as a civil right' set a new tone in the education debate that went beyond questions purely about the new recruiting of 'human capital'.[44]

Tightly bound to the debate over the necessary construction of the education system was, in both German states, the development of professionalized consulting and expert bodies. The business cycle of education economists began with the attempt to determine, from an extrapolation of economic growth, the demand for university graduates or, as the case may be, to deduce the attractiveness of university careers from social processes, such as expectations of individual mobility and advancement. Although the planning perspective in the Federal Republic had been discredited by the GDR example and found no place in the liberal market platform of the CDU, the Scientific Council, for example, was founded in 1957.[45] In addition, attempts at planning sprung up in various departments at the beginning of the 1960s. Many examples demonstrate, however, that the planning approach and the belief in the prognostic capacity of scientific experts developed in no way parallel to their institutionalization.[46] Above all, conservative camps were sceptical of the democratic legitimacy of professional experts.

The SPD dwelled for a certain period in planning euphoria. But soon the limited range of sweeping planning-based designs was made clear, and the opposition of the civil service had gained the upper hand over the academic competition. Nevertheless, sociologists and political scientists in the 1960s had prepared a vocabulary and knowledge base that could be used to analyse developments within the Federal Republic and in an international context. The transfer of planning models from the Anglo-Saxon, and, above all, US realm stood on the agenda, and international comparison, in which the institutions of the Federal Republic would be put to the test, now belonged to the arsenal of 'comparative politics'. This internationalization of domestic and social problems in the Federal Republic surely counts among the most lasting effects of the broad debate over policy planning, expert knowledge, and future prognoses. In Czechoslovakia and the GDR, similar debates took place. The parallels between the themes are, indeed, astonishing. In the place of sociology and systems theory stood Marxist social science and cybernetics. Above all, though, party and national leaders tried to use the debates regarding methods of development and the necessity of changes to concentrate power and not to carry them publicly out. This appears to have occurred with varying degrees of success. The GDR leadership organized the debates over consumption and societal politics in research groups, which informed the party leaders, without allowing the groups to submit their results for discussion in accessible publications.

In Czechoslovakia, the homogeneity and the level of organization of the national and party leadership were less great, either because an intellectual opposition elite existed within the party, or because different groups in the debates over personality cults and Stalinism could be distinguished. In any case, this strongly polycentric structure led to political, that is, controversial and public discussions, and thus also laid the foundation for an at least partially existing political public in Czechoslovakia. Because critiques and alternative visions were also quickly publicized in the West, the discussion space expanded beyond national boundaries. From this perspective, it becomes understandable how the Prague Spring and the fearful separation of the GDR from Czechoslovakian development came to be. Christoph Boyer points out, however, that the debates in the intellectual public were not identical to the discontent that was felt by broad levels of the population.[47] Among workers, the market-based reform recommendations proposed by the CSSR reformers were met with scepticism and opposition, because they were meant to change the existing circumstances without promising any tangible improvements. This structurally rather conservative mindset was also widespread among GDR workers and supported through Honecker's policy in the GDR after 1970. The debate over the origins of different developmental paths in the GDR and Czechoslovakia cannot remain solely as a strong political and elite-historical analysis of the party leadership, it must take other factors into account.

Cultural Revolutions

The reality that the new youth culture of the 1960s was a transnational phenomenon is obvious and often has been pointed out. Thus, Eric Hobsbawm noted that rock music and blue jeans, even in states where they were not tolerated, like the Soviet Union, were the hallmark of 'modern' youth.[48] These cross-systemic commonalities of a 'cultural revolution' should not, however, overshadow the dramatic differences among the 'cultural uprisings' taking place in the respective systems, or even in the respective individual societies. Even the question of to what extent the different 'cultural uprisings', which called into question the social developments in their respective societies, were able to be integrated or ultimately effected change can have exceedingly different answers.

Looking at the GDR, this uprising belonged doubtlessly in the context of the increasing self-consciousness that followed the building of the Wall. From this event, both the national leadership and bureaucracy, as well as artists, drew the conclusion that within the GDR, experiments and innovations were possible. The *Bitterfeld Weg*, which was implemented in the beginning of the 1960s, aimed to propagate the social and political basis of the regime through the fusion of labour and artistic intelligence. The frequent use of generational and youth metaphors in artistic works and cultural-political writings suggested an attempt at a new quasi-justification of the GDR.[49] Thus, it is important to keep in mind that these dynamics of change originated not on the fringes of the artistic and literary spectrum, or even in the opposition, but rather in the state-supportive middle, which demonstrated, in various fields, a will toward formation and change. In architecture, music, and poetry, as in prose, these projects emerged from an intimate bond between socialist values and optimistic expectations for the future.[50] The national and party leadership were skilful in including prominent artists and writers in the circle of 'planners and leaders' by making them familiar with economic duties and responsibilities through 'personal discussions'. The attempt to extend the 'New Economic System of Planning and Management' (NÖSPL) into the realm of 'cultural creativity' in order to hold cultural processes under control was thus not only undeniable, but also successful. Already in the first half of the 1960s, though, the appeal *Kumpel, greif zur Feder* (friend, take up your pen) was ebbing, and the symbiosis between working life and art administratively was narrowed. Instead of an unrestricted search for new forms of expression, control and steering of cultural politics was henceforth the order of the day. When it became clear that the staged cultural movement began to take its own momentum, the state and party leaders terminated these developments completely. The resolution of the 11. Plenum of the SED in 1965 reduced literature back to its instructional function.[51]

Institutional reorganization in the realm of cultural politics during the 1960s revealed a strengthening of those political forces that regarded every independent movement with distrust and argued for unconditional control. Thus, in 1963, the Cultural Commission of the SED Politburo was established through the Ideological Commission under the leadership of Kurt Hager; in 1964, the new Department XX (for art and artists) was founded in the Ministry of State Security. Art and culture had thus become security risks. Nevertheless, that meant, vice versa, that culture was finally credited as a force capable of undermining the system.

Even though essentially similar structures and developments existed in the other socialist states, a comparison quickly reveals that the range of freedom for writers and artists in the GDR was especially narrow. Contemporaneously with developments in the GDR, a comparable pluralizing of cultural life occurred in Czechoslovakia, which did not last much longer, but should be understood in completely different measure as an independent development.[52] The systemic crisis of the late 1950s can be seen as a point of origin that led to far-reaching debates and new departures in the economy, on the one hand, and culture, on the other. Different strategic proposals and projects were discussed, not only within the narrow power circle of the Communist Party. Magazines, films, books, and forums of different kinds emerged, in which—in contrast to situation in the GDR—an intelligence independent of the party leadership articulated itself and proclaimed another version of socialism.[53] This was characterized not, as in the GDR, by a radicalization of youth and revolutionary pathos, but, rather, by challenging these phenomena. The ambivalence toward the new, the brittleness of progress, and the brokenness of new socialist beings became the themes that undercut the official planning and progress ideology. Given the internally divided state and party bureaucracy, perspectives critical of the state could spread in circles. They were also supported by the import of foreign literature and visits of Western artists, who moulded cultural life in Czechoslovakia much more so than in the GDR. With the abatement of the Prague Spring in 1968, the cultural revolution and all cultural momentum experienced an abrupt end in Czechoslovakia. The demand for control of cultural developments no longer differed meaningfully from that in the GDR. From the perspective of the government, the explosive political and social force of cultural developments had become all too clear.

A similar explosive socio-political force was also called upon by the protagonists of the 'cultural revolution' in the West. From there, also, the cultural uprising of the 1960s was perceived by many as a system-overarching phenomenon. Differently than in the socialist societies, this uprising did not, however, prove to be system shaping in Western societies. It is clear that the optimism toward progress from the new left was similar to that of the technocrats. Herbert Marcuse and others did, indeed, ridicule the 'enslavement' and 'alienation' of people under the dictation of technical progress and technical rationality, but they did not dispute the fundamental phenomena themselves.[54] Erich Fromm was concerned with the 'humanization of technological society'.; he had no doubts about the future significance of societal planning on the basis of the cybernetic model.[55] Marcuse and Fromm placed great faith in the ability of societies radically to be changed, rather than in the promise of technical progress. Technical critique was not an integral part of the Western student and civil rights movements. The unbroken belief in the beneficial impact of atomic energy can be seen in the Port Huron Statement of the US SDS, as much as the hope for technical solutions of everyday problems was part of the worldview of Rudi Dutschke and other spokesmen of the student movement.[56]

A document, equally fascinating as it is strange, that speaks to the enmeshing of sub-cultural currents with unbridled optimism in progress is the vision of the US 'Drug Pope', Timothy Leary, from the year 1966. Leary commented on the future meaning of drugs, postulating that:

> LSD is only the first of many new chemicals, which in the coming years will ease learning, expand consciousness and deepen memory. These chemicals will inevitably revolutionize our methods of raising children and of social behaviour. Within a generation, these chemical keys to the nervous system will be used as regular instruments for learning. When the children come home, one will not ask them, 'Which book did you read?', but rather, 'Which molecules are you taking to open up new Libraries of Congress in your nervous system?' There is no doubt that chemicals will be the central educational method of the future'.[57]

So absurd was this pronouncement that it overlaid a bizarre combination of belief in progress, (sub)cultural uprising, and consumerism. An array of studies about the relationship between the (youth) uprising of the 1960s and the consumer industry emphasized that 'subcultural impulses integrate amazingly easily into that universal commercialization spiral which deepened the consumer society and advanced globalization'.[58] According to the art and cultural historian Walter Grasskamp, the political expectations of the protagonists of the youth-oriented protest culture were shaped not just by consumer experiences to a much greater extent than the protagonists were aware.[59] Rather, everything that originated in the fringe or in subcultures 'was intercepted, studied, repackaged and promptly marketed by the advertising agencies, record companies, and media bureaus'.[60] Youth (protest) culture, cultural industry, consumer experiences, and consumer expectations were thus directly linked to one another. Where the potential struggle for cultural freedom and its accompanying lifestyle was always viewed as system-threatening in the socialist states, the struggle for an individual lifestyle and every protesting pose of defiance in the West, as long as they could be integrated directly into the consumer society, remained forceless. Even ostentatious anti-consumerism remained bound to the consumer society.

Conclusion

In retrospect, from the perspective of the early twenty-first century, the 1960s appear to be a time steeped to an astonishing extent in visions of the feasibility, the 'ability to plan', and the changeability of economic and societal circumstances. The quick and steady economic recovery following the Second World War, the outlook toward a tangible 'conquest' of space, and, last but not least, the approaching of year 2000 catalysed fantasies of the future, not only in the West, but also in the socialist states. The rise of convergence theory in this time is thus less an indication of an actual harmonization of the systems than evidence that, in light of the fascinating prospects and challenges of the future, the systemic contradiction appeared, to many contemporaries, as bridgeable. Moreover, the rise of youth culture, 'the years of 68' from Berkeley to Prague, inspired the impression of a large, worldwide movement from a completely different perspective.

The awakening from the dream turned out to be sobering for both societal systems. This sobering, however, had a distinctly different quality in the states of the 'Eastern Bloc'. Bound to the invasion of Warsaw Pact troops was an immediate and lasting loss of utopia, which let any hope for a reform of the system die. The significance of the scholars from the Prague Spring was unambiguous for the potentates of the socialist states: all discussions that detracted from the primacy of policy by definition planted the seed of systemic subversion and had to be eliminated. The projections developed partially in the West of a new, stronger, technocratically outfitted elite, oriented more toward practical problems than ideological guidelines, was thus put aside. All considerations of a convergence of systems were thrown away. In the West, the sobering up from convergence dreams occurred somewhat later, took place more slowly, and had much less dramatic consequences. The political ability to plan societal processes proved to be, for the most part, an illusion. Little can be said of the 'scientification' of policy. Although increased scientific advising of policy through experts served primarily to increase legitimacy, experts in no way took the place of political decision makers. Technical and scientific progress was in no way linear, rapid, and unproblematic, as the majority of experts had predicted in the 1960s. The expansion of education improved the general level of education, but did little to change the societal hierarchy. Above all, the basis for all optimistic predictions—perpetual, controllable economic growth—collapsed abruptly in 1973 with the oil crisis.[61] In light of such results, if one is amused today by the affinity for utopian visions during the period or finds its hope for the feasibility and malleability of history excessive, then this is a product of the contemporary experience, in which the future is less imaginable and planning is either met with scepticism or associated with bad policy.

What is truly of concern in the results and perspectives of a comparison between the differently structured societies can be laid out in three points, which are both methodological and content-based. As non-comprehensive as an asymmetrical comparison may be, it indicates firstly, that in a comparison of the GDR with other socialist states, the peculiarities of the SED Regime within the 'Eastern Bloc' is more sharply pronounced. It would certainly be more precise to investigate individually if the range of discussion, whether in the area of economics or culture, were in reality much narrower in the GDR than in Czechoslovakia and Poland.

Secondly, the comparison offers insight into the complex relations and mutual observations among the respective states. One can see the extent to which states, especially those of the Warsaw Pact, reacted sensibly to changes in the 'brother countries' and how they attempted to integrate or exclude different groups with different interests. Along with this, the comparison also highlights how there was in no way a complete consonance of development for the socialist states. They proved to be different in their reactions to the arguments and guidelines of the Soviet Union. The same significance of the comparative approach applies to the West: even if the structure of the argument is very different, the question of how the individual countries engaged with the issue of economic planning or future research, or how comprehensive cultural changes would find their own character in the different countries, demonstrates the extent upon which transnational and comparative research is to be relied. The cross-systemic perspective focuses on the interesting phenomenon that developments derive their particular significance precisely from their apparent existence across both systems.

Thirdly, criteria, which up until now, have not played a role in the history of the 1960s move to the foreground with this perspective. Thus, this phase no longer appears in the long, continuity-based and success-focused perspective of Western societies. Instead, discontinuities occupy the foreground and demonstrate at which impasses unsolvable problems and contradictions arose, not only in the discussions in the socialist states, but also in Western societies. It also demonstrates how little the planning approach, under democratic-pluralist conditions, was able to incorporate or limit the market power of businesses. As much as convergence theory was incorrect in its predictions, it nevertheless reflects a phase in which both great systems were, at least in their unbroken belief in progress, astoundingly close to one another. In this respect as well, the theory proves to be an artefact of a bygone era.

Notes

1. For a basic breakdown of issues, see J. Kocka, 'Nationalsozialismus und SED-Diktatur im Vergleich', in Kocka, *Vereinigungskrise* (Göttingen, 1995), 91–101. For a general overview of research in the field of comparative dictatorship with a relevant bibliography: D. Schmiechen-Ackermann, *Diktaturen im Vergleich* (Darmstadt, 2002). SED stands for *Sozialistische Einheitspartei Deutschlands* (Socialist Unity Party of Germany).

2. Examples are comparative resistance research or research on the roll of the church. See R. Eckert, 'Die Vergleichbarkeit des Unvergleichbaren. Die Widerstandsforschung über die NS-Zeit als methodisches Beispiel', in *Zwischen Selbstbehauptung und Anpassung. Formen des Widerstandes und der Opposition in der DDR*, eds. U. Poppe et al. (Berlin, 1995), 68–84; G. Heydemann and L. Kettenacker, eds., *Kirchen in der Diktatur. Drittes Reich und SED-Staat* (Göttingen, 1993).
3. For relevant conceptual considerations, see M. Brie, 'Staatssozialistische Länder Europas im Vergleich. Alternative Herrschaftsstrategien und divergente Typen', in *Einheit als Privileg. Vergleichende Perspektiven auf die Transformation Ostdeutschlands*, ed. H. Wiesenthal (Frankfurt, 1996), 39–104; also M. Csanádi, *A comparative model of party-states: the structural reasons behind similarities and differences in self-reproduction, reforms and transformation* (Budapest, 2004); M. Csanádi, 'Reforms and transformation paths in comparative perspective: challenging comparative views on East European and Chinese reforms', *Acta oeconomica: Periodical of the Hungarian Academy of Sciences* 55 (2005): 171–99. For more recent individual studies cf., for example, J. Connelly, *Captive university: the Sovietization of East German, Czech and Polish higher education, 1945–1956* (Chapel Hill, 2000); H. Rothermel, *Aufbau, Entwicklung und Verfall kommunistischer Parteiherrschaft in Polen und der DDR: zur gesellschaftlichen Dynamik in post-totalitären sozialistischen Systemen* (Pfaffenweiler, 1997); important newer volumes with comparative perspectives: P. Hübner, C. Kleßmann, and K. Tenfelde, eds., *Arbeiter im Staatssozialismus. Ideologischer Anspruch und soziale Wirklichkeit* (Cologne, 2005); C. Brenner and P. Heumos, eds., *Sozialgeschichtliche Kommunismusforschung. Tschechoslowakei, Polen, Ungarn und DDR, 1948–1968* (Munich, 2005).
4. These system-comprehensive perspectives are taken up in J.C. Behrends, Á. von Klimó, and P. Poutros, eds., *Antiamerikanismus im 20. Jahrhundert: Studien zu Ost- und Westeuropa* (Bonn, 2005); also spanning systems in its points of departure is K. Jarausch and H. Siegrist, eds., *Amerikanisierung und Sowjetisierung in Deutschland 194 –1970* (Frankfurt a.M., 1997).
5. In this sense: C. Kleßmann, 'Verflechtung und Abgrenzung. Aspekte der geteilten und zusammengehörigen deutschen Nachkriegsgeschichte', *Aus Politik und Zeitgeschichte*, 29–30 (1993): 30–41. Building on this also the volume by A. Bauerkämper, M. Sabrow, and B. Stöver, eds., *Doppelte Zeitgeschichte. Deutsch-Deutsche Beziehungen 1945–1990* (Bonn, 1998).
6. K. Maase, 'Körper, Konsum, Genuss—Jugendkultur und mentaler Wandel in den beiden deutschen Gesellschaften', *Aus Politik und Zeitgeschichte*, 45 (2003): 9–16, here 9. Maase references here D. Mühlberg, 'Von der Arbeitsgesellschaft in die Konsum-, Freizeit- und Erlebnisgesellschaft', in *Deutsche Vergangenheiten—eine gemeinsame Herausforderung*, eds. C. Kleßmann, H. Misselwitz, and G. Wichert (Berlin, 1999), 176–205.
7. As a concise summary of the references, see P.C. Ludz, 'Konvergenz, Konvergenztheorie', in *Sowjetsystem und demokratische Gesellschaft. Eine vergleichende Enzyclopädie*, ed. G.D. Kernig, 3 vols. (Freiburg, 1969), vol. 3: 889–904.

8. D. Farber, *The Age of Great Dreams. America in the sixties* (New York, 1994); with a similar direction: M. Dickstein, *Gates of Eden. American Culture in the Sixties* (New York, 1977).
9. J. Fourastié, *Les trente glorieuses ou la révolution invisible de 1946 à 1975* (Paris, 1979); B. Lutz, *Der kurze Traum immerwährender Prosperität. Eine Neuinterpretation der industriell-kapitalistischen Entwicklung im Europa des 20. Jahrhunderts* (Frankfurt a.M., 1984).
10. See also C. Kleßmann, *Zwei Staaten, eine Nation. Deutsche Geschichte 1955–1970* (Göttingen, 1970), 340.
11. The article relies much on the findings of the volume published by myself and H.-G. Haupt, *Aufbruch in die Zukunft. Die 1960er Jahre zwischen Planungseuphorie und kulturellem Wandel. DDR, UdSSR und Bundesrepublik Deutschland im Vergleich* (Göttingen, 2004).
12. W.W. Rostow, *The Stages of Economic Growth. A non-communist manifesto* (Cambridge, 1960). On Rostow's political and scholarly career, see L. Tanzer, *Die Männer um Kennedy* (Stuttgart, 1963), 69ff.
13. Rostow, *Stages*, 162f.
14. Ibid., 136.
15. G. Rose, *'Industriegesellschaft' und Konvergenztheorie. Genesis, Strukturen, Funktionen*, 2nd. ed. (Berlin, 1974), 223, 319.
16. Ibid., 279.
17. Z. Brzezinski and S.P. Huntingtion, *Politische Macht USA/UdSSR* (Cologne, 1966).
18. On the effects of the Sputnik shock and its apparent economic success of the Soviet Union on politics in the USA, see R.M. Collins, 'Growth Liberalism in the Sixties. Great Societies at Home and Grand Designs Abroad', in *The Sixties. From Memory to History*, ed. D. Farber (Chapel Hill, 1994), 11–44.
19. See R.M. Collins, 'Growth Liberalism in the Sixties', 15f.
20. See J.K. Galbraith, *The new industrial state* (London, 1967), also published in German as *Die moderne Industriegesellschaft* (Munich, 1968); see also *The Affluent Society* (Boston, 1958); and further: C. Thalheim, 'Annäherung von Plan- und Marktwirtschaft. A comparative analysis', *Österreichische Osthefte* 9 (1967): 96–112.
21. R. Aron, *Dix-huit lecons sur la société industrielle* (Paris, 1963). The book is based on lectures given by Aron in 1956.
22. See here the work of J. Tinbergen, *Central Planing* (London, 1964); Tinbergen et al., eds., *Convergence of Economic Systems in East and West* (Rotterdam, 1964); Tinbergen, 'Do Communist and Free Economies Show a Converging Pattern?', *Soviet Studies* 12 (1961): 333–41, German translation: Tinbergen, 'Kommt es zu einer Annäherung zwischen den kommunistischen und den freiheitlichen Wirtschaftsordnungen?', *Hamburger Jahrbuch für Wirtschafts- und Gesellschaftspolitik* 8 (1963): 11–20; K.P. Hensel, 'Strukturgegensätze oder Angleichungstendenzen der Wirtschafts- und Gesellschaftssysteme in Ost und West', *Ordo* 12 (1960/61): 305–29; R. Dubs, 'Konvergieren die Wirtschaftsordnungen in Ost und West?', *Außenpolitik* 18(1) (1967): 5–15; I. Weinberg, 'The

Problem of the Convergence of Industrial Societies. A critical look at the state of a theory', *Comparative Sudies in Society and History* 11(1969): 1–15.
23. See here the works of Polish economist W. Brus, as well as his Czechoslovakian colleague O. Šik, among others. W. Brus, *Funktionsprobleme der sozialistischen Wirtschaft* (Polish ed., 1961; German ed., 1971); O. Šik, 'Problems of the New System of Planned Management', *Czechoslovak Economic Papers* 1965: 7–33; M. Bornstein, *Plan and Market. Economic Reform in Eastern Europe* (New Haven/London, 1973); P. Dobias, *Die Wirtschaftssysteme Osteuropas* (Darmstadt, 1986); H. Buck, *Technik der Wirtschaftslenkung in kommunistischen Staaten* (Coburg, 1970); H.-H. Höhmann, M. Kaser, and K. Thalheim, eds., *Die Wirtschaftsordnungen Osteuropas im Wandel, Ergebnisse und Probleme der Wirtschaftsreformen*, vol.1 (Freiburg, 1972). A first-rate selection of articles by Czech authors published at the end of the 1960s and 1970s can be found in the interesting West European publication (available in English and German), H. Leipold and T. Eger, eds., *Sozialistische Marktwirtschaften, Konzeptionen und Lenkungsprobleme* (Munich, 1975); further articles in *Jahrbücher für Nationalökonomie und Statistik* (1971); *Österreichische Osthefte* 9(1967).
24. For a historical perspective, see W. Brus, *Geschichte der Wirtschaftspolitik in Osteuropa* (Cologne, 1987). For debates in each of the three countries: for the GDR the work of A. Steiner, esp. Steiner, *Die DDR-Wirtschaftsreform der sechziger Jahre. Konflikt zwischen Effizienz- und Machtkalkül* (Berlin, 1999); A. Steiner, '"Umfassender Aufbau des Sozialismus" oder "Anleihe beim Kapitalismus"?' On the concept of GDR economic reform, see G. Diesener and R. Gries, eds., *Propaganda in Deutschland. Zur Geschichte der politischen Massenbeeinflussung im 20.Jahrhundert* (Darmstadt, 1996), 146–57; on Poland: D. Jaseśniak-Quast, 'Die ersten Versuche der Dezentralisierung der sozialistischen Planwirtschaft in Polen. Höhepunkte der Debatten über die Wirtschaftsreformen (1956–1968)', in Haupt and Requate, *Aufbruch in die Zukunft*, 89–106; on Czechoslovakia: M. Köhler-Baur, 'Von der "Vervollkommnung" der Planwirtschaft in der ČSSR zum "Neuen System der Lenkung". Wirtschaftsreformen als Impuls für politische Veränderungen?', in Haupt and Requate, *Aufbruch in die Zukunft*, 65–87.
25. Köhler-Baur; Steiner.
26. See the work of Steiner.
27. See Jaseśniak-Quast.
28. From the broad contemporary debate, see here: A. Plitzko, *Planung ohne Planwirtschaft* (Tübingen, 1964); K. Lenk, 'Aspekte der gegenwärtigen Planungsdiskussion in der Bundesrepublik', *Politische Vierteljahresschrift* 7 (1966): 364–76; J.H. Kaiser, ed., *Begriff und Institut des Plans* (Planung, vol. 2) (Baden-Baden, 1966); H.C. Rieger, *Begriff und Logik der Planung* (Wiesbaden, 1967); F. Naschold and W. Väth, eds., *Politische Planungssysteme* (Opladen, 1973); for the discursive history of the term 'Planung': M. Ruck, 'Ein kurzer Sommer der konkreten Utopie—Zur westdeutschen Planungsgeschichte der langen 60er Jahre', in *Dynamische Zeiten: die 60er Jahre in den beiden deutschen Gesellschaften*, eds. A. Schildt et al. (Hamburg, 2000), 362–401.

29. G. Altmann, *Aktive Arbeitsmarktpolitik. Entstehung und Wirkung eines Reformkonzepts in der Bundesrepublik Deutschland* (Stuttgart, 2004).
30. On its origins and development see L. Hölscher, *Die Entdeckung der Zukunft* (Frankfurt a.M., 1999).
31. As only a small selection of publications on the year 2000, see: H. Kahn, *The Year Two Thousand: a Framework for Speculation on the Next 33 Years* (New York, 1967); R. Jungk, ed., *Mankind 2000* (Oslo, 1969); H. Hamm-Brücher, *Aufbruch ins Jahr 2000 oder Erziehung im technischen Zeitalter* (Reinbek b. Hamburg, 1967); *A Policies Plan for the Year 2000. The Nation's Capital*, Prepared by National Capital Planning Commission (Washington, DC, 1961); T. Husén, *Education in the Year 2000. Extracts from a Research Project Report* (Stockholm, 1971); M.E. Wolfgang, ed., *The Future Society: Aspects of America in the Year 2000* (Philadelphia, 1973).
32. On the boom in future research, see: A. Schmidt-Gernig, 'Scenarios of Europe's Future. Western Future Studies of the Sixties and Seventies as an Example of a Transnational Public Sphere of Experts', *Journal of European Integration History* 18 (2002): 69–91; Schmidt-Gernig, '"Futurologie"—Zukunftsforschung und ihre Kritiker in der Bundesrepublik der 60er Jahre', in Haupt and Requate, *Aufbruch in die Zukunft*, 109–31.
33. The concept and practice of 'planification' already played a central role in France in the 1950s. See the following from the contemporary literature: R. Houin, 'La Planification Française', in *Begriff und Institut des Plans*, ed. J.H. Kaiser (Baden-Baden, 1966), 149–88; P. Bauchet, *La planification française* (Paris, 1962; 1966); H. Teitgen, 'Les Instruments dont dispose la France pour assurer l'Exécution de la Planification Communautaire', in *Planung international*, ed. J.H. Kaiser (Baden-Baden, 1970), 21–40; P.W.L. Edelmann, *Möglichkeiten und Grenzen der französischen Planification. Ein Beispiel staatlicher Rahmenplanung in der Marktwirtschaft* (Bern/Frankfurt, 1971).
34. See Schmidt-Gernig, '"Futurologie"', 111.
35. See M. Marien, *Societal Directions and Alternatives. A Critical Guide to the Literature* (New York, 1976), esp. 7–15 and 384ff.
36. On the development of 'think tanks' in the USA and the Federal Republic, see W. Gellner, *Ideenagenturen für Politik und Öffentlichkeit. Think Tanks in den USA und in Deutschland* (Opladen, 1995).
37. See Kommission der Europäischen Gemeinschaften, *Europa plus 30 Jahre* (Cologne, 1976), Appendix I.
38. See H.-E. Friedrich, *Science Fiction in der deutschsprachigen Literatur* (Tübingen, 1995); as well as '"One Hundred Years from this Day..."—Zur Semantik der Zukunft in den 1960er Jahren. Science Fiction in der Bundesrepublik Deutschland und Wissenschaftliche Phantastik der DDR', in Haupt and Requate, *Aufbruch in die Zukunft*, 133–64.
39. See among others: G. Klaus, *Was ist, was soll Kybernetik?* (Leipzig, 1968); G. Klaus, *Wörterbuch der Kybernetik* (Berlin (Ost), 1968); G. Klaus, *Kybernetik—eine neue Universalphilosophie der Gesellschaft?* (Frankfurt a.M., 1973); G. Klaus, *Kybernetik und Gesellschaft* (Berlin (Ost), 1964). For the cybernetics

debate in the FRG, cf. esp. the work of K. Steinbuch, *Über Kybernetik. Kybernetische Systeme des menschlichen Organismus* (Cologne, 1963); K. Steinbuch, ed., *Neuere Ergebnisse der Kybernetik: Bericht über die Tagung Karlsruhe 1963 der Deutschen Arbeitsgemeinschaft Kybernetik* (Munich, 1964); furthermore, with multiple editions, F. von Cube, *Was ist Kybernetik? Grundbegriffe, Methoden, Anwendungen* (Bremen, 1967).

40. S. Mallet, *La nouvelle classe ouvrière* (Paris, 1963).
41. On this and its effects see R. Jessen, 'Zwischen Bildungsökonomie und zivilgesellschaftlicher Mobilisierung. Die doppelte deutsche Bildungsdebatte der sechziger Jahre', in Haupt and Requate, *Aufbruch in die Zukunft*, 209–31.
42. G. Picht, *Die deutsche Bildungskatastrophe. Analyse und Dokumentation* (Olten, 1964).
43. On the history of education reform in the Federal Republic, see L. v. Friedeburg, *Bildungsreform in Deutschland. Geschichte und gesellschaftlicher Widerspruch* (Frankfurt, 1989).
44. See here esp R. Dahrendorf, *Bildung ist Bürgerrecht—Plädoyer für eine aktive Bildungspolitik* (Hamburg, 1965).
45. On this, as well as on the parallel debates in the Federal Republic and the GDR: Jessen, 'Zwischen Bildungsökonomie', 215f.
46. See Ruck in Schildt et al., *Dynamische Zeiten*, 362–401; as well as Ruck, 'Westdeutsche Planungsdiskurse und Planungspraxis der 1960er Jahre im internationalen Kontext', in Haupt and Requate, *Aufbruch in die Zukunft*, 289–325; G. Metzler, 'Demokratisierung durch Experten? Aspekte politischer Planung in der Bundesrepublik', in Haupt and Requate, *Aufbruch in die Zukunft*, 267–87; Metzler, *Konzeptionen politischen Handelns von Adenauer bis Brandt. Politische Planung in der pluralistischen Gesellschaft* (Paderborn, 2005).
47. C. Boyer, 'Sozialistische Sozialpolitik und Gesellschaftsreform in den sechziger Jahren: DDR und ČSSR im Vergleich', in Haupt and Reqaute, *Aufbruch in die Zukunft*, 249–65.
48. E. Hobsbawm, *Age of Extremes. The Short Twentieth Century, 1914–1991* (New York, 1995), 327; see also F. Starr, *Red and Hot. The Fate of Jazz in the Soviet Union 1917–1980* (New York, 1983), 287ff.
49. On the significance of generational metaphors in the GDR, see D. Wierling, 'Erzieher und Erzogene. Zu Generationenprofilen in der DDR der 60er Jahre', in Schildt et al., *Dynamische Zeiten*, 624–41.
50. B. Dahlke, '"Ich bin so alt wie die Republik!" Die 60er Jahre: Aufbruch einer Generation', in Haupt and Requate, *Aufbruch in die Zukunft*, 329–44.
51. On the decision, see G. Adge, ed., *Kahlschlag. Das 11. Plenum des ZK der SED 1965. Studien und Dokumente* (Berlin, 1991).
52. See U. Rassloff, 'Gegenwelten—Kultureller Wandel in der Slowakei der 1960er Jahre', in Haupt and Requate, *Aufbruch in die Zukunft*, 345–60.
53. On the development of 'counter culture' in Czechoslocakia and other states of the 'Eastern Bloc' see: L. Richter and H. Olschowsky, eds., *Im Dissens zur Macht. Samizdat und Exilliteratur der Länder Ostmittel- und Südosteuropas*

(Berlin, 1995); W. Eichwede, ed., *Samizdat. Alternative Kultur in Zentral- und Osteuropa: Die 60er bis 80er Jahre* (Bremen, 2000).
54. See H. Marcuse, *One-dimensional man. Studies in the Ideology of Advanced Industrial Society* (London, 1964).
55. E. Fromm, *The Revolution of Hope. Toward a Humanized Technology* (New York, 1968), esp. 93ff.
56. The Port Huron Statement is included in J. Miller, *'Democracy is in the Streets.' From Port Huron to the Siege of Chicago* (Cambridge, MA, 1994), 329–75, and expresses his hope that atomic energy will solve all future energy problems; see ibid., 330. On the German context see 'Ein Gespräch über die Zukunft mit Rudi Dutschke, Bernd Rabehl und Christian Semmler', in *Kursbuch* 14 (1968): 146–74, esp. 167f. Rabehl speaks here of the 'optimal application of technology as an instrument of emancipation from repressive work', and Semler holds the computer as the foundation for a future governance.
57. T. Leary, *Politik der Ekstase* (Hamburg, 1970), 53. The citation is originally from an interview Leary gave to *Playboy* in 1966.
58. J. Tanner, '"The Times They are A-Changin". On the subcultural dynamics of the 68 Movements', in *1968. Vom Ereignis zum Gegenstand der Geschichtswissenschaft*, ed. I. Gilcher-Holtey (Göttingen, 1998), 206–23, here 208.
59. W. Grasskamp, *Der lange Marsch durch die Illusionen. Über Kunst und Politik* (Munich, 1995), 20.
60. Ibid., 16.
61. Central to this relationship is also the report of the Club of Rome: D.H. Meadows, *The limits to growth. A Report for the Club of Rome's project on the Predicament of Mankind* (New York, 1972).

CHAPTER 9

Comparisons, Cultural Transfers, and the Study of Networks

Toward a Transnational History of Europe

PHILIPP THER

There is a very vivid debate among European historians on how to transcend the national paradigm in historiography. Since the institutionalization of history in the nineteenth century, the nation state or the territory inhabited by the own national group has served as the main point of reference for historians. Major developments in the history of the European nations and nation states have been researched and explained with an internalist perspective. One can characterize this as 'methodological nationalism', which has particularly influenced the 'big' nations of Europe, their historiography, and also their traditions of comparative history.[1] Not surprisingly, in recent years the debate about 'transnational history' has been especially intensive in France and even more so in Germany.[2]

This chapter begins by introducing this debate, which has so far been mostly a Franco-German debate, but has begun to be followed up by historians in the United States.[3] One of the results of the debate has been a reconceptualization of the comparative method, which is also the topic of this volume. It has been influenced in particular by the proponents of the model of 'cultural transfers', who were centred originally in Paris. This reconceptualization and the resulting proposal of a *histoire croisée* might also be relevant to readers from neighbouring disciplines such as sociology or literary studies, which frequently use comparisons.

All three approaches—the comparative method, the model of cultural transfers, and *histoire croisée*—form the methodological core of 'transnational' history. This fashionable term has the potential for being a new paradigm for historiography, because it serves as a common denominator for historians of very different backgrounds and interests who want to go beyond the national paradigm and the traditional setup of comparisons.

The danger lies in the fact that so far, there have been few attempts to define the term 'transnational' or to apply it in empirical studies.[4] Some authors see the new paradigm as a possibility for leaving behind the national framing of historiography; others regard it as an extension of national history.[5] There is a consensus that transnational history does not mean international or diplomatic history. It concentrates on the relations between cultures, societies or groups of societies and intentionally transcends the boundaries of one culture or country. This chapter will present the argument that the principles of transnational history were used already in area studies such as East Central European history, which recently have been complemented by a concept of a Franco-German history. These area studies are by necessity comparative and take into account cultural transfers. They could also form the basis of a transnational history of Europe.

So far, the debate about transnational history has been mostly theoretical. There have been few empirical transnational studies, although there were previous attempts in historiography to overcome the national paradigm. One possibility for applying the keyword of transnational history in empirical practice is the study of networks.[6] Networks were the basis of communication and learning processes over large distances, which have been of particular relevance for Central and Eastern Europe. Since the second half of the nineteenth century, there were also a sharply increasing number of networks on a European level, which can serve as empirical evidence for a transnational European history.

The Debate About Historical Comparison and the History of Cultural Transfers

The debate about transnational history has its roots in a sometimes polemical quarrel between adherents of the traditional historical comparison method and the proponents of the model of transfer history, which broke out in the 1990s.[7] The French historian Michel Espagne attacked the comparatists for juxtaposing artificially isolated national cases and overlooking the mutual contacts between cultures.[8] He also criticized the fact that comparisons are static and concentrate too much on structures instead of agency. This line of conflict reflects the fact that most comparatists in Germany and France have a background in social history, while the proponents of the model of transfer history have a propensity toward cultural history and are influenced by postmodernism.

Indeed, the great number of comparative studies that were produced by the Bielefeld school of social history in the 1980s and 1990s were based mostly on national cases.[9] The main purpose of these comparisons was to analyze differences and commonalities and to generate causal explanations. One major field of interest was the intensely discussed question of why Germany got on its *Sonderweg*, which lead to National Socialism.[10] Germany was therefore contrasted with the United States, England or France in order to generate a better causal explanation for a perceived German exceptionalism in the late nineteenth and early twentieth centuries.[11] Some prominent comparatists, such as the English historian John Breuilly, argued explicitly for the isolation of the analysed cases and regarded the comparative method as the closest equivalent of historical science with experiments in natural sciences.[12]

However, diverse research in social and cultural history has shown that contacts and exchange between cultures, societies, and states deeply can influence their development. This is now shown briefly with the three examples of 'high culture', welfare systems and education. Opera is commonly categorized in national terms such as Italian, French or German opera, but, in fact, the national and international reception of operas was driven by cultural transfers. An excellent case with which to show this is Wagner and 'Wagnerism'. After several decades of rejection, in the 1890s, French audiences came to adore the music of Richard Wagner. The reception of Wagner influenced French composers in many ways, even though Debussy and other colleagues deliberately rejected his principles of composition.[13] Yet, the obsession with Wagner and his works was based on previous cultural transfers from France to Germany. One of the most important stages for German operas in the nineteenth century was the court theatre in Dresden. If one takes a closer look at the famous German opera department directed by Carl Maria von Weber in the early nineteenth century, most operas staged by him in the German language were, in fact, translated French operas.[14] One generation later, Richard Wagner's operas were heavily influenced by the example of the French *Grand Opéra*. One could summarize that the international success of German opera was based on French examples and their impact several decades earlier. Moreover, the popularity of Wagner was influenced by the reception in France. When his work was rejected in a scandalous staging of the opera *Tannhäuser* in Paris in 1861, German audiences applauded his work demonstratively and began to view him for the first time as a symbol of German culture.

Another example for the relevance of cultural transfers is welfare systems. In recent debates about welfare reforms, there were frequent arguments about the superior effectiveness of the Dutch and the Scandinavian models; there was even talk of a European Social Model.[15] But it was already common practice to refer to foreign models in order to argue for changes in social policy in the nineteenth century.[16] In the twentieth century, the openly discussed or implicit competition between countries again has been a driving force in establishing new welfare benefits.[17]

Another example of continuous and intensive cultural transfers is education. The French university system was deeply influenced by the German, or Humboldtian, model in the second half of the nineteenth century.[18] If one were to juxtapose these social security or university systems according to a traditional comparison, one would find many differences and then probably conclude that one country was more advanced or backward than the other one. But it would be hard to come up with a convincing explanation of how the European countries built up such high level of social security and why the French universities changed so much in the second half of the nineteenth century. Universities and Wagnerism were paradigmatic for the entire relationship between those two countries. Throughout modern history, the French and the Germans closely observed their neighbour(s), partly copying and using, but also rejecting, elements of the neighbouring culture.

Similar conclusions can be made about Polish-German relations, which were so deeply intertwined that they were interdependent.[19] The ways in which Germans came to define themselves as a modern nation in the course of the nineteenth century, pivotal areas of politics of the German Empire, and the blockade of democratization in Prussia were deeply connected with the partition of Poland, the presence of a strong Polish minority in Germany, and, hence, Poles as agents of German history.

The very formation of the modern European nations can only be understood if one analyses the complex interaction of European nationalisms. In other words, even the phenomenon of nationalism requires a transnational approach. These empirical findings can be transmitted also to a more abstract level. Any differentiation is built upon systems of reference and therefore requires more than an internalist perspective. External factors on a given European history have to be more thoroughly analysed and considered, as opposed to the internalism of master narratives, which were still being published in France and Germany in the 1980s and early 1990s.

The approach of cultural transfers does not idealize the 'uncovered' contacts between two countries or cultures in the way that can sometimes be seen in so-called 'shared' or 'entangled' history.[20] It includes the deliberate exclusion and rejection of elements of culture that were perceived as foreign. As the example of the French university system or of opera has shown, countries, societies, but also smaller entities such as cities or institutions observed and partially adapted foreign examples and transformed them for their own purposes. These transfers were based on comparative observations in the given period. Especially territorial entities and groups that perceived themselves as backward had a strong tendency to look over borders, to import and adapt cultural goods from abroad. The 'reforms from above', which were so typical for the states of Central and Eastern Europe in the long nineteenth century, were a reaction to a perceived backwardness and were aimed at catching up with economic and cultural pioneer countries such as France or England. This contributed to major changes. As is widely known, Germany became a very strong economic competitor for England, and the Habsburg Empire, remarkably, caught up with the more industrialized countries of Europe.[21] In the twentieth century, many countries and societies compared themselves with a presumably more advanced 'West'. This has been crucial for the forced industrialization policy in the Soviet Union, the socialist countries in Central Europe, and in many postcolonial states. Comparisons also have been a crucial factor for the process of transformation in the former communist countries since 1989. The major geographical categories in Europe, such as 'West' or 'East' and Occidentalism and Orientalism with its European variants, are inherently comparative. To summarize, the study of cultural transfers reveals the *historicity of comparisons*. Hence, making comparisons is not only an abstract method, but is also a long established historical practice that caused cultural transfers.

This is only one historical argument for combining the comparative method with the approach of cultural transfers. The sometimes sharp polemics between the proponents of historical comparison and those of cultural transfers have concealed the fact that both approaches are highly constructivist, since they both combine the study of units that have to be distinguished from their context and that are put into a relation by the researcher. In general, the analysis of cultural transfers forces one to delineate a boundary between the transmitting and the receiving culture and to define 'the own' and 'the other'.

Both approaches—historical comparison and transfer history—have concentrated for a long time on national units of analysis. This is also true for comparative sociology or economic studies. While in the case of comparative history, the main objects of interest have been nation states and societies, transfer history dealt mostly with national cultures, in particular the cultures of France and Germany. Since the mid 1990s, Espagne and Matthias Middell have widened the scope and analysed cultural transfers from and to regions, in particular Saxony.[22] But regions are constructed entities, like nation states, and thus are not fundamentally different on a theoretical level. They are still in line with the traditional territorialized thinking developed in modern Europe.[23]

Moreover, both approaches have the common goal of producing a historiography that transcends the present national borders. The difference is, rather, on a level of operationalization than of theory. As stated previously, it is the purpose of scientific comparisons to measure differences and commonalities and to reach causal explanations. But the latter purpose often can be fulfilled only if one takes into account previous cultural transfers. According to the model developed by Espagne and Middell, their analysis relies on knowledge about the transmitting and the receiving cultures in order to understand why a certain cultural import was perceived as being necessary or beneficial or was renounced. It follows from this that both units, the exporting and the receiving culture, have to be compared.[24]

The French historian Michael Werner has concluded that comparative history and the study of cultural transfers belong to a 'family of relational approaches'.[25] He introduced into the debate the term *histoire croisée*, which can be translated literally as 'crossed history'. *Croiser* has two dimensions. Like Espagne, Werner argues that German and French histories are deeply connected. This is in line with concepts such as entangled history. But he also states explicitly that the historian should connect these two histories. Hence, Werner is outspoken about the constructivist character of his approach. Together with his co-author Bénédicte Zimmermann, he dedicates ample reflections to the position of the historian vis-à-vis his object of analysis. This demand of self-reflexivity, which is stated very prominently, shows the influence of postmodernism and postcolonialism.[26]

So far, none of the protagonists of the debate have drawn parallels between this theoretical discussion and the political development of Europe. In the 1970s and 1980s, when social history comparisons reached their peak, the European Community was still conceptualized, according to Adenauer and De Gaulle, as a union of fatherlands. The European order of nation states is also reflected in the structure of most larger history departments in the United States, which usually split up the field of European history into chairs for French, German, English, Russian, and some other national histories. Hence, the juxtaposition of national cases in comparative social history was in concordance with the political status quo of the postwar period. In Germany, there also was a strong transatlantic dimension in comparative history.[27] In general, the strong emphasis on comparison with Western countries reflects the strong will of the political and intellectual elite of the Federal Republic to complete its 'long way to the West', as a recent book was titled.[28] German historians undertook hardly any comparisons with Central and Eastern European countries,[29] although, for example, the inclusion of Czech history would have put into question key arguments of the *Sonderweg* thesis.[30]

There also appears to be a political background for the study of cultural transfers. When the protagonists of this approach stressed the connections between German and French history,[31] both countries were on their way to prepare the Maastricht treaty, which set the pace for the Euro and a closer integration of Western Europe. Although this is not addressed openly, the approach delivers a historical blueprint for the present integration of Germany and France and the deepening of the European Union. Michael Werner's proposal for a *histoire croisée*, which is also based on the cases of France and Germany, coincided with a deep conflict between the United States and Europe because of the war against Iraq, the Kyoto protocol, and other issues. This inspired an even closer Franco-German alliance, which reached its peak in 2003, when Germany at times even delegated the representation of its national interest at the UN to France. Michael Werner's proposal for a *histoire croisée* would result in a historiography of European countries that are integrated so closely that they do not need separate national histories anymore. Yet one should not carry the parallels between historiography and politics too far. Michael Werner thought about his *histoire croisée* already before the Bush presidency provoked attempts of closer European integration. Historians are not the tools of politicians and sometimes they write books under adverse circumstances.

When Lucien Febvre published his book about the river Rhine more than seventy years ago, the Nazis had just taken power and were about to provoke another war with France. This book by one of the founders of the *Annales* school deserves special attention, because it integrates both sides of the contested border region into one transnational history.[32] Furthermore, the book is based on a regional approach and thus already overcame the nation state paradigm. The Czech historian Josef Pekář did not go as far as Febvre, but he also had thoughts that today could be termed transnational. He argued in his programmatic book about the *Sense of Czech History* that foreign, Byzantine, West European, German, and Hungarian influences were of paramount importance for Czech history. Pekář also concluded that these external factors at times shaped the history of the Czechs more than internal developments.[33] These examples of interwar historiography show that demands for transcending the national paradigm of history are not a novelty. Although the term 'transnational' was not used yet, there were earlier attempts to overcome the national, and then still mostly nationalist, tradition of historiography.

While in the interwar period nationalism in Europe was at its peak, currently few historians argue openly for a national paradigm. In Canada and the United States, sympathies for national histories are expressed in a rebuke of multiculturalism, political correctness, and topics such as diasporas, minority cultures, postcolonialism or world history.[34] In Europe as well, the pleas for a national paradigm are usually made implicitly or indirectly. It is brought forward that the history of the nation is still relevant—which is indisputable, that it was the nations that shaped European history, that the welfare state was built up by nation states, etc. The national paradigm is also supported by conventional narrative structures. For example, in Hans-Ulrich Wehler's history of German society, Poles, Czechs or other groups that were ruled by Prussia and Germany, but who also formed the history of these states and their majority societies, are hardly treated at all and are thus excluded from his book. Most 'master narratives' in postwar Europe have a national bias that results in the exclusion of minority groups.[35]

In contrast to the implicitness of national history, transnational history has to be explicit. In his proposal of a *histoire croisée* and his empirical studies about cultural transfers, Michael Werner has developed, in effect, a Carolingian vision of German and French history. This is now being realized in a new book series as *Deutsch-französische Geschichte*.[36] If one carries his article and the concept of this book series a bit further, the study of these two countries is moulded into a new kind of Western or West Central European area studies.

Transnational Area Studies

Werner's proposal could be connected with already developed approaches for the history of Central Europe. According to common understanding, this part of Europe comprises the countries and regions between Germany in the West and Russia in the East. In the postwar period, the exiled Polish historian Oskar Halecki, the German historian Klaus Zernack, the Hungarian historian Jenö Szücs, and other scholars have made great efforts to define the historical region of 'Central Europe', which, in German, has often been labelled as *Ostmitteleuropa* (*East* Central Europe).[37]

These founding fathers of Central European history as area studies based their characterization on social and political structures, a framework of *Strukturgeschichte*. Accordingly, East Central Europe was driven by Western Christianization and the establishment of relatively autonomous cities according to the Magdeburg laws. There was an extraordinary intense and long tradition of feudalism, a strong nobility, and a relatively weak bourgeoisie. Therefore, agrarian economies and values remained intact relatively long, while industrialization occurred late. Another characteristic often attributed to *Ostmitteleuropa* is ethnic diversity, which resulted in nationalism, armed conflicts, and wars.[38]

These structures were based on comparative studies and attributed to an area that reaches from the river Elbe in Germany to the western frontier of Russia. Most parts of Germany were included, which also corresponds to the mapping of the most pre-eminent English language journal of the region, *Central European History*. The structures of Central Europe were often viewed normatively. Hence, they have been termed as late, untimely, backward, superficial, distorted, along with other negative expressions in terms of time or values. These negative judgements, which are especially pronounced among Szücs, are a result of comparisons with a 'normal' development in the West. Hence, there are certain parallels to the *Sonderweg* argument, which accentuated the exceptionalism of Germany vis-à-vis the West. But the aforementioned authors have also drawn an even thicker line between Central Europe on the one hand, and an East Slavonic, Orthodox, and, since 1917, Soviet part of Europe, on the other. This distinction was again influenced by political considerations, especially the attempt to distinguish the Soviet-dominated sphere of influence from the Soviet Union itself.

Because most comparisons in Central European history concentrated on the region itself, it has gone unnoticed that it had many similarities with some parts of Western Europe. Catalonia, for example, was influenced by very similar structures, had a long history of feudalism, was ruled by an empire (the Spanish one), was for a long time economically backward if compared with France or England, had a relatively late but ethnically defined national movement, and a cultural history that was very similar to 'small' nations such as the Czechs.[39] There are also certain similarities in the cultural and social history of Poland and Ireland.[40] Hence, it is hard to uphold the exceptionalism that is present in many studies about Central Europe. It also is not useful to understand area studies—which are a good tool for teaching students—as fixed geographical units with clear borders that are valid over centuries. The *longue durée* perspective that is underlying in the structural definition of *Ostmitteleuropa* is based on the assumption that the aforementioned characteristics shaped the history of the region from the Middle Ages until recent times. But especially Bohemia can hardly be regarded as agrarian in the modern period—the feudal landowners were a major force of modernization in the nineteenth century,[41] and even the ethnic conflicts were a result of the modern nation building process, rather than of the ethnic mixture as such. At least from a perspective that does not ignore all of the insights of postmodernism and that includes cultural history, it is clear that this structural definition has to be amended.

In Austria, there has been an additional attempt to define Central Europe. The cultural historian Moritz Csáky developed a cultural definition of the region that was amply used in the 'special research scheme' (*Spezialforschungsbereich*), *Moderne. Wien und Zentraleuropa um 1900*, at the University of Graz. According to Csáky, Central Europe was partially united by the aforementioned structures, but even more so by culture on various levels, ranging from food to high arts. He also stresses the relevance of communication and cultural transfers within the region[42] and contends that there was a degree of common identification in the late Habsburg Empire.[43]

Csáky's cultural concept of Central European studies has the advantage that it is more flexible and inclusive. According to the structural definition of Central Europe, Ukraine would be excluded because of its long Russian rule, its Eastern Slavonic culture, the dominance of the Orthodox Church, and structural commonalities with Russia. Following a culturally based concept of area studies, Ukraine can be integrated into the study of Central Europe in the early modern period. There was intensive communication with the West through Poland, resulting in a Ukrainian version of the Counter-Reformation, Jesuit activities, and influences of the Enlightenment.[44] These connections were so strong that one can regard Ukraine as a part of Central Europe until the late eighteenth century.[45] Similar arguments could be made for Germany, which is rarely treated as a part of modern *Ostmitteleuropa*.[46] The cases of early modern Ukraine and of modern Germany highlight the fact that until 1914, political, social, and cultural boundaries in Europe were volatile and permeable. This is not only true for states and other territorial units, but also for social groups and even individuals. Cultural barriers were frequently weakened by bi- or multilingualism. At least until 1914, crossing state borders and societal boundaries was common practice. However, it was also a result of the creation of new borders between states, societies, and cultures in an age of nationalism.

Area studies that are based on communication and interaction rather than on social structures have the additional advantage that the various spaces do not have to be treated as mutually exclusive territorial units. There are, for example, geographical and topographical areas of overlap between Michael Werner's Carolingian West Central Europe and a Germano-Slavic East Central Europe. Metropoles especially functioned as centres of communication for several cultural spaces and as nodes of cultural exchange. This can be shown using the example of Vienna, which was obviously a capital for Central Europe and therefore must have a prominent position in these area studies. But Vienna also played an important role for German culture and politics and should therefore be integrated into Michael Werner's Franco-German *histoire croisée*. Because of its status in music and opera production and at times as a political capital, Vienna is also a part of Italian or southern European cultural history. Another example for the multi-spatial relevance of a metropole is the port city of Hamburg. On the one hand, it is located in the west of Germany and has always played a major role in the exchange with the Netherlands and England and on the Northern Atlantic. On the other hand, Hamburg was a major port of emigration and of trade for the east Elbian areas of Prussia, for Bohemia, and Poland. In the history of opera and theatre, Hamburg cooperated closely and competed with the cities of Leipzig, Dresden, Prague, Vienna, and Budapest. Thus, it was the starting point of an axis of cultural transfers that reached to the southeast of Europe.[47] There was an intense exchange of composers, conductors, costumes, music scores, singers, and actors on this route. It was as important for trade of economic goods and for labour migrants.

The concept of cultural spaces can contribute to a new mental mapping of Europe, where places and axes of cultural exchange shape the map of the continent, rather than the nation state or other territorial units of analysis. It needs to be stressed that this vision is not driven by antipathy against nation states, but follows Charles Maier's observation that the highpoint of the territorialized state was reached between 1860 and the 1960s. Since then, Europe and the world are entering a post-territorial age. Moreover, the period when an order of nation states structured the entire map of Central and Eastern Europe began, in fact, only in 1918[48]; thus, the age of modern nationalism and nation states is relatively short. This is yet another purely historical reason for why the national framing of historiography should be overcome, or at least reduced. Area studies, which inevitably are transnational, would be an already well-established way to move in this direction. Framing historiography in these grand regions of Europe might not be productive for every topic of research, because the spatial dimension always depends on the area. But it is certainly useful in teaching and would produce students who know several languages and cultures and who are familiar with the "family of relational approaches".

Conclusions for 'European History'

Traditionally, Europe is understood in public debates and in historiography as a territorial entity with fixed borders. If it is treated like this, there is a danger that fundamental problems of national history are transposed onto a European level. Europe would be a territorial 'container' that is filled with historical events and peoples. A container-history of Europe would result also in a Eurocentrism that is similar to the internalism and ethnocentrism of national history. Moreover, there is a risk that European history would be confined to the member countries of the enlarged EU and exclude Russia. In non-academic literature, one finds many attempts to construct such a Europe and to underpin it with normatively charged elements of culture, such as the tradition of the Occident, Christianity or Christiano-Judaism, writing in Latin, the traditions of Roman law, Enlightenment, secularism, having overcome nationalism, etc.[50] This results in an affirmative Euro-essentialism in which Mark Mazower's 'dark continent' could hardly be integrated.

If cultural history is used as a basis of area studies, a different picture of Europe and European history arises. For the early modern period and the long nineteenth century, one can distinguish between a partially overlapping West Central and East Central Europe, an eastern European, and also a southern European or Mediterranean cultural space.[49] Over these culturally defined regions ranges Europe, which served as a point of reference and common denominator in all sub-regions. Europe itself can be regarded as a cultural space held together by communication and interaction. In this view, Europe is a process, a result of communication and interaction.

Understanding Europe as a space of communication and interaction would allow for study not only of its intensive internal, but also of its external cultural exchange. There is, for example, a strong transatlantic dimension of European history, which Daniel Rodgers has shown in his book about social politics and reformers.[51] Since Russia's victory over the Tatars in the sixteenth century, there was also a vital cultural exchange between Eastern Europe and Asia. Postcolonial studies have shown many influences of the former colonies on Europe.[52] They also demonstrated that countries and societies appearing to be far away can be intensively intertwined and remain connected even after the end of colonialism. This is of more than empirical relevance because, so far, comparisons, transfer history, and the concept of *histoire croisée* have been applied mostly to close or neighbouring countries and cultures.

Postcolonialism has raised sensitivity to the fact that cultural relations rely rarely on roughly equal partners such as France and Germany. The political and social asymmetry between cultures is also a problem for the study of Central Europe, where the long dominance of German culture and rule created many conflicts. But even imperialism and colonialism resulted in learning processes that cannot be seen only in negative terms. For example, the Polish national movement in the Prussian partition utilized successfully presumably German values, such as good work ethics and discipline, in order to shake off German rule. There also were responses in the area of culture. Gustav Freytag, the most popular German novelist of the nineteenth century, portrayed Poles as a minor race having no capability to build up a high culture and a state. The Polish writer and Nobel Prize winner Sienkiewicz responded to this by writing the novel *Krzyżacy* (*The Crusaders*), which presented Germans as cruel colonizers and militarists. Moreover, as Franco Moretti has shown, there were novels from single countries that were read all over Europe. This European market of novels expanded greatly in the nineteenth century and supports the thesis that Europe was a process and not an ontological category.[53]

Not only in literature, but also in all areas of the arts one can observe a massive growth of cultural exchange over large distances. This is particularly obvious in music and opera. In the eighteenth century, the production and staging of music was already highly internationalized. Italian opera was a synonym for opera, and so composers, star singers, and sometimes musicians or small ensembles travelled through Europe. In the nineteenth century, entire opera companies, stage sets, and orchestras were on their way through Europe. Invitations for composers and star singers became a part of the daily routine of all of the bigger theatres. The audiences were connected through daily newspapers and cultural periodicals. Theatre and music journals, such as the *Wiener Allgemeine Theaterzeitung* and the *Allgemeine Musikalische Zeitung* in Leipzig, already had built up a network of correspondents by the first half of the nineteenth century. These networks covered every large city of Europe.[54] The readership went far beyond a specialized audience and was informed about all important premiers, scandals, trends, and fashions. These journals and their readers increasingly developed a common understanding of European civilization and culture. It was also labelled as such, in spite of all national strife and competition. The travelling artists, the art critics, and their audiences formed a nucleus of a European public. In Poland and Russia, the journals had special rubrics and columns 'from Europe' and thus already imagined and established a common cultural space.[55]

The character of these networks of music and music audiences changed, however. In the first half of the nineteenth century, Paris still had a unique status as a cultural capital of Europe. It was followed closely by Vienna, by London as the capital of commerce, and a few other European cities, such as Milan. Later on, several additional cultural metropoles became centres of European or regional networks. Leipzig and Berlin were increasingly important for musical education and printing, Dresden and Prague for premiers of operas, and Budapest for operettas. The musical Europe became more differentiated, pluralistic, and multicentred.

In summary, the amount and intensity of cultural contacts grew exponentially in the second half of the nineteenth century. Thus, Europe increasingly became a point of reference, a space of experience and of agency (*Erfahrungsraum* and *Handlungsraum*). Europe also expanded in terms of space. While in the eighteenth century the cultural map of Europe was shaped by one or two dozen cultural metropoles, mostly the capitals of empires and other residential cities, in the late nineteenth century, the Europe of operas and concert halls included trans-Caucasian cities such as Tbilissi and Baku and reached over the Atlantic to Philadelphia, New York, Havanna, Buenos Aires, and Montevideo. The career of the Czech composer Antonín Dvořák, who was invited to the United States to help establish a distinct and yet Europeanized American tradition of music and who came back to Europe with his *Symphony from the New World*, is exemplary of these transatlantic connections.[56]

The communication and cultural exchange within Europe profited from structural changes. While Mozart and the composers of his time had to use uncomfortable coaches, Verdi, Wagner, and the following generations of composers travelled comfortably with steamships and on trains. The invention of modern means of transportation connected western, central, and, a little later, also eastern Europe. Since then, not only music scores, composers, and musicians, but also costumes and stage sets were transported throughout Europe. In the 1880s, a train with five wagons transported 134 musicians and supportive staff for the staging of Wagner's *Ring des Nibelungen*. This train went to all of the big cities of Italy, and then travelled to Central Europe and Russia.[57] The European reception of Wagner's main work depended on these modern means of transportation.

The result of these multiple cultural transfers was an increasing convergence of European opera repertoires. In the late nineteenth century, one can observe the development of a European standard repertoire. The change of styles also became synchronized. Franco Moretti has shown similar development for literature, and it could be demonstrated as well in architecture and the arts. Simultaneously, there was also a convergence within Central Europe, where the opera houses developed a canon of national and international operas. Moreover, cultural institutions gained a much higher status within the societies than in England or North America, a tradition that is vivid until present times.

This Europeanization was not restricted to 'high' culture, which is a standard topic of the study of cultural transfers. It can also be observed on a different level of society and area of history: migration. As Klaus Bade has put it, Europe was 'a continent on the move'.[58] The migrants often remained connected with their home places. They gave advice to relatives and friends on whether to follow them, the best way of transportation, where to look for work in the cities and countries of arrival, etc. This knowledge was communicated over large distances and contributed to patterns of migration that were often based on gender, relatives, neighbourhoods or village communities. Studies from Sicily and the Carpathian Mountains, two areas of especially high emigration, have shown that even return migration was very frequent.[59] Just like the agents of culture, these migrants also formed networks that were kept up over large distances and longer periods of time.

While we have shown empirically the increasing density and relevance of networks, it is now time to define this term. According to the sociologist Manuel Castells, networks can be defined as 'a set of interconnected nodes'.[60] They are a form of social organization that can be spread out over large distances and are based on temporary consolidation and a minimal level of institutionalization. This is very important, because, so far, historians have avoided discussing what constitutes a cultural transfer. Because of this, even a short-term communication between two individuals could be regarded as a cultural transfer. This means that it would be very difficult to study any area of history that does not constitute a cultural transfer. But a scientific concept can only be applied if it is clear where it can be utilized with a specific value. This is also an imminent problem of the paradigm of transnational history, which is built upon cultural transfers. The study of networks offers the opportunity to study not just any communication over large distance, but to concentrate on institutionalized and consolidated forms of cultural exchange, which rests on interaction between two or more sides.

Networks also offer the chance to study the increase and decrease of communication over large distances. So far, many studies about cultural transfers have been arbitrary. Most publications have concentrated so far on Germany and France in the modern period, but it has been much less researched whether and when there were cultural transfers in other parts of Europe. The historical region of Central Europe also constituted an area of intensive communication and interaction. The study of networks would allow one to measure the intensity and direction of cultural exchanges within Central Europe. Similar to cultural spaces, networks are not mutually exclusive. So nodes of a Central European network could also be integrated into a European network. This again can be exemplified with musical institutions. Opera houses such as those in Prague, Lemberg, and other Central European metropoles were, on the one hand, oriented toward Vienna as the musical capital of the region; on the other hand, they closely observed premieres in Paris and sometimes imported them directly. The study of networks would allow measurement of when and why the orientation toward Vienna or Paris was increasing and whether the flow of cultural goods occurred in one or two directions.

Last but not least, networks are a useful tool for avoiding the hidden teleology of European history. At the moment, the historiography about Europe is driven by a presentist impulse.[61] It is clear that the European integration, which culminated in the creation of the Euro and the enlargement of the EU in May 2004, requires a different historiography. But the study of networks also allows one to analyse periods of disintegration, separation, and even conflict. For example, networks of culture and migration suffered a severe setback after the First World War. The Cold War brought about another period of decreased contacts. Yet the breakdown of communism was influenced by contacts that went beyond the Iron Curtain. The debate about Central Europe, although it was largely constrained to cultural elites and small circles of dissidents, marked the beginning of the accession of the East Central European countries to a wider European Community. The mode of 'comparing oneself' also played an important role in Western Europe, especially in the creation of welfare systems.

Furthermore, the study of networks would have the potential to create a radically different mapping of a Europe that does not resemble a territorialized entity anymore, but that would, rather, resemble a satellite picture taken at night. This picture is not structured by state boundaries anymore, but instead is shaped by brightly illuminated nodes of cultural exchange and the lines of communication between them.

The final argument for networks is that they facilitate the analysis of the present European integration and enlargement in a historical perspective. The period between 1848 (or even since the Napoleonic Wars) and 1914 can be regarded as a first phase of Europeanization, which, as today, was accompanied by globalization. Already at that point in time, this process was based on relatively open borders, increasing cultural exchange, an international share of labour and mass labour migration. This contributed to social disintegration in the countries and regions involved in the process of Europeanization. Rising nationalism and attempts to create homogenous nation states or to create homogenous national societies at the end of the nineteenth century can be seen as a response to this challenge. It remains to be seen how the present phase of Europeanization will develop in the decades to come.

Notes

1. For a critique of this perspective see the introduction to S. Conrad und J. Osterhammel, eds., *Das Kaiserreich transnational. Deutschland in der Welt 1871–1914* (Göttingen, 2004), 7–28.
2. The main forums of this debate have been the journals *Geschichte und Gesellschaft* and *Comparativ* in Germany, and the *Annales* in France. The debate has also resulted in the establishment of the internet forum 'geschichte .transnational'. Most recently, H-German has opened a similar forum for the English-speaking community.
3. Independently of the debates in Europe, there were already discussions about transnational history in the United States in the beginning of the 1990s. See the October issue of *AHR* in 1991 and the articles by I. Tyrrell, 'American Exceptionalism in an Age of International History', *AHR* 96 (1991): 1031–55; and M. McGerr, 'The Price of the "New Transnational History"', *AHR* 96 (1991): 1056–67. These discussions were revived by T. Bender, ed., *Rethinking American History in a Global Age* (Berkeley, 2002). The approach has also been applied by D.T. Rodgers in his book *Atlantic Crossings: Social Politics in a Progressive Age* (Cambridge, MA, 1998). See more recently the "AHR Conversation: on Transnational History" *AHR* 111 (2006), 1440–64.

4. For a definition and a summary of the debate see M. Middell, 'Transnationale Geschichte als transnationales Projekt? Zur Einführung in die Diskussion', in Geschichte.transnational (Forum), 15 January 2005. All articles in Geschichte. transnational, which are quoted in this article, can be found on the webpage: http://geschichte-transnational.clio-online.net/forum/type=artikel (last accessed on 15 February 2006). See for the relationship between the history of cultural transfers and transnational history M. Middell, "Kulturtransfer und transnationale Geschichte" in Idem, ed., *Dimensionen der Kultur- und Gesellschaftsgeschichte* (Leipzig, 2007), 49–72.
5. See K. Patel, 'Transnationale Geschichte—ein neues Paradigma?', in *Geschichte. transnational* (Forum), 2 February 2005.
6. Here the article relies on the definition given by M. Castells, 'Materials for an exploratory theory of the network society', *British Journal of Sociology* 51 (2000): 5–24, here 15.
7. This quarrel and the conclusions to be drawn from it are well summarized in a recent publication by H. Kaelble, 'Die Debatte über Vergleich und Transfer und was jetzt?', in Geschichte.transnational (Forum), 8 February 2005. http://geschichte-transnational.clio-online.net/forum/2005-02-002.pdf.
8. See a summary of this critique, which began in the early nineties, in M. Espagne, *Les transferts culturels franco-allemands* (Paris, 1999). The critique was repeated by M. Middell, the most prominent proponent of the 'Kulturtransfer' or 'Transfergeschichte' in Germany. See M. Middell, 'Kulturtransfer und Historische Komparatistik—Thesen zu ihrem Verhältnis', *Comparativ* 10 (2000): 7–41.
9. See a typical example of this research design J. Kocka, ed., *Bürgertum im 19. Jahrhundert. Deutschland im europäischen Vergleich*, 3 vols. (Munich, 1988).
10. See J. Kocka, 'Asymmetrical Historical Comparison: The Case of the German *Sonderweg*', *History and Theory* 38 (1999): 40–51.
11. Because of restrictions of space it is impossible to provide an overview over the very fruitful comparative research generated by the Bielefeld school of social history and associated historians. This is provided in a very widely read publication by H.-G. Haupt and J. Kocka, eds., *Geschichte und Vergleich. Ansätze und Ergebnisse international vergleichender Geschichtsschreibung* (Frankfurt a.M., 1996). See also H. Kaelble, *Der historische Vergleich. Eine Einführung zum 19. und 20. Jahrhundert* (Frankfurt a.M., 1999).
12. See J. Breuilly, 'Introduction: Making Comparisons in History', in J. Breuilly, *Labour and Liberalism in Nineteenth Century Europe: Essays in Comparative History* (Manchester, 1992), 1–25, here 3. A similar argument can be found in Haupt and Kocka, *Geschichte und Vergleich*, 7.
13. S. Wolff, *L'opéra au Palais Garnier (1875–1962)* (Paris, 1962), 135. For the perception of Wagner in France see M. Kahane and N. Wildt, *Wagner et la France* (Paris, 1983).
14. For the French influence on the German opera in Dresden and the birth of German opera see A. Mungen, 'Morlacchi, Weber und die Dresdner Oper', in

Die Dresdner Oper im 19. Jahrhundert, eds. M. Heinemann and H. John (Laaber, 1995), 85–106, here 92–94.

15. The biannual meeting of the German Historical Association in Halle in 2002 offered a panel organized by Hans-Jürgen Puhle, which discussed the European welfare state as a 'model for the world' (the original title was 'Der Sozialstaat—ein europäisches Modell für die Welt?'). A strong sense of crisis was conveyed in M. Jepsen, A. Pascual, eds., *Unwrappig the European Social Model* (Bristol, 2006).
16. See S. Kott, 'Gemeinschaft oder Solidarität. Unterschiedliche Modelle der französischen und deutschen Sozialpolitik am Ende des 19. Jahrhunderts', *Geschichte und Gesellschaft* 22 (1996): 311–30. Earlier had appeared E.P. Hennock, *British Social Reform and German Antecedents: The Case of Social Insurance 1880–1914* (Oxford, 1987). These studies demonstrate again that there were already transnational studies when this keyword was not in fashion yet.
17. This is particularly true for West Germany and the GDR in the postwar period. See A. Bauerkämpfer, *Sozialgeschichte der DDR* (Munich, 2005). Simultaneously, there was a competition between the European Community countries and the Eastern Bloc countries about levels of social development and security.
18. M. Werner, 'Die Auswirkungen der preußischen Universitätsreform auf das französische Hochschulwesen (1850–1900)', in *'Einsamkeit und Freiheit neu besichtigt.' Universitätsreformen und Disziplinbildung in Preußen als Modell für Wissenschaftspolitik im Europa des 19. Jahrhunderts*, ed. G. Schubring (Stuttgart, 1990), 99–114; M. Espagne, ed., *L'Ecole normale supérieure et l'Allemagne* (Leipzig, 1995).
19. For the connections between Polish and German history, see P. Ther, 'Beyond the Nation: the Relational Basis of a Comparative History of Germany and Europe', *Central European History* 36 (2003): 45–74.
20. See for this concept S. Conrad und S. Randeria, 'Einleitung. Geteilte Geschichten—Europa in einer postkolonialen Welt', in *Jenseits des Eurozentrismus. Postkoloniale Perspektiven in den Geschichts- und Kulturwissenschaften*, eds. S. Conrad and S. Randeria (Frankfurt a.M., 2002), 9–49, here 18–20.
21. Although he still views Central European history as 'derailed', this is a main conclusion of I. Berendt, *History Derailed: Central and Eastern Europe in the Long Nineteenth Century* (Berkeley, 2003).
22. See for this the many publications in the book series *Deutsch-Französische Kulturbibliothek*, which is published in Leipzig, and also M. Espagne's monograph *Le creuset allemand. Histoire interculturelle de la Saxe (XVIIIe-XIXe siècle)* (Paris, 2000). There also are arguments to build European history on more regional studies. See C. Applegate, 'A Europe of Regions: Reflections on the Historiography of Sub-National Places in Modern Times', *AHR* 104 (Oct. 1999): 1157–82; P. Ther, 'Einleitung: Sprachliche, kulturelle und ethnische "Zwischenräume" als Zugang zu einer transnationalen Geschichte Europas', in *Regionale Bewegungen und Regionalismen in europäischen Zwischenräumen*

seit der Mitte des 19. Jahrhunderts, eds. Ther and H. Sundhaussen (Marburg, 2003), ix–xxix.
23. See C.S. Maier, 'Consigning the Twentieth Century to History: Alternative Narratives for the Modern Era', *AHR* 105 (2000): 807–31.
24. This is what Hartmut Kaelble argues in his introduction into comparative history. See Kaelble, *Der historische Vergleich*, 19–21.
25. See M. Werner and B. Zimmermann, 'Penser l'histoire croisée: entre empirie et réflexivité', *Annales HSS* 58 (2003): 7–36, here 8. There also is a slightly different German version of the article with the title: 'Vergleich, Transfer, Verflechtung. Der Ansatz der Histoire croisée und die Herausforderung des Transnationalen', *Geschichte und Gesellschaft* 28 (2002): 607–36.
26. A similar demand, which is absent in earlier comparative history, is also made by H. Siegrist, 'Perspektiven der vergleichenden Geschichtswissenschaft. Gesellschaft, Kultur, Raum', in *Vergleich und Transfer. Komparatistik in den Sozial-, Geschichts- und Kulturwissenschaften*, eds. H. Kaelble and J. Schriewer (Frankfurt a.M., 2003), 307–28.
27. See for example the works of J. Kocka and T. Welskopp.
28. See H.A. Winkler, *Der lange Weg nach Westen*, 2 vols. (Munich, 2000).
29. In this regard, Jürgen Kocka's three-volume history of the *Bürgertum* in nineteenth century Europe was a pioneering work, because it contained articles about the Czech, Polish, and Hungarian bourgeoisie. The work of Eastern Europeanists in Germany also had a strong comparative dimension. See especially the publication by Klaus Zernack, who combined the study of Polish and Prussian history, and later Polish and Russian history. See K. Zernack, *Preußen—Deutschland—Polen. Aufsätze zur Geschichte der deutsch-polnischen Beziehungen* (Berlin, 1991); K. Zernack, *Polen und Russland: Zwei Wege in der europäischen Geschichte* (Berlin, 1994).
30. Arguments for the *Sonderweg* thesis are the traditions of the 'Obrigkeitsstaat', the effects of bureaucratization, and the simultaneity of deep structural changes in politics, society, and the economy. See J. Kocka, 'Asymmetrical Historical Comparison: The Case of the German *Sonderweg*', *History and Theory* 38(1) (1999): 40–51, here 41–43. All of these factors were valid in Czech history as well, and yet the Czechs developed one of the few and the most stable democracies in interwar Europe.
31. Two publications of the late 1980s already quite fully developed the program of 'transferts culturels' in the late 1980s. See M. Espagne and M. Werner, 'La construction d'une référence culturelle allemande en France—Génèse et Histoire (1750–1914)', *Annales E.S.C.* (Jul./Aug. 1987): 969–92; M. Espagne and M. Werner, eds., *Transferts. Les relations interculturelles dans l'espace franco-allemand* (Paris, 1988). For an entire genealogy of the approach of cultural transfers until recent times, see M. Middell's introduction into the internet forum Geschichte.transnational.
32. See L. Febvre, *Le Rhin: Problemes d'histoire et d'economie* (Paris, 1935). The book has been translated into German as *Der Rhein und seine Geschichte* (Frankfurt a.M., 1994).

33. J. Pekař, 'Smysl českých dějin', in J. Pekař, *O smyslu českých dějin*, 3rd ed. (Prague, 1990), 383–405, here 394–401.
34. Chris Lorenz even sees a danger of a re-nationalization of historiography in North America. See C. Lorenz, 'Comparative Historiography: Problems and Perspectives', *History and Theory* 38(1) (1999): 25–39, here 26.
35. See C. Conrad and S. Conrad, eds., *Die Nation schreiben. Geschichtswissenschaft im internationalen Vergleich* (Göttingen, 2002). Still, Wehler insists on the relevance of the nation state for historiography. See H.-U. Wehler, "Transnationale Geschichte – der neue Königsweg historischer Forschung", in G. Budde, S. Conrad, O. Janz, eds. *Transnationale Geschichte. Themen, Tendenzen unde Theorien* (Göttingen, 2006), 164–74, here 173.
36. This new series is edited by W. Paravicini and M. Werner and published by the *Wissenschaftliche Buchgesellschaft* in Darmstadt. So far, two volumes have appeared covering the period between 800–1214 and 1500–1648. Since the early 1990s, there also is the book series, *Deutsch-Französische Kulturbibliothek*, published at the University of Leipzig.
37. This variation in historical geography has political reasons. The term 'Mitteleuropa' was misused by the National Socialists. Therefore, it has been shunned by most professional historians in Germany in the postwar period. It was revived in the so-called '*Mitteleuropadebatte*' driven by intellectuals in the successor states of the Habsburg Empire in the 1980s. For the discourse about 'Mitteleuropa' see T. Judt, 'The Rediscovery of Central Europe', *Daedalus* 119(1) (1990): 23–54.
38. This is only a very abbreviated version of the structural definition. For a more comprehensive account, see Zernack, *Preußen—Deutschland—Polen;* Szücs; W. Eberhard et al., eds., *Westmitteleuropa—Ostmitteleuropa. Vergleiche und Beziehungen* (Munich, 1992).
39. See J. Fradera, 'Regionalism and Nationalism: Catalonia within Modern Spain', in *Regionale Bewegungen und Regionalismen in europäischen Zwischenräumen seit der Mitte des 19. Jahrhunderts*, eds. P. Ther and H. Sundhaussen (Marburg, 2003), 3–18. For the rich cultural history of Catalonia, see the multivolume edition by G. Pere, ed., *Historia de la cultura catalana*, 10 vols. (Barcelona, 1994–1998).
40. These similarities were the basis of a project that compared Ireland and Poland. See J. Belchem and K. Tenfelde, eds., *Irish and Polish Migration in Comparative Perspective* (Essen, 2003).
41. See M.G. Müller, 'Adel und Elitenwandel in Ostmitteleuropa: Fragen an die polnische Adelsgeschichte im ausgehenden 18. und 19. Jahrhundert', *Zeitschrift für Ostmitteleuropaforschung* 50 (2001): 497–513.
42. See a comprehensive overview of his definition of Central Europe in M. Csáky, *Ideologie der Operette und Wiener Moderne. Ein kulturhistorischer Essay*, 2nd. ed. (Vienna, 1998), 169. In contrast to his German colleagues, Csáky stresses the relevance of dynasties for the history of Central Europe, especially the Habsburgs.
43. Ibid., 172.

44. For the relations of Ukraine with the West see R. Szporluk, 'The Making of Modern Ukraine: The Western Dimension', *Harvard Ukrainian Studies* 25 (2001): 57–90; and several articles in G. Kasianov, P. Ther, eds., *A Laboratory of Transnational History: Ukraine and Recent Ukrainian Historiography* (Budapest, 2009).
45. This is accomplished in a recent history of early modern Poland, which could be labelled as transnational. See A.S. Kamiński, *Historia rzeczypospolitej wielu narodów 1505–1795. Obywatele, ich państwa, społeczeństwo, kultura* (Lublin, 2000).
46. There are, however, many studies by Klaus Zernack that combine Polish and German history. See among many publications his collection of essays *Preußen—Deutschland—Polen. Aufsätze zur Geschichte der deutsch-polnischen Beziehungen* (Berlin, 1991).
47. See for this axis of cultural exchange P. Ther, *In der Mitte der Gesellschaft. Operntheater in Zentraleuropa 1815–1914* (Vienna, 2006), 411–12.
48. For the imperial shape of the Eastern half of Europe, see A. Miller and A. Rieber, eds., *Imperial Rule* (Budapest, 2004).
50. See for example H. Schmidt, *Die Selbstbehauptung Europas. Perspektiven für das 21. Jahrhundert* (Stuttgart, 2000). Recent concepts for comparisons between civilizations (*Zivilisationsvergleich*) have also excluded Russia and constructed an Eastern Slavonic, orthodox or Soviet civilization, which is juxtaposed with Europe. See for example J. Osterhammel, *Geschichtswissenschaft jenseits des Nationalstaats. Studien zu Beziehungsgeschichte und Zivilisationsvergleich* (Göttingen, 2001). The case of Ukraine or of Greece and other zones of overlapping influences probably suffice as a way to point at the problems of such an approach.
49. In addition to Braudel's early modern Mediteranée, the concept of Southern Europe was utilized at a conference at the Berlin College for Comparative History of Europe (BKVGE) in 2005. The title of the conference was: 'Der Süden Europas—Strukturraum, Wahrnehmungsraum, Handlungsraum?'; a book will appear in 2006.
51. See D.T. Rodgers, *Atlantic Crossings: Social Politics in a Progressive Age* (Cambridge, MA, 1998).
52. For a postcolonial perspective on European history see Conrad and Randeria, 'Einleitung', *Geteilte Geschichten*, 22–42. Postcolonial approaches can also be fruitfully applied for Central European history. See J. Feichtinger, U. Prutsch, and M. Csáky, eds., *Habsburg postcolonial. Machtstrukturen und kollektives Gedächtnis* (Innsbruck, 2003); see for Prussia and the German Empire and the following references to Polish-German relations P. Ther, 'Deutsche Geschichte als imperiale Geschichte. Polen, slawophone Minderheiten und das Kaiserreich als kontinentales Empire', in S. Conrad and J. Osterhammel, *Das Kaiserreich transnational*, 129–48.
53. See F. Moretti, *Atlas des europäischen Romans. Wo die Literatur spielte* (Cologne, 1999).

54. See for these networks of music and opera Ther, *In der Mitte der Gesellschaft*, 395–421.
55. For the formation of a European public see H. Kaelble, *Europäer über Europa. Die Entstehung des europäischen Selbstverständnisses im 19. und 20. Jahrhundert* (Frankfurt a.M., 2001).
56. See for Dvořák's career and his stay in America M. Beckerman, ed., *Dvořák and his World* (Princeton, 1993).
57. See K. Geitel, 'Angelo Neumanns "Wanderndes Richard Wagner Theater"', *Theater und Zeit* 12(2) (Oct. 1964): 21–27.
58. See K. J. Bade, *Europa in Bewegung. Migration vom späten 18. Jahrhundert bis zur Gegenwart* (Munich, 2000).
59. Several cases of remigration are compiled in a collective volume edited by D. Hoerder, ed., *Labor migration in the Atlantic economies: The European und North American working classes during the period of industrialization* (Westport, 1985), here 353–434 (part II of the volume). For the Germans see also K. Schniedewind, 'Fremde in der Alten Welt: die tranatlantische Rückwanderung', in *Deutsche im Ausland—Fremde in Deutschland. Migration in Geschichte und Gegenwart*, ed. K. Bade (Munich, 1992), 179–85. For southeastern Europe see J. Puskás, *Overseas Migration from East-Central and South-Eastern Europe 1880–1940* (Budapest, 1990).
60. M. Castells, 'Materials for an exploratory theory of the network society', here 15. For this article there also has been used the first of three volumes of Castells' book about the 'network society'. German version as M. Castells, *Der Aufstieg der Netzwerkgesellschaft. Teil 1 der Trilogie. Das Informationszeitalter* (Opladen, 2004).
61. For a detailed account between the different ways and traditions of writing European history see the special issue of the journal *Comparativ: Comparativ* 14(3) (2004) about problems and perspectives of European historiography, especially the introduction by H. Siegrist and R. Petri and the articles by M.G. Müller and H.-G. Haupt in this volume (on 7–14, 72–97). See also H. Duchhardt, ed., *'Europäische Geschichte' als historiographisches Problem* (Mainz, 1997). There is much more literature about the problem of historiography of Europe in German and in other languages that cannot be cited in this short article.

CHAPTER 10

Germany and Africa in the Late Nineteenth and Twentieth Centuries

An Entangled History?[1]

ANDREAS ECKERT

I.

Until very recently, Germany's colonial past was more or less ignored by both professional academics and the wider public.[2] This ignorance had to do with the widespread conviction that colonialism had to be equated with colonial rule. Thus, Germany only was allocated a place at the margins of colonial involvement. There is no doubt, of course, that the German colonial empire was not very important in economic terms and only lasted for little more than three decades, between the 1880s and the First World War. Still, it would be wrong to argue that because German colonial rule was so short-lived, it also was irrelevant to German history. Colonial possessions are one thing, colonialism and colonial thinking another. Charles Maier argued a few years ago that the creation of nation states and colonial imperialism were but two sides of the same coin, but also that the colonial project was a western project, shared by most people in Europe.[3] Even those who did not take part directly in this project approved it, because it promised markets and raw material, knowledge, progress, and civilization. Thus, one could argue that Germany with and without colonies was a close ally to the colonial project, and that the effects of the colonial experience considerably influenced German culture and society, not only during the period when Germany possessed colonies, but also after the First World War.[4] A particularly controversial discussion recently arose around the question of what German colonialism had to do with National Socialism, to what extent colonial racial doctrines and practices, especially the genocide of the Herero in German South West Africa, shaped the Nazi wars of extermination and the Holocaust.[5] It should be added that the repercussions of the colonial experience to metropolitan politics, economics, and, above all, culture are by now a long established topic in the historiography on other European colonial powers, especially Great Britain.[6]

The reluctance of German historians to deal with colonialism is closely connected with the strong focus on the nation state in German modern history, but it also results from the strong focus on the history of everyday life, the *Alltagsgeschichte*, which favored German localities and thus unwillingly further promoted a certain provincialization of knowledge. To put it somewhat roughly, the attitude of the German *Alltagsgeschichte* was like this: why should we work on cocoa?—German workers consumed potatoes and never cocoa, thus research on potatoes is more important than research on cocoa. As the German colonial empire was short-lived and economically marginal, there were obviously no reasons for German historians, with their focus on the history of the nation state, to explore the potential of this field of research. The overall importance of the Holocaust and the German *Sonderweg* for the critical historians of the 1960s, 1970s, and 1980s,[7] but also the fact that in Germany after 1945, there were only few national or colonial minorities who could call for their histories, further marginalized colonialism as a scholarly or media topic.[8]

Not surprisingly, all too often the history of German colonialism is treated as an appendix of the German *Kaiserreich*. It should be added that the ways German historians dealt with colonialism corresponded widely with the attitude of politicians. While, for example, France after 1945 was shaken by a huge decolonization crisis,[9] Germany was apparently left untouched by the problematic consequences of colonial rule. The 'coping' with the Nazi past and with the Holocaust, as well as the integration into the West in the context of the Cold War, ranked high on the political agenda. In this context, German politicians were prepared to concede—at least to a certain extent—the fatal role of anti-Semitism in German history; colonial racism and the economic exploitation of Africa, Asia, and Latin America, however, were seen as something with which the other European states had to cope. This attitude is still widespread among German politicians and the media. Take, for example, the reaction to the speech of the German Minister of Foreign Affairs, Joschka Fischer, at the Durban conference against racism in September 2001, where Fischer excused himself in the name of Germany for slavery and colonialism. The *Frankfurter Allgemeine Zeitung* informed Fischer, 'Unlike Great Britain, Spain, Portugal, France and the Netherlands, Germany does not look back on a distinct colonial past', and sneered at Fischer's attempts 'to take the blame for whatever evils Germany performed'[10]. And when in August 2004, the German Minister for Development and Cooperation, Heide Wieczorek-Zeul, publicly and very emotionally declared that the war of the Germans against the Herero and Nama in German South West Africa between 1904 and 1908 could be defined as a genocide,[11] Christian Ruck, a politician of the Christian Democratic Party, immediately launched a press release in the name of his parliamentary party, which stated, 'Emotional outburst of Minister for Development can cost millions to German taxpayers', arguing that Wieczorek-Zeul's excuse could provide the legal base for Herero claims for reparations.[12]

After the Second World War, the Federal Republic of Germany was even able to present itself as a guiltless partner in development politics, with politicians free of neo-colonial aims. The formerly lamented 'loss' of the colonies was reinterpreted as a virtue. In 1959, for instance, permanent secretary Hasso von Etzdorf noted, 'We have a great advantage in Africa—the loss of our colonies forty years ago'.[13] On the other hand, the German Democratic Republic regarded itself the 'natural partner' of the 'national liberation movements' in Africa and tried to uncover the neo-colonial efforts of the government in Bonn. The whole complex of development politics and policies provides, indeed, a good example for the fact that even many decades after the formal end of German colonialism, German policies were still involved in structures that were, in turn, part of the colonial project. The development initiatives after the Second World War were children of late colonialism and of the crises in the colonial empires of France and Great Britain.[14] Many of the ideologies and practices relevant then are still—in slightly modified form—relevant for the development policies of European countries today—just think of the belief in the superiority of Europe or of the neglect of local African knowledge.[15] At the economic level, many German firms took great advantages from 'colonial situations and constellations' in the world economy, for example, from the fact that Africa is still only the producer of raw material without any important processing industries.

Recent 'colonial studies' on Germany, however, are not interested in economics. Some literary scholars and anthropologists, mainly from the German departments in the United States, quite recently have established new attempts that can be subsumed under the field of postcolonial studies. Often on the basis of a relatively small set of contemporary texts, these scholars attempt to uncover the 'colonial discourse' in imperial Germany. Though most of this work on colonial discourses and fantasies ignores the empirical data available and shows a tendency to self-loved over-theorization, as well as a certain ignorance of the more violent realities of colonial rule, it opens up a new and interesting field of questions, for example, of race and gender, aspects which have been neglected so far in the relevant German historiography. Moreover, these studies refer to the fact that colonial imaginations were not limited to geographical and temporal boundaries. Still, a somewhat puzzling feature of this historiography is the more or less complete absence of the colonized as agents of history. The request of

Frederick Cooper and Ann Stoler to treat metropole and colony in a single analytical field is often quoted but seldom realized, at least in the case of German colonialism.[16] Even empirically well-grounded studies emphasize the metropolitan side of colonialism and show little or no interest in the 'colonial situation' and the colonized populations (besides in their function as 'projection surface' for the colonizers' fantasies and projects).[17] It is without any doubt important to study—also in the German case—the repercussions of colonial experiences and fantasies to European societies, but the place of the colonized in the history of colonialism should be kept in mind as well.

This leads us to the concept of 'entangled' or 'shared histories'.[18] This concept implies, on the one hand, the idea that the creation and development of the modern world can be conceptualized as a 'shared history', in which different cultures and societies shared a number of central experiences and through their interactions and interdependence commonly created the modern world. On the other hand, the growing circulation of goods, people, and ideas not only produced common ground, but at the same time created disassociations and differences, the need for particularities, and the hypostatization of dichotomous structures. Moreover, the reference to 'interaction' should not imply the ignorance of inequality, power, and violence. Relations between Europe and the non-European world were often hierarchical or even repressive. 'Europe was made by its imperial projects, as much as colonial encounters were shaped by conflicts within Europe itself.'[19] It is impossible to conceptualize European modernity and leave out colonialism and imperialism. Europe realized itself in the world by arguing and disputing with other societies beyond its own boundaries. European expansion changed the world, and it changed Europe. European expansion not only affected the conquered and colonized territories overseas, it also affected the metropolitan states. This was also true for Germany, which—with and without colonies—was part of the European colonial project. The following pages represent a still provisional effort to discuss the concept of 'entangled histories' with the example of Germany and Africa. German colonial possessions were concentrated on Africa, and in the course of the twentieth century, in Germany, colonialism and Africa became more or less synonymous.[20] This article focuses on the ways in which experiences with and images of or fantasies about Africa or Africans shaped German history.

II.

Recent debates about colonialism in Africa (and elsewhere) stress the agency of the colonized Africans and conceptualize the colonial situation as a process of manifold as well as contradictory struggles.[21] In this context, Africans made efforts to use all resources available that the European presence offered. African rulers and slave owners, as much as peasants and slaves, redefined their relationship into something other than that of employer and worker. Germans as well as other colonial rulers soon found that 'they could only maintain order by forging alliances with the very elites whose tyranny they had railed against, and colonialism in most of the continent soon settled for living off the surplus production of peasants or extracting surplus value from labourers who retained a strong foothold in their villages and thus gave only part of their being to the demands of capitalist production'.[22] However, Jacob Ajayi's famous dictum of the 1960s, that colonialism was only an episode in the continuous flow of African history, is difficult to accept today.[23] There is no doubt that the effects and consequences of colonial rule on Africa considerably and deeply changed African societies and landscapes. The colonial experience changed the colonizers as well. The whole domain of social discipline was a particularly important element of the colonial experience. Ideas about racial orders and discourses about sexuality in the European bourgeois order often received their inspiration from colonial contexts. Moreover, colonies marked a place beyond the inhibitions of the increasingly bourgeois cultures of Europe. Thus, colonies were sites of unfettered economic and sexual opportunity, where masculine self-indulgence could be given free vent. Furthermore, colonies have been seen as laboratories of modernity, where missionaries, educators, and doctors could carry out experiments in social engineering without confronting the popular resistances and bourgeois rigidities of European society at home.[24]

It would be extremely useful to test this catalogue in the German case. Some recent work makes attempts to stress the connections between colonialism and the order of society in Germany. One particularly interesting dimension is the legal one. A number of legal measures, especially the revised version of the 'Nationality Law' from 1913, need to be contextualized in the colonial setting.[25] During the long debates about this law in the German parliament, specific colonial questions played an important role. A fierce debate was raised around the ban of so-called mixed marriages and the possibility of establishing racial criteria in the nationality law. In the end, due to numerous administrative problems, problems of definition, and due to massive opposition from the Social Democrats and some other parties, the related regulations did not find their way into the legal text. The valid model of a patrilineal nationality was successful once more; the 'male state' prevailed over the racial state, so to speak.[26] Another regulation, also closely connected with the colonies, became a part of the revised nationality law. This regulation is still relevant today—the key word here is *Spätaussiedler*, or 'late emigrants', which means emigrants of German origin from Eastern European States. From 1913 on, the right to German nationality did not expire after ten years, and this right was even transferable to descendants. With this measure, the German government wanted to make sure that the German people and the German economy would not lose German settlers in the non-European possessions.

Women organized in the colonial movement were among the fiercest advocates of the ban of mixed marriages.[27] An 'appeal to all German-minded men and women' from October 1912, mainly signed by bourgeois women, stated, 'Should German women and girls silently tolerate that they are put on the same level as members of the lowest races? Should they sit back and watch while their sons and brothers have intimate relations with women of this race, relations that can stand up against the law as marriage, but that morally superior men can and should never accept?'[28] The racial hierarchy of a male-dominated imagination was taken over here; one could argue that the 'colonial equality' for German women was linked to the subjugation of the local population in the colonies.[29] The role of women in the colonial project was highly ambivalent and reflects central aspects of the struggles over gender roles in Wilhelminian Germany. On the one hand, attempts to settle more women in the colonies were based upon the efforts to take specific attitudes about domesticity and family into the colonies.[30] On the other hand, many women regarded their participation in colonialism and racial rule as an indication of their 'national usefulness', which went far beyond the usual domestic duties.[31] The writer Frieda von Bülow described her stay in East Africa even as liberation from paternalistic ties and as a possibility for self-responsible female activities. Her impressions from the colony were, in fact, suitable for destroying whatever confidence she may have had in male superiority. Instead of aristocratic self-control and virility, she mainly found faint-heartedness, greed, and inefficiency on the one hand, and brutal violence, on the other.[32]

Colonies not only served as cultural and social laboratories, but also as 'scientific' laboratories, particularly in the field of medical research. For instance, German medical researchers made experiments with typhoid inoculation during the Herero war in German South West Africa (today Namibia) and used African war prisoners as human experimentees.[33] The fame of Robert Koch, the great bacteriologist, is based, among other things, upon his research in German East Africa. Medical researchers especially felt the end of the German colonial empire as a dramatic loss of working and experimental opportunities. Doctors became an important part of the revisionist syndrome of the Weimar Republic. They employed a rhetoric of delay, arguing, for example, that in medical and other scientific research, Germany would fall behind the leading nations. Doctors also stand for a certain continuity between colonialism and National Socialism, both at a personal and at a more structural level, for instance, in regard to human experiments.³⁴ The continuity between imperialism and racism, between colonial wars and the Holocaust, was emphasized many years ago by Hannah Arendt.³⁵ Among other things, Hannah Arendt stressed that the Herero War in Namibia was something like a 'preliminary stage' of the Holocaust.

Some recent studies haven taken up this idea. Jürgen Zimmerer argues in several publications that the Nazi wars of conquest and extermination, with their central terms of 'race' and 'space', stand in a line of tradition with European colonialism.³⁶ However, according to Zimmerer, the Holocaust is not a simple copy of the European conquest of America, Australia, and South Africa, but an extremely radicalized variant at best. The Nazi crimes cannot be traced back straightforwardly to colonialism; both in ideology and policy, National Socialism was far too complex and eclectic. However, Zimmerer argues that colonialism stands for breaking the last taboo—that is, not only to think about the extermination of other ethnic groups, but also to act accordingly. Without this consequence, the assassination of the European Jews probably would have been unthinkable. There is, according to Zimmerer, one decisive difference between colonialism and National Socialism, and this is the different role the state played in colonial genocides. The bureaucratic and state-organized killing depended upon the stage of development of the state. While at the New England frontier we had massacres carried out by settlers and militia, the embryonic modern administrative state in German South West Africa established prisoner camps as sites of extermination activities. The genocide of the Herero was not an active, industrial killing, but there death had occurred already through neglect. For instance, the German administration introduced pre-printed death certificates with the inscription 'death through exhaustion'. As Arendt offered little empirical evidence and failed to specify the institutional and cultural mechanisms by which ideas and practices developed in the imperial realm were transmitted back to Europe and became the bases for policies instituted decades later, new research investigates the imperial experience of ex-colonial actors and their career paths in the Weimar and Nazi period. This research particularly looks at institutions, such as military training camps and colonial associations, as key sites for the transmission of racially based ideas and strategies developed in the imperial realm before 1918 to new cohorts of officers and officials.³⁷

Is there even a connection between the loss of the colonies and the rise of Nazism? Many years ago, Frantz Fanon, the radical theorist of an anti-colonial revolution, insisted that fascism in essence was a European imperialism turned inward—that is why fascism was most successful in Germany, which had lost its colonies in 1918.³⁸ One could fiercely debate this idea; there is no doubt, at least, that after the First World War, colonial projects and fantasies continued to shape German society and politics in many ways. Ironically, there was never so much agreement on the importance of colonies in Germany as after the loss of colonial territories in the First World War. We can observe for the period between the two World Wars something that Dirk van Laak has labelled the 'imaginary elaboration of an imperial infrastructure'.[39] Many Germans were very angry about the verdict of the Allies in the Treaty of Versailles, which stated that Germany had proved incapable of colonizing. As if to prove the opposite, during the Weimar Republic a number of individuals presented fantastic ideas and projects about how to make Africa productive and link it to Europe. A particularly remarkable proposal was made by the Munich architect Hermann Sörgel, who intended to partially drain the Mediterranean Sea in order to link Europe and Africa to a single continent: 'Alantropa'.[40]

Interwar Africa remained an important element of German expansion fantasies and plans, at times even more important—and more popular— than Eastern Europe. In the late 1930s, the Nazi government initiated intensive plans and preparations for a future German colonial empire. Compared to parallel projects for a new order in Eastern Europe, plans for a colonial German Africa were comparatively moderate. In this context, one could ask, by the way, why the German expansion in Eastern Europe was never systematically analysed as part of the German colonial project. In any case, the end of the German war expansion to the East marked by Stalingrad also meant the official end of any colonial activities. In 1943, the Nazi authorities officially ordered the end of all colonial planning activities. At this point, the German colonial empire was nearly completed on the drawing board. The historian Wolf Schmokel sarcastically notes that there was never a non-existing empire that was better administered than this one.[41] Until this date, the Africans living in Germany were mostly excluded from systematic persecution. This was due to the fact that they were regarded as potential middlemen in a future German colonial empire in Africa.

III.

The migration of Africans to Germany to a larger extent only began during the period of formal German colonialism in the late nineteenth and early twentieth centuries.[42] After 1884, mainly male individuals from Germany's African colonies temporarily or permanently established their home in Germany, most of them in the big cities of Berlin and Hamburg.[43] Their overall number is very difficult to determine. Estimates in the secondary literature differ considerably. They range from 500 colonial migrants from the period 1885 to 1945, to around 3,000 individuals only for the 1920s and 1930s.⁴⁴ In any case, the number of Africans in Germany remained very small. Compared to France and Great Britain, the impact of Africans on German society was less significant, and there was never a 'Black Berlin' or a 'Black Hamburg' comparable to the 'Black Paris' before the Second World War.⁴⁵ Nevertheless, the lives and experiences of Africans in Germany constitute an important and hitherto little-known chapter at the intersection of African history, German history, and the history of the African diaspora.

Africans in Germany formed a rather heterogeneous group, and they came for very different reasons. During the three decades of German colonial rule in Africa, some—especially chiefs' sons—were brought or sent as children or young adults for training at Christian mission societies and trade workshops; others taught African languages at the universities and colonial institutes of Berlin and Hamburg; some accompanied returning colonial officers as servants or were recruited for one of the ethnographic exhibitions (*Völkerschauen*), which became very popular in Germany at the end of the nineteenth century.⁴⁶ Some Africans tried their luck as businessmen;⁴⁷ many, especially after 1918, worked as servants or in the field of entertainment. In most cases, African migration to Germany took place occasionally and without force.

The history of African migration to, and African presence in, Germany from the late nineteenth century until the Second World War can be divided into three phases:

1. Before the First World War, in general, colonial migrants were regarded as an unwelcome side effect of colonial politics. This led to increased efforts by the colonial administration to restrict the influx of Africans. German authorities tried to make sure that no African would stay in Germany permanently. From the perspective of these authorities, the unclarified legal status of African migrants constituted a major problem. The specific legal status of Africans as 'natives' (*Eingeborene*) was only in force in the colonies. During their stay in Germany, Africans had to be treated either as 'domestic citizens' (*Inländer*) or as 'expatriates', but more rights were attached to both statuses than colonial administrations had provided for their 'native subjects' in the colonies. During the colonial period, the state kept close watch on Africans in Germany, attempting to control as much of their movements as possible because of the potential political threat they posed. Those Africans who exposed themselves politically and self-consciously claimed rights and status had to face massive reprisals. Mpundu Akwa, the son of an important Cameroonian chief from Douala, spent the years between 1902 and 1911 in

Germany, where he tried to support the protest of the Duala against German misrule in Cameroon, but also—not very successfully—tried his hand at doing business. However, Mpundu became a figure of considerable notoriety in Germany. The public seems to have been 'highly entertained by the image, portrayed in both newspaper interviews and music hall burlesques, of a black man speaking excellent German, wearing a monocle and formal attire, who gave himself the airs of both metropolitan *Herr* and an African prince'.[48] But his claims to be treated as the peer of European authorities and, probably even worse, his appearances as the public escort and possibly private lover of bourgeoisie and even aristocratic European women seemed to threaten the very foundations of racial order. A retired naval captain, Liersemann, went so far as to accuse him of grand larceny and brothel keeping. Mpundu Akwa combated this charge with a lawsuit. In the course of the trial, Liersemann withdrew most of his accusations, but Mpundu's long record of financial embarrassment came to light. Mpundu won the first round of his case, but in two subsequent appeals, Liersemann was acquitted entirely, on the grounds that 'the concept of sensitivity to honour is not as developed among Negroes as among *Kulturmenschen*'.[49] Mpundu returned to Cameroon and was eventually imprisoned by the colonial authorities.[50]

2. With the end of the German empire in 1919, migrants from the former German colonies became subjects of the new mandatory powers, Great Britain, France, Belgium, and South Africa. In legal terms, this change meant that Africans in Germany came nearer to the status of expatriates. However, the Weimar authorities, and especially the relevant department of the Foreign Office, strictly refused to naturalize Africans. Africans either got the label 'stateless' in their passport, or they got a certificate as 'formerly belonging to a German protectorate' or as 'former German *protégé*' (*Schutzbefohlener*). Thus, the legal status of Africans in Germany remained unclear. Some Africans started to establish cultural and political networks in order to look after their rights and interests. For instance, in 1918, the Cameroonian Peter Makembe founded in Hamburg the 'African Aid Association' (*Afrikanischer Hilfsverein*). One of the tasks of this organization was to support Africans in finding a job and accommodation or to help them in dealing with German authorities and employers. German politicians had mixed feelings about the presence of the more or less right-less but increasingly self-confident Africans. While some officials preferred to 'carry these people directly back to Africa',[51] others regarded the small African diaspora in Germany as a positive factor.

As these latter officials were convinced that one day Germany would get back their colonies, the Africans living in metropolitan Germany were seen as potential multipliers who, once back in Africa, would spread a positive image of Germany. Thus, for the time being, forced deportation was out of the question. The Foreign Office employed a strategy that was meant to encourage Africans to leave the country 'voluntarily'. At the same time, the authorities took care to secure the livelihoods of Africans during the remaining time of their stay in Germany. For this purpose, the 'German Society for the Study of Natives' (*Deutsche Gesellschaft für Eingeborenenkunde*) was engaged to support needy Africans.[52]

Even those German officials who found it useful to treat Africans well, however, vehemently rejected relationships between African men and German women, although there was no legal hold on African-German marriages in Germany. In the years after the First World War, there were heightened 'race anxieties' due to the so-called 'Black Horror on the Rhine'—the presence of several thousand African soldiers among the French troops that occupied the Rhineland—as well as a prevalent sense that the 'proper racial order' had been inverted by the Versailles treaty, which treated Germany as an 'object' rather than a full subject of international law, and by the 'reverse colonization' of the Rhineland with French colonial soldiers.[53] In the German public, the African soldiers were presented as 'cannibals' and rapists. To quote only one of many similar examples, the *Ärztliche Rundschau*, a medical journal, wrote in 1920, 'Shall we silently endure that in future days not the light songs of white, beautiful, well-built, intelligent, agile, healthy Germans will ring on the shores of the Rhine, but the croaking sounds of greyish, low-browed, broad-muzzled, plump, bestial, syphilitic mulattos?'[54]

Since the mid 1920s, Germany, especially Berlin and Hamburg, became an important scene for the activities of 'black revolutionaries', in many cases supported by the Soviet Union and the Comintern.[55] According to the Trinidadian George Padmore, a leading figure in the Pan-Africanist movement who for many years was a leader of the Comintern, Moscow did not want to bring attention to itself and carefully chose Germany as the centre of anti-imperial activities:

> They assigned the responsibility of organizing the new anti-imperialist movement to the German Communists.... Shorn of her African and other colonies' defeat in the First World War, Germany was no longer a colonial power; and it was thought that an anti-

imperialist call from Berlin would arouse less suspicion among colonial and dependent peoples than one coming from Western European capitals—London or Paris—possessing overseas empires.[56]

The so called 'Negro Bureau', established in Hamburg in 1930, served as a centre for the exchange of information. Directives from Moscow came there, and political operations were planned and directed. The rise of the Nazis to power in 1933 put an end to these activities.

3. After 1933, a number of African political activists migrated from Germany to France. For those who stayed in Germany, the situation deteriorated. The German government declared nearly all 'members of the German protectorates' as 'stateless', and, due to the increasingly open racism of the German population, it became impossible for most Africans to continue working as artists, etc., in the public. Still, many old colonials were concerned about the negative impact that Nazi race policies might have on former colonial subjects.[57] They argued that at least some Africans in Germany had earned membership in German society by virtue of their service as colonial soldiers. As former 'comrades in the protectorate', they deserved jobs, and it was more desirable to employ former colonial subjects than to let them become burdens to society. These arguments eventually convinced some higher Nazi leaders, and in 1936, a circular was sent to all district leaders (*Gauleiter*), stating:

> About fifty *Neger* from our former colonies live with their families in Germany. These natives are almost entirely without secure jobs, and when they find work, the employer is treated with such hostility that he is forced to let the *Neger* go. I point out that these *Neger* must be offered a means of living in Germany. It must also be taken into consideration ... that some of the *Neger* remain in contact with their homelands and will report their about their treatment in Germany. The Foreign Minister and I have therefore agreed that it must be determined which *Neger* are to be put under special protection for their deployment for Germany. These will then be given a permit from the Foreign Office roughly stating that there are no reservations about their employment.[58]

The idea was that these Africans would serve as colonial propagandists for Germany. For this purpose, the German Africa Show was founded, a travelling exhibit that employed black performers, some of whom were German citizens and almost all of whom had spent many years in Germany, but who played the part of 'Africans' for the

German crowds.⁵⁹ The show offered a means of survival to a number of blacks in Germany, who found it nearly impossible to find employment under the repressive regime established by the Nuremberg Laws. In exchange, however, they were forced to bring forward the political message of colonial revisionists: that German colonizers had not been brutal to their colonial subjects, as the Versailles Treaty has claimed, but rather had been especially benevolent and caring, for which reason Africans wanted nothing more than for Germany to recolonize their continent.

The show was shut down in 1940. With the outbreak of the Second World War, and especially after the German government gave up its colonial ambitions after the defeat in Stalingrad in 1943, there were no reasons left to create space for Africans and to exclude them from persecution. In the end, however, as von Joeden-Forgey states, 'the Nazis never created a coherent racial policy for Africans and other blacks in Germany.'⁶⁰ The Africa Show's cancellation in 1940 was supposed to be part of a wider prohibition against the public appearance of blacks. Although the Reich Theatre Chamber officially forbade such appearances, many African show performers still found jobs in the theatre. Others found parts in state-sponsored colonial nostalgia films that became popular during the war. Despite the availability of film and theatre jobs, many African Germans, especially those categorized as *Mischlinge*, were forced into concentration camps. The total number of blacks who were murdered in the camps is disputed; some estimates mention the number of about two thousand.⁶¹ In any case, there are documents indicating that individual Africans got death sentences or were murdered in concentration camps for alleged 'attempted rape' or for *Rassenschande* ('racial pollution').⁶² Despite the space created for Africans due to an incoherent race policy, 'the Nazi State still reserved the right to murder them on an individual basis as unwanted race aliens.'⁶³

IV.

Even after the Second World War, German yearning for Africa flared up once more, this time in the context of the newly designed European Union. As a partner of France, West Germany participated in plans to more systematically open up Africa's raw materials. Political journalists formulated new visions to push forward the opening up of Africa as a common task of Europe. The widely read journalist A.E. Johann stated:

> The world is not yet portioned, quite the contrary! The world is about to be partitioned again. For Europe, and especially for us Germans, the quickly developing African continent offers new and exciting possibilities. But we must realize this; we must realize that there are more important and exciting perspectives than inner-German politics. Africa is a common European task, but it is especially a German task. And this is true of Egypt to Cape Town, and from Dakar to Zanzibar and Madagascar.[64]

Africa also played an important part in the German-German relations.[65] West German attitudes toward the new African states were determined by the so-called Hallstein Doctrine. Hallstein was a permanent secretary in the Ministry of Foreign Affairs. This doctrine implied that the diplomatic acceptance of the GDR by the new African states was regarded by Bonn as an 'unfriendly act' that had to be sanctioned, for example, by cutting development aid. So not only did the two superpowers and the former colonial powers France and Great Britain take the cold war to Africa—Germany did it as well.

Very little research has been done on the importance of the anti-colonial liberation movement and the decolonization process for so-called 'Third World Groups' and solidarity movements in Germany.[66] Church groups and theologians played an important role in this context. Again, it could be argued that the West German solidarity movements were in some ways the late result of the missionary activities. The Third World Movement could be seen as important evidence for a long-term transculturation process caused by colonialism. The effects of this transculturation process went far beyond the boundaries of the Church. Furthermore, mission history, far more than political history, underlines the fact that the colonial project had transnational features right from the beginning. German missionary societies were not just active in German colonies, but also in other parts of Africa. Moreover, English, French, and Swiss mission societies often recruited their personnel in Germany.

Finally, the special attachment many Germans seem to have to the tropical rainforest can also be read as evidence for the fact that colonialism was a point of reference for cultural phenomena and practices in the Federal Republic of Germany. Two icons of the post-Second World War period may illustrate this argument. The first is Albert Schweitzer, who spent a considerable part of his life as a doctor in Lambarene in French Equatorial Africa.[67] After 1945, the then already elderly 'jungle doctor' Schweitzer rose from the jungle, so to speak, and was celebrated by many Europeans, and especially in Germany, as an incarnation of the good Samaritan and alter ego. Moreover, Lambarene became a mythical site, a place where 'German culture' survived during 'the dark years', the 'bad times'. Born in Alsace,

Schweitzer was a French citizen; this did not prevent Germans from celebrating him as 'their' hero. The journalist Rolf Italiander wrote in 1954 that: 'Lambarene is not only a hospital under the equatorial sun, but far more: a bulwark of good old Europe. For this we not only have to thank Albert Schweitzer, we also have to make efforts to emulate Schweitzer and his exceptional moral force.'[68] Here, it is obvious again that the idea of Africa as a continent without culture made Africa a particularly suitable site for utopia and dreams—for worse or for better. The second icon, the extremely popular animal film director Bernhard Grzimek—who won, in 1959, an Academy Award for *Serengeti Must Not Die*—leads us back to colonial dreaming. In his movies, such as *No Place for Wild Animals*, he constructed the tropical rainforest as a stage on which the German search for a place in the sun was re-arranged in the world of animals. The old idea of the 'people without space' was transferred in an amazingly open way to the African fauna.[69]

Colonial images are still very much with us—just have a look at schoolbooks or at travel reports published in newspapers and weeklies, not to mention the statements of German politicians when they talk about Africa once there is no microphone or camera around. A recent investigation about the presentation of Africa in German mass media and teaching manuals concluded: 'Especially as far as Africa is concerned, highly problematic ways of presenting the continent continue. This is especially true for schoolbooks on subjects that covered Africa already in colonial times—biology and geography, for example.'[70]

V.

It would be certainly misleading to overestimate the impact of colonial experience in Africa on German metropolitan history. The sometimes exaggerated enthusiasm of some authors, who now everywhere discover colonial traces in German history, can be explained at least partly by the long and complete neglect of the colonial dimension of German history. This article has tried to provide some ideas and evidence for the fact that Africa and Africans during and after colonial rule shaped German history in many ways and in various degrees. One could certainly argue about the 'relevance' of specific phenomena presented in this article, and further research and more empirical data are definitely needed. Still, there should be no doubt that African and German histories overlapped at various levels and influenced each other. Their 'shared histories' were characterized by violence, racism, and hierarchies. Few people would deny that African history cannot be conceptualized without colonialism. This article attempted to provide arguments for the claim that German history cannot be conceptualized without taking into consideration colonial experiences in Africa and elsewhere.

Notes

1. This article draws in part from A. Eckert and A. Wirz, 'Wir nicht, die Anderen auch. Deutschland und der Kolonialismus', in *Jenseits des Eurozentrismus. Postkoloniale Perspektiven in den Geschichts- und Kulturwissenschaften*, eds. S. Conrad and S. Randeria (Frankfurt, 2002), 372–92.
2. Good examples for this ignorance are widely acclaimed syntheses of German history such as H.-U. Wehler, *Deutsche Gesellschaftsgeschichte*, vol. 3 (Munich, 1995); H. Schulze, *Kleine deutsche Geschichte* (Munich, 1998).
3. C.S. Maier, 'Consigning the Twentieth Century to History. Alternative Narratives for the Modern Era', *American Historical Review* 105(3) (2000): 807–31.
4. S. Conrad, 'Doppelte Marginalisierung. Plädoyer für eine transnationale Perspektive auf die deutsche Geschichte', *Geschichte und Gesellschaft* 28(1) (2002): 145–69; S. Conrad and J. Osterhammel, eds., *Das Kaiserreich transnational. Deutschland in der Welt 1871–1914* (Göttingen, 2004); B. Kundrus, *Moderne Imperialisten. Das Kaiserreich im Spiegel seiner Kolonien* (Cologne, 2003); B. Kundrus, ed., *Phantasiereiche. Zur Kulturgeschichte des deutschen Kolonialismus* (Frankfurt a.M., 2003); S. Friedrichsmeyer, S. Lennox, and S. Zantop, eds., *The Imperialist Imagination. German Colonialism and Its Legacy* (Ann Arbor, 1998); E. Ames, M. Klotz, and L. Wildenthal, eds., *Germany's Colonial Past* (London/Lincoln, 2005); D. van Laak, *Imperiale Infrastruktur. Deutsche Planungen für eine Erschließung Afrikas 1880–1960* (Paderborn, 2004); L. Wildenthal, *German Women for Empire, 1884–1945* (Durham, NC, 2001); S. Conrad, *Globalisierung und Nation im deutshcnen kaiserreich* (München, 2006). Fierce criticism of these and other publications, which all stress the importance of the German colonial empire for German history, has recently been brought forward by H.-U. Wehler, 'Transnationale Geschichte—der neue Königsweg historischer Forschung?', in *Transnationale Geschichte. Themen, Tendenzen und Theorien*, eds. G. Budde et al. (Göttingen, 2006), 161–74.
5. See P. Grosse, 'What Does German Colonialism Have to Do with National Socialism? A Conceptual Framework', in Ames, Klotz, and Wildenthal, *Germany's Colonial Past*, 115–34. For the Herero case, see the numerous publications by J. Zimmerer, for instance his 'Die Geburt des Ostlandes aus dem Geist des Kolonialismus. Die nationalsozialistische Eroberungs- und Beherrschungspolitik in (post-)kolonialer Perspektive', in *Sozial.Geschichte* 19(2004): 10–43; J. Zimmerer, 'Krieg, KZ und Völkermord in Südwestafrika. Der erste deutsche Genozid', in *Völkermord in Deutsch-Südwestafrika. Der Kolonialkrieg (1904– 1908) in Namibia und seine Folgen*, eds. J. Zimmerer and J. Zeller (Berlin, 2003), 45–63. For a substantial critique of Zimmerer's approach see: S. Ma-

linowski, R. Gerwarth, 'Der Holocaust als "kolonialer genozid"? Europaische kolonialgewalt und nationalsozialistischer Vernichtungskrieg', *Geschichte und Gesellschaft* 33(3) (2007): 439–66.

6. See especially the influential studies in J. MacKenzies *Studies in Imperialism* series, published by Manchester University Press, for instance: J. MacKenzie, ed., *Imperialism and Popular Culture* (Manchester, 1986); J. MacKenzie, *Propaganda and Empire: The Manipulation of British Public Opinion 1880–1960* (Manchester, 1984); C. Hall, *Civilising Subjects: Metropole and Colony in the English Imagination 1830–1867* (London, 2002); for a sceptical voice, which argues that the empire had a far lower profile in Great Britain than it had abroad, see B. Porter, *The Absent-Minded Imperialists. Empire, Society, and Culture in Britain* (Oxford, 2004).

7. P. Nolte, 'Die Historiker der Bundesrepublik. Rückblick auf eine lange Generation', *Merkur* 53 (1999): 423–32.

8. S. Friedrichsmeyer et al., 'Introduction', *Imperialist Imagination*. In the mid 1980s, a group of feminist African-German women who operated largely outside established academic circles, attempted to connect the formation of an African-German identity with the struggle against racism and discrimination in contemporary Germany. Their main concern was to challenge the widespread idea that 'black' and 'German' constituted an irreconcilable contrast and to establish a counter-discourse to the dominant nationalist paradigm, which excluded the experiences of Africans. See M. Opitz et al., eds., *Farbe bekennen: Afro-deutsche Frauen auf den Spuren ihrer Geschichte* (Berlin, 1986); English version as *Showing Our Color: Afro-German Women Speak Out* (Amherst, 1992).

9. See, for instance, H. Lebovics, *Bringing the Empire Back Home. France in the Global Age* (Durham, NC, 2004); K. Ross, *Fast Cars, Clean Bodies. Decolonization and the Reordering of French Culture* (Cambridge, MA, 1995).

10. *Frankfurter Allgemeine Zeitung* (6 Sept. 2001).

11. *Frankfurter Allgemeine Zeitung* (16 Aug. 2004).

12. J. Böhlke-Itzen, 'Die bundesdeutsche Diskussion und die Reparationsfrage. Ein "ganz normaler Kolonialkrieg?"', in *Genozid und Gedenken. Namibisch-deutsche Geschichte und Gegenwart*, ed. H. Melber (Frankfurt a.M., 2005), 117f.

13. Quoted in U. Engel, *Die Afrikapolitik der Bundesrepublik Deutschland 1949–1999. Rollen und Identitäten* (Münster/Hamburg, 2000), 40.

14. See F. Cooper, *Decolonization and African Society. The Labor Question in British and French Africa* (Cambridge, 1996).

15. See for example E.G. Norris, 'Die Unfähigkeit der Entwicklungshilfe, aus ihrer eigenen Geschichte zu lernen: Die vergessenen Erfahrungen der deutschen kolonialen Ackerbauschule in Togo', in *Entwicklungshilfe und ihre Folgen. Ergebnisse empirischer Untersuchungen in Afrika*, eds. T. Bierschenk and G. Elwert (Frankfurt a.M., 1993), 143–54.

16. A.L. Stoler and F. Cooper, 'Between Metropole and Colony. Rethinking a Research Agenda', in *Tensions of Empire. Colonial Cultures in a Bourgeois World*, eds. A.L. Stoler and F. Cooper (Berkeley, 1997), 4.

17. See, for instance, the otherwise stimulating studies by D. van Laak, *Imperiale Infrastruktur*. S. Conrad, *Globalisierung und Nation*.
18. See S. Randeria, 'Geteilte Geschichte und verwobene Moderne', in *Zukunftsentwürfe. Ideen für eine Kultur der Veränderung*, eds. J. Rüsen et al. (Frankfurt a.M., 1999), 87–96; Conrad and Randeria, *Geteilte Geschichten*, 17–19.
19. Stoler and Cooper, 'Between Metropole and Colony', 1.
20. On German colonialism in other parts of the world and its impact on metropolitan Germany see K. Mühlhahn, *Herrschaft und Widerstand in der 'Musterkolonie' Kiautschou. Interaktionen zwischen China und Deutschland, 1897–1914* (Munich, 2000); M. Fuhrmann, *Der Traum vom deutschen Orient. Zwei deutsche Kolonien im Osmanischen Reich 1851–1918* (Frankfurt, 2006).
21. A. Eckert, *Kolonialismus* (Frankfurt, 2006).
22. F. Cooper, 'Africa in a Capitalist World', in *Crossing Boundaries. Comparative History of Black People in Diaspora*, eds. D. Clark Hine et al. (Bloomington, 1999), 400f.
23. See J.F. Ade Ajayi, 'The Continuity of African Institutions under Colonialism', in *Emerging Themes in African History*, ed. T.O. Ranger (Nairobi, 1968), 189–200.
24. For this catalogue see Stoler and Cooper, 'Between Metropole and Colony', 4f. For a critical discussion of the concept of colonies as laboratories of modernity see D. van Laak, 'Kolonien als "Laboratorien der Moderne"', in: Conrad and Osterhammel, *Das Kaiserreich transnational*, 257–79.
25. See P. Grosse, *Kolonialismus, Eugenik und bürgerliche Gesellschaft in Deutschland, 1850–1918* (Frankfurt, 2000), 160–68; F. El-Tayeb, *Schwarze Deutsche. Der Diskurs um 'Rasse' und nationale Identität 1890–1933* (Frankfurt, 2001), 92ff.; D. Gosewinkel, *Einbürgern und Ausschließen. Die Nationalisierung der Staatsangehörigkeit vom Deutschen Bund bis zur Bundesrepublik Deutschland* (Göttingen, 2001), 303–309; Kundrus, *Moderne Imperialisten*; C. Essner, 'Zwischen Vernunft und Gefühl- Die Reichstagsdebatten von 1912 um koloniale "Rassenmischehen" und "Sexualität"', *Zeitschrift für Geschichtswissenschaft* 45 (1997): 503–19; F.-J. Schulte-Althoff, 'Rassenmischung im kolonialen System. Zur deutschen Kolonialpolitik im letzten Jahrzehnt vor dem Ersten Weltkrieg', *Historisches Jahrbuch* 105 (1985): 52–94.
26. Gosewinkel, *Einbürgern*, 309. In another article, Gosewinkel explicitly states that the Nationality Law is no evidence for the transfer of colonial racial politics to the metropolitan legal order. See Gosewinkel, 'Rückwirkungen des kolonialen Rasserechts? Deutsche Staatsangehörigkeit zwischen Rassestaat und Rechtsstaat', in: Conrad and Osterhammel, *Das Kaiserreich transnational*, 254. Yet it is important to note that the colonial context is important in order to understand the related debates.
27. See Wildenthal, *German Women*.
28. Quoted in Gosewinkel, *Einbürgern*, 307.
29. Ibid., 308. See also M. Maozai, *Herrenmenschen. Frauen im deutschen Kolonialismus* (Reinbek, 1982). More general A.L. Stoler, 'Making Empire Respecta-

ble. The Politics of Race and Sexual Morality in 20th Century Colonial Cultures', *American Ethnologist* 16 (1989): 634–60.
30. See Wildenthal, *German Women;* R. Chickering, "'Casting Their Gaze More Broadly". Women's Patriotic Activism in Imperial Germany', *Past and Present* 186 (1988): 156–85.
31. Gosewinkel, *Einbürgern,* 308.
32. F. Freiin von Bülow, *Reiseskizzen und Tagebuchblätter aus Deutsch-Ostafrika* (Berlin, 1889); F. Freiin von Bülow, *Tropenkoller. Episode aus dem Kolonialleben* (Berlin, 1896); R. Berman, *Enlightenment or Empire. Colonial Discourse in German Culture* (Lincoln/London, 1998), 171ff.; F. Eigler, 'Engendering German Nationalism. Gender and Race in Frieda von Bülow's Colonial Writings', in Friedrichsmeyer et al., *Imperialist Imagination,* 69–86.
33. See W.U. Eckart, *Medizin und Kolonialimperialismus. Deutschland 1884–1945* (Paderborn, 1997), 276f.
34. Ibid., 505ff. However, Eckart can only refer to a few examples that may verify this continuity.
35. H. Arendt, *Elemente und Ursprünge totaler Herrschaft* (Munich, 1986 [1951]).
36. See literature mentioned in endnote 5.
37. E. Weitz from the University of Minnesota is currently undertaking a project in order to search for the missing link between colonial genocidal violence and Nazi crimes.
38. See F. Fanon, *Les damnés de la terre* (Paris, 1961).
39. D. van Laak, *Imperiale Infrastruktur;* D. van Laak, "'Ist je ein Reich, dass es nicht gab, so gut verwaltet worden?" Der imaginäre Ausbau der imperialen Infrastruktur in Deutschland nach 1918', in Kundrus, *Phantasiereiche,* 71–90.
40. D. van Laak, *Weiße Elefanten. Anspruch und Scheitern technischer Großprojekte im 20. Jahrhundert* (Stuttgart, 1999), 166–73.
41. W.W. Schmokel, *Der Traum vom Reich. Der deutsche Kolonialismus zwischen 1919 und 1945* (Gütersloh, 1967).
42. For the history of Africans in Germany before the 1880s, see P. Martin, *Schwarze Teufel, Edle Mohren: Afrikaner in Geschichte und Bewusstsein der Deutschen* (Hamburg, 1993); H.W. Debrunner, *Presence and Prestige. Africans in Europe. A History of Africans in Europe before 1918* (Basel, 1979). For later periods see: K. Oguntoye, *Eine Afro-Deutsche Geschichte. Zur Lebenssituation von Afrikanern und Afro-Deutschen in Deutschland von 1884 bis 1950* (Berlin, 1997); P. Mazón and R. Steingröver, eds., *Not so Plain as Black and White. Afro-German Culture and History, 1890–2000* (Rochester, 2005); M. Bechhaus-Gerst and R. Klein-Arendt, eds., *Die (koloniale) Begegnung. AfrikanerInnen in Deutschland 1880–1945. Deutsche in Afrika 1880–1918* (Frankfurt, 2003); M. Bechhaus-Gerst and R. Klein-Arendt, eds., *AfrikanerInnen in Deutschland und schwarze Deutsche—Geschichte und Gegenwart* (Münster, 2004); T.M. Campt, *Other Germans. Black Germans and the Politics of Race, Gender, and Memory in the Third Reich* (Ann Arbor, 2004).
43. See U. van der Heyden and J. Zeller, eds., *Kolonialmetropole Berlin. Eine Spurensuche* (Berlin, 2002); H. Möhle, ed., *Branntwein, Bibeln und Bananen. Der*

Deutsche Kolonialismus in Afrika. Eine Spurensuche in Hamburg (Hamburg, 1999).
44. For the first estimate see P. Grosse, 'Zwischen Privatheit und Öffentlichkeit. Kolonialmigration in Deutschland, 1900–1940', in Kundrus, *Phantasiereiche*, 91–109, here 107n1; the latter is from P. Martin and C. Alonzo, eds., *Zwischen Charleston und Stechschritt. Schwarze im Nationalsozialismus* (Hamburg, 2004), 9.
45. T. Stovall, *Paris Noir. African Americans in the City of Lights* (New York, 1996).
46. The literature on these exhibitions is quite vast. The most recent study is A. Dreesbach, *Gezähmte Wilde. Die Zurschaustellung 'exotischer' Menschen in Deutschland 1870–1940* (Frankfurt, 2005).
47. L. Hopkins, 'Einbürgerungsakte 1154: Heinrich Ernst Wilhelm Anumu, African Businessman im Imperial Hamburg', in Bechhaus-Gerst and Klein-Arendt, *Koloniale Begegnung*, 161–70.
48. R.A. Austen, 'Cameroon and Cameroonians in Wilhelminian Innenpolitik. Grande Histoire and Petite Histoire', in *L'Afrique et l'Allemagne de la Colonisation à la Coopération, 1884–1986. Le cas du Cameroun*, ed. Kum'a Ndumbe III (Yaoundé, 1986), 204–26, here 219.
49. Quoted in ibid.
50. See A. Eckert, *Die Duala und die Kolonialmächte* (Münster, 1991).
51. The former German Govenor in Cameroon and German South West Africa, Theodor Seitz, as quoted in El-Tayeb, *Schwarze Deutsche*, 108.
52. H. Möhle, 'Betreuung, Erfassung, Kontrolle. Afrikaner aus den deutschen Kolonien und die "Deutsche Gesellschaft für Eingeborenkunde" in der Weimarer Republik', in Bechhaus-Gerst and Klein-Arendt, *Koloniale Begegnung*, 225–36.
53. The literature on this topic is vast. See, for instance, C. Koller, *'Von Wilden aller Rassen niedergemetzelt.' Die Diskussion um die Verwendung von Kolonialtruppen in Europa zwischen Rassismus, Kolonial- und Militärpolitik (1914–1930)* (Stuttgart, 2001). I. Wigger, *Die 'Schwarze Schmach' am Rhein* (Münster 2007).
54. Quoted in F. El-Tayeb, 'Dangerous Liaisons. Race, Nation, and German Identity', in Mazón and Steingröver, *Not so Plain as Black and White*, 27–60, here 49.
55. For brief summaries of their activities see P. Martin, 'Schwarze Sowjets an Elbe und Spree?', in Martin and Alonzo, *Zwischen Charleston und Stechschritt*, 178–93; I. Geiss, *The Pan-African Movement* (London, 1974), ch. 16. An interesting case study: R. Aitken, 'From Cameroon to Germany and Back via Moscow and Paris: The Political Career of Joseph Bile' (1892–1959): Performer, "Negerarbeiter" and Comintern Activist', *Journal of Contemporary History* 43(4) (2008): 597–616.
56. G. Padmore, *Pan-Africanism or Communism: The Coming Struggle for Africa* (London, 1956), 323.
57. For the following paragraph see E. von Joeden-Forgey, 'Race Power in Postcolonial Germany. The German Africa Show and the National Socialist State,

1935–40', in Ames, Klotz, and Wildenthal, *Germany's Colonial Past*, 167–88, esp. 172f.
58. Quoted by ibid., 173.
59. See S. Lewerenz, *Die Deutsche Afrika-Schau (1935–1940). Rassismus, Kolonialrevisionismzus und postkoloniale Auseinandersetzungen im nationalsozialistischen Deutschland* (Frankfurt, 2006); E. Forgey, '"Die große Negertrommel der kolonialen Werbung": Die Deutsche Afrika-Schau 1935–1943', *Werkstatt Geschichte* 3(9) (1994): 25–33.
60. Von Joeden-Forgey, 'Race Power', 180f.
61. Ibid., 181.
62. See M. Bechhaus-Gerst, 'Alexander N'doki. Ein Opfer nationalsozialistischer Justiz', in Martin and Alonzo, *Zwischen Charleston und Stechschritt*, 557–65.
63. Von Joeden-Forgey, 'Race Power', 181.
64. Quoted in Van Laak, *Imperiale Infrastruktur*, 345f.
65. See U. Engel and H.-G. Schleicher, *Die beiden deutschen Staaten in Afrika. Zwischen Konkurrenz und Koexistenz, 1949–1990* (Hamburg, 1998); B.H. Schulz, *Development Policy in the Cold War Era. The Two Germanies and Sub-Saharan Africa, 1960–1985* (Hamburg, 1995).
66. For some information see R. Kößler and H. Melber, *Globale Solidarität? Eine Streitschrift* (Frankfurt, 2002).
67. C. Fetscher, 'Lambarene und der Dschungel der Deutschen', in *Der deutsche Tropenwald. Bilder, Mythen, Politik*, ed. M. Flitner (Frankfurt, 2002), 225–43.
68. Quoted in ibid., 233.
69. See M. Flitner, 'Vom "Platz an der Sonne" zum "Platz für Tiere"', in Flitner, *Der deutsche Tropenwald*, 244–62; on Grzimek see also F. Toma, *Eine Naturschutzkampagne in der Ära Adenauer. Bernhard Grzimeks Afrikafilme in den Medien der 1950er Jahre* (Munich, 2004).
70. A. Poenicke, *Afrika in den deutschen Medien und Schulbüchern* (St. Augustin, 2001), 52; more generally on this: S. Arndt, ed., *AfrikaBilder. Studien zu Rassismus in Deutschland* (Münster, 2003).

CHAPTER 11

Losing National Identity or Gaining Transcultural Competence

Changing Approaches in Migration History

DIRK HOERDER

The migration of men and women—whether individually, in families or in cultural groups—connects societies. The study of migration might thus have been comparative or transsocietal by definition. However, scholars' socialization in one particular culture and their embeddedness in the respective polity's discourse prevented them from noticing the obvious. Approaches reflected the period's climate of opinion (Carl Becker) or frames of reference (Maurice Halbwachs).[1] Unless they totally overlooked it, European historians traditionally have studied emigration from each and every nation state separately, and their North American peers have studied immigration by distinct ethnic group. In this nation-centred reading of the two *ends* of a continuous process, the move across the Atlantic turned men and women from nationals into ethnics; it was a 'nation to ethnic enclave approach'. Only in the 1970s did international cooperation fuse the emigration-immigration dichotomy into one migration history and, in the 1990s, into transnational and transcultural approaches. I will, first, discuss the development of the field before the 1970s in Germany and the United States to outline achievements and limitations; intensive transatlantic interaction between scholars mandates such transnational approach to historiography. Secondly, I will turn to developments in Germany from the late 1970s to the 1980s, and thirdly, I will discuss the reconceptualization of nation-centred research to complex migration systems in the North Atlantic world. Fourthly, the introduction of the 'transnational migration' paradigm in the early 1990s will be evaluated critically, and concepts of transregionalism and transculturalism will be proposed: namely, the emergence of an empirically tenable approach to migration between cultural regions in which crossing of *inter*national borders leads to *trans*cultural lives and transborder linkages. I will propose a Transcultural Societal Studies approach. In conclusion, I will illustrate to what degree public memory of migration in Germany, and, consequently, its scholarship, were deficient.

The study of migration in the nineteenth-century Germanies and the German-language region of Central Europe during the Second German Reich–Weimar Republic–Third Reich period, as well as in the Federal Republic of Germany and the German Democratic Republic, has a complex history. Several characteristics stand out: firstly, rather than study outbound migration comprehensively in a worldwide perspective, scholars specialized by destination either on east- or westward moves or on colony-bound migrations. Second, outbound and inbound migrations were distinct fields of research: Huguenots arriving from France were not compared to Protestants departing for Pennsylvania, nor were Polish-cultured labourers in Mecklenburg or the Ruhr District compared to German-cultured ones from Mecklenburg in Chicago or Milwaukee. Historians fragmented the field.

After 1945, scholarship's corruption under fascism[2] resulted in a post-fascist dearth of research on demographic issues, including migration.[3] A historiography of emigration re-emerged in the 1970s, if at first restricted to a factographic mould. Since most scholars specialized in *Amerikawanderung* (migration to the United States),[4] interaction with US (and later Canadian) researchers led to fruitful exchanges of concepts, methods, and theories. As a consequence, the transatlantic exchanges will range foremost in this essay. However, research on internal migrations and on in- and out-migration to and from other regions of the world will be related to the continental and transatlantic moves.

Migration historiography, like the research of German Africanists, Asianists, and North and South Americanists, has remained separate from political historiography in German scholarship, as well as from the 'nation-centred social history' (Lutz Raphael). The practitioners of these fields turned to their colleagues in other historiographies for intellectual exchange. As late as 1999/2001, the editorial board of *Geschichte und Gesellschaft* had to issue an invitation to conceptualize German history transnationally in relation to the neighbouring and more distant worlds. Philipp Ther's thoughtful plea of 2003 to understand Germany history from a 'relational basis' as including Poles and other peoples (settled 'minorities') and neighbouring regions still included no reference to migration. About 7 million men and women from the Germanies left for other parts of the world. The nationalist historiography of the Second German Reich, since 1871, had exorcised emigrants—as well as the many-cultured immigrants—from historical memory or had turned them into *Auslandsdeutsche*. In contrast, economic history, a once important, then an increasingly marginalized compartment of German historiography, had occasionally included migrants, but always had conceptualized economic regions as larger than and different from nation states' bounded territories. Only in the early 2000s does a new, less self-referential debate begin to emerge.[5]

The Data and the Discourses: A Critique of pre–1960s Migration Research

In traditional understanding, the trajectories of migrants occurring between nation states were international: from Germany (or another state) to the United States, Canada, Russia or elsewhere. This terminology posits states as distinct entities and emphasizes the borderlines separating them. Socialized into national identities and discourses, historians emphasized the space 'between' cultures and considered migrants to be 'in between', 'in limbo', 'suspended'. However, official governmental statistics available as early as 1911 indicated that, at that time, 94 per cent of all US-bound European migrants headed for places where earlier migrating family members (79 per cent) or friends (15 per cent) lived.[6] With such transatlantic family structures, where is 'in limbo' except in non-migrating scholars' mental worlds?

Emigrants left a state—their nation?—and crossed an international border, where data on migration used to be collected, and then vanished from the records as well as, often, from memory. The German language does not even provide terms for such lifecourse cultural change. Designations refer to origins: *Deutsche in der Fremde, deutsche Reichsbürger im Ausland, Auslandsdeutsche, Brückenköpfe für deutsche Wirtschaftsinteressen, Träger germanischen Blutes und deutscher Kultur* or, in contrast, *vaterlandslose Gesellen, Verräter, Verlust deutschen Blutes*.[7] The German 'mother tongue' imposed one particular—and incomplete—perspective and so did data collection. If migrants are counted at interstate borders only, then a quantitative database for research on internal migration is missing.[8] The term 'inter*national*' migration before 1914 was also misleading, since the vast majority of Europe's emigrants came from empires comprising many ethno-cultural groups: four peoples in the case of the Windsor one, several in the case of the Hohenzollern one, many in the cases of the Romanov one, and the Habsburg *Vielvölkerstaat* (state of many peoples). In addition, 'nation' as a concept or a cultural group was never clearly defined: Switzerland contains four cultural and linguistic groups, Belgium, two. The commonly cited models of nation building—Britain and France—have always been many-cultured. In the UK, Scots, English, Welsh, and Irish share the structures of the state; in France, Basques and Bretons remain distinct, but the different language and culture of the south (*langue d'oc*) was destroyed centuries ago.

Internal migrations within the German Reich, established with a Polish segment in 1870/71, or in the North American societies of destination were hardly recorded. Did migrants stay put in a frontier settlement or in an urban neighbourhood after arrival? Centering data collection on a nation state or an empire is but one of many possible forms of organization of data. Public discourse was similarly narrow: *Auf nach Amerika*—'Let's go to [an imagined] America'—indicated a vague hope, neither a place nor social space, and, surprisingly, in view of the contemporary emphasis on state and nation, referred neither to the US nor to Canada nor to any other specific country in the Americas. The mental maps of common people had not been nationalized in this period.

When language and mental images misrepresent, empirically untenable conceptualizations result. As regards gender, emigrants were imagined as generically male. Only in the numerous pictorial renderings of departure and travel did women have a place: during the actual voyage they left the 'home', where men's imaginations and power placed them, and, thus, they became—briefly—visible.[9] According to the data, nineteenth-century men and women migrated in a proportion of 60 to 40 on average. The change from one mentality-constrained language to another changes clichés, connotations, and interpretations. In the language of the state of arrival, the very same men, women, and children who were emigrants became immigrants said to be deeply impressed by the Statue of Liberty and expected to move into an ethnic enclave or ghetto or, in the period of agricultural settlement, to 'the frontier'. The sometimes-decried 'linguistic turn' does have the advantage of making historians aware of their particular language and discourse limitations. Comparative approaches become imperative for self-liberation from national perspectives and restrictions of the mother tongue.

The immigration mode of thought, like the emigration mode, by turning terms into paradigms, determined researchers' questions. In the US, data on departures (return migration) were not collected before 1907 because, in the self-referential and pervasive immigration discourse, out-migration was inconceivable. The 'ethnics-not-yet-nationals' hierarchization had immigrants move into Little Germanies, Italies or Portugals, or from China into Chinatowns, while immigrants from the English, Welsh, and Scottish sections of the UK were not located in Little Englands or Scotlands, but were designated the founders of New England or Nova Scotia. Gatekeepers with the power to define and to name determined who was part of the nation and who an enclave-dweller. In contrast, the highly educated women who, in the 1890s, gathered the empirical data for the Chicago Survey of immigrant living conditions realized that migrants lived interspersed rather than ethno-culturally segregated.[10]

In the US context, half a century after the government's Americanization project around 1900 and the Jewish immigrant Zangwill's use of the term 'melting pot' in 1909, Oscar Handlin from Harvard used the term 'the uprooted' for immigrants. This label for three decades became *the* paradigm of migration history and influenced German as well as European scholarship in general. Somewhat later, Milton M. Gordon's concept of *Assimilation in American Life* (1964) became a sacred text or, more profanely, the centre of a citation cluster. He posited a mono-cultural society, *e pluribus unum*, in which the *unum* was never defined but was implicitly white, Protestant, of European origin, and English-speaking.[11] The hold of the catchphrase-paradigm 'assimilating the uprooted' lasted even though Handlin himself had provided a clue to its flaw by recognizing that 'the great migrations made the American people'.[12] In critical retrospect, it appears that he succumbed to the discourse of a specific conjuncture: at the time of his writing, about half a million 'Displaced Persons' from Europe's war-ravaged societies and Nazi Germany's forced labour camps arrived in the United States,[13] and scholars, like politicians and the general public, were intensely concerned with uprooting and with traumatized personalities.

Another conceptual problem emerges from the practice in US and German scholarship of subdividing research into ever smaller compartments: the history of immigration, labour, forced labour, slavery, etc. Although necessary to achieve precision in data collection and in interpretation, this fragments a complex process. In received language's connotations, immigrants arrive of their own free choice, forced labourers are transported, slaves are deprived of agency. This terminology implies that some migrants will make it on their own and, thus, may be accepted,[14] while others—for example, East European *Fremdarbeiter* (foreign workers before the 1930s) and *Zwangsarbeiter* (forced labourers, especially between 1939 and 1945) or Asian indentured labourers are incapable of taking care of themselves, live degraded lives, and develop deviant personalities.[15]

In contrast to this conglomerate of conceptual shortcomings, highly differentiated concepts of migrant insertion and cultural interaction were developed since the 1930s outside of the core of the Atlantic world's intellectual life: the United States, Great Britain, France, and Germany. In Canada's bicultural Montreal, Helen MacGill Hughes and Everett Hughes recognized that societies do not provide single models for immigrant acculturation; rather, newcomers face regional and class-specific cultures.[16] In Brazil, Gilberto Freyre discussed power relations in cultural interaction, and in Cuba, Fernando Ortiz developed a concept of transculturation in many-cultured societies. These scholars were conscious that cultures did not end at a state's borders. Rather, human beings, commercial goods, and ideas cross borders and are transcultural.[17] Core-based scholars did not care to take note of these innovative ideas from the alleged periphery of the Western world's knowledge production.

White academic men in the core also disregarded the publications of women and of non-white scholars in their own countries. More than a decade before Handlin's uprootedness-version of migration history at Harvard, Caroline F. Ware from Columbia University published a sensitive community study of Greenwich Village, New York City, in which she emphasized continuity and adaptation among Irish and Italian immigrants and discussed intergenerational cultural transfer and change. Not even the revisionist social historians of the 1970s and 1980s cited this study. Her anthology, *The Cultural Approach to History* (1940), did become a classic, however.[18] In Europe, intellectuals of African origin in Paris and intellectuals of Indian origin at British universities developed major concepts of migrants' cultural adaptation under unequal power relations in the 1930s. They too were not accepted into academic institutions. Thus, complex concepts of migration, insertion, and transculturation were available on the marketplace of ideas, but mainstream scholars engaged in a consumer boycott.[19]

Expanding Nation State Centredness through the Study of International Migrations

In the 1970s and 1980s, research on migration into, within, and out of Germany resumed slowly. Wolfgang Köllmann and Peter Marschalck, as historians and demographers, provided a narrative and quantitative summary of internal as well as out-bound migrations. Their work was encouraged by the US editors of *Perspectives in American History*, who, in 1973, published essays on migration written by experts in the field on a state-by-state basis.[20] In the early 1980s, Klaus J. Bade (Osnabrück) began his prolific career by questioning bordered states as frames of reference. In seminal studies, he connected German-language artisans' migrations across Europe with the German Reich's late-nineteenth-century intercultural east-west labour migrations of 'foreign' and 'Prussian' Poles and these, in turn, with regional German rural-urban migrations as well as with emigration.[21] Bade moved the field ahead by combining economic with political history, by deemphasizing nation, and pointing to the entwined Polish and German migration histories. He discussed the German state's shifting macro-regional position as reflected in the change from East Central European *Fremdarbeiter* to Mediterranean Europe's *Gastarbeiter* migrations. Bordered states are inextricably linked to larger regions. Bade's analysis of the Reich's *Abwehrpolitik* (to keep Poles out of the Reich) may be considered a precursor to the exclusion and inclusion approaches to national belonging of the 1990s.[22]

At the same time, transatlantic emigration—at first almost exclusively to the United States—became the subject of Günter Moltmann's research at the University of Hamburg. While his emphasis on emigration and on Germans as a group without class or gender differentiation was traditional, he and his students emphasized the process of emigration as a move from country of origin via the trip through Dutch or North German ports to assimilation in Little Germanies or German quarters in North American cities. In this respect, his research was ahead of those US scholars who, for lack of language capabilities other than English, pursued an 'arrival at Ellis Island with cultural baggage'-approach but could not analyse non-English cultures.[23] A new analytical level emerged through the projects of Hartmut Keil and others and, later, of Christiane Harzig,[24] who differentiated the German-American ethno-cultural group by emphasizing class—German workers in Chicago—and gender—women in the emigration from Germany. Keil and collaborators pointed to a distinct working-class culture among German-Americans as part of an international labour movement, but not necessarily as an indicator of internationalist-mindedness. Harzig demonstrated that women developed migration networks of their own and benefited from the less confining gender roles in the United States. With Monika Blaschke, she placed German women's migrations in a worldwide perspective.[25] This research began to emphasize distinct regional cultures within states and described men and women capable of adjusting their pre-migration characteristics and capabilities in order to lead satisfactory lives in the society of their choice.[26] The international or interstate character of migration still framed analyses, even if continuities in migrants' lives came to the fore, as expressed in Bodnar's term 'the transplanted'. In Germany, a first collaborative synthesis was achieved at a conference organized by K.J. Bade in 1982, which also overcame the compartmentalization into distinct emigration, internal migration, and immigration research.[27]

With some 55 million men, women, and children leaving the states of Europe between 1815 and 1939, the apologists of national identities and narrow nation state histories might have realized that their narrative lacked analytical rigour. Nevertheless, they left it to migration historians to cross nation states' borders. While all of the elements for a *transnational* approach were present, however, historians did not theorize mobility in such terms.

From Nation States to North Atlantic World(s): Re-conceptualizing Migrant Agency within Migration Systems

A new development in the history of transatlantic migrations was suggested by a perspective from North America: a study of the labour movements and working-class cultures indicated that US and Canadian historians' emphasis on class and labour unions, which often paid but lip service to the role of migrants, could not reflect the input and diversity of Europeans' pre-migration cultures, working-class experiences, and practices of rural resistance. The view from multi-ethnic labour movements rather than from allegedly distinct ethno-culturally bordered neighbourhoods made clear that research had to consider out-migration from the whole of Europe.[28] Thus, in a cooperative project coordinated by myself at the University of Bremen, scholars from all European cultures (not merely all states) west of the Soviet Union and north of the Iberian corporatist states—in which no emigration research was permitted—as well as from the US and Canada, pooled their knowledge and approaches. They developed the concept of migration in the Atlantic economies, in which migrants aim for internationally accessible segments of labour markets commensurate with their skills, education (or lack thereof), and language knowledge (or lack thereof), mediated through kin and friendship networks. Economic history, labour market theory, and family studies became part of this interdisciplinary approach. Competence and capabilities of migrants were emphasized.[29]

The importance of borders and of the nation state approach began to recede in research on nineteenth-century migration. After the mid century, most dynastic states no longer required departure permissions, and the North American receiving societies pursued open door policies with but few exclusionary regulations for migrants from Europe.[30] Furthermore, the new Europe-wide railroad and travel agency system facilitated mobility. After arriving in the community (rather than society or country) of destination and achieving minimal economic security, migrants organized by region (rather than state) of origin. Designations like 'German-Americans' were ascriptions from the outside, used by neighbours of the mainstream and other immigrant cultures who could not keep the German-language regions and their specific cultures apart. However, to develop political clout through voting, numbers were important, and migrants with regional identifications began to organize themselves as German (or German-American) or as Italian (or Italian-American). National belonging was constructed *after* migration for utilitarian purposes. From the binational 'country of departure/country of destination'-perspective, migration research had moved to analysing cultural regions und interaction between these regions. A comparative project on women's migration (Harzig) compared four different emigration regions in Europe—including Mecklenburg—and the reinsertion of the 'German', 'Irish', 'Swedish', and 'Polish' migrant women in particular Chicago neighbourhoods.[31] Borderlines became fuzzy. In borderlands, German-speaking, Czech-cultured potential migrants, for example, learned about routes and options from their German-language neighbours and, later, informed their eastern Slovak-language coresidents of the same when these began to consider departure. In 1992, David Thelen, criticizing the self-centredness of US historiography, generalized the migration historians' concept: 'People, ideas and institutions do not have clear national identities. Rather, people may translate and assemble pieces from different cultures. Instead of assuming that something was distinctively American [or German, French, ...], we might assume that elements of it began or ended somewhere else'.[32]

A conceptual innovation emerged in parallel in the Netherlands from Jan Lucassen's research on labour migration in imperial Napoleonic Europe. He aggregated multiple migrations to a particular region of destination into 'migration systems'. This groundbreaking concept was expanded by Leslie Page Moch to cover Western Europe since the seventeenth century and, by Hoerder, first for the Atlantic World and Eurasia, and then across the globe. Migration systems, which link regions of different cultures, empirically are observable, with interconnected patterns of mobility that continue over time. They involve two-directional information flows between regions of departure and of arrival. They connect labour market segments in free migrations or non-matching regions of supply and demand in forced migrations. After arrival, labour migrants have to earn a living or, if not free, have to produce for the investors/rulers. Whatever their legal condition, however, they also have to develop the capacities to lead meaningful lives in the new culture, with its options and constraints.[33]

This global approach, that deemphasized borders, was developed by historians concentrating on migrations in and before the nineteenth century. From the 1880s, when the exclusionist aspects of nationhood increased even in Europe's empires of many peoples, states began to insert themselves into the medium-distance, continent-wide, and transoceanic migrations. Migration historiography is acutely aware of the nation state concept's internal contradiction: the state was to treat inhabitants as equal before the law, but the concept of nation privileged one cultural group over all others and implied inequality of other-cultured minorities and migrants. For the national group, it was a means of gaining ascendancy in resource allocation, as well as in defining belonging; migrants who had arrived in dynastic societies merely had to swear allegiance as subjects to the respective ruler and, like the Huguenots, could retain their culture. Under the new nationhood ideology, they were expected to Americanize, Germanize, etc. Cultural difference, acceptable among a dynasty's subjects, became unacceptable in nations and was instrumentalized as a means of exclusion of those defined as non-nationals. States increased border controls and established passport systems. Later, the nation state developed institutions—including social security systems—that were not necessarily open to newcomers or accessible to 'minorities'.[34]

Noting the dividing lines, migration historians' systems approach to migration began to focus attention on cultural macro-regions, like Europe as a whole, and on migrant agency contextualized in micro-regional living conditions before departure—which reasons induced men and women to leave? Did they leave family economies as individuals, or did they form new families before departure? Did they have prior, intrastate migration experiences? Who left; who stayed? At first, this involved a comparative analysis of the regional societies of departure (by the scholars from the Bremen project); then, macro-regional migration histories appeared (by Leslie Page Moch for Western Europe).[35] In a further step of transnational cooperation and parallel to Raphael's, Kocka's, and Osterhammel's critique of nation-centred social history, scholars adapted Canadian models of rewriting 'national' history to incorporate the many-cultured input from which societies, whether called Canadian, German or European, emerged. The focus on internal and multi-directional migrations brought to the fore both historical diversity and the social construction of diversity in the present.[36] Finally, a synthesis of European migrations appeared,[37] and state-wide new history texts reinserted the agency of the many constituent cultures.[38] When borders were being challenged in the process of reintegrating Europe into a European Union and when fears of the external Others led to calls for a 'fortress Europe', scholars reinserted migration and diversity into historical memory. Sweden and the Netherlands not only redefined themselves as multicultural societies; they had been many-cultured in the past.[39] Other societies refused to face the diversity of their past and the present intercultural mobility.

Transnational or Transcultural: Re-Conceptualizing Migration

While historians reconstructed Europe's history from nation-centredness to overlapping spaces, anthropologists and sociologists specializing on south-north migration in the Americas suddenly noticed the cultural continuities and multiple many-directional moves therein and inserted the term 'transnationalism' into the debate in 1992.[40] Historians of the Atlantic migrations could have done the same so much earlier had they been willing to abandon the nation state frame of reference when empirically describing the phenomenon. The new concept was adopted by US sociologist Alejandro Portes and his collaborators, who emphasized new, faster modes of transportation of people and of messages (communication) as well as the role of second-generation migrants. In historical contexts, slower communication (letters) and transportation networks with multiple voyages had never prevented migrants from living transcultural lives. The term quickly became fashionable, and a citation cluster developed around Portes' work.

The concept presented an important step in re-conceptualization: 'international' posits distinct entities with dividing, clearly defined borderlines, as well as exchanges formalized by diplomacy, trade protocols, etc. 'Transnational', in contrast, posits continuities across similar, yet distinct *spaces* rather than bounded *territories*. Ludger Pries and Thomas Faist introduced the term and the international debate into German research.[41]

Portes's concept, however, as Peter Kivisto has pointed out, had several shortcomings:[42] it stuck to the concept of 'nation state' even though concepts of belonging and embeddedness were changing, and the hold of states over their citizens was declining. In Canadian sociologist Lloyd L. Wong's words: 'The deterritorialisation of social identity challenges the nation-state's claim of making exclusive citizenship a defining focus of allegiance and fidelity, in contrast to the overlapping, permeable and multiple forms of identity.'[43] Portes' approach neither incorporated differentiation by region or everyday culture nor studies of borderlands. Subsequently, the German political scientist, Thomas Faist (Bremen/Bielefeld), proposed the most historically grounded and theoretically advanced concept of transnationalism. Building on previous models of migration and centre-periphery models, he argues that border-crossing migrants create integrated social spaces that follow a logic other than that of nation states. As historians had noted, they develop mental maps that compress or enlarge 'distance' and 'time' when, moving between geographic places, they also moved between stages of economic and societal development. 'Transnational' takes into account that not only goods and migrants cross national boundaries, but that an overlay of webs of personal relationships to kin and friends and of diasporic affiliations exists. Researchers deal with the levels of individuals and families, of groups and classes, and of state structures and civic societies; they differentiate between social and symbolic ties, and they reveal transnational circuits and communities. Following Salman Rushdie, Faist calls migrants 'translated' rather than 'transplanted' people. While societies ascribe cultures to migrants, migrants engage in a continuous process of translating patterns of everyday life—whether material or spiritual, normative or ephemeral, intellectual or emotional, social or symbolic—between societies.[44] Other scholars have used concepts of 'negotiating' between societies or of 'brokering' different cultural patterns; Pries has emphasized the time-space continuum. As in the concept of diaspora, the continued linkages to the society of origin and to other destinations of co-ethnics, as well as, perhaps, to people at transitory intermediate stopovers, are central to the concept of transnationality. The mediating images of migrant letters, oral accounts or modern electronic media also do not stop at political boundaries, which often reflect but an arbitrary division at some accidental historical caesura frozen in time.[45]

The concept of 'transculturalism' avoids the implication of political borders and bounded territories, but it is aware of social spaces and cultural differences.[46] Since affiliations of migrants originate in a region—Bavaria, Baden, the Rhineland, Mecklenburg or the Hanseatic North Sea ports, etc.— 'transregional' provides another empirically grounded option.[47] These concepts move the debate away from polities and their boundaries and permit selective reference to specific regions, borderlands or supranational macro-regions.[48] Furthermore, for life-course projects and belongings, states have begun to take second place to urban spheres, to 'a chain of cosmopolitan cities and an increasing proliferation of subnational and transnational identities'. Such belongings are now being studied among the many-cultured youth in urban agglomeration as well as in hinterlands. Rather than losing one national identity, most migrants gain transcultural competence.[49]

On the basis of migration research, Canadian regionalism, and the study of multicultural living in Canada as well as in historic Europe,[50] I developed a Transcultural Societal Studies approach.[51] If culture is a complex system that includes tools, spoken and body language, arts and beliefs created by human beings who must provide for their material, emotional, and intellectual needs in order to survive, then transculturalism denotes the competence to live in two or more differing cultures and, in the process, create a transcultural space. Strategic transcultural competence involves conceptualizations of life projects in multiple cultures and choice between cultural options. Transculturation is the process of individuals and societies to change themselves by integration of diverse cultural ways of life into a dynamic new whole. Subsequent interactions and transcultural lives will again change this new—and transitory—culture.

'Transcultural' societal spaces are described and defined by empirical observation; contact zones come to the fore. People act out their life-projects or, at a minimum, *re*act on a day-to-day basis to circumstances within the limits of the capabilities acquired through their socialization in family, local community, regional society, and economy—in more than one location. A regional cultural space as the immediate life-world of people provides the frame for their agency by specific everyday norms, as well as from opportunity or constraint structures. The latter permit life-projects or, sometimes, lead to involuntary trajectories or to stagnation. Such cultural spaces are located within structures and institutions of a polity, but, when crossing an international border, people move into another *society* and its norms and practices. In a global perspective, supra-state macro-regions determine life chances, whether they are low wage segments of the world's global economic sphere, cultural-economic remnants of the historic British, French or Spanish empires or the modern zones of mass-media hegemony, like those of CNN, BBC or Al-Jazeera.

In the case of Canada, the cultural actors living in the same overlapping spaces were particularly diverse. 'The Indians' redefined themselves as 'First Peoples'; 'the nation' was said to consist of two cultures of European origin but of different language and customs and, thus, was a bi-nation; the inhabitants included newcomers from the many cultural spaces of Europe, the United States, Asia, the Caribbean, Latin America, and Africa. The dual claim for nationality and the multiplicity of cultural groups prevented the emergence of a hegemonic nationalism and of a mono-cultural nation state paradigm. Nineteenth-century Canadians lived transcultural lives, as their memoirs indicate. Research needs to address different cultures under the concept of *alterity* rather than of exclusion, alienation or Othering. In distinction to the German assumption of a stable society with marginal minorities and marginalized immigrants in cultural, social, and political limbo, the concept of transcultural lives in flexible social spaces posits that native-born and long-term residents take part in interaction and change rather than forming a cultural backdrop against which to measure immigrant adaptation.

Applied to German history, its contracting and expanding borders as well as its trans-European emperors, this approach includes, to give only a few examples, African influences from Saint Mauritius, patron of the Magdeburg cathedral; Dürer's African merchant in southern Germany; Danish-Afro-Caribbean manumitted slaves that Christianized and married in Hamburg; Huguenots; Sephardic as well as Askenazi Jews, and the many other immigrants.[52] Similarly, and with no nationalist pretensions involved, German history never ended at the principalities or Reich's borders. German-language people settled in Europe and in other parts of the world and shared their particular regional culture and adapted aspects of the Others'/their new neighbours' ways of life.[53]

'Transcultural Societal Studies' integrates the traditional discourse-based humanities, the data-based social sciences, the habitus-centred behavioural approaches, normative disciplines of law, ethics, and religion, the life sciences, the environmental sciences, as well as other fields into a transdisciplinary whole. It provides a transdisciplinary approach to whole societies rather than to particular fragments of them—workers, women, men, Bavarians or Thuringians, etc. Cultural transfer has often been understood as occurring in hierarchies, from (German) nationals to immigrants, from (mature adult) parents to (immature) children, and, in a variation, from men to women by the legal construction common in the Western world up to the 1960s, that a married woman's national or ethnic identity is derived from that of her husband, regardless of her culture of birth. Such views of transfer assume an unmediated, 'straight' passing on or handing *down*—note the hierarchy—with neither resistance nor adaptation, as well as demarcated, internally homogeneous cultural (-genetic) groups. Cultural theory, however, points to an encoding of cultural preferences, a transmission of these messages, and a process of receiving and decoding by the less powerful—immigrants, women, youths—in their own terms of reference.

Young people in Germany, for example, face complex, encoded, multiple-meaning messages from parents, grandparents, and other relatives, as well as from the acquaintances of their elders and their community. They engage in an active process of self-creation by selecting between different products in the market supply of the previous generation's cultural models. In addition, two other relational suppliers of cultural frames of reference are on the market: the regional or national education system mediated through the local teaching personnel, as well as the peer group, a group composed of young people of many birth-cultures in most societies of the present. All of these face a multitude of transnational media influences and multinational companies' consumer goods marketing strategies. Attitudinal differences between young and old within one cultural group, regardless of origin, have always been larger than between different ethnic groups.[54] Comparative evaluation of options of young people's strategic competence to develop life-projects in the transcultural societies indicates that the vast majority of youth accept neither master narratives that—like freeways—lead in one direction only, nor do they accept cultural no-access zones. Multiculturality refers to many pieces composing a mosaic, transculturality to lived and changing relationships.[55]

The research on migrant cultures recognized that transculturation was not merely one of economic, social, and political adaptation, but involved resistance and recreation in the 'transfer', or, even better, translation, of cultural patterns. Such mixed existence, neither white nor black, neither Turkish nor German, has been pronounced in a Cultural Studies jargon as 'homelessness as human condition'. Homi Bhaba's conceptualization of a 'third space', something new regarding codes as well as material lives, is far more useful.[56] In interviews and life-writings, migrants only rarely report feelings of having been uprooted, lost in space or time or of lack of positioning identifications. The Cultural Studies' slogan 'neither here nor there' merely reiterates the old-fashioned 'uprooted' paradigm of 1950s migration historiography. People of all age groups and genders engaged in transculturation create new spaces, spaces that are not progressing as mechanistically as the Marxian sequence of thesis, antithesis, and synthesis. Transculturation, as first conceptualized by Ortiz, offers many options and has many potential outcomes, but those who live several cultures as a process experience power strategies of hierarchization, of inclusion or exclusion of groups and individuals—as first discussed by Freyre. They, like societies as a whole, also react to internal economic and political and external input, be it from immigrants, cultural imports or globalization of production.[57]

Migrant men and women, throughout the centuries and in the present, lived and live transcultural lives. Scholarship in the Atlantic core has incorporated such transcultural perspectives late, but most of the early theoreticians in the vanguard of transcending nation state constructs and of conceptualizing multiple discursive strategies lived in more than one culture. Of the French-language theorists, Roland Barthes lived in Romania and Egypt, Frantz Fanon in Martinique and Algeria, Jacques Derrida and Pierre Bourdieu in Algeria. Other theorists experienced two (or more) social regimes in one society: Antonio Gramsci and Mikhail Bakhtin, for example, experienced the transformation of regimes to fascism and to Stalinism, respectively. Michel Foucault observed the multiple discourses of schizophrenic men and women and of those who did not live according to assigned sexual roles. In Great Britain, Stuart and Catherine Hall, the former non-white and of Jamaican origin, questioned imperial and national discourses. Experiences in more than one culture provide increased options and positions for interpretation of life-worlds. Kiran K. Patel has recently conceptualized this in Germany.[58]

Public Memory: German Attitudes to Migrants and Cultural Difference

If scholarship was slow in reconceptualizing migration from a binary e/im-migration perspective to transcultural lives, and if scholars through their socialization reflect attitudes permeating their societies, in conclusion, a look at two vignettes of the hegemonic discourses and constructions of public memory in Germany may highlight the problems.

Migrants remained in contact with their families and friends in the cultures of origin, whether through voyages back and forth, through sequential (or chain) migration, through remittances of savings, and—most importantly—through letters. Of the emigration research of the 1980s, Wolfgang Helbich's and Walter Kamphoefner's study of emigrant letters demonstrated that from 1820 to 1914, some 250 to 300 million letters from the US arrived in Germany. In the 1870s, when the Reich's population stood at 41 million, about 2 million letters arrived annually; in the 1880s, the number doubled. Contrary to the assumption that emigrants sent rosy accounts of their successes, the letters gave a realistic description of achievements and options, discussed who might follow, inquired about parents and other kin 'at home'—a 'home' often without perspectives for satisfactory lives—and reported on family developments in the new social space: the birth of children, emotions, happiness about achievements or dejection after reversals. The letters are testimony to family lives extending over particular regions of two continents; they indicate transregional and transcultural experiences. Given the dearth of references to political life, they refute the hypothesis of a primacy of national identification.[59] At the same time, in official pronouncements in Germany, the United States or the vague *Amerika* appeared, in conservative circles, as a dangerously democratic society or, among innovators, as a highly dynamic, technologically advanced society providing jobs and incomes.[60] While diplomacy was international between the empire and the 'immigrant nation', lives and images were transcultural or transregional. Thus, German (and other) historians, empirically, might have established concepts of transnationalism, transculturalism, and transregionalism long ago.

How, then, are historians' minds formed or formatted? This is not a question of the conscious acceptance of a particular ideology or political persuasion, whether nationalism or conservatism. Rather, it is the unconscious imbuing of discourses and public historical memory in childhood, adolescence, and adult life. I will discuss this issue through an autobiographical reflection on the post-Second World War decades. I was socialized in 1950s Altona, a quarter in the city of Hamburg close to the port. In the primary school's *Heimatkunde* (lessons on the immediate *Heimat*), we were taught that, as inhabitants of Altona, we were distinct and separate from people in neighbouring districts as well as from those of historic Hamburg. But, as inhabitants of this historic Hanseatic city of Hamburg, we were different from—perhaps superior to—inhabitants of other parts of Germany. After class, we passed on the jokes of our elders, which always happened to juxtapose an Englishman, a Frenchman (sometimes), an American, and a German who all bragged about the achievements of their country. In the jokes, the German always came out winning. Why ruins lined our way to school was not explained. That Hamburg had been a major port of emigration was not mentioned. Nor was there an explanation why Altona had a 'Jewish cemetery'. The latter, I only realized as an adult historian, was the last *lieu de mémoire* of a Sephardic Jewish community, which, expelled from Portugal, had settled in Amsterdam and had formed a branch community in Altona. Without this knowledge, the history of Hamburg lacked a major component: this Portuguese-Dutch-Jewish community had laid one of the foundations of Hamburg's wealth by reorienting the (stagnating) Hanseatic Baltic and North Sea trades to colonial Dutch South America. The community had dissolved in the late nineteenth century, but the economic connections to South America lasted. The *Heimatkunde* of the 1950s also involved a tour through the port. Having learnt in these Cold War years that Russians were dangerous, as were the foreign sailors we met on the streets, I noticed that in the economic sphere a different discourse reigned (as economic historians had argued—but were never included into school texts). Incoming ships were greeted with the country's national anthem. Arriving from all over the world, they were personalized and male: depending on the flag, a ship would be *der Amerikaner, der Engländer, der Russe*. In the harbour, the Cold War was on leave: the guide would explain that in trade, everybody was treated as equal, 'the Russian' included.

When, later, I moved to a small town north of Bremen, within a circle of less than a hundred kilometres in diameter, I could visit the hidden or belatedly erected migration memorials: internal migration—the region, once a peat bog, had been settled only some two hundred years ago; local emigration—a mere hundred years later, migrants had gone to North America from the villages; global connections—the neighbouring district centre's small town industry had exported and imported specialized products worldwide; forced migration—Third Reich military installations and the graveyards of the slave labourers; involuntary wartime mobility—a camp for prisoners of war from which the men had been detached to labour in all of the surrounding villages; Europe's mass emigration, flight from fascist Germany after 1933, and the Displaced Persons' departures—through Bremerhaven, some 5 million Europeans had left the continent (and many had returned); intra-European voluntary migration—the emigration port's first docks had been planned by a nineteenth-century immigrant Dutch engineer, and the later expansion for the huge transatlantic liners of the 1890s had been the labour of Polish migrating workers; 'guestworker' migrations—in a suburb of the city of Bremen, a mosque signified their presence. To exclude all of this from received national master narratives involved a massive effort of falsifying the historical record. In German history, regardless of the particular region, the signs of migration in its many variants as well as of cultural exchange and transcultural lives are visible. Historiography has, finally, come to accept the empirical data and the concept.

Notes

1. C.L. Becker, *Everyman His Own Historian: Essays on History and Politics* (New York, 1935; repr. Chicago, 1966); M. Halbwachs, *La mémoire collective* (Paris, 1950; new ed., rev. and augmented, Paris, 1997), English version as *The Collective Memory* (New York, 1980).
2. After 1933, internationally renowned migration historian Friedrich Burgdörfer ('Die Wanderungen über die deutschen Reichsgrenzen im letzten Jahrhundert', *Allgemeines Statistisches Archiv* 20 (1930): 161–96, 383–419, 537–51) published *Völker am Abgrund* (1937) and *Volk ohne Jugend. Geburtenschwund und Überalterung des deutschen Volkskörpers. Ein Problem der Volkswirtschaft, der Sozialpolitik der nationalen Zukunft* (1938). Heinz Kloss, since the 1930s,

pursued his 'Germans abroad' approach regardless of political systems: *Atlas der im 19. und frühen 20. Jahrhundert entstandenen deutschen Siedlungen in USA* (Marburg, 1974).
3. P. Marschalck, 'Kontinuitäten und Brüche im bevölkerungswissenschaftlichen und bevölkerungspolitischen Denken in Deutschland während der letzten zwei Jahrhunderte', in *Acta Demographica* (1992): 117–30; D. Oberndörfer, 'Politische Annahmen in der Demografie Herwig Birgs und Charlotte Höhns, Vortrag anlässlich der Tagung des Rates für Migration', *Demografie und Demagogie* (11 Sept. 2005).
4. Language is imprecise in regard to geographic place, social space, and mental maps. The commonly used 'Amerika' for the United States (as even in *'Deutsche Gesellschaft für Amerikastudien'*) is conceptually misleading and has often been criticized. In this essay, 'America' will refer to the double continent, 'Amerika' to a nineteenth-century image of a better world, 'North America' to the United States and Canada.
5. L. Raphael, 'Nationalzentrierte Sozialgeschichte in programmatischer Absicht. Die Zeitschrift "Geschichte und Gesellschaft. Zeitschrift für Historische Sozialwissenschaft" in den ersten 25 Jahren ihres Bestehens', *Geschichte und Gesellschaft* 25 (1999): 5–37; J. Kocka, 'Historische Sozialwissenschaft heute', in *Perspektiven einer Gesellschaftsgeschichte*, eds. P. Nolte et al. (Munich, 2000), 5–24, esp. 21–22; and Kocka, 'Einladung zur Diskussion', *Geschichte und Gesellschaft* 27 (2001): 463; J. Osterhammel, 'Transnationale Gesellschaftsgeschichte: Erweiterung oder Alternative?', *Geschichte und Gesellschaft* 27 (2001): 464–79, esp. 465, 470; P. Ther, 'Beyond the Nation: The Relational Basis of a Comparative History of Germany and Europe', *Central European History* 36 (2003): 45–73; W. Fischer, ed., *Handbuch der europäischen Wirtschafts- und Sozialgeschichte*, 6 vols. (Stuttgart 1980–1990).
6. *Reports of the Immigration (= Dillingham) Commission*, 41 vols. (Washington, DC, 1911–1912), 3: 358–59, 362–65.
7. In English: Germans abroad, citizens of the German Reich in foreign states, German nationals abroad, bridgeheads for German economic interests, carriers of Teutonic blood and German culture, *or* fellows without a fatherland, traitors, loss of German blood.
8. An early and isolated exception was D. Langewiesche, 'Wanderungsbewegungen in der Hochindustrialisierungsphase. Regionale, interstädtische und innerstädtische Mobilität in Deutschland 1880–1914', *Vierteljahrschrift für Sozial- und Wirtschaftsgeschichte* 64 (1977): 1–40.
9. See, for example, S. Stölting, *Auswanderer auf alter Zeitungsgraphik* (Worpswede, 1987).
10. *Hull-House Maps and Papers. A Presentation of Nationalities and Wages in a Congested District of Chicago, together with comments on problems growing out of social conditions, by Residents of Hull-House. A Social Settlement* (New York, 1895; repr. New York, 1970).
11. I. Zangwill, *The Melting Pot: Drama in Four Acts* (New York, 1909); O. Handlin, *The Uprooted: The Epic Story of the Great Migrations that Made the Ameri-*

can People (Boston, 1951); M.M. Gordon, *Assimilation in American Life. The Role of Race, Religion, and National Origins* (New York, 1964). For a critique of unconditional 'assimilation' see D. Hoerder, 'From Migrants to Ethnics: Acculturation in a Societal Framework', in *European Migrants: Global and Local Perspectives*, eds. Hoerder and L.P. Moch (Boston, 1996), 211–62.

12. Three-and-a-half decades later, John Bodnar still had to challenge the 'uprooted' concept by calling his study *The Transplanted. A History of Immigrants in Urban America* (Bloomington, 1985). Rudolph J. Vecoli's, 'The *Contadini* in Chicago: A Critique of *The Uprooted*' (*Journal of American History* 51(1964): 404–17) pointed to new directions early—but was also limited by the discourse of the times: for him, gender was not a category. To insert women into the story of Italian migration was left to Donna Gabaccia in *From Sicily to Elizabeth Street: Housing and Social Change Among Italian Immigrants, 1880–1930* (New York, 1984). Gabaccia influenced German research as an associate professor at the Free Univ. Berlin and, later, as a Fulbright professor at the Univ. of Bremen.

13. W. Jacobmeyer, *Vom Zwangsarbeiter zum Heimatlosen Ausländer. Die Displaced Persons in Westdeutschland, 1945–1951* (Göttingen, 1985); M. Wyman, *DP. Europe's Displaced Persons, 1945–1951* (Philadelphia, 1988).

14. But see J. Higham, *Strangers in the Land: Patterns of American Nativism, 1860–1925* (New York, 1963), for hostility to migrants from Europe, Germans and Irish in particular.

15. The research on forced migration in East and West Germany remained separate from research on free transatlantic migrations. See L. Elsner, ed., *Fremdarbeiterpolitik des Imperialismus*, 20 vols. (Rostock, 1976–1988), renamed in a critique of the field's compartmentalization *Migrationsforschung* since 1989; C. Kleßmann, *Polnische Bergarbeiter im Ruhrgebiet 1870–1945. Soziale Integration und nationale Subkultur einer ethnischen Minderheit in der deutschen Industriegesellschaft* (Göttingen, 1978). For surveys in both Germanies see U. Herbert, *Geschichte der Ausländerbeschäftigung in Deutschland 1880 bis 1980. Saisonarbeiter, Zwangsarbeiter, Gastarbeiter* (Berlin-West, 1986), Trans. by W. Templer as *A History of Foreign Labor in Germany 1880–1980. Seasonal Workers—Forced Laborers—Guest Workers* (Ann Arbor, 1991); and L. Elsner and J. Lehmann, *Ausländische Arbeiter unter dem deutschen Imperialismus 1900 bis 1985* (Berlin-Ost, 1988).

16. E.C. Hughes, 'The Study of Ethnic Relations', *Dalhousie Rev.* 27 (1948): 477–82; E.C. Hughes and H. MacGill Hughes, *Where Peoples Meet: Racial and Ethnic Frontiers* (Glencoe, IL, 1952).

17. G. Freyre, *Casa-Grande e senzala: introd. à historia da societa patriarcal no Brasil; farmação da familia brasileira solo o regime de economia patriarchal* (Rio de Janeiro, 1935), English trans. from the fourth and definitive edition by S. Putnam, *The Masters and the Slaves. A Study in the Development of Brazilian Civilization* (New York, 1946; rev. ed., Berkeley, 1986); F. Ortiz, 'Del fenómeno de la transculturación y su importancia en Cuba', *Revista Bimestre Cubana* 27 (1940): 273–78, repr. in: Ortiz, *Contrapunteo cubano del tabaco y*

el azúcar (1940) and trans. by H. de Onis as *Cuban Counterpoint: Tobacco and Sugar,* introduction by B. Malinowski (New York, 1947; repr. with new introduction, Durham, NC, 1995).

18. Ware, *Greenwich Village, 1920–1930: a Comment on American Civilization in the Post-war Years* (Boston, 1935; pbk. ed., 1965; expanded repr. Berkeley, 1994); Ware, ed., *The Cultural Approach to History,* ed. for the AHA (New York, 1940). In the second edition of *The Uprooted* in 1973, while still not citing Ware's study, Handlin admitted that he had not taken family into account even though it was in his sources.

19. P. Dewitte, *Les Mouvements nègres en France 1919–1939* (Paris, 1985); J.-R. Bennetta, *Black Paris. The African Writers' Landscape* (Urbana, 1998); B.-P. Lange and M. Pandurang, 'Dialectics of Empire and Complexities of Culture: British Men in India, Indian Experiences of Britain', in *The Historical Practice of Diversity: Transcultural Interactions from the Early Modern Mediterranean to the Postcolonial World,* eds. D. Hoerder, C. Harzig, and A. Shubert (New York, 2003), 177–200.

20. Köllmann and Marschalck, 'German Emigration to the United States', *Perspectives in American History* 7 (1973): 499–544, and, connecting internal to international migrations: Köllmann, 'Industrialisierung, Binnenwanderung und soziale Frage', in *Bevölkerung in der industriellen Revolution,* ed. Köllmann (Göttingen, 1974); Marschalck, *Deutsche Überseewanderung im 19. Jahrhundert: Ein Beitrag zur soziologischen Theorie der Bevölkerung* (Stuttgart, 1973); and Marschalck, *Bevölkerungsgeschichte Deutschlands im 19. und 20. Jahrhundert* (Frankfurt, 1984).

21. The German language does not provide a terminology of Polish-Germans or Turkish-Germans similar to the English language's German-Americans or Chinese-Americans. The terminology segregates 'Poles in Germany' or 'Turks in Germany'. In contrast, French language incorporates immigrants as *Français et Françaises issues de l'immigration.*

22. K.J. Bade's publications include: 'German Emigration to the United States and Continental Immigration to Germany, 1879–1914', *Central European History* 13 (1980): 348–77; 'Altes Handwerk, Wanderzwang und Gute Policey: Gesellenwanderung zwischen Zunftökonomie und Gewerbereform', *Vierteljahrschrift für Sozial- und Wirtschaftsgeschichte* 69 (1982): 1–37; 'Massenwanderung und Arbeitsmarkt im deutschen Nordosten von 1880 bis zum Ersten Weltkrieg', *Archiv für Sozialgeschichte* 20 (1980): 265–323; '"Preußengänger" und "Abwehrpolitik": Ausländerbeschäftigung, Ausländerpolitik und Ausländerkontrolle auf dem Arbeitsmarkt in Preußen vor dem Ersten Weltkrieg', *Archiv für Sozialgeschichte* 24 (1984): 91–283; *Vom Auswanderungsland zum Einwanderungsland? Deutschland 1880–1980* (Berlin, 1983); ed., *Population, Labour and Migration in 19th and 20th Century Germany* (New York, 1986).

23. Moltmann, ed., *Deutsche Amerikaauswanderung im 19. Jahrhundert: Sozialgeschichtliche Beiträge* (Stuttgart, 1976); Moltmann, ed., *Germans to America: 300 Years of Immigration, 1683–1983* (Stuttgart, 1982); German translation in *Zeitschrift für Kulturaustausch* 32 (1982): 305–452, and many others. The

dissertations of his students—H. Bickelmann, A. Bretting, B. Gelberg, H.-J. Grabbe, M. Just, I. Schöberl—provided a first social history of emigration.
24. The *Stiftung Volkswagenwerk* funded the projects of Moltmann, H. Keil and J. Jentz (Munich), W.P. Adams (FU Berlin), W. Helbich and W. Kamphoefner (Bochum / College Station Texas), and D. Hoerder (Bremen). The foundation assumed a role in integrating German and US research by changing its practice of relying on anonymous referees from a closed circle of 'Americanists' in German academia to include, on the request of Keil and Hoerder, anonymous US referees and thus open the program to the new social history approaches then current in US academia.
25. Keil and J.B. Jentz, eds., *German Workers in Industrial Chicago, 1850–1910: A Comparative Perspective* (DeKalb, IL, 1983), and other publications; Harzig, *Familie, Arbeit und weibliche Öffentlichkeit in einer Einwanderungsstadt: Deutschamerikanerinnen in Chicago um die Jahrhundertwende* (St. Katherinen, 1991), and other publications; M. Blaschke and C. Harzig, eds., *Frauen wandern aus: Deutsche Migrantinnen im 19. und 20. Jahrhundert* (Bremen, 1990).
26. For migration into agricultural regions and Midwestern cities, the continuities were emphasized by two US scholars: W.D. Kamphoefner, *The Westfalians: From Germany to Missouri* (Princeton, 1987); K.N. Conzen, *Immigrant Milwaukee, 1836–1860. Accommodation and Community in a Frontier City* (Cambridge, MA, 1976), and her work on German immigrants in the rural Midwest.
27. Bade, ed., *Auswanderer—Wanderarbeiter—Gastarbeiter*, 2 vols. (Ostfildern, 1984), and, after ten more years of research, D. Hoerder and J. Nagler, eds., *People in Transit. German Migrants in Comparative Perspective, 1820–1930* (Cambridge, 1995), with a review of the scholarship (Hoerder, 'Introduction' and 'Research on the German Migrations, 1820s to 1930s: A Report on the State of German Scholarship', 1–16, 399–421). The latter volume was published by the German Historical Institute, Washington, DC, which has played an important role in internationalizing German historiography.
28. Hoerder, ed., *American Labor and Immigration History, 1877–1920s: Recent European Research* (Urbana, IL, 1982); and Hoerder, ed., *'Struggle a Hard Battle'—Essays on Working-Class Immigrants* (DeKalb, IL, 1986).
29. Hoerder, ed., *Labor Migration in the Atlantic Economies. The European and North American Working Classes during the Period of Industrialization* (Westport, CT, 1985). In the Labor Migration Project, from 1978–1993, scholars from some forty European cultures cooperated.
30. Pervasive racism led to different developments in Pacific ports in regard to immigration from the several Asian cultures.
31. Harzig, ed., *Peasant Maids, City Women. From the European Countryside to Urban America* (Ithaca, NY, 1997).
32. D. Thelen, 'Of Audiences, Borderlands, and Comparisons: Toward the Internationalization of American History', *Journ. Am. Hist.* 79 (1992): 432–62, quote 436.

33. J. Lucassen, *Migrant Labour in Europe, 1600–1900: The Drift to the North Sea* (London, 1987; Dutch original 1984); L. Page Moch, *Moving Europeans: Migration in Western Europe since 1650* (Bloomington, 1992; 2nd rev. ed. 2003); J.H. Jackson, Jr., and Moch, 'Migration and the Social History of Modern Europe', in Hoerder and Moch, *European Migrants*, 52–69; Hoerder, 'Migration in the Atlantic Economies: Regional European Origins and Worldwide Expansion', Hoerder and Moch, *European Migrants*, 21–51; Hoerder, 'Changing Paradigms in Migration History: From "To America" to Worldwide Systems', *Canadian Review of American Studies* 24(2) (Spring 1994): 105–26.
34. J. Torpey, *The Invention of the Passport. Surveillance, Citizenship and the State* (Cambridge, 2000); A. Fahrmeir, O. Faron, and P. Weil, eds., *Migration Control in the North Atlantic World: The Evolution of State Practices in Europe and the United States from the French Revolution to the Inter-War Period* (New York, 2003).
35. D. Hoerder, I. Blank, and H. Rößler, eds., *Roots of the Transplanted*, 2 vols. (Boulder and New York, 1994); Moch, *Moving Europeans*.
36. 'Recasting European and Canadian History: National Consciousness, Migration, Multicultural Lives', Symposium, European Network for Canadian Studies, Bremen, May 2000. 'Negotiating Nations: Exclusions, Networks, Inclusions / Nations en transition: exclusions, réseaux, inclusions', eds. C. Harzig, D. Hoerder, and A. Shubert, *Histoire sociale—Social History* 34 (2000); Hoerder, with Harzig and Shubert, eds., *Diversity in History: Transcultural Interactions from the Early Modern Mediterranean World to the 20th-Century Postcolonial World* (New York, 2003); Harzig, D. Juteau, with I. Schmitt, eds., *The Social Construction of Diversity: Recasting the Master Narrative of Industrial Nations* (New York, 2003).
37. K.J. Bade, *Europa in Bewegung: Migration vom späten 18. Jahrhundert bis zur Gegenwart* (München, 2000); Trans. by A. Brown as *Migration in European History* (Oxford, 2003); Italian ed. (2001); French ed. (2002); Spanish ed. (2003). K.J. Bade, P.C. Emmer, L. Lucassen, and J. Oltmer, eds., *Migration—Integration—Minderheiten seit dem 17. Jahrhundert: eine europäische Enzyklopädie* (Paderborn/München, forthcoming 2006); English version as *Migration—Integration—Minorities since the 17th Century: A European Encyclopaedia* (Cambridge, forthcoming 2010).
38. Works in this area have become too numerous to list. For France, as one example, see Y. Lequin, ed., *La mosaïque France: histoire des étrangers et de l'immigration* (Paris, 1988), rev. under the title *Histoire des étrangers et de l'immigration en France* (Paris, 1992); and *Toute la France. Histoire de l'immigration en France au XXe siècle*, eds. L.Gervereau, P. Milza, and E. Temime (Paris, 1998). For Britain, see, among many others, R. Cohen, 'Fuzzy Frontiers of Identity: the British Case', *Social Identities* 1 (1995): 35–62.
39. C. Harzig, *Einwanderung und Politik. Historische Erinnerung und Politische Kultur als Gestaltungsressourcen in den Niederlanden, Schweden und Kanada* (Immigration and Policy-Making. Historical Memory and Political Culture as a Creative Strategic Resource in the Netherlands, Sweden, and Canada), Transkulturelle Perspektiven 1 (Göttingen, 2004).

40. N. Glick Schiller, L. Basch, and C. Blanc-Szanton, eds., *Towards a Transnational Perspective on Migration: Race, Class, Ethnicity and Nationalism Reconsidered* (New York, 1992); and Glick Schiller, Basch, and Blanc-Szanton, 'From Immigrant to Transmigrant: Theorizing Transnational Migration', *Anthropological Quarterly* 68 (1995): 48–63; A. Portes, L.E. Guarnizo, and P. Landolt, 'The Study of Transnationalism: Pitfalls and Promise of an Emergent Research Field', *Ethnic and Racial Studies* 22 (1999): 217–37; Portes, 'Conclusion: Toward a New World: The Origins and Effects of Transnational Activities', *Ethnic and Racial Studies* 22 (1999): 463–77. K.K. Patel, in *Nach der Nationalfixiertheit. Perspektiven einer transnationalen Geschichte* (Berlin, 2004), 5–7, has traced earlier usages of the term in specific compartments of historiography.
41. L. Pries, ed., *Transnationale Migration* (Baden-Baden, 1997), esp. his 'Neue Migration im transnationalen Raum', 14–44; T. Faist, 'International Migration and Transnational Social Spaces: The Turkish-German Example', paper presented at the 3rd Conference of the European Sociological Association, Aug. 1997.
42. P. Kivisto, 'Theorizing Transnational Immigration: A Critical Review of Current Efforts', *Ethnic and Racial Studies* 24(4) (July 2001): 549–77; and Kivisto, 'Social Spaces, Transnational Immigrant Communities, and the Politics of Incorporation', *Ethnicities* 3(1) (2003): 5–28. Before Kivisto, L.E. Guarnizo and M.P. Smith in 'The Locations of Transnationalism', had argued for a *Transnationalism from Below*, eds. Guarnizo and Smith (New Brunswick, 1998), 5–34.
43. L.L. Wong, 'Home Away from Home: Deterritorialized Identity and State Citizenship Policy', unpublished paper presented at the 15th Biennial Conference of the Canadian Studies Association, Toronto, March 2000 (quote, unnumbered pages); Wong, 'Home Away from Home? Transnationalism and the Canadian Citizenship Regime', in V. Roudometof and P. Kennedy, eds., *Communities across Borders: New Immigrants and Transnational Cultures* (London, 2002), 169–81; A. Ong, 'On the Edge of Empires: Flexible Citizenship among Chinese in the Diaspora', *Positions* 1(3) (1993): 745–78.
44. T. Faist, *The Volume and Dynamics of International Migration and Transnational Social Spaces* (Oxford, 2000), esp. 197–210.
45. See, for example, R. Cohen, *Global Diasporas: An Introduction* (Seattle, 1997); A. Walaszek, 'Labor Diasporas in Comparative Perspective: Polish and Italian Migrant Workers in the Atlantic Wold between the 1870s and the 1920s', in Hoerder, Harzig, and Shubert, *The Historical Practice of Diversity*, 152–76; P. Li, 'The Chinese Diaspora in Occidental Societies: Canada and Europe', Hoerder, Harzig, and Shubert, *The Historical Practice of Diversity*, 134–51; D.R. Gabaccia and F. Ottanelli, eds., *Italian Workers of the World: Labor, Migration and the Making of Multi-Ethnic States* (Urbana, 2001).
46. See also Osterhammel's call for open, radiating, and absorbing social macrospaces ('Transnationale Gesellschaftsgeschichte', 478).
47. Regionalism has been far more intensively discussed for Italy and for Canada than for Germany or France.
48. See among many others A. Appadurai, *Modernity at Large. Cultural Dimension of Globalization* (Minneapolis, 1996); U. Hannerz, *Cultural Complexity:*

Studies in Social Organization of Meaning (New York, 1999); research by a team of the International Council for Canadian Studies on 'transculturalisms', directed by Z. Bernd, S. Gunew, C.M. Hall, S. Harel, and D. Hoerder, 2000–2005; P. Anctil and Z. Bernd, 'Canada from the Outside', in *New Trends in Canadian Studies* (Bruessel, 2006).

49. Cohen, *Global Diasporas*, 175; Y. Hébert, 'The Accumulation of Social Capital among Canadian Youth (native-born and globally mobile)', outline of a research project, Oct. 2002, and Hébert, 'Identity, Diversity, and Education: A Critical Review of the Literature', *Canadian Ethnic Studies* 33(2) (2001): 155–85.
50. Hoerder, *Creating Societies: Immigrant Lives in Canada* (Montreal, 1999).
51. Hoerder, *'To Know Our Many Selves Changing Across Time and Space': From the Study of Canada to Canadian Studies* (Augsburg, 2005), 316–26.
52. P. Martin, *Schwarze Teufel, edle Mohren. Afrikaner in Bewusstsein und Geschichte der Deutschen* (Hamburg, 1993), provided a first contribution history. A. Mielke, *Nigra sum et formosa. Afrikanerinnen in der deutschen Literatur des Mittelalters* (Stuttgart, 1992). A. Kuhlmann-Smirnov (Univ. of Bremen) is preparing a research monograph on Africans in German-language Central Europe (and beyond) in the early modern period.
53. P. Marschalck, ed., *Europa als Wanderungsziel. Ansiedlung und Integration von Deutschen im 19. Jahrhundert*, IMIS-Beiträge no. 14 (Osnabrück, 2000); Hoerder, 'The German-Language Diasporas. A Survey, Critique, and Interpretation', *Diaspora: A Journal of Transnational Studies* 11(1) (Spring 2002): 7–44.
54. J.S. Frideres, 'Edging into the Mainstream: A Comparison of Values and Attitudes of Recent Immigrants, their Children and Canadia-born Adults', in *Multiculturalism in North America and Europe. Comparative Perspectives on Interethnic Relations and Social Incorporation*, ed. W.W. Isajiw (Toronto, 1997), 537–61.
55. This has been analysed first by the researchers of the Birmingham Centre for Contemporary Cultural Studies. See, more recently, comparative research on immigrant and native-born youth in Hamburg, Germany, and London, Britain. P. Cohen, M. Keith, L. Back, *Issues of Theory and Method*, Working Paper 1 (mimeographed) (London, 1996); N. Räthzel, 'Young People of Many Cultures in Hamburg: Racialized Space and the Appropriation of Places', in *Socio-Cultural Problems in the Metropolis. Comparative Analyses*, eds. D. Hoerder and R.-O. Schultze (Augsburg, 2000), 37–56.
56. H.K. Bhabha, 'DissemiNation: Time, Narrative, And the Margins of the Modern Nation', in *Nation and Narration*, ed. Bhabha (London, 1990), 291–322; Bhabha, *The Location of Culture* (London, 1994).
57. Globalization has become a catchword. It requires a reminder that the seventeenth-century fur trade was a global activity in the northern hemisphere, that the nineteenth-century plantation belt circles the globe, and that from the 1880s on, German consumers bought a part of their food in stores, whose designation *Kolonialwaren* indicated the worldwide origins of elements of a 'typically German' diet prepared by allegedly kitchen-centred German housewives.

58. Patel, *Nach der Nationalfixiertheit.*
59. W. Helbich, W.D. Kamphoefner, and U. Sommer, eds., *Briefe aus Amerika. Deutsche Auswanderer schreiben aus der Neuen Welt, 1830–1930* (München, 1988); Trans. by S. Carter Vogel as *News from the Land of Freedom. German Immigrants Write Home* (Ithaca, NY, 1991), data on the number of letters, English ed., 27–28.
60. Hoerder, 'Labour Migrants' Views of "America"', *Renaissance and Modern Studies* 35 (1992): 1–17; and Hoerder and H. Rössler, eds., *Distant Magnets: Expectations and Realities in the Immigrant Experience* (New York, 1993). See also Hoerder, ed., *Plutokraten und Sozialisten. Berichte deutscher Diplomaten und Agenten über die amerikanische Arbeiterbewegung 1878–1917* (Plutocrats and Socialists. Reports by German Diplomats and Agents on the American Labor Movement) (München, 1981).

≣ CONTRIBUTORS ≣

Sebastian Conrad is Professor of Modern History at the European University Institute in Florence, Italy. He was Fellow at the Center for Advanced Study (Wissenschaftskolleg) in Berlin. His publications include *Auf der Suche nach der verlorenen Nation. Geschichtsschreibung in Westdeutschland und Japan, 1945–1960* (1999); *Globalisierung und Nation im Deutschen Kaiserreich* (2006); *Deutsche Kolonialgeschichte* (2008) and the edited volumes *Globalgeschichte. Theorien, Ansätze, Themen* (2007, with Andreas Eckert, Ulrike Freitag) and *Competing Visions of World Order: Global Moments and Movements, 1880s–1930s* (2007, with Dominic Sachsenmaier).

Andreas Eckert is Professor of African History at Humboldt University Berlin. He holds visiting professorships in Bloomington, Harvard, and the Maison des Sciences de l'Homme in Paris. He is Fellow of the Royal Historical Society (UK), chair of the study group of modern social history (*Arbeitskreis für Moderne Sozialgeschichte*), and currently editor of the *Journal of African History*. His main research areas are nineteenth and twentieth century African history, colonialism, the history of historiography, and global labor history. Among his recent publications are *Kolonialismus* (2006); *Herrschen und Verwalten. Afrikanische Bürokraten, staatliche Ordnung und Politik in Tanzania, 1920–1970* (2007); and *Vom Imperialismus zum Empire. Nicht-westliche Perspektiven auf die Globalisierung* (2008, ed. with Shalini Randeria).

Heinz-Gerhard Haupt is Professor of Social History at the University of Bielefeld, currently teaching at the European University Institute, Florence. He has published widely in the fields of the comparative history of the European middle classes, nationalism, and political violence.

Dirk Hoerder teaches North American social history, history of global migrations, and borderland issues at Arizona State University. His areas of interest are labor migration in the Atlantic economies, worldwide migration systems, and sociology of migrant acculturation. He has taught at York University, Toronto, Duke University, Durham NC, Université de Paris 8—

Saint Denis, and the University of Toronto. His publications include *Cultures in Contact: World Migration/ in the Second Millennium* (2002), which has received the Social Science History Association's Sharlin Prize, and the coedited *The Historical Practice of Diversity: Transcultural Interactions from the Early Modern Mediterranean to the Postcolonial World* (2003).

Monica Juneja is Professor of Global Art History at the University of Heidelberg. She has been a Professor at the Universities of Delhi, and Visiting Professor at the Universities of Hannover, Vienna, and at Emory University, Atlanta. Her research and writing focus on transculturality and visual representation, disciplinary practices in the art history of Western Europe and South Asia, and Christianization and religious identities in India. Her publications include *Peindre le paysan. L'image rurale dans la peinture française de Millet à Van Gogh* (Paris, 1998); *Architecture in medieval India. Forms, Contexts, Histories* (Reader South Asia. Histories and Interpretations, 2001); *BildGeschichten. Das Verhältnis von Bild und Text in den Berichten zu außereuropaeische Welten* (Theme issue of Zeitenblicke, 2008, edited together with Barbara Potthast); *Religion und Grenzen in Indien und Deutschland: Auf dem Weg zu einer transnationalen Historiografie* (edited with Margrit Pernau, 2008). Her next monograph is entitled *Christianisierung als globaler Prozess* (co-authored with Kirsten Rüther).

Hartmut Kaelble, since 1990, is Professor for social history at the Humboldt University. He has been a Professor, from 1971–1990, at Free University of Berlin, fellow at Harvard University, St. Anthony's College, Oxford, MSH Paris, Sorbonne Paris I. His main publications are: *Social Mobility in the 19th and 20th Centuries: Europe and America in Comparative Perspective* (1985); *A Social History of Western Europe, 1880–1980* (1990); *Nachbarn am Rhein. Entfremdung und Annäherung der französischen und deutschen Gesellschaft seit 1880* (1991); *Der historische Vergleich* (1999); *Social history of Europe since 1945* (2009).

Jürgen Kocka was Professor of History of the Industrial World at the Free University of Berlin and Research Professor at the Berlin Social Science Research Centre (WZB) until 2009. Among his publications are: *White Collar Workers in America 1890–1940* (1980); *Les employés en Allemagne 1850–1980* (1989); *Facing Total War. German Society 1914–1918* (1984); *Arbeitsverhältnisse und Arbeiterexistenzen. Grundlagen der Klassenbildung im 19. Jahrhundert* (1990); *Industrial Culture and Bourgeois Society. Business, Labor, and Bureaucracy in Modern Germany* (1999); *Das lange 19. Jahrhundert* (2001); *Civil Society and Dictatorship in Modern German History* (2010).

Dieter Langewiesche was Chair for modern history at the University of Tuebingen until 2008. Among his publications are: *Liberalism in Germany* (2000); *Liberalismus und Sozialismus* (2003); *Nation, Nationalismus, Nationalstaat in Deutschland und Europa* (2000); *Europa zwischen Restauration und Revolution 1815–1849*, (5th ed., 2007); *Reich, Nation, Föderation. Deutschland und Europa* (2008); *Zeitwende. Geschichtsdenken heute* (2008); Ed., *Europe 1848. Revolution and Reform* (2001); *Formen des Krieges. Von der Antike bis zur Gegenwart* (2007).

Jürgen Osterhammel is Professor of Modern and Contemporary History at the University of Konstanz (Germany). He is also a member of the Center of Excellence 'Cultural Foundations of Integration' at that University. His publications since 2000 include *Geschichtswissenschaft jenseits des Nationalstaats: Studien zu Beziehungsgeschichte und Zivilisationsvergleich* (Göttingen, 2001); co-authored with Niels P. Petersson, *Globalization: A Short History* (Princeton, NJ, 2005); edited with Boris Barth, *Zivilisierungsmissionen* (Konstanz, 2005); edited, *Weltgeschichte* (Stuttgart, 2008); *Die Verwandlung der Welt: Eine Geschichte des 19. Jahrhunderts* (Munich, 2009). He is currently directing the research program 'Dynamics of transnational action.'

Margrit Pernau is Leader of a Research Group at the Centre for the History of Emotions at the Max-Planck-Institute for Human Development, Berlin. She had been Research Fellow at the Social Sciences Research Center (WZB), Berlin (2006) and at the Center for Modern Oriental Studies (ZMO), Berlin (2006–2007). Her most important publications include: *Bürger mit Turban. Muslime in Delhi im 19. Jahrhundert* (Göttingen: Vandenhoeck & Ruprecht, 2008; Ed., *The Delhi College. Traditional Elites, the Colonial State, and Education before 1857* (Delhi: Oxford University Press, 2006); *Family and Gender. Changing patterns of family and gender values in Europe and India* (edited with Imtiaz Ahmad and Helmut Reifeld) (Delhi: Sage, 2002) and, edited with Monica Juneja, *Religion und Grenzen. Studien auf dem Weg zu einer transnationalen Historiographie* (forthcoming); 'Gab es eine indische Zivilgesellschaft im 19. Jh.? Überlegungen zum Verhältnis von Globalgeschichte und historischer Semantik,' in *Traverse*, 3.2007: 51–67; 'Transkulturelle Geschichte und das Problem der universalen Begriffe. Muslimische Bürger im Delhi des 19. Jahrhunderts,' in *Area Studies und die Welt. Weltregionen und neue Globalgeschichte*, ed. Birgit Schäbler (Wien: Mandelbaum Verlag, 2007), 117–50.

Shalini Randeria is Professor of Social and Cultural Anthropology at the University of Zurich. She is currently president of the European Association of Social Anthropologists (EASA) and member of the Senate of the German Research Foundation (DFG). She studied Sociology and Social

Anthropology at the Universities of Delhi and Heidelberg and completed her Ph.D and habilitation at the Free University of Berlin. She was a Rhodes scholar at the University of Oxford, a Fellow of the Wissenschaftskolleg zu Berlin, Max Weber Professor for Sociology at the University of Munich, and Full Professor and Chair of the Department of Sociology and Social Anthropology of the Central European University Budapest. Her research interests include anthropology of law and governance, the transformation of the nation state, the role of civil society actors, a critical analysis of processes of globalization as well as multiple modernities and postcolonial theory. The regional focus of her research is on South Asia. Latest Publication: *Vom Imperialismus zum Empire: Globalisierung aus nicht-europäischer Sicht*, ed. with Andreas Eckert (Frankfurt/Main, 2008).

Jörg Requate is Oberassistent an der Fakultät für Geschichtswissenschaft Philosophie und Theologie der Universität Bielefeld. His publications include: *Journalismus als Beruf. Die Entstehung des Journalistenberufs im 19. Jahrhundert Deutschland im internationalen Vergleich* (Göttingen, 1995); ed., with Martin Schulze Wessel, *Europäische Öffentlichkeit. Transnationale Kommunikation seit dem 18. Jahrhundert* (Frankfurt a.M., 2002); ed., with Heinz-Gerhard Haupt, *Aufbruch in die Zukunft. Die 1960er Jahre zwischen Planungseuphorie und kulturellem Wandel. DDR, CSSR und Bundesrepublik Deutschland im Vergleich* (Göttingen, 2004).

Philipp Ther teaches modern European history at the Department of History and Civilization at the EUI in Florence. His fields of interest are comparative social and cultural history and its methodological foundations, music and history, comparative nationalism studies, ethnic cleansing, genocide, and collective memory. Among his books are: *In der Mitte der Gesellschaft. Operntheater in Zentraleuropa 1815–1914* (Vienna, 2006); *Robbery and Restitution. The Conflict over Jewish Property in Europe* (Providence, 2007) (co-editor); *Redrawing Nations: Ethnic Cleansing in East-Central Europe 1944–1948* (Lanham, 2001) (co-editor).

Thomas Welskopp is Professor for the History of Modern Societies at Bielefeld University; 2003–2004: Fellow at the Center for Advanced Study in the Behavioral Sciences, Stanford, California; 2008–2009: Fellow of the Historisches Kolleg in Munich. His major publications are: *Der Migros-Kosmos. Zur Geschichte eines außergewöhnlichen Schweizer Unternehmens* (Co-ed., 2003); *Das Banner der Brüderlichkeit. Die deutsche Sozialdemokratie vom Vormärz bis zum Sozialistengesetz* (2000); *Geschichte zwischen Kultur und Gesellschaft. Beiträge zur Theoriedebatte* (Co-ed., 1997); *Arbeit und Macht im Hüttenwerk. Die deutsche und amerikanische Eisen- und Stahlindustrie von den 1860er bis zu den 1930er Jahren* (1994).

SELECT BIBLIOGRAPHY

Abelshauser, W. *Kulturkampf. Der deutsche Weg in die Neue Wirtschaft und die amerikanische Herausforderung.* Berlin, 2003.
Adams, J., E.S. Clemens, and A.S. Orloff, eds. *Remaking Modernity: Politics, History, and Sociology.* Durham, NC, 2005.
Ahmad, I., ed. *Modernization and Social Change among Muslims in India.* Delhi, 1983.
Ames, E., M. Klotz, and L. Wildenthal, eds. *Germany's Colonial Past.* London/Lincoln, 2005.
Amin, S. *L'eurocentrisme. Critique d'une idéologie.* Paris, 1988.
Anderson, B. *Imagined Communities. Reflections on the Origin and Spread of Nationalism.* London, 1983.
———. *The Spectre of Comparisons. Nationalism, Southeast Asia and the World.* London/New York, 1998.
Angster, J. *Konsenskapitalismus und Sozialdemokratie. Die Westernisierung von SPD und DGB.* Munich, 2003.
Appadurai, A. *Modernity at Large. Cultural Dimension of Globalization.* Minneapolis, 1996.
Applegate, C. 'A Europe of Regions: Reflections on the Historiography of Sub-National Places in Modern Times'. *AHR* 104 (1999): 1157–82.
Arendt, H. *Elemente und Ursprünge totaler Herrschaft* (1955/1966). München, 1986.
Arndt, S., ed. *AfrikaBilder. Studien zu Rassismus in Deutschland.* Münster, 2003.
Ashcroft, B. et al., eds. *The Post-Colonial Studies Reader.* London, 1995.
Bade, K.J. *Migration in European History.* Oxford, 2003.
———, P.C. Emmer, L. Lucassen, and J. Oltmer, eds. *Migration—Integration—Minderheiten seit dem 17. Jahrhundert: eine europäische Enzyklopädie.* Paderborn/München, 2007; English version as *Migration—Integration—Minorities since the 17th Century: A European Encyclopaedia.* Cambridge, forthcoming.
Baldwin, P. *The Narcissism of Minor Differences. How America and Europe Are Alike.* Oxford, 2009.
Barbier, F. *L'Empire du livre. Le livre imprimé et la construction de l'Allemagne contemporaine.* Paris, 1995.
Bauer, O. *Die Nationalitätenfrage und die Sozialdemokratie.* 2nd ed., Vienna, 1924; 1st ed., 1907. English translation as *Question of Nationalities and Social Democracy* (2000).
Bauerkämper, A., M. Sabrow, and B. Stöver, eds. *Doppelte Zeitgeschichte. Deutsch-Deutsche Beziehungen 1945–1990.* Bonn, 1998.

Baumgart, W. *Deutschland im Zeitalter des Imperialismus 1890–1914. Grundkräfte, Thesen und Strukturen.* Stuttgart, 1982.
Bayly, C.A. *The Birth of the Modern World 1780–1914.* Malden and Oxford, 2004.
Bechhaus-Gerst, M. and R. Klein-Arendt, eds. *AfrikanerInnen in Deutschland und schwarze Deutsche—Geschichte und Gegenwart.* Münster, 2004.
Behrends, J.C., Á. von Klimó, and P. Poutros, eds. *Antiamerikanismus im 20. Jahrhundert: Studien zu Ost- und Westeuropa.* Bonn, 2005.
Belchem, J. and K. Tenfelde, eds. *Irish and Polish Migration in Comparative Perspective.* Essen, 2003.
Bender, T., ed. *Rethinking American History in a Global Age.* Berkeley, 2002.
Bennetta, J.-R. *Black Paris. The African Writer' Landscape.* Urbana, 1998.
Bentley, J. *Old World Encounters. Cross-Cultural Contacts and Exchanges in the Pre-Modern Times.* Oxford, 1993.
Berendt, I. *History Derailed: Central and Eastern Europe in the Long Nineteenth Century.* Berkeley, 2003.
Berg, E. and M. Fuchs, eds. *Kultur, soziale Praxis, Text. Die Krise der ethnographischen Repräsentation.* Frankfurt a.M., 1999.
Berger, S. *The Search for Normality. National Identity and Historical Consciousness in Germany since 1800.* Oxford, 1997.
Berman, N. *Orientalismus, Kolonialismus und Moderne. Zum Bild des Orients in der deutschsprachigen Literatur um 1900.* Stuttgart, 1996.
Berman, R. *Enlightenment or Empire. Colonial Discourse in German Culture.* Lincoln/London, 1998.
Béteille, A. *Civil Society and its Institutions.* First Fulbright Memorial Lecture, Calcutta, 1996.
Bhabha, H. *The Location of Cultures.* London, 1994.
Bierschenk, T. and G. Elwert, eds. *Entwicklungshilfe und ihre Folgen. Ergebnisse empirischer Untersuchungen in Afrika.* Frankfurt a.M., 1993.
Bitterli, U. *Die 'Wilden' und die 'Zivilisierten'. Grundzüge einer Geistes- und Kulturgeschichte der europäisch-überseeischen Begegnung.* Munich, 1976.
Blaut, J. *The Colonizer's Model of the World. Geographical Diffusionism and Eurocentric History.* New York, 1993.
Bley, H. *Kolonialherrschaft und Sozialstruktur in Deutsch-Südwestafrika 1894–1914.* Hamburg, 1968.
Bloch, M. 'Pour une Histoire comparée des Sociétés européennes' (1928). In Bloch, *Mélanges historiques.* Vol. 1, 16–40. Paris, 1963. English translation in M. Aymard and H. Mukhia, eds., *French Studies in History,* Vol. 1: The Inheritance, 35–68. New Delhi, 1988.
Bodnar, J. *The Transplanted. A History of Immigrants in Urban America.* Bloomington, 1985.
Boll. *Arbeitskämpfe und Gewerkschaften in Deutschland, England und Frankreich. Ihre Entwicklung vom 19. zum 20. Jahrhundert.* Bonn, 1992.
Brenner, C. and P. Heumos, eds. *Sozialgeschichtliche Kommunismusforschung. Tschechoslowakei, Polen, Ungarn und DDR, 1948–1968.* Munich, 2005.
Breuilly, J. 'Introduction: Making Comparisons in History'. In J. Breuilly, *Labour*

and Liberalism in Nineteenth Century Europe: Essays in Comparative History, 1–25. Manchester, 1992.

Brie, M. 'Staatssozialistische Länder Europas im Vergleich. Alternative Herrschaftsstrategien und divergente Typen'. In *Einheit als Privileg. Vergleichende Perspektiven auf die Transformation Ostdeutschlands*, edited by H. Wiesenthal, 39–104. Frankfurt, 1996.

Bright, C. and M. Geyer. 'Globalgeschichte und die Einheit der Welt im 20. Jahrhundert'. *Comparativ* 4(5) (1994): 13–45.

Budde, G. et al., eds. *Transnationale Geschichte. Themen, Tendenzen und Theorien*. Göttingen, 2006.

Burton, A. *Burdens of History. British Feminists, Indian Women and Imperial Culture, 1865–1915*. London, 1994.

Buschmann, N. and D. Langewiesche, eds. *Der Krieg in den Gründungsmythen europäischer Nationen und der USA*. Frankfurt a.M., 2004.

Campt, T.M. *Other Germans. Black Germans and the Politics of Race, Gender, and Memory in the Third Reich*. Ann Arbor, 2004.

Carl, H., H.-H. Kortüm, D. Langewiesche, and F. Lenger, eds. *Kriegsniederlagen. Erfahrungen und Erinnerungen*. Berlin, 2004.

Castel, R. *Die Metamorphosen der sozialen Frage. Eine Chronik der Lohnarbeit*. Konstanz, 2000.

Chakrabarty, D. *Provincializing Europe. Postcolonial thought and historical difference*. Princeton/New Delhi, 2000.

Chambers, S. and W. Kymlicka, eds. *Alternative Conceptions of Civil Society*. Princeton, 2002.

Charle, C. *La république des universitaires 1870–1940*. Paris, 1994.

Chatterjee, P. *The Nation and its Fragments. Colonial and Postcolonial Histories*. Princeton, 1993.

Chickering, R. *We Men Who Feel Most German. A Cultural Study of the Pan-German League, 1886–1914*. London, 1984.

Cohen, R. 'Fuzzy Frontiers of Identity: the British Case'. *Social Identities* 1(1995): 35–62.

———. *Global Diasporas: An Introduction*. Seattle, 1997.

Cohn, B. *Colonialism and its Forms of Knowledge. The British in India*. Delhi, 1997.

Collins, R.M. Growth Liberalism in the Sixties. Great Societies at Home and Grand Designs Abroad. In *The Sixties. From Memory to History*, edited by D. Farber, 11–44. Chapel Hill, 1994.

Comaroff, J.L. and Jean Comaroff, eds. *Civil Society and the Political Imagination in Africa*. Chicago, 1999.

Connelly, J. *Captive university: the Sovietization of East German, Czech and Polish higher education, 1945–1956*. Chapel Hill, 2000.

Conrad, C. and S. Conrad, eds. *Die Nation schreiben. Geschichtswissenschaft im internationalen Vergleich*. Göttingen, 2002.

Conrad, S. *Globalisierung und Nation im Deutschen Kaiserreich*. München, 2006.

———. 'What Time is Japan? Problems of Comparative (Intercultural) Historiography'. *History and Theory* 38(1999): 67–83.

—— and J. Osterhammel, eds. *Das Kaiserreich transnational. Deutschland in der Welt 1871–1914*. Göttingen, 2004.

—— and S. Randeria. *Jenseits des Eurozentrismus. Postkoloniale Perspektive in den Geschichts- und Kulturwissenschaften*. Frankfurt a.M./New York, 2002.

Cooper, F. 'Africa in a Capitalist World'. In *Crossing Boundaries. Comparative History of Black People in Diaspora*, edited by D. Clark Hine et al. Bloomington, 1999.

——. *Decolonization and African Society. The Labor Question in British and French Africa*. Cambridge, 1996.

—— and A. Stoler, ed. *Tensions of Empire. Colonial Cultures in a Bourgeois World*. Berkeley, 1997.

Csanádi, M. *A comparative model of party-states: the structural reasons behind similarities and differences in self-reproduction, reforms and transformation*. Budapest, 2004.

Curtin, P.D. *Cross-Cultural Trade in World History*. Cambridge, 1984.

Debrunner, H.W. *Presence and Prestige. Africans in Europe. A History of Africans in Europe before 1918*. Basel, 1979.

Debusmann, R. and J. Riesz, eds. *Kolonialausstellungen—Begegnungen mit Afrika?* Frankfurt, 1995.

Dewitte, P. *Les Mouvements nègres en France 1919–1939*. Paris, 1985.

Didry, C. et al., eds. *Arbeit und Nationalstaat. Frankreich und Deutschland in europäischer Perspektive*. Frankfurt, 2000.

Diesener, G. and R. Gries, eds. *Propaganda in Deutschland. Zur Geschichte der politischen Massenbeeinflussung im 20. Jahrhundert*. Darmstadt, 1996.

Dirlik, A., V. Bahl, and P. Gran, eds. *History after the Three Worlds. Post-Eurocentric Historiographies*. Lanham, 2000.

Dreesbach, A. *Gezähmte Wilde. Die Zurschaustellung 'exotischer' Menschen in Deutschland 1870–1940*. Frankfurt, 2005.

Drescher, S. 'Capitalism and Slavery after Fifty Years'. *Slavery and Abolition* 18(1997): 212–27.

Duara, P. *Rescuing History from the Nation. Questioning Narratives of Modern China*. Chicago, 1995.

Duchhardt, H., ed. *'Europäische Geschichte' als historiographisches Problem*. Mainz, 1997.

Eberhard, W. et al., eds. *Westmitteleuropa—Ostmitteleuropa. Vergleiche und Beziehungen*. Munich, 1992.

Eckart, W. *Medizin und Kolonialimperialismus. Deutschland 1884–1945*. Paderborn, 1996.

Eckert, A. *Kolonialismus*. Frankfurt a.M., 2006.

Eckert, R. 'Die Vergleichbarkeit des Unvergleichbaren. Die Widerstandsforschung über die NS-Zeit als methodisches Beispiel'. In *Zwischen Selbstbehauptung und Anpassung. Formen des Widerstandes und der Opposition in der DDR*, edited by U. Poppe et al., 68–84. Berlin, 1995.

Eichwede, W., ed. *Samizdat. Alternative Kultur in Zentral- und Osteuropa: Die 60er bis 80er Jahre*. Bremen, 2000.

Eisenstadt, S.N. 'Multiple Modernities'. In *Daedalus* 129 (1)(2000): 1–29.

El-Tayeb, F. *Schwarze Deutsche. Der Diskurs um 'Rasse' und nationale Identität 1890–1933*. Frankfurt, 2001.
Engel, U. and H.-G. Schleicher. *Die beiden deutschen Staaten in Afrika. Zwischen Konkurrenz und Koexistenz, 1949–1990*. Hamburg, 1998.
Espagne, M. *Les transferts culturels franco-allemands*. Paris, 1999.
———. 'Sur les limites du comparatisme en histoire culturelle'. *Genèses* 17 (Sept. 1994): 112–21.
——— and M. Werner, eds. *Transferts. Les relations interculturelles dans l'espace franco-allemand*. Paris, 1988.
Essner, C. 'Zwischen Vernunft und Gefühl- Die Reichstagsdebatten von 1912 um koloniale "Rassenmischehen" und "Sexualität". *Zeitschrift für Geschichtswissenschaft* 45(1997): 503–19.
Fahrmeir, A., O. Faron, and P. Weil, eds. *Migration Control in the North Atlantic World: The Evolution of State Practices in Europe and the United States from the French Revolution to the Inter-War Period*. New York, 2003.
Faist, T. *The Volume and Dynamics of International Migration and Transnational Social Spaces*. Oxford, 2000.
Fanon, F. *Les damnés de la terre*. Paris, 1961.
Febvre, L. *Le Rhin: Problèmes d'histoire et d'économie*. Paris, 1935.
Feichtinger, J., U. Prutsch, and M. Csáky, eds. *Habsburg postcolonial. Machtstrukturen und kollektives Gedächtnis*. Innsbruck, 2003.
Feldbauer, P., M. Mitterauer, and W. Schwentker, eds. *Die vormoderne Stadt. Asien und Europa im Vergleich*. Vienna/Munich, 2002.
Fisch, J. 'Zivilisation, Kultur'. In *Geschichtliche Grundbegriffe. Historisches Lexikon zur politisch-sozialen Sprache in Deutschland*, edited by O. Brunner, W. Conze, and R. Koselleck. 7 vols. Vol. 7: 679–774. Stuttgart, 1972–1997.
Fischer, W., ed. *Handbuch der europäischen Wirtschafts- und Sozialgeschichte*. 6 vols. Stuttgart, 1980–1990.
Fletcher, I.C., L.E.N. Mayhall, and P. Levine, eds. *Women's Suffrage in the British Empire: Citizenship, Nation, and Race*. London/New York, 2000.
Flitner, M., ed. *Der deutsche Tropenwald. Bilder, Mythen, Politik*. Frankfurt, 2000.
François, E., ed. *Sociabilité et société bourgeoise en France, en Allemagne et en Suisse (1750–1850)*. Paris, 1986.
François, E., H. Siegrist, and J. Vogel, eds. *Nation und Emotion. Deutschland und Frankreich im Vergleich*. Göttingen, 1995.
Freedman, J. 'Zwischen Frankreich und Deutschland. Buchhändler als Kulturvermittler'. In *Kulturtransfer im Epochenumbruch. Frankreich und Deutschland 1770 bis 1815*, edited by H.-J. Lüsebrink and R. Reichardt, 445–98. Leipzig, 1997.
Friedemann, P. and L. Hölscher. 'Internationale, International, Internationalismus'. In *Geschichtliche Grundbegriffe. Historisches Lexikon zur politisch-sozialen Sprache in Deutschland*, edited by O. Brunner, W. Conze and R. Koselleck, vol. 3, 367–97. Stuttgart, 1982.
Fuhrmann, M. *Der Traum vom deutschen Orient. Zwei deutsche Kolonien im Osmanischen Reich 1851–1918*. Frankfurt, 2006.

Gabaccia, D.R. and F. Ottanelli, eds. *Italian Workers of the World: Labor, Migration and the Making of Multi-Ethnic States.* Urbana, 2001.
Gandhi, L. *Postcolonial Theory.* New York, 1998.
Gellner, W. *Ideenagenturen für Politik und Öffentlichkeit. Think Tanks in den USA und in Deutschland.* Opladen, 1995.
Geyer, M. and C. Bright. 'World History in a Global Age'. *AHR* 100 (1995): 1034–60.
Geyer, M.H. and J. Paulmann, eds. *The Mechanics of Internationalism: Culture, Society, and Politics from the 1840s to the First World War.* Oxford, 2001.
Glick Schiller, N., L. Basch, and C. Blanc-Szanton, eds. *Towards a Transnational Perspective on Migration: Race, Class, Ethnicity and Nationalism Reconsidered.* New York, 1992.
Gosewinkel, D. *Einbürgern und ausschließen. Die Nationalisierung der Staatsangehörigkeit vom Deutschen Bund bis zur Bundesrepublik Deutschland.* Göttingen, 2001.
Grosse, P. *Kolonialismus, Eugenik und bürgerliche Gesellschaft in Deutschland 1850–1918.* Frankfurt a.M., 2000.
Gründer, H. Geschichte der deutschen Kolonien, Paderborn, 2000.
———. 'Indianer, Afrikaner und Südseebewohner in Europa: Zur Vorgeschichte der Völkerschauen und Kolonialausstellungen'. *Jahrbuch für Europäische Überseegeschichte* 3 (2003): 65–88.
Halbwachs, M. *La mémoire collective.* Paris, 1950. New and rev. ed., Paris 1997. English version as *The Collective Memory.* New York, 1980.
Hall, J.A., eds. *Civil Society: Theory, History and Comparison.* Cambridge, 1995.
Hann, C. and E. Dunn, eds. *Civil Society: Challenging Western Models.* London, 1996.
Hardtwig, W. and H.-U. Wehler, eds. *Kulturgeschichte heute.* Göttingen, 1996.
Harzig, C. *Einwanderung und Politik. Historische Erinnerung und Politische Kultur als Gestaltungsressourcen in den Niederlanden, Schweden und Kanada.* Transkulturelle Perspektiven 1. Göttingen, 2004.
———, ed. *Peasant Maids, City Women. From the European Countryside to Urban America.* Ithaca, NY, 1997.
———, D. Juteau, with I. Schmitt, eds. *The Social Construction of Diversity: Recasting the Master Narrative of Industrial Nations.* New York, 2003.
Haupt, H.-G. *Aufbruch in die Zukunft. Die 1960er Jahre zwischen Planungseuphorie und kulturellem Wandel. DDR, ČSSR und Bundesrepublik Deutschland im Vergleich.* Göttingen, 2004.
———. 'Comparative history'. In *International Encyclopedia of the social and behavioral sciences,* vol. 4, 2397–2403. Amsterdam, 2001.
——— and J. Kocka. 'Comparative History. Methods, Aims, Problems'. In *Comparison and History. Europe in Cross-National Perspective,* edited by D. Cohen and M. O'Connor, 23–39. London, 2004.
——— and J. Kocka, eds. *Geschichte und Vergleich. Ansätze und Ergebnisse internationaler vergleichender Geschichtsschreibung.* Frankfurt, 1996.
——— and D. Langewiesche, eds. *Nation und Religion in Europa. Mehrkonfessionelle Gesellschaften im 19. und 20. Jahrhundert.* Frankfurt a.M., 2004.

Heins, V. *Der Neue Transnationalismus. Nichtregierungsorganisationen und Firmen im Konflikt um die Rohstoffe der Biotechnologie.* Frankfurt/New York, 2001.

Heintz, B., R. Münch, and H. Tyrell, eds. *Weltgesellschaft.* Stuttgart, 2005.

Hennock, E.P. *British Social Reform and German Antecedents: The Case of Social Insurance 1880–1914.* Oxford, 1987.

Herbert, U. *A History of Foreign Labor in Germany 1880–1980. Seasonal Workers— Forced Laborers—Guest Workers.* Translated by W. Templer. Ann Arbor, 1991.

Heydemann, G. and L. Kettenacker, eds. *Kirchen in der Diktatur. Drittes Reich und SED-Staat.* Göttingen, 1993.

Hildebrand, K. *Das vergangene Reich. Deutsche Außenpolitik von Bismarck bis Hitler 1871–1945.* Stuttgart, 1995.

Hildermeier, M. et al., eds. *Europäische Zivilgesellschaft in Ost und West. Begriff, Geschichte, Chancen.* Frankfurt a.M., 2000.

Hirschhausen, U. v. and J. Leonhard, eds. *Nationalismus in Europa. West- und Osteuropa im Vergleich.* Göttingen, 2001.

Hobsbawm, E. *Age of Extremes. The Short Twentieth Century, 1914–1991.* New York, 1994.

Hoerder, D. *Cultures in Contact: World Migration in the Second Millenium.* Durham, NC, 2002.

——, C. Harzig, and A. Shubert, eds. *The Historical Practice of Diversity: Transcultural Interactions from the Early Modern Mediterranean World to the 20th-Century Postcolonial World.* New York, 2003.

—— and J. Nagler, eds. *People in Transit. German Migrants in Comparative Perspective, 1820–1930.* Cambridge, 1995.

Hommelhoff, P. and P. Kirchhoff, eds. *Der Staatenverbund der Europäischen Union.* Heidelberg, 1994.

Honold, A. and K.R. Scherpe, eds. *Mit Deutschland um die Welt. Eine Kulturgeschichte des Fremden in der Kolonialzeit.* Stuttgart, 2004.

Höpel, T. *Emigranten der Französischen Revolution in Preußen 1789–1806. Eine Studie in vergleichender Perspektive.* Leipzig, 2000.

Hoston, G.A. *The State, Identity, and the National Question in China and Japan.* Princeton, 1994.

Hübner, P., C. Kleßmann, and K. Tenfelde, eds. *Arbeiter im Staatssozialismus. Ideologischer Anspruch und soziale Wirklichkeit.* Cologne, 2005.

Isajiw, W.W., ed. *Multiculturalism in North America and Europe. Comparative Perspectives on Interethnic Relations and Social Incorporation.* Toronto, 1997.

Jacobmeyer, W. *Vom Zwangsarbeiter zum Heimatlosen Ausländer. Die Displaced Persons in Westdeutschland, 1945–1951.* Göttingen, 1985.

Jarausch, K. and H. Siegrist, eds. *Amerikanisierung und Sowjetisierung in Deutschland 1945–1970.* Frankfurt a.M., 1997.

Jeismann, M. *Das Vaterland der Feinde. Studien zum nationalen Feindbegriff und Selbstverständnis in Deutschland und Frankreich 1792–1918.* Stuttgart, 1992.

Judt, T. 'The Rediscovery of Central Europe'. *Daedalus* 119(1) (1990): 23–54.

Juneja, M. and M. Pernau, eds. *Religion und Grenzen in Indien und Deutschland. Studien auf dem Weg zu einer transnationalen Historiographie.* Frankfurt a.M./New York, 2009.

Kaelble, H. *Der historische Vergleich. Eine Einführung zum 19. und 20. Jahrhundert.* Frankfurt a.M./New York, 1999.

———. *Europäer über Europa. Die Entstehung des europäischen Selbstverständnisses im 19. und 20. Jahrhundert.* Frankfurt a.M., 2001.

———, ed. *The European Way: European Societies during the Nineteenth and Twentieth Centuries.* New York, 2004.

——— and J. Schriewer, eds. *Vergleich und Transfer. Komparatistik in den Sozial-, Geschichts- und Kulturwissenschaften.* Frankfurt, 2003.

Kaiser, K. 'Transnationale Politik'. In *Die anachronistische Souveränität*, edited by E.-O. Czempiel, 80–109. Cologne/Opladen, 1969.

Kalberg, St. *Max Weber's Comparative-Historical Sociology.* Cambridge, 1994.

Kamphoefner, W.D. *The Westfalians: From Germany to Missouri.* Princeton, 1987.

Kaviraj, S. and Khilnani, S., eds. *Civil Society. History and Possibilities.* Cambridge, 2001.

Kedar, K.Z., ed. *Explorations in Comparative History.* Jerusalem, 2009.

Keil and J.B. Jentz, eds. *German Workers in Industrial Chicago, 1850–1910: A Comparative Perspective.* DeKalb, 1983.

Keohane, R.O., ed. *Transnational Relations and World Politics.* Cambridge, MA, 1972.

Kivisto, P. 'Social Spaces, Transnational Immigrant Communities, and the Politics of Incorporation'. *Ethnicities* 3(1) (2003): 5–28.

Kleßmann, C. *Polnische Bergarbeiter im Ruhrgebiet 1870–1945. Soziale Integration und nationale Subkultur einer ethnischen Minderheit in der deutschen Industriegesellschaft.* Göttingen, 1978.

———. 'Verflechtung und Abgrenzung. Aspekte der geteilten und zusammengehörigen deutschen Nachkriegsgeschichte'. *Aus Politik und Zeitgeschichte* 29–30 (1993): 30–41.

———. *Zwei Staaten, eine Nation. Deutsche Geschichte 1955–1970.* Göttingen, 1970.

Kloosterhuis, J. *'Friedliche Imperialisten'. Deutsche Auslandsvereine und auswärtige Kulturpolitik.* 2 vols. Frankfurt a.M., 1994.

Knoll, A.J. and L.H. Gann, eds. *Germans in the Tropics. Essays in German Colonial History.* New York, 1987.

Kocka, J. *Arbeitsverhältnisse und Arbeiterexistenzen. Grundlagen der Klassenbildung im 19. Jahrhundert.* Bonn, 1990.

———. 'Asymmetrical Historical Comparison: The Case of the German *Sonderweg*'. *History and Theory* 38(1) (1999): 40–51.

———. *Bürgertum im 19. Jahrhundert: Deutschland im europäischen Vergleich.* 3 vols. Göttingen, 1995.

———. 'Comparison and beyond'. In *History and Theory* 42.2003: 39–44.

———. 'Nationalsozialismus und SED-Diktatur im Vergleich'. In Kocka, *Vereinigungskrise*, 91–101. Göttingen, 1995.

——— and H. Siegrist. *Die Arbeitsstelle für Vergleichende Gesellschaftsgeschichte an der Freien Universität Berlin 1992–1997.* Berlin, 1997.

Koller, C. *'Von Wilden aller Rassen niedergemetzelt'. Die Diskussion um die Verwendung von Kolonialtruppen in Europa zwischen Rassismus, Kolonial- und Militärpolitik (1914–1930).* Stuttgart, 2001.

Koselleck, R., U. Spree, and W. Steinmetz. 'Drei bürgerliche Welten? Zur vergleichenden Semantik der bürgerlichen Gesellschaft in Deutschland, England und Frankreich'. In *Bürger in der Gesellschaft der Neuzeit. Wirtschaft—Politik—Kultur,* edited by H.-J. Puhle, 14–58. Göttingen, 1991.

Kößler, R. and H. Melber. *Globale Solidarität? Eine Streitschrift.* Frankfurt, 2002.

Kothari, R. 'Human Rights: A Movement in Search of a Theory'. In S. Kothari and H. Sethi, *Human Rights: Challenges for Theory and Action,* 151–62. New York, 1991.

Kott, S. 'Gemeinschaft oder Solidarität. Unterschiedliche Modelle der französischen und deutschen Sozialpolitik am Ende des 19. Jahrhunderts'. *Geschichte und Gesellschaft* 22 (1996): 311–30.

Kum'a N'Dumbe III, A. *Was wollte Hitler in Afrika? NS-Planungen für eine faschistische Neugestaltung Afrikas.* Frankfurt a.M., 1993.

Kundrus, B., ed. *Phantasiereiche. Zur Kulturgeschichte des deutschen Kolonialismus.* Frankfurt a.M., 2003.

Kundrus, B. *Moderne Imperialisten. Das Kaiserreich im Spiegel seiner Kolonien.* Cologne, 2003.

Langewiesche, D. 'Zentralstaat—Föderativstaat: Nationalstaatsmodelle in Europa im 19. und 20. Jahrhundert'. *Zeitschrift für Staats- und Europawissenschaften* 2 (2004): 173–90.

———. 'Zum Wandel von Krieg und Kriegslegitimation in der Neuzeit'. *Journal of Modern European History* 2 (2004): 5–27.

Lebovics, H. *Bringing the Empire Back Home. France in the Global Age.* Durham, NC, 2004.

Lehmann, H. *Wege zu einer neuen Kulturgeschichte.* Göttingen, 1995.

Lequin, Y., ed. *La mosaïque France: histoire des étrangers et de l'immigration.* Paris, 1988.

Lewerenz, S. *Die Deutsche Afrika-Schau (1935–1940). Rassismus, Kolonialrevisionismus und postkoloniale Auseinandersetzungen im nationalsozialistischen Deutschland.* Frankfurt a.M., 2006.

Lingelbach, G. *Klio macht Karriere. Die Institutionalisierung der Geschichtswissenschaft in Frankreich und den USA in der zweiten Hälfte des 19. Jahrhunderts.* Göttingen, 2003.

Lorenz, C. 'Comparative Historiography: Problems and Perspectives'. *History and Theory* 38(1) (1999): 25–39.

Loth, W. and J. Osterhammel, eds. *Internationale Geschichte. Themen—Ergebnisse—Aussichten.* Munich, 2000.

Lucassen, J. *Migrant Labour in Europe, 1600–1900: The Drift to the North Sea,* London 1987.

Luhmann, N. *Die Gesellschaft der Gesellschaft,* Frankfurt a.M., 1997.

Lundgreen, P., ed. *Sozial- und Kulturgeschichte des Bürgertums. Eine Bilanz des Bielefelder Sonderforschungsbereichs (1986–1997).* Göttingen, 2000.

Maase, K. 'Körper, Konsum, Genuss—Jugendkultur und mentaler Wandel in den beiden deutschen Gesellschaften'. *Aus Politik und Zeitgeschichte,* 45 (2003): 9–16.

Maier, C.S. 'Consigning the Twentieth Century to History. Alternative Narratives for the Modern Era'. *American Historical Review* 105(3) (2000): 807–31.
Mann, M. *The Sources of Power. Vol. II: The rise of classes and nation-states, 1760–1914.* Cambridge, 1993.
Martin, P. *Schwarze Teufel, Edle Mohren: Afrikaner in Geschichte und Bewusstsein der Deutschen.* Hamburg, 1993.
Matthes, J., ed. *Zwischen den Kulturen?. Die Sozialwissenschaften vor dem Problem des Kulturvergleichs.* Göttingen, 1992.
Mazón, P. and R. Steingröver, eds. *Not so Plain as Black and White. Afro-German Culture and History, 1890–2000.* Rochester, 2005.
McGerr, M. 'The Price of the "New Transnational History"'. *AHR* 96 (1991): 1056–67.
Melber, H., ed. *Genozid und Gedenken. Namibisch-deutsche Geschichte und Gegenwart.* Frankfurt a.M., 2005.
Middell, M., ed. *Historische Zeitschriften im internationalen Vergleich.* Leipzig, 1999.
Middell, M. 'Kulturtransfer und Historische Komparatistik—Thesen zu ihrem Verhältnis'. *Comparativ* 10 (2000): 7–41.
Middell, M. 'Transnationale Geschichte als transnationales Projekt? Zur Einführung in die Diskussion'. In *Geschichte.transnational (Forum)*, 15 January 2005.
Middell, M. 'Kulturtransfer und historische Komparatistik. Thesen zu ihrem Verhältnis'. In *Kulturtransfer und Vergleich*, edited by M. Middell, 7–41. Leipzig, 2000.
Mitchell, T. *Colonizing Egypt.* Berkeley, 1991.
Mitchell, W.J.T. 'Translator translated. An Interview with cultural theorist Homi Bhabha'. *Artforum* 33 (1995): 80–84.
Möhle, H., ed. *Branntwein, Bibeln und Bananen. Der Deutsche Kolonialismus in Afrika. Eine Spurensuche in Hamburg.* Hamburg, 1999.
Mollat Du Jourdin, M. *Europa und das Meer.* München, 1993.
Moltmann, ed. *Germans to America: 300 Years of Immigration, 1683–1983.* Stuttgart, 1982.
Mommsen, W.J. *Der europäische Imperialismus.* Göttingen, 1979.
Montgomery, D. *The Fall of the House of Labor. The Workplace, the State, and American Labor Activism, 1865–1925.* Cambridge, 1987.
Mühlhahn, K. *Herrschaft und Widerstand in der 'Musterkolonie' Kiautschou. Interaktionen zwischen China und Deutschland, 1897–1914.* Munich, 2000.
O'Hanlon, R. and D. Washbrook. 'After Orientalism. Culture, Criticism and Politics in the Third World'. *Comparative Studies in Society and History* (1992): 141–67.
Oberkrome, W. *Volksgeschichte. Methodische Innovation und völkische Ideologisierung in der deutschen Geschichtswissenschaft 1918–1945.* Göttingen, 1993.
Offe, C. 'Homogeneity and Constitutional Democracy: Group Rights as an Answer to Identity Conflicts'. In *Rules, Laws and Constitutions*, eds. S. Sabarwal and H. Sievers, 188–208. New Delhi, 1998.
Olin Hill, A. and B. Hill. 'Marc Bloch and Comparative History'. *American Historical Review* 85 (1980): 829–84.

Opitz, M. et al., eds. *Farbe bekennen: Afro-deutsche Frauen auf den Spuren ihrer Geschichte.* Berlin, 1986. English version as *Showing Our Color: Afro-German Women Speak Out.* Amherst, 1992.

Osterhammel, J. *Die Entzauberung Asiens. Europa und die asiatischen Reiche im 18. Jahrhundert.* Munich, 1998.

——. *Die Verwandlung der Welt Eine Geschichte des 19. Jahrhunderts.* Munich, 2009.

——. 'Europamodelle und imperiale Kontexte.' *Journal of Modern European History* 2 (2004): 157–81.

——. *Geschichtswissenschaft jenseits des Nationalstaats. Studien zu Beziehungsgeschichte und Zivilisationsvergleich.* Göttingen, 2001.

——. 'Sozialgeschichte im Zivilisationsvergleich. Zu künftigen Möglichkeiten komparativer Geschichtswissenschaft.' *Geschichte und Gesellschaft* 22(2) (1996): 143–64.

——. '"Weltgeschichte". Ein Propädeutikum.' *Geschichte in Wissenschaft und Unterricht* 56 (2005): 452–79.

—— and N.P. Petersson. *Globalization: A Short History.* Translated by D. Geyer. Princeton, 2005.

Page Moch, L. *Moving Europeans: Migration in Western Europe since 1650.* Bloomington, 1992; 2nd rev. ed. 2003.

Patel, K.K. *Nach der Nationalfixiertheit. Perspektiven einer transnationalen Geschichte.* Berlin, 2004.

——. 'Transnationale Geschichte—ein neues Paradigma?' In *Geschichte.transnational (Forum),* 2 February 2005.

Patlagean, E. 'Europe, seigneurie, féodalité. Marc Bloch et les limites orientales d'un espace de comparaison.' In *Marc Bloch aujourd'hui: Histoire comparée et Sciences sociales,* edited by H. Atsma and A. Burguière, 297–98. Paris, 1990.

Paulmann, J. 'Internationaler Vergleich und interkultureller Transfer. Zwei Forschungsansätze zur europäischen Geschichte des 18. bis 20. Jahrhunderts.' *Historische Zeitschrift* 267 (1998): 649–85.

Pelzer, E. *Die Wiederkehr des girondistischen Helden. Deutsche Intellektuelle als kulturelle Mittler zwischen Deutschland und Frankreich während der Französischen Revolution.* Bonn, 1998.

Pernau, M., ed. *The Delhi College. Traditional Elites, the Colonial State and Education before 1857.* Oxford, 2006.

——. *Der Bürger mit Turban. Muslime in Delhi im 19. Jahrhundert.* Göttingen, 2008.

Poenicke, A. *Afrika in den deutschen Medien und Schulbüchern.* St. Augustin, 2001.

Pomeranz, K. *The Great Divergence. China, Europe, and the Making of the Modern World Economy.* Princeton, 2000.

Porter, B. *The Absent-Minded Imperialists. Empire, Society, and Culture in Britain.* Oxford, 2004.

Portes, A., L.E. Guarnizo, and P. Landolt. 'The Study of Transnationalism: Pitfalls and Promise of an Emergent Research Field.' *Ethnic and Racial Studies* 22 (1999): 217–37.

Puskás, J. *Overseas Migration from East-Central and South-Eastern Europe 1880–1940.* Budapest, 1990.
Radkau, J. *Natur und Macht. Eine Weltgeschichte der Umwelt.* Munich, 2000.
Randeria, S. 'Geteilte Geschichte und verwobene Moderne'. In *Zukunftsentwürfe. Ideen für eine Kultur der Veränderung,* edited by J. Rüsen et al. Frankfurt a.M., 1999.
――. 'Jenseits von Soziologie und soziokultureller Anthropologie: Zur Ortsbestimmung der nichtwestlichen Welt in einer zukünftigen Sozialtheorie'. *Soziale Welt* 50 (4)(1999): 373–82.
――. 'Zivilgesellschaft in postkolonialer Perspektive'. In Jürgen Kocka et al., Neues über Zivilgesellschaft aus historisch-sozialwissenschaftlichem Blickwinkel. *WZB Arbeitspapier p01–801,* (Berlin 2001): 81–103.
Rassloff, U. 'Gegenwelten—Kultureller Wandel in der Slowakei der 1960er Jahre'. In *Im Dissens zur Macht. Samizdat und Exilliteratur der Länder Ostmittel- und Südosteuropas,* edited by L. Richter et al. Berlin, 1995.
Rees, J. *Managing the Mills. Labor Policy in the American Steel Industry during the Nonunion Era.* Dallas, 2004.
Reinhard, W. *Geschichte der Staatsgewalt. Eine vergleichende Verfassungsgeschichte Europas von den Anfängen bis zur Gegenwart.* Munich, 1999.
Renn, J., J. Straub, and S. Shimada, eds. *Übersetzung als Medium des Kulturverstehens und sozialer Integration.* Frankfurt a.M., 2002.
Risse-Kappen, T., ed. *Bringing Transnational Relations Back In: Non-State Actors, Domestic Structures and International Institutions.* Cambridge, 1995.
Rodgers, D.T. *Atlantic Crossings: Social Politics in a Progressive Age.* Cambridge, MA, 1998.
Rothermel, H. *Aufbau, Entwicklung und Verfall kommunistischer Parteiherrschaft in Polen und der DDR: zur gesellschaftlichen Dynamik in post-totalitären sozialistischen Systemen.* Pfaffenweiler, 1997.
Said, E. *Culture and Imperialism.* New York, 1993.
――. *Orientalism.* New York, 1978.
Sandner, G. and M. Rössler. 'Geography and Empire in Germany, 1871–1945'. In *Geography and Empire,* edited by A. Godlewska and N. Smith, 115–27. Oxford, 1994.
Schäbler, B., ed. *Area Studies und die Welt. Weltregionen und neue Globalgeschichte.* Wien, 2007.
Schlögel, K. *Im Raume lesen wir die Zeit. Über Zivilisationsgeschichte und Geopolitik.* Munich, 2003.
Schmidt, H. *Die Selbstbehauptung Europas. Perspektiven für das 21. Jahrhundert.* Stuttgart, 2000.
Schmidt, J. *Zivilgesellschaft. Bürgerschaftliches Engagement von der Antike bis zur Gegenwart. Texte und Kommentare.* Reinbek, 2007.
Schmidt-Gernig, A. 'Scenarios of Europe's Future. Western Future Studies of the Sixties and Seventies as an Example of a Transnational Public Sphere of Experts'. *Journal of European Integration History* 18 (2002): 69–91.
Schmiechen-Ackermann, D. *Diktaturen im Vergleich.* Darmstadt, 2002.

Schöllgen, G. *Imperialismus und Gleichgewicht. Deutschland, England und die orientalische Frage 1871–1914*. München, 1984.
Schulz, B.H. *Development Policy in the Cold War Era. The Two Germanies and Sub-Saharan Africa, 1960–1985*. Hamburg, 1995.
Schwentker, W. *Max Weber in Japan. Eine Untersuchung zur Wirkungsgeschichte 1905–1995*. Tübingen, 1998.
Sewell, W.J. 'Marc Bloch and the Logic of Comparative History'. *History and Theory* 6(2) (1967): 208–18.
Shimada, S. *Die Erfindung Japans. Kulturelle Wechselwirkung und nationale Identitätskonstruktion*. Frankfurt a.M., 2000.
Siegrist, H. *Advokat, Bürger und Staat. Sozialgeschichte der Rechtsanwälte in Deutschland, Italien und der Schweiz (18.-20. Jh.)*. Frankfurt a.M., 1996.
Sinha, M. *Colonial Masculinity. The 'manly Englishman' and the 'effeminate Bengali' in the late nineteenth century*. Manchester, 1995.
Sombart, W. *Warum gibt es in den Vereinigten Staaten keinen Sozialismus?* Tübingen, 1906.
Spiliotis, S. 'Wo findet Gesellschaft statt? oder Das Konzept der Transterritorialität'. *Geschichte und Gesellschaft* 27(2001): 480–88.
Spohn, W., ed. *Kulturanalyse und vergleichende Forschung in Sozialgeschichte und historischer Soziologie*. Leipzig, 1998. (*Comparativ* 1 (1998)).
Staehelin, B. *Völkerschauen im Zoologischen Garten Basel 1879–1935*. Basel, 1993.
Starr, F. *Red and Hot. The Fate of Jazz in the Soviet Union 1917–1980*. New York, 1983.
Steinisch, I. *Arbeitszeitverkürzung und sozialer Wandel. Der Kampf um die Achtstundenschicht in der deutschen und amerikanischen Eisen- und Stahlindustrie 1880–1929*. Berlin/New York, 1986.
Stoler, A.L. and F. Cooper, eds. *Tensions of Empire. Colonial Cultures in a Bourgeois World*. Berkeley, 1997.
Stovall, T. *Paris Noir. African Americans in the City of Lights*. New York, 1996.
Subrahmanyam, S. *Explorations in Connected History. From the Tagus to the Ganges*. Delhi, 2005.
———. *Explorations in Connected History. Mughals and Franks*. Delhi, 2005.
Sutcliffe, A. *Towards the Planned City. Germany, Britain, the United States, and France, 1780–1914*. Oxford, 1981.
Szporluk, R. 'The Making of Modern Ukraine: The Western Dimension'. *Harvard Ukrainian Studies* 25 (2001): 57–90.
Tenbruck, F.H. 'Gesellschaftsgeschichte oder Weltgeschichte?' *Kölner Zeitschrift für Soziologie und Sozialpsychologie*, 41(3) (1989): 417–39. English version as 'Internal History of Society or Universal History?' *Theory, Culture and Society: Explorations in Critical Social Science*, 11(1) (1994): 75–94.
Thelen, D. 'Of Audiences, Borderlands, and Comparisons: Toward the Internationalization of American History'. *Journal of American History* 79 (1992): 432–62.
Ther, P. 'Beyond the Nation: the Relational Basis of a Comparative History of Germany and Europe'. *Central European History* 36 (2003): 45–74.

———. *In der Mitte der Gesellschaft. Operntheater in Zentraleuropa 1815–1914.* Vienna, 2006.

——— and H. Sundhaussen, eds. *Regionale Bewegungen und Regionalismen in europäischen Zwischenräumen seit der Mitte des 19. Jahrhunderts.* Marburg, 2003.

Thiemeyer, G. 'Supranationalität als Novum in der Geschichte der internationalen Politik der fünfziger Jahre'. *Journal of European Integration History* 4 (1998): 5–21.

Torp, C. *Die Herausforderung der Globalisierung. Wirtschaft und Politik in Deutschland 1860–1914.* Göttingen, 2005.

Torpey, J. *The Invention of the Passport. Surveillance, Citizenship and the State.* Cambridge, 2000.

Tyrrell, I. 'American Exceptionalism in an Age of International History'. *AHR* 96 (1991): 1031–55.

van der Heyden, U. and J. Zeller, eds. *Kolonialmetropole Berlin. Eine Spurensuche.* Berlin, 2002.

van der Veer, P. *Imperial Encounters. Religion and Modernity in India and Britain.* Princeton, 2001.

Van Laak, D. *Imperiale Infrastruktur. Deutsche Planungen für eine Erschließung Afrikas 1880 bis 1960.* Paderborn, 2004.

———. *Weiße Elefanten. Anspruch und Scheitern technischer Großprojekte im 20. Jahrhundert.* Stuttgart, 1999.

Wagner, P., C. Didry, and B. Zimmermann. *Arbeit und Nationalstaat: Frankreich und Deutschland in europäischer Perspektive.* Frankfurt a.M., 2000.

Wahl, R. *Verfassungsstaat, Europäisierung, Internationalisierung.* Frankfurt a.M., 2003.

Wallerstein, I. *The Modern World System.* 3 vols. New York, 1974–1989.

Wehler, H.-U. *Deutsche Gesellschaftsgeschichte.* 5 vols. Munich, 1987–2008.

Welskopp, T. *Arbeit und Macht im Hüttenwerk. Arbeits- und industrielle Beziehungen in der deutschen und amerikanischen Eisen- und Stahlindustrie von den 1860er bis zu den 1930er Jahren.* Bonn, 1994.

———. *Das Banner der Brüderlichkeit. Die deutsche Sozialdemokratie vom Vormärz bis zum Sozialistengesetz.* Bonn, 2000.

———. 'Stolpersteine auf dem Königsweg. Methodenkritische Anmerkungen zum internationalen Vergleich in der Gesellschaftsgeschichte'. *Archiv für Sozialgeschichte* 25 (1995): 339–67.

Werner, Michael. 'Maßstab und Untersuchungsebene. Zu einem Grundproblem der vergleichenden Kulturtransfer-Forschung'. In *Nationale Grenzen und internationaler Austausch. Studien zum Kultur- und Wissenschaftstransfer in Europa,* edited by L. Jordan and B. Kortländer, 20–33. Tübingen, 1995.

——— and B. Zimmermann. 'Beyond Comparison. Histoire Croisée and the Challenge of Reflexivity'. *History and Theory* 45 (2006): 30–50.

——— and B. Zimmermann. 'Vergleich, Transfer, Verflechtung. Ansatz der *Histoire croisée* und die Herausforderung des Transnationalen'. *Geschichte und Gesellschaft* 28 (2002): 607–36.

———— and B. Zimmermann, 'Penser l'histoire croisée: entre empirie et réflexivité', in *Annales* 58 (2003): 7–36.
Wilson, K., ed. *A New Imperial History. Culture, Identity and modernity in Britain and the Empire*. Cambridge, 2004.
Wilson, T.M. and H. Donnan, eds. *Border Identities: Nation and State at International Frontiers*. Cambridge, 1998.
Winkler, H.A. *Der lange Weg nach Westen. Deutsche Geschichte*. 2 vols. München, 2000.
Wirz, A. 'Für eine transnationale Gesellschaftsgeschichte'. *Geschichte und Gesellschaft* 27 (2001): 489–98.
————. *Sklaverei und kapitalistisches Weltsystem*. Frankfurt a.M., 1984.
Wright, G. *The Politics of Design in French Colonial Urbanism*. Chicago, 1991.
Wyman, M. *DP. Europe's Displaced Persons, 1945–1951*. Philadelphia, 1988.
Young, R.J.C. *Postcolonialism. An Historical Introduction*. Oxford, 2001.
Zernack, K. *Polen und Russland: Zwei Wege in der europäischen Geschichte*. Berlin, 1994.
Zimmerer, J. and Joachim Zeller, eds. *Völkermord in Deutsch-Südwestafrika. Der Kolonialkrieg (1904–1908) in Namibia und seine Folgen*. Berlin, 2003.

INDEX

A
Africa, 53–54, 59, 61, 63–66, 80–81, 154, 226–40, 248, 252, 259
African Diaspora, 234–35
American Federation of Labor (AFL), 154–56, 158, 160–61, 168–70
Anthropology, 42, 56
Asymmetry, 56–58, 215

B
Begriffsgeschichte (see history of concepts)
Betriebsräte (works councils), 164, 169, 171–72
Bhabha, Homi, 114
Bloch, Marc, 3–4, 19, 33, 108–09
Bohemia, 212–13
borders/boundaries, 19, 39, 42–43, 45–47, 67–68, 80–83, 91–94, 106–123, 120, 139, 142–43, 184, 192, 205, 208, 212–14, 219, 228, 238, 249, 253–59
British Empire, 39
Bürgertum (bourgeoisie, middle class), 3, 16, 40, 107, 115, 117, 211, 221, 235

C
Canada, 210, 249–51, 258–59
Carolingian, 211, 213
Catholicism/Catholics, 46, 121
Chakrabarty, Dipesh, 110
Christianity/Christians, 2, 78, 121–22, 214
civil society, 8, 21, 48, 77–100, 117
closed shop, 151, 170
Cold War, 175, 218, 227, 239, 262–63
colonial power, 20, 56, 59, 68, 116, 138, 227, 236, 239
Colonial Studies, 228
colonialism/colonies, 20–21, 34, 42, 48, 54, 56, 58–69, 79, 84, 86, 90, 109, 112, 117–18, 210, 215, 226–33, 239–40
communism, 182, 189, 218
company unions, 160, 167–68
Competition/systemic competition, 44, 138–40, 143, 151, 157, 167, 174, 190–91, 207, 216
Congress of Industrial Organizations (CIO), 168–70
consumption/consumer society, 181–82, 191, 195
convergence/convergence theory, 10, 19, 21, 35, 83, 91, 179–84, 187, 196–97, 217
craft unionism, 151, 154, 160, 174
Cultural Revolution, 154, 181, 192–94
cybernetics, 189, 191
Czechoslovakia, 22, 180, 183–85, 187, 189, 191–94

D
decolonization, 142, 227, 239
democratization, 10, 141, 172, 190, 207
dialogue, 36, 38, 106, 111–14, 116, 119–20, 123

E
Eastern Bloc, 178–79, 183, 188, 196
enemy, 63, 143, 188
entangled history, 22, 33–34, 37, 39, 68, 107, 208, 227

entanglement, 8, 19–22, 44, 80, 106, 117–19, 122
equality, 89, 93, 94, 138, 43, 231
ethnic cleansing, 144
ethnic community, 134
ethnic history, 136
European expansion, 43, 59, 68, 229
European Union, 36, 37, 137, 142, 144–45, 210, 238, 256
Europeanization, 19, 28, 217, 219

F
Febvre, Lucien, 210
Federal Republic of Germany, 180, 228, 239, 248
First World War, 42, 62, 66, 68, 138, 154–60, 181, 218, 226
Future prognosis, 186

G
Genocid, 63, 226, 228, 232
German Africa Show, 237
German colonial empire, 61, 64, 66–67, 226–273 231, 233
German Democratic Republic, 22, 171, 173, 178, 180, 183–85, 187–94, 196, 228, 239, 248
German *Sonderweg* (see *Sonderweg*)
Gesellschaftsgeschichte (history of society), 40–49
global history, 20, 110, 123
globalisation, 36

H
Habsburg Empire, 208, 214
Hamburg, 152, 173, 213, 233–37, 253, 262
Heimatkunde, 262
Herero, 62–63, 66, 226–28, 231
Hinduism/Hindus, 78, 81, 91, 93, 121
Histoire croisée, 1, 2, 20, 33–35, 37, 53, 134, 204, 209–11, 213, 215
History of concepts (*Begriffsgeschichte*), 18, 56

Holocaust, 63, 226–27, 232
homogeneity, 11, 78, 121, 137–38, 144, 192

I
identity, 11, 81–83, 91–94, 98, 111, 120, 122, 133, 135, 139, 257, 259
imperialism, 41, 54, 62, 64–65, 68, 80, 84, 138, 215, 226, 229, 232
India, 8, 48, 57, 59, 78–97, 100, 105, 112–13, 115–17, 119–23, 174, 252, 259
industrial unionism, 160, 162, 167–68
international relations theory, 45
Iron Curtain, 180, 186–87, 218
Islam/Muslims, 2, 78, 80–81, 121

J
Jewish nation, 134, 140

K
Knights of Labor, 154

L
language, 18, 20, 35, 37, 77, 80, 87, 106, 110–16, 120, 123, 133, 143, 144, 188, 206, 211, 214, 234, 248–51, 253–55, 259
legitimacy, 91, 95, 137, 164, 184, 191, 196
Linguistic turn, 106, 109, 111–12, 250

M
Maastricht, 209
Marxist theory, 138
Migration, 21, 43, 45, 68, 78, 123, 174, 217–19, 233–34, 247–58, 261–264
mission, 122, 234, 239
Mitbestimmung (co-determination), 172, 189
Modernization, 5, 7–10, 17, 42, 48, 54–55, 58, 60, 77, 79–80, 89, 100, 105, 121 ,179, 190, 212

N

nation state, 7, 11, 16, 43, 45, 48, 52, 64, 69, 80, 84, 91, 97, 107, 119, 134, 137–45, 150, 210, 227, 253–57, 259, 261
national cult, 135
national history, 6, 14, 19, 34, 40, 43, 52–53, 61, 69, 205, 211, 214, 256
national identity, 133, 136, 247
National Labor Relations Board, 167
National Socialism, 63, 69, 171, 206, 226, 232
nationalism, 19, 22, 41, 53, 79–80, 93, 123, 133–35, 137, 143, 204, 207, 210–11, 213–15, 219, 259, 262
network, 43, 47–48, 54, 68, 77, 82, 99, 121, 136, 155, 161, 163–64, 167, 171, 205, 216–19, 235, 253–54, 256
New Deal, 165–68
New Economic System, 185, 193
NGO (Non-Governmental Organization), 45, 84, 95–97
Non-Western (non-occidental) history, 44
North America, 42, 49, 217, 247, 250, 253–54, 263

O

Opera, 206–07, 213, 215–18
Orientalism, 48, 61, 63, 116, 208

P

Participation, 64, 66, 98, 137–38, 141, 157, 164, 172, 231
planned economy/planning euphoria, 183–84, 186, 188, 191
Poland, 64, 184–87, 197, 207, 212–13, 216
Postcolonialis, m, 109, 209–10, 215
Prague Spring, 189, 192, 194, 196

R

reform/reform euphoria, 59–60, 66, 78, 116, 184–86, 192, 196

representation, 35, 55, 58, 61, 63, 65, 83, 90, 106, 111–12, 114–16, 118–19, 154, 158, 160, 210
Romania, 187, 260

S

Saxony, 152, 208
Second World War, 17, 116, 140, 163, 169, 187, 195, 228, 233–36, 238–39, 262
secularization, 86, 141
security, 137–39, 142–43, 166, 170, 193, 207, 254–55
Social Democracy, 154, 157–58
socialism, 63, 149, 152–54, 171, 194, 206, 226, 232
societies
    European, 3, 10, 16–17, 22, 34, 42, 54, 68, 79–80, 85–86, 110–11, 229
    non-European, 34, 42, 54, 86, 110–11, 118, 123, 229
    non-Western, 5, 10, 42, 44, 79–87, 89–94, 119
    postcolonial, 79, 83, 87, 89, 91, 96, 100, 208
    Western, 42, 44, 78–82, 84–87, 90, 194, 197
Sonderweg, 5–6, 107, 206, 209, 212, 227
strikes, 17, 150–51, 153–57, 159–62, 165–66, 168–71
Strukturgeschichte (structural history), 211

T

Taft-Hartley Act, 169–72
technical intelligence, 190
technocracy/technocrats, 186, 194
Third Space, 115, 260
transfers, 2, 20, 22, 33–38, 43, 48, 109–10, 120, 204–13, 217–18
translation, 84–85, 105, 112–23, 260
Trente glorieuses, 179

U

union shop, 151, 156–60, 170, 173

V

Vienna, 213, 216, 218
violence, 86–87, 89, 142, 144–45, 166, 229, 231, 240
Völkerschauen, 58, 65, 234

W

Wagner, Richard, 206, 217
Wagnerism, 206–07
Weber, Max, 9–10, 41, 54–55, 98, 144, 206
Wehler, Hans-Ulrich, 40, 42, 48, 62, 211
welfare state, 8–9, 15, 17, 48, 83, 88, 142, 210
West (the), Occident (the), 5, 7, 9, 20, 47, 77, 80–81, 84–87, 94, 106, 113, 122, 140, 161, 171, 180, 184, 188–90, 194–97, 208, 211–14
Western exceptionalism, 5, 140, 206, 212
workers' associations, 152
world history, 9–10, 46, 54, 80, 86, 137, 140, 210

www.ingramcontent.com/pod-product-compliance
Lightning Source LLC
Chambersburg PA
CBHW071956290426
44109CB00018B/2035